Understanding
Violence

Understanding
Violence

GRAEME NEWMAN
State University of New York at Albany

J. B. Lippincott Company
New York, Hagerstown, Philadelphia, San Francisco, London

To Tamsin and Clancy

Sponsoring Editor: Alan M. Spiegel
Project Editor: David Nickol
Production Manager: Jeanie Berke
Compositor: York Composition Co., Inc.
Printer and binder: The Maple Press Company

UNDERSTANDING VIOLENCE

Library of Congress Cataloging in Publication Data
Newman, Graeme R
    Understanding violence.

    Includes index.
    1. Violence. I. Title.
HM291.N49   301.6′33   79-11845
ISBN 0-397-47396-6

Permission to use copyright material has been received from the following authors and publishers.
    Joan McCord for *The Psychopath: An Essay on the Criminal Mind* by W. McCord and J. McCord, Van Nostrand Co. *The Bulletin of Los Angeles Neurological Society*, Californian Neuropsychiatric Institute, Center for Health Services. "Terror in Brooklyn: Youth Gangs Take Over" by Dena Kleinman, October 26, 1977, © The New York Times Company. Harper & Row Publishers, Inc., for *Psychiatry and the Dilemmas of Crime* by S. Halleck © 1967, Hoeber Medical Division, Harper & Row; *The Psychobiology of Aggression* by K. E. Moyer © 1976, K. E. Moyer; *The Murdering Mind* by David Abrahamsen; *Our Violent Society* by David Abrahamsen; and *Political Violence and Civil Disobedience* by Ernest van den Haag. Arno Press for *The Molly Maguire Riots: Industrial Conflict in the Pennsylvania Coal Region* by Walter J. Coleman, reprinted by Arno Press, 1969. Routledge and Kegan Paul Ltd., for *Crime and Personality* by H. J. Eysenck. For *The Liberation of Brazil* translated by John Butt and Rosemary Sheed (Pelican Latin American Library, 1971), pages 94–95, Copyright © John Butt and Rosemary Sheed, 1971, reprinted by permission of Penguin Books Ltd. George Wiedenfeld and Nicholson Ltd., for *The Glory Game* by H. Davies. W. W. Norton and Co., Inc., for *Crusaders, Criminal Crazies* by F. J. Hacker. Crown Publishers, Inc., for *Terror in the Name of God* by Simma Holt, Copyright © 1964, 1965 by Simma Holt, used by permission of Crown Publishers. Tavistock Publications Ltd., for *The Subculture of Violence* by M. Wolfgang and F. Ferracuti. *The Young Child: Reviews of Research—Volume 1* by W. Hartup and N. L. Smothergill, Copyright © 1967, National Association for the Education of Young Children, 1834 Connecticut Ave., N. W., Washington, D. C. 20009. Texas State Historical Association for *George Washington's Account of the Great Hanging at Gainesville, 1862* by S. Acheson and J. H. O'Connell. John Wiley and Sons for *The Police: Six Sociological Essays* by D. Bordua. Glide Urban Center Publications for *Battered Wives* by Del Martin, price $7.95 plus $.60 postage. Hans Toch for *Violent Men*. Harvard University Press for *The Militant South* by J. H. Franklin. University of North Carolina Press for *Homicide in the United States* by H. C. Brearley. Rand McNally and Co. for "Assaultive Offences" in Daniel Glaser (ed.), *Handbook of Criminology* © Rand McNally College Publishing Company. New York State Department of Mental Hygiene, Hudson River Psychiatric Center for *Psychiatric Quarterly*, pp. 65–69, 1971. Bantam Publishers for *Rivers of Blood, Years of Darkness* by R. E. Conot. Donald T. Lund for *Murder and Madness*.
    I am also pleased to acknowledge the assistance of Richard Moran of Mt. Holyoke College for furnishing me with a bibliography on sport and violence, and to Betty Kemmer whose *Rape: A Bibliography*, was of considerable assistance. Cheryl Haft Picker also gathered material on feuding and violence.

Contents

Preface

My previous books, Comparative Deviance *and* The Punishment
Response, *were written as complementary investigations into certain
questions having to do with moral order. I was able to break new
ground in those books because the areas of subject matter through
which I addressed the question of morality were relatively untrodden
by social scientists. The contrary is the case with violence; there is so
much subject matter that one flounders around as if in a bog.*

*There is no mistaking that the job had to be done, as far as my own
life as a theorist is concerned. Violence is no stranger to morality, nor
to immorality. We ought to understand it more clearly and, more im-
portantly, understand how it is currently comprehended in contemporary
culture. I hold the view that our "scientific" understanding of violence
is not necessarily or wholly cumulative in the sense in which natural
science uses this term. Social science is closely wedded to culture, and
as such may reflect certain preoccupations of contemporary culture, as
well as feed into it. Social scientific explanations are therefore constantly
on the brink of becoming grand self-deceptions. This is why we must
stop every now and again and take stock of our combined efforts at
explanation.*

*Disciplinary prejudices abound in the study of violence. Many
sociologists have an emotional block against biologically based explanations. Psychologists think sociologists' explanations are superficial.
And one could go on. Each discipline levels fierce criticisms at the
methodology of the other. To get beyond this unsettling state of affairs,
I have adopted a policy of presenting theories and descriptive data in a
positive light, keeping criticism to a minimum. Of course, I have had to*

be selective and have had to interpret research material. And where excessively unsubstantiated myths have arisen, it has been necessary to deflate them.

Maintaining a sensible balance between these competing demands became at times almost paralyzing. I am sure that I would not have brought the book to a standard that satisfied me had it not been for the substantial and constructive criticisms provided me by my friend and colleague Hans Toch. He is not, of course, responsible for the content of the book and its shortcomings, but he probably is responsible for my having finished it! Bob Meier, who has also become something of a constant critic of my manuscripts provided very substantial criticisms and advice, for which I am very grateful. I am also happy to acknowledge an intellectual debt to my former teachers and current friends, Franco Ferracuti and Marvin Wolfgang, whose classic, The Subculture of Violence, *remains an indispensable source.*

I am pleased to thank once again Jo Anne DeSilva who transformed my illegible scrawl into a beautifully typed manuscript, and several times over at that! She is irreplaceable, and I thank her very much.

GRAEME NEWMAN

Introduction

Definitions of Violence

The word "violence" has many meanings and conjures up a variety of images. Although it is easy to get "lost in meaning" if one takes definitions too seriously, I propose to outline the basic definitions of violence and related terms and the contexts within which these words are most commonly used. Although psychologists and other social scientists usually claim that their words have specific scientific meanings, my review of definitions is of common usage, since it is my aim in this book to apply what we have found out about violence to what we commonly think of as violence.

The following definitions of violence are basically restatements of those found in the *Oxford Dictionary*.[1]

THE USE OF PHYSICAL FORCE: "The exercise of physical force so as to inflict injury on, or cause damage to, persons or property." This is the broadest and most common use of the term in relation to human behavior. There are, however, some difficulties with it. It would seem to require a face-to-face contact or near physical contact between the aggressor and the object of violence. The pushing of a button deep down in a missile silo is ruled out, even though it is human behavior that may result in enormous destruction. A more difficult case is the use of a gun in a coolly calculated murder. It is difficult to see how squeezing the trigger of a gun is "physical force," as far as human behavior is concerned. The criminal law has dealt with this problem as we shall see in Chapter 3. If one broadens the meaning of the term "physical force" to

1

encompass other than human behavior, then it is easy to accept the proposition that the bullet which kills the victim is "physical force." This leads to the definition of violence as a "natural" element.

THE VIOLENCE OF NATURE: There is a long usage of the term to refer to the violence of the forces or elements of nature such as wind, rain, fire, or earthquakes. We often refer to a "violent storm." This is an important meaning of the word, because we shall see that it has sometimes been applied, often implicitly, to violence perpetrated by humans, as though this were a force of nature. Instinct theories discussed in Chapter 10 are an excellent example.

VEHEMENCE OF PERSONAL FEELING OR ACTION: This definition combines the first definition to convey the image of violence that most of us have in regard to human behavior: the heated, vehement expression of personal feeling conveyed to victims and onlookers through action that inflicts injury or damage. It is an important definition because it seems to rule out, or ignore, the possibility that violence may be used *coolly,* or, to use the term commonly used by psychologists, *instrumentally*. The distinction between instrumental and expressive violence, while it seems stark here, is not easy to make in many situations. We will see in Chapter 3 that the criminal law uses such concepts as threat, intent, and other rules in making the distinction; whereas in Chapter 11, psychologists have tried to test expressive and instrumental models of aggression in the laboratory, finding support for both.

All of these definitions clearly refer to one central element of violence, which is *intensity*—intensity described as extreme feelings, actions, or sensations. The Oxford Dictionary lists a wide variety of examples: violent heat, violent poison, violent love, violent odor, violent lines (as in art), violent winds, violent sound, violent hands. It can be seen that used in this variety of contexts, violence may or may not imply damage, injury, or destruction.

In this book we are concerned more with violence defined as that which leads to physical injury or damage, since historically and statistically it is the only aspect of violence that we are able to observe and record. There are no statistics or historical records of people's violent feelings. We must infer them, often backwards from what we see as violent events.

The question of "violent feelings" is, of course, the object of study by psychologists, which is reviewed in Chapters 10 and 11. There are three related terms which are often, but not necessarily, related to violence. These are anger, hate, and rage.

RAGE: The Oxford Dictionary defines rage as "violent anger, furious passion, usually manifested in looks, words, and action."[2] It may also refer to the "fury" of things, such as the wind or sea. This word comes closest to the meaning of the word violence, with its emphasis on intensity of feeling. There is, however, no aspect of its definition that refers to physical injury or damage of others, although this may very well result.

ANGER: Oxford defines anger as "the active feeling provoked against the agent; passion; rage; wrath; ire; hot displeasure." And John Locke in 1690 noted: "Anger is uneasiness or discomposure of the mind upon receipt of any injury, with a present purpose of revenge."[3] The specific attribute of anger is that it is *provoked* by another, and therefore has a strong element of moral justification (revenge). Once again, physical injury or damage does not necessarily follow from anger (I may shout at the person who provoked me, or write him a heated letter), which sets the anger apart from violence. However, it is the moral undertone of anger that has often been used as a justification for violence, as we shall see, especially in Chapter 1 and throughout Part 3.

HATE: "An emotion of extreme dislike or aversion."[4] Clearly hate does not necessarily lead to violence, but once again it may be part of the social and psychological process that makes violence a more acceptable form of behavior, mainly because hate must be directed specifically against a person or group of persons. The process which allows for the infliction of violence upon specific classes of persons is a theme which crops up through the entire book.

Distorted Definitions

TO DO VIOLENCE: The word violence is commonly used in this sense to refer to *violation* of someone, something, or a particular norm. Professor van den Haag has pointed out that this use of the word is very different from those that I have described above. The above definitions of violence are those whose Latin root is *violentia* (physical force). But the usage here is that referring to the Latin root *violatio,* which means "violation."[5] A confusion often occurs because acts of violence are often (but not always) also violations of norms (e.g., "he violated her"). Professor van den Haag has suggested that this conflation of meanings has led some to refer to violations of their standards of justice as "violence" even when no force is used. As a result, accusations have been made against various political and social systems that they are "violent systems."

INSTITUTIONAL VIOLENCE: In the 1960s, a common catchcry was that the capitalistic system had institutionalized violence in the sense that it had produced a poverty-stricken class which suffered physical loss and damage. What these people meant, in fact, is that poverty is a violation of their standards of justice. It cannot be shown that poverty is equivalent in any way to violence as defined earlier: there is no intensity of feeling, no purposive or direct infliction of physical injury or damage. That the poor end up suffering is more by default than intent.

This distortion occurs in various forms. A common distortion is to refer to the treatment of blacks in the United States as "genocide." It is clear enough that this is a "violation" of the term's meaning. Genocide refers to the planned, intentional, purposeful extermination of a race. Only by incredible stretches of the imagination could one say that such a program exists in the U. S. Again, blacks suffer by default, not by design.

The reply to this might be that there is direct injury, because the laws are set up in such a way that the poor are those who must break them more often, and that it is physical violence that backs up the enforcement of laws. But the error in this argument is that physical violence is used ultimately to back up *all* social orders, as we shall see in Chapter 1, and may (theoretically) be used against individuals at every level of the social structure, whether a rich man trying to get richer, or a poor man trying to escape poverty. It may be reasonable to say that the use of physical force by a policeman against a poor offender or suspect is "violence," but that applies to any offender, whether rich or poor, and only to that specific situation. One cannot infer, because of inequalities in the social order, that it is therefore a "violent system," since all social orders are based on violence. A social order may be unfair or unjust, but it is not helpful to describe it as a "violent system,"[6] simply on the basis of inequality. This is not to say that there can be no such thing as a violent political system. Of course there can, as we shall see in Chapter 1. But the application of the label "violent system" in this case is made according to factors apart from inequality.

In this book, I have not addressed myself directly to either of these distorted uses of the term "violence," although an implicit theme that recurs throughout the book is that there is a relationship between inequality and violence; but the kinds of violence that may result from inequalities may be of other kinds besides "political violence," which is essentially the violence that the critics of "institutional violence" are talking about.

Organization of the Book

Focused research in social science of the kind addressing itself to the "problem of violence" must face up to an inbuilt bias: by focusing theory and research on a particular problem, one tilts the conceptualization of it to one which assumes that the object under study is unitary. It may be assumed to be unitary in two ways. One may see "it" (violence) as a single phenomenon which may be explained by either single or multiple causal theories. Or, one may see the phenomenon as varied, but explainable by a single or very few causal factors. Presented as a stark dichotomy, both of these approaches seem, separately, narrow and therefore unacceptable.

In this book, I have set out to review "what we know" about "violence," upon the assumption that it makes sense to do just that, so that some understanding of violence in general may accrue. Thus, it is implied that violence is to some extent unitary. Yet it is also my thesis that violence is *not* a unitary phenomenon, that it occurs in an incredible variety of forms, contexts, and conditions, and that there are multiple explanations as well. How can one write a book perched upon such an uneasy contradiction?

The answer is to write a book without making either of these assumptions in advance, allowing the material to decide, treating both possibilities as hypotheses to be tested by a review of the available theoretical and research evidence. One must therefore present a mixture, ideally a blending, of both theoretical and descriptive material.

This approach has largely dictated both the structure and breadth of the book. To allow for the variability of violence, I have covered the gamut: from political violence, through the violence of occupations, criminal violence, violence in the home, to the violence of those who are sick, and many other different forms of violence. To allow for the unitary aspects of violence, I have reviewed carefully those theories and research that deal with it as unitary: instinct theories, some culture theories, some biological theories. To allow for the possibility of single or limited cause models, I have not only reviewed such literature (e.g., frustration-aggression theory) but have tried where appropriate to apply it to explain violence in diverse settings. This is why, although the chapter titles do clearly identify the gamut of explanations and variability in violent forms, I have nevertheless here and there purposely blended aspects of what is popularly called "collective violence" with "individual violence." While the division between collective and individual violence is perhaps didactically useful, it is in my view somewhat arbitrary, tending to split off explanations which might ordinarily apply to both types of violence. Furthermore, I have purposely mixed some particular explanations of violence which are popularly (at least in criminology) assumed to have nothing to do with each other, such as the biological and the cultural. The reader will see that I have supplemented cultural explanations of violence with biological ones when it seemed appropriate, and this is achieved especially in Chapter 5.

Chapter 1 reviews material on political violence, analyzing its ideological explanations but also trying to assess the psychological and social underpinnings of these ideologies. It becomes clear that political violence is like food: it is a basic necessity for all societies; it may be in content good or bad, or put to good or bad use. An understanding of the broad justifications for its use and the psychological processes underlying political violence leads to a review, in Chapter 2, of violence in American history. Here we find that it has been used in an incredibly wide variety of circumstances, and that there is some evidence of continuity in certain aspects of violence in American history but not in others. Some aspects of this continuity of violence, it is suggested, may have contributed to particular variations in levels of criminal violence in America. This proposition is considered along with many other factors in Chapter 3, which reviews the levels and patterning of violence in America since 1900. This completes Part One, which has already surveyed a wide variety of violent behavior, but has also concentrated upon isolating any single or continuous factors that may explain these varieties of violence.

Part Two develops conclusions reached at the end of the review of criminal violence: the suggestion that there may be basic cultural or subcultural factors that contribute to various types of violence. Chapter 4 looks at the subcultural factors related to ethnicity, religion, and social class and assesses the extent to which these factors contribute to variations in criminal violence, as well as the extent to which these factors represent unitary or continuous explanations, as against culturally specific explanations. Chapter 5 continues this search, by identifying age and sex as the biological bases of culture and assessing the transcultural or universalistic aspects of age and sex that may contribute to variations in violent behavior. An attempt is made to separate out those factors related to age and sex that are culturally specific in contributing to violent behavior. Another basic unit of culture is the family, so it is family violence that we turn to next in Chapter 6. We find that even within such a closed social unit, a broad range of theories and research may be used to explain this quite specific but basic type of violence.

A conclusion reached in the chapter on family violence is that the context of violence may be a significant factor in explaining violence, so that we move on to Part Three, which surveys violence in many different settings. Types of violent settings covered here are those relating to cops and criminals, prisoners and guards, teachers and pupils, sports, gangs and mobs, and the violence of strangers. Perhaps a little in contrast to Part Two, Part Three emphasizes the diverse and variable nature of violence.

But a theme which runs through Part Three is that, although there may be many contextual, or situational, factors at work in generating many different kinds of violence, nevertheless, violence is perpetrated *by individuals* in these situations; it never simply "erupts" without an individual or two actually starting it. This leads us to a consideration, in Part Four, of the individualistic aspects of violence. Chapter 10 reviews research on instinct and biologically based theories. It is apparent, however, especially from the work reviewed in Part Two, that many instinct and biologically based theories have far-reaching cultural implications. Chapter Eleven then builds upon these individually oriented explanations by reviewing much of the work in psychology and social psychology concerning the dynamics of aggression—how people seem to use it; under what conditions they will express it; the extent to which it is the behavior of "normals" as against "abnormals."

THE CONCLUSIONS. The diverse and unitary aspects of violence are reconsidered; and we find that this tour-de-force has brought to light some interesting new questions, identified important directions for future violence research, and assessed the possibilities for its control.

Part One

The Violent Scene

Political Violence: Revolution and Repression

EXITUS ACTUM PROBAT (The end justifies the means)
Motto on George Washington's Coat of Arms

Political violence is instrumental violence. It is violence used to achieve a particular political end—whether a radical change in the authority structure or a reaffirmation of authority. It may be a means to power, but it may also be a way of exercising power. The concepts of power and authority are central to an understanding of political violence.

Professor van den Haag in his *Political Violence and Civil Disobedience* outlines the essential distinctions between these terms:[1]

1. Authority (the legal aspect): the right of office-holders to order, and the duty of those subject to their authority to comply.
2. Authority (the consensual aspect): the effective exercise of authority by the officials vested with it, and acceptance by those subject to it.
3. Power: the ability to compel others to comply with one's wishes, regardless of authority.
4. Influence: the ability to make others acquiesce (by persuasion, prestige, or loyalty) without relying altogether on authority or on actual power.
5. Violence: "physical force used by a person, directly or through a weapon, to hurt, destroy, or control another or to damage, destroy, or control an object (e.g., territory or property). Violence can be used for the acquisition and exercise of power and to challenge authority or to enforce it."

Professor van den Haag has identified four political uses of violence: (1) to acquire power; (2) to exercise power; (3) to challenge authority; and (4) to enforce authority. Bearing in mind that these are distinctions made for conceptual clarity, it should be possible nevertheless to identify

11

and classify the many politically violent groups—referred to these days under the general rubric of "terrorist groups"—according to the emphasis that their activities or ideologies give to each of these instrumental aims of political violence.

Violence to Enforce Authority

The distinction made between the legal and consensual meaning of authority is crucial in regard to political violence. It is clear, for example, that violence used by a legal authority is by definition "legitimate violence." This applies, of course, only insofar as the legal authority uses violence according to what is legally permissible. For example, violence used by a police officer to prevent a homicidal maniac from murdering a hostage may be legitimate violence, but violence used to extract a confession would be illegitimate.

We know also that there are many different kinds of social orders, some clearly more, or clearly less, just or moral than others. In some social orders, for example, those of feudal or traditional structure, there is a direct relationship between legal and consensual authority. That is, the people totally acquiesce, or "believe in" complete authority, and never question its moral base. In fact, the consensus may be so deep that there is no need for a formal legal authority at all.[2] But in other social orders (most, in fact) there is never this clear agreement between the two. Although people will recognize the legal right of officeholders to command obedience, they will nevertheless disobey because they do not always agree with the moral or political base of the social order upon which legal authority rests. Perhaps the extreme examples of this process are those who use civil disobedience, who purposely break laws, with the full expectation of being punished—who would in fact see it as a denial of their "rights" if they were not punished—hoping that by doing so they will invoke or lay bare the lack of consensus underlying particular laws.

Although it is somewhat controversial in theory, I am inclined to accept the proposition that in practice all modern social orders rest upon the ultimate use of physical force (violence) as the source of their authority. This view of the basis of social order has been around for a long time, probably reaching its peak with the utilitarian ideas of Hobbes and the "social contract": we pursue pleasure, and, so that we may do so without society's dissolving into chaos, we must give up to the state a little of our freedom to pursue pleasure. Thus the state is legitimized (i.e., it has the consensual authority) to enforce its laws. Whether we are all motivated by pleasure and bent upon the destruction of others, as the Hobbesians and many since have thought (we shall discuss these questions in the final section of this book), the fact of the matter is that there is no modern regime, nor has there been one in Western civilization, that has not depended upon an armed force (whether a modern police force, of comparatively recent origin; a secret police, of ancient origin developed to its finesse during the Italian and Spanish Inquisitions; or a military or paramilitary band) as the final arbiter of "justice." Certainly, the history of Western criminal law attests clearly to the long tradition of violence as the enforcer of legal authority.[3]

We can see that the only conditions under which legal authority might not need to fall back on violence to enforce authority would be a social order in which there was total consensus and acceptance of legal authority. Such a society would, I suggest, be one composed either of mindless people who were incapable of perceiving or envisaging alternative social orders or imperfections in the existing one, or it would be a utopia in which the social order was perfect, so that there was nothing to disagree with. Neither of these two possibilities is likely. It follows that all social orders, no matter how "democratic" or how "benign," must rest in the long run upon violence as the ultimate back-up to legal authority.

It is important, also, to recognize that I make this assessment, not on the basis of the assumption that "man is a wolf to man," and therefore is controllable ultimately only by violence, the argument made by most supporters of the social contract philosophy, but rather on an assessment of the cognitive prowess of man: his ability to perceive (and misperceive) justices and injustices; his ability to dream of alternative and better ways of living; in short his idealism, his romanticism. As the anarchist Errico Malatesta observed: "Everything depends on what the people are capable of wanting."[4]

Another important caveat is that there is a tendency for radical opponents of existing orders to characterize any state as violent in and of itself, suggesting that everything it does is therefore violent in consequence, that it is embarked daily upon an unbridled pursuit of violence.

These charges are usually overstated or at least inaccurate. Most modern established states have a legal system which clearly forbids the unbridled use of violence by those in authority, and this includes the South American states where there is said to be widespread torture of suspects. The use of violence by such torturers must be seen as illegitimate violence since it is violence that exceeds the limitations imposed upon it by the legal codes. Therefore, because in some states, those in legal authority exceed the limitations on the use of violence placed upon them by the law, we should not leap to the conclusion that therefore all states can survive over time only because they have an unbridled or unconstrained access to violence. Most, in fact, are severely constrained, and this places them, sometimes, at the mercy of terrorists, as we shall see. It is only in times of severe political crisis that a state may break these constraints, and it is to these situations that we now turn.

Violence to Challenge Authority

"One can do anything with bayonets except sit on them," observed Count Cavour, the great Italian leader who unified Italy in the nineteenth century. He meant that authority must have the consensual support of the people, or it will come undone. It cannot rest solely upon violence, because if it does, the chances are that the famous Maoist maxim "Power grows out of the barrel of a gun" would indeed turn out to be true: that is, anyone who gets hold of the weapons of violence, and uses them, gains power. Violence is, in this context, the deadly opposite to authority.

We may identify three forms of political violence which are used periodically to challenge authority. These are riots, anarchist violence, and modern terrorism. I have excluded full scale revolutionary violence from this category of political violence, since in my assessment "orthodox" violent revolutionaries seek to *acquire power,* whereas in contrast, the activities of rioters, anarchists, and terrorists are more destructive and less "creative." The latter groups seek either to challenge or to destroy authority, but not to "take over." In fact, some terrorist groups are remarkable for their lack of a coherent ideology and for their utter disregard for the ultimate consequences of destroying an existing authority.

Rɪoᴛs. Although we shall look at a little of the social psychology of riots in a later chapter, we are interested here in the political aspects of violent riots. The question we must address here is: are violent riots the product of purposeful political "consciousness"?

Probably the most common theory of violent riot behavior is the "riffraff theory": that riots are the result of a small, delinquent, criminal, or irresponsible subgroup of a disaffected ethnic or political group. The theory further purports that violent riots are by and large disowned and unequivocally opposed by 99% of the minority group from whose ranks the majority of the rioters usually come.

This is an old theory. One can trace it back at least as far as the time of the Gordon Riots in England, a period when the idea of public protest as a political method was emerging. These riots, probably the worst of the eighteenth century in London, were characterized until very recently as products of the disheveled, criminal, alcoholic mob. Only recently has it been pointed out that they were started by reasonably well established persons from the trades and professions.[5]

In his review of the public reaction to the race riots of the sixties—those of Los Angeles (1965), Newark (1967), Detroit (1967), Washington, D.C. (1968), Rochester (1964), Chicago (1965), Boston (1967)—Robert Fogelson[6] shows that the riffraff theory was by far the one most commonly used by the media and public figures to explain the riots. Based upon opinion surveys and arrest data concerning these riots, Fogelson concluded that the rioters were "a small but significant minority of the black population, fairly representative of the ghetto residents, and especially of the young adult males, and tacitly supported by at least a large minority of the black community."[7] In a Harris survey, for example, Fogelson reports that only 61% of the blacks said they would *not* join a riot. This leaves a substantial number "at risk," certainly more than the riffraff theory claims. Fogelson concludes from this analysis that violent riots are therefore political protest against the conditions of life in the ghetto, "an indication of the necessity of fundamental changes in American society."[8]

But there is a problem with viewing this kind of violence as *political* violence. Political violence is instrumental violence: it is employed to achieve a particular end. Some would argue that many of these riots were in part "spontaneous," or at least, "set off" by particular precipitating events, and we shall see in Chapter 8 that this was probably so in some or even many instances. Nor does Fogelson show that the "leaders" of these riots were motivated by a coherent or explicit political end or ideology. We must conclude that this kind of violence is symptomatic of various shortcomings in the social order, and, although its consequences may have far-reaching political implications, it is more accurately classified as "pre-political violence."[9] Indeed, it was not until the rise of the Black Panthers that race riots, if they were ever led by Black Panthers, could be said to be truly political violence. Yet, it is also apparent that the Black Panthers did not engage so much in riots, as in a mild form of terrorism.

ANARCHIST VIOLENCE. Many, many books have been written on anarchism, and I cannot hope to do justice to the topic in the small space at my disposal. As a philosophy, it can be traced from as far back as the middle ages, to its peak in Germany with Stirner and Proudhon in the first half of the 19th century. We are, perhaps, more acquainted in this century with the anarchist writings of the Russians Kropotkin and Bakunin. There have been many different conceptions and theories of anarchy and many groups that have tried to carry out these theories into action.

Some, because their theories grew out of their early contact with Marxist thought, have perhaps been much maligned and feared as crazed persons bent upon the total destruction of society. Indeed, anarchy in the popular mind is equated with chaos. Yet, almost to a man, the anarchist theorists have had the completely opposite image of society in mind— an almost heavenly society, where men lived for each other rather than against each other. This view is well demonstrated in Kropotkin's classic, *Mutual Aid,* a treatise designed to refute Aldous Huxley's interpretation of Darwin's "survival of the fittest."

Anarchy, in its ideal sense, means ". . . the perfect, unfettered self-government of the individual, and, consequently, the absence of any kind of external government."[10] Leaving aside the question of whether the idea of anarchy is so romantic as to be hopelessly utopian, what is of interest to us in anarchist theory is its strange contradiction between pacifism and violence. To a man, anarchists envisage a society (if one can even use that word) after "the revolution" which will be nonviolent, dominated by good will. Malatesta says, "the revolution must of necessity be violent, even though violence is itself an evil,"[11] and he goes on to justify violence on the basis that the privileged classes use violence against the "slave class," so that it is only fair that violence be used against them. Revolutionary violence, he and other anarchists argue, is the only way to put an end to the "permanent violence" of the existing state and class dominated society.

The misuse of the term "violence" here is of course quite clear: the now familiar accusation that a system is violent if it has within it poor or lower classes, regardless of whether it uses physical force or not. We saw in the Introduction how the use of the term "violent" in this sense is purely rhetorical and abuses the meaning of the word. This linguistic elasticity, however, has made it possible for many anarchists to rationalize their use of violence, while at the same time insisting that they are non-violent. Alexander Berkman notes:

> Anarchists have no monopoly on violence. On the contrary, the teachings of anarchism are those of peace and harmony, of non-invasion, of the sacredness of life and liberty . . . but . . . anarchists are more sensitive to wrong and injustice.[12]

Berkman elsewhere uses the familiar rationalization:

> I know that all life under capitalism is violence . . . everyone of
> you is guilty . . . of violence and outrage in the protection of *his*
> interests. Well . . . labor defends its interests with the weapons
> you use against it.[13]

There is a further feature to much anarchist violence, and that is the
belief that violence in and of itself is a *creative force*. Again we see a
strange contradiction, as Bakunin pronounced: *"Destruction is the Beginning of Construction*. There can be no revolution without a sweeping
and passionate destruction, since by means of such destruction new
worlds are born and come into existence."[14]

A final central feature of violence in the service of anarchists was its
conceptualization as a perfect leveler, the most direct way to eradicate
authority—whether legal or consensual authority. This anarchist view of
violence is most eloquently expressed in Albert Parson's speech, upon
being sentenced to hang in 1886:[15]

> Dynamite is the diffusion of power. It is democratic; it makes
> everybody equal. . . . Nothing can meet it. The Pinkertons, the
> police, the militia are absolutely worthless in the presence of dyna-
> mite. . . . It is the equilibrium. It is the annihilator. It is the
> disseminator of power. It is the downfall of oppression. It is the
> abolition of authority; it is the dawn of peace; it is the end of war,
> because war cannot exist unless there is somebody to make war
> upon, and dynamite makes that unsafe.

Dynamite, the great leveler, was fervently believed in by the American
anarchists of that period, as their various exhortations in the anarchist
periodical the Chicago *Alarm* (edited by Albert Parsons) illustrates:[16]

> Workingmen of America, learn the manufacture and use of
> dynamite. It will be your most powerful weapon; a weapon of the
> weak against the strong. . . . Then use it unstintingly, unsparingly.
> The battle for bread is the battle for life. . . . Death and destruc-
> tion to the system and its upholders, which plunders and enslaves
> the men, women, and children of toil.

*   *   *

> Dynamite! Of all the good stuff, this is the stuff. Stuff several
> pounds of this sublime stuff into an inch pipe (gas or water-pipe),
> plug up both ends, insert a cap with a fuse attached, place this in
> the immediate neighborhood of a lot of rich loafers who live by the
> sweat of other people's brows, and light the fuse. A most cheerful
> and gratifying result will follow. In giving dynamite to the down-

> trodden millions of the globe, science has done its best work. . . .
> It is a formidable weapon against any force of militia, police, or
> detectives that may want to stifle the cry for justice that goes forth
> from the plundered slaves. It is something not very ornamental but
> exceedingly useful. . . . It is a genuine boon for the disinherited,
> while it brings terror and fear to the robbers. . . . A pound of this
> good stuff beats a bushel of ballots all hollow, and don't you forget
> it. Our lawmakers might as well try to sit down on a crater of a
> volcano.

These "traditional" anarchists of the late nineteenth and early twentieth centuries were, without doubt, responsible for a great deal of destruction, bombings, and killings. Their fanatacism was such as to elicit from the great grandfather of modern criminology, Lombroso, the cry, "A hundred fanatics are found to support a theological or metaphysical statement, but not one for a geometric theorem." [17] Yet at least it may be said of the old anarchists that they had an ideal, their utopian anarchy of life without external constraints. Modern anarchists, it seems, have no such dream. They are not idealists. They are nihilists. They wish to destroy for the sake of destruction, or at least with no consideration of the future at all.

MODERN TERRORISM. The prototype of this type of anarchist violence is that of the Baader-Meinhof gang in Germany. Although much of the activity of this gang has been terroristic, in the sense that terror strategies have been used to bring down authority, and it would appear that the gang was also trained in the Arab guerilla camps of Al Fatah, this gang can be distinguished from other terrorists groups, on a number of points.

First, it is composed of individuals of the disaffected middle class, not of an ethnic or subcultural minority. Second, the gang does not indulge in extensive ideological rhetoric as do most terrorist groups. Police have reported that the apartments of these terrorists are no longer full of ideological literature; in fact, they have found few books at all, suggesting that there is a strong nihilist streak to their activities. One researcher has argued that the Baader-Meinhof terrorists were motivated by alienation from society, the feeling that life is meaningless.[18] Certainly this explains their cold-bloodedness in the taking of hostages and execution of prominent citizens, since, if one decides that life is meaningless, the taking of lives is not an especially significant act.

The Baader gang left a trail of blood and destruction throughout the seventies. On May 14, 1970, the gang was "born" when Ulrike Meinhof, a sociology teacher, liberated Baader by shooting it out with police. During the next one and a half years, the gang bombed an American colonel, the Springer Press Building in Hamburg, and the U. S. Army headquarters in Heidelberg and carried out many other killings and bomb attacks. Of considerable interest is the fact that throughout this period, the gang enjoyed support from "left wing intellectuals," especially because the more terror this gang perpetrated, the more the "establishment" Germans called for strong retaliation. There was great fear that Germany would once again become an oppressive, Nazi-like state.

Meinhof was eventually caught and sentenced to eight years imprisonment for her part in the rescue of Baader. A prominent German judge, who had nothing to do with the case, was promptly assassinated by one of the gang, as reprisal. Meinhof hanged herself in her Stuttgart cell in May, 1976. She had, by the way, been operated on some several years before for a brain tumor, and her suicide has been attributed to "feelings of growing hopelessness or to her unbroken rebellious desire for spectacular self-sacrifice."[19] In 1977, the remnants of this gang continued to wreak havoc with the West German Government, and dissension rang strongly within the government about whether a "heavy hand" should be used to eliminate the terrorists. Then came the suicides of Baader and the core of his gang within the multimillion dollar specially built maximum security prison. At the very same time, a German Commando group rescued hostages from a hijacked plane in Somalia. Public suspicion grew. Had the government, the *democratic* government, allowed the use of violence against Baader and Meinhof? The situation in West Germany was one of incredible drama. The young West German government was literally taunted to breaking point by the Baader gang.

Why was this Baader gang so "successful" in comparison with the anarchists of the nineteenth century? There are two main reasons. The first and most obvious is that they enjoyed considerable popular support, which naturally made them a greater threat to a democratic government. The second is their training in terrorism. Compared to the classic anarchists, the violence of these nihilistic anarchists does not appear as sporadic or disorganized. The old anarchists had developed no strategy based upon what violence could do. In short, they put too much store in the effect of a violent act itself (e.g., "dynamite") instead of seeing violence as a *strategy* which required planning, organization, and careful selection of political targets. As we shall see below, it has been the terrorist groups who have refined political violence in this way.

Professor Ralph Dahrendorf, a former Secretary of State in the West German foreign ministry and a well-known sociologist, asked, why Germany? His answer was that the phenomenon has grown out of a process of soul-searching in the German culture. There is still the Nazi war to live down as far as the older generation is concerned. And the younger generation does not seem to have forgiven its elders for their mistakes, either of the past or the present. Germany's identity as *nation* is ambiguous, either as a protector of other people's rights, or as being solely concerned with the prosperity of its own citizens. It cannot be either of these, says Dahrendorf, and so it blunders ahead seeking an identity:

> I do not suggest that there is any link between terrorism and these questions—but the inability to answer them contributes to the insecurity, the sense of self-doubt, that pervades the country. As a country—dare I say "Nation"?—Germany has so far found neither purpose nor identity.[20]

Of course, it is not only Germany where terrorism has taken hold. But Dahrendorf has put his finger on an important psychological ingredient of terroristic activities: the search for identity. More on this shortly.

Violence to Acquire Power: Terrorism and Revolution

Terrorists use violence not chiefly as a "cleanser" or a "leveler" (although they may often use the rhetoric related to that anarchist ideology), but rather as a direct tool to invoke *fear* or *terror* in the hearts of those in power or those who would support authority. Thus they seek to maneuver authority into overstepping itself, into falling back too easily upon the use of physical force—all of which unleashes more repression. Another essential ingredient to successful terrorism is publicity, because, it is believed, the more publicity, the more fear and terror will be spread, and the more the repressive reactions of authority will be exposed.

The ideological underpinning of these terroristic strategies is traceable easily enough to Marxist revolutionary theory, although today these terroristic strategies are used by a wide range of terrorist groups, many of them having very little in common with Marxist ideology. It may even be argued, in fact, that terrorism is a distortion of Marx and certainly is contradictory to the basic principles of orthodox Marxist theory. This is why a great deal of argument went on among those whom I would call the fathers of modern terrorism—Fidel Castro, his brother Raul and Che Guevara—as to what revisions of Marx would be necessary to bring about a successful revolution in Cuba. Marxist theory, deliciously ambiguous concerning the nature of historical determinism, had traditionally been interpreted as relegating violence to a second, or at least incidental place: the famous analogy to childbirth, where pain is the necessary concomitant, but not the focus of the activity (according to the male Marx, that is!). Furthermore, the revolution could not occur until both "objective" (i.e., economic) and "subjective" (i.e., consciousness of the masses) conditions occurred. Therefore, up until Castro, the habit had always existed among traditional Marxists (and anarchists, too) of "waiting around" for the revolution to come. Castro and Guevara came to the conclusion that if they waited, nothing would happen. Instead, they chose to make things happen and theorized that once the violent revolution began, this would inspire the poor to take part. Castro's was essentially a rurally based revolution, the theory being that (1) guerilla activity needed the advantages of terrain to be able to ambush, kill, and retreat; and (2) the poor peasants, as they saw the successes of the guerilla band, would gradually join forces, so that eventually the "army of the people" would storm the main capital of the country.[21] Indeed, this is what happened in Cuba. Attempts to apply this essentially elitist theory of revolution in other parts of South America and elsewhere have failed. The most decisive failure was the hunting down of Guevara in Colombia by a trained and experienced anti-guerilla band.

We can see that, in contrast to orthodox Marxist theory, this is essentially an elitist theory of revolution, since it depends upon a small group which is ideologically "superior" to decide when and how violence will be employed, "for the good" of the poor, or of whatever group on whose behalf it is decided to revolutionize. It does not depend upon a widespread collective action of the masses of the downtrodden, which is, in my opinion, the kind of revolution that was envisaged by Marx. All modern terrorist groups which operate on the grounds that they are liberating someone or something are essentially elitist in this regard.

Upon the failure of Guevara in Colombia, a new theory was developed. This time, the strategy was outlined by Carlos Marighela in his *Mini Manual of the Urban Guerilla*. A maxim summed up the position: "Where the population is, there resides the revolution." The idea was for a small elite band of guerillas to begin insurrection in the city, to live in the lap of the repressive political organization of the State. In response to terrorist activities, the government would be forced into more and more repressive responses in an effort to crack down on the terrorism. The result would be that more and more innocent citizens' liberties would be infringed, so that they would eventually go over to the liberation army. These are Marighela's words:

> From the moment a large proportion of the population begin to take his activities seriously, his success is assured. The Government can only intensify its repression, thus making the life of its citizens

harder than ever: homes will be broken into, police searches organized, innocent people arrested and communications broken; police terror will become the order of the day, and there will be more and more political murders—in short a massive political persecution. . . . The political situation of the country will become a military situation.[22]

The activities of the urban guerilla were oriented towards not only the physical liquidation of its enemies through attacking property owners and big business, robbing banks, and stealing arms, but also the psychological destruction of the political establishment by an extensive propaganda campaign which uncovers the government's use of violence and thus demonstrates its dictatorial nature.

Marighela wrote his "manifesto" in 1971, yet similar urban guerilla insurrections had already failed in the early sixties in Guatemala and Venezuela. Marighela also failed in Brazil. There were many reasons for the failures. First, the guerillas found themselves up against rulers who were not as stupid as was Battista in Cuba. Second, they found themselves up against right wing terrorist groups, the prototype of which is the Brazilian Death Squad, a cadre of police and other right wing individuals who "unofficially" systematically sought out and executed revolutionaries, using violent methods that the governments are less in a position to adopt.[23]

In Venezuela, Bettancourt tried to avoid as much as possible overreaction by his government to the urban terrorists. Many local people turned against the guerillas, seeing *them* as the source of violence and infringement of liberties. In Guatemala, a combination of official government troops (with Green Beret U. S. Army advisers) and free-lance antiCommunist groups hunted down the guerillas, and internal dissension in the guerilla ranks (old guard Trotskyites against young idealists) led to its destruction.[24]

In fact, the use of ancillary, or "informal," squads to quash urban guerillas may have been a direct outcome of the Marighela emphasis upon provoking government oppression. In Brazil, the Death Squad during the period 1964–1970 was probably responsible for 1,000 killings of left wing terrorists.[25]

An interesting case, both because of partial success and the changes brought about, is that of the Tupamaros[26] in Uruguay. The Tupamaros were much more flexible in their use of violence, and although generally siding with the view that strategy should still be an urban strategy similar to Marighela's, they nevertheless saw the rural scene as one that would keep the government forces busy in dealing with armed raids.

From 1965–1967, they gained considerable publicity from "expropriating" money from banks, infiltrating universities and corporations. Their ranks became swelled by predominantly middle-class persons—civil servants, university professors, and students, later rather caustically termed "career revolutionaries" by Sir Geoffrey Jackson, the English diplomat who was kept prisoner for ransom in their "people's prison" for 244 days.[27] The Tupamaros also indulged in various "Robin Hood" activities, stealing provisions and redistributing them to the poor. They gained considerable publicity, investigations were made of their infiltration of the government, and chicanery was found in high places. Eventually there was no way to deal with the Tupamaros but to curb the traditional liberties of democracy (e.g., freedom of the press, no detention without trial). After an election in 1972 the new President, Borduberry, declared a state of internal war, and by October, 1972, over 2,400 suspects were in prison. On June 27, 1973, Borduberry dissolved Congress, and the expected "People's Democracy" fought for by the Tupamaros became a "Generals' Democracy."

Another failure. Yet the Tupamaros created an exciting vision of terrorism and demonstrated clearly that violence can indeed bring a government to the brink of desperation. They have been copied all over the world, the most clear and direct application of their methods being that of the Baader-Meinhof Gang in West Germany.[28]

The ultimate lesson that has been learned from all of these guerilla activities in South America is that the majority of them, although bringing down destruction on the guerillas themselves, did bring about change. Unfortunately, the changes were nothing like what these guerillas had anticipated: many governments became weakened only to be toppled by more repressive regimes.[29]

Perhaps the reason why urban terrorism has not brought about the kinds of total change that its proponents have hoped for has been its own strategy—its utter dependency upon the use of terror—and the way in which this strategy has been coldly and logically played out. While the terrorists confined themselves to the assassination and kidnapping of prominent businessmen they at least provided the possibility of a rationalization for the act, for those who felt economically oppressed, since they could easily see that the government cared more for the individual lives of "capitalists" than for the mass of workers. One might (only might) expect under these circumstances some popular sympathy for the terrorists. But the logic of terror, as we shall see when we look at violence in the exercise of power, is that it be used *indiscriminately, unpredictably,* against innocent people. Thus, the terrorists have leaned more and more to the kidnapping of planes, trains, and buses where innocent persons have been senselessly killed or maimed. It is difficult to see how such actions can gain popular sympathy. They produce nothing but public terror. In contrast, a rural guerilla insurrection depends upon the countryside and not the population, which lives largely in the cities and has little direct contact with rural guerilla activity. In fact, when one surveys the successful revolutions, most of them were essentially rural based: this includes the U.S.S.R., China, Cuba, and more recently Angola (which perhaps explains the heavy involvement of the Cubans).

So far, the excessive use of provocative violence has not been experienced in the United States. In spite of attempts by the FBI and other official sources to characterize the underground or revolutionary movements of the 1960s in the U. S. as terroristic or guerilla-like, compared to terrorist and guerilla movements elsewhere in the world—especially South America—the Weathermen and Black Power Movements, and the Yippies especially, have been very mild.[30] In the sixties they were certainly responsible for many riots and some bombings. But not at any time did their activities reach anything like the level of guerilla activity that has been achieved by such groups as the Tupamaros. There may be a number of reasons for this:

1. Some have suggested that the reason why terrorism has developed with such flair and to such serious proportions in South America, is that it is endemic to Latin American culture. It is a culture that is receptive to the spectacular and the daring, to the worship of folk heroes, and to the display of the Latin American macho image. This observation is buttressed by the fact that for the moment, many of these urban terrorist groups do not seem bent on gaining complete power, only flaunting it through disparate acts of violence.[31]

2. The repressive machinery of America's democratic politics overreacted to the slightest of provocations, so that the Weathermen, Yippies, and others needed to do little in the way of really violent revolutionary activity. Often, words were enough. Another reason may have been that the ideological underpinnings of many of the revolutionary factions were idealistically "love-oriented." Such an ideology, in its extreme form as espoused by the Yippies, was essentially an ideology of self-love. But in its less extreme form, it required love of others, making it difficult to shoot or kill indiscriminately. It is significant, in fact, that most of the American revolutionaries of the 1960s shied away from indiscriminate killing of innocents[32] (with the possible exception of the Manson clan—but there is some argument about whether this group is properly classi-

fied as "revolutionary"), and instead adopted an ideology of "we" versus "the pigs" (police, military, politicians, etc.). This was the first small step towards terrorism, but only a small step, and could hardly be interpreted as a systematic campaign of terror.

3. Another reason is that of the historical nature of the societies in which terrorism occurs. Most common is the presence of a "subculture" (about which we will speak in Chapter 4) which is either ethnically or religiously segregated as a minority, and which has a long history of oppression (whether real or perceived) and feelings of economic deprivation. An excellent example of this is Northern Ireland, where there is a long tradition of violence both by the Irish against the British and by the British against the Irish (this goes back at least as far as the massacres of the Irish by Oliver Cromwell in the seventeenth century). However, there are many subcultures that respond to oppression in ways other than terrorism. Such a group may develop a system of parallel governance which reaches a "compromise" with the "outside" government, such as has occurred with the Mafia organizations in Sicily over the last century,[33] and various other forms of "self-governance" that avoid open rebellion. One expert on terrorism has identified two decisive factors in propelling an oppressed minority towards open terrorism against the dominant culture: (1) encouragement by an external source, which may provide both ideological (e.g., Trotskyist) and material (e.g., weapons) support, and (2) the presence of a frustrated elite that is "prepared to overcome the natural distaste . . . to initiate violence by giving it an ideological justification."[34]

There are, of course, many variations of these themes. An interesting borderline case of an originally nonviolent subculture which became violent is that of the Doukhobor Sons of Freedom in Canada, which I will describe in detail in Chapter 4. It is a borderline case because its acts of terror were not primarily political but had a psychological and religious motivation. But the Doukhobors' actions did indeed evoke quite explicit political retaliation. Although it began as an essentially nonviolent religious community, a strange set of political, psychological, and social reasons and the influence of a series of rather weird "religious" leaders contributed to its becoming terroristic. In fact, the situation reached one of incredibility when the Canadian government seriously considered the question of whether the Doukhobors could claim exemption from military service on the grounds of a religious belief in pacifism, when at the same time they were bombing and burning public and private buildings![35] Furthermore, the Doukhobors, because they believed in parading nude, managed to incite the Canadian government to enact a three-year prison sentence for public nudity. Authority was once again easily maneuvered into overstepping itself and simply contributed to the Doukhobors' deeply held belief of their constant and malicious oppression by the Canadian government.

We might also note, by the way, that the problem of this terrorist group was exascerbated by sympathy for their position expressed by a number of academics who wished to preserve and respect Doukhobor culture. In fact, one can quite easily find books written by academics on the Doukhobors which do not mention at all their violent activities.[36]

Violence in the Exercise of Power

We tend to use the word "terrorism" to refer to oppressed minorities which use violence to "liberate" either themselves or others. Their violence may be seen as used to inflict terror from below. But there is also terror from above, the reign of terror. Although we find the spectacle of terrorism employed by rebels very frightening, the fact that it is used by a small minority that has, in most respects, very little power, allows us to relegate it to a place of lesser importance when compared to violence in the exercise of power. For here we have a situation in which a person or persons have already acquired power (through whatever means—it may be violence or simply an inherited position) and who use excessive violence to exercise it. Such a political structure is inherently weak in the sense that we can infer, from our earlier distinction between power and authority, that such rulers rule on the basis of very little consensual authority—hence their need to continually exercise their monopoly on physical force. The extreme of such a political use of violence is that of the reign of terror, in which violence is perpetrated indiscriminately and unpredictably upon the people. In this way, *all* people live literally in fear of their lives. The reigns of Stalin and Ahmin are probably excellent examples of this form of terror.

There are, of course, many variations in the use of terror from above. A shrewd tyrant will choose a hated minority upon whom to apply his indiscriminate violence, which leaves the rest of the masses untouched, safe, "pure." Hitler made the most sophisticated use of this form of terror. It is apparent that terror used by those in power can reach the most horrible proportions, such proportions that it is entirely understandable that the oppressed would want to become terrorists, rise up, and overthrow the tyrants. And here we have turned full circle. The big question is, and always has been: When are conditions so bad that one is justified in using violence to bring about change?

I cannot (and do not want to!) answer this question in a book such as this. Yet we must be aware that this question must be the basic one that all serious political activists have asked themselves. It follows, however, that since we are interested in understanding violence, we should perhaps look at the psychological aspects of political violence, which may at least help us to understand what moves political activists towards violence.

The Psychology of Political Violence

The Manichaean World

Franz Fanon[37] in his classic *The Wretched of the Earth* has, perhaps, exposed most successfully the psychological underpinnings of revolutionary violence. Revolutionary violence always occurs in what he calls a Manichaean World, by which he means that the "world" (i.e., culture, which includes the "mind") is divided into two compartments, each of which is the reflection of the other and uses its opposite to define itself. Nietzsche[38] was perhaps the first to berate Christians for defining what was good only by referring to what was evil. Marx set the bourgeoisie in contraposition to the proletariat. Genet gibes the judge who needs criminals so that he can identify himself as noncriminal.[39] Fanon shows that the white man defines himself as clean, intelligent, and good by identifying the black man as evil, stupid, and dirty. We can at once see how it is that people are able to commit such terrible acts of violence upon each other. Although in revolution violence is always for a lofty cause, the actual performance of a terrible act of violence is made much easier when the object of the attack is seen as being evil, unworthy—in fact less than human. It is no coincidence that soldiers in Vietnam referred to the enemy as "gooks," that protestors in the 1960s referred to police as "pigs," or that law enforcers have commonly referred to criminals as "animals" and "scum."[40]

But the Manichaean psychology goes deeper than this since it is clear that there is a strange interdependence of one side upon the other. Each relies upon the other for its identity. Both parties, therefore, have deep psychological reasons for the continuance of this Manichaean culture. This is why a potential revolutionary must undergo a considerable transformation if he is to break out of his dependence upon his oppressor for his identity. The solution that Fanon relies upon is also paradoxical—violence; yet it is this very behavior that the oppressors of the black man point to as evidence that he is a "wild animal." It is at this point that political violence is claimed to have inherent properties of psychological liberation.

Sartre writes in his preface to Fanon's *The Wretched of the Earth:* "To shoot down a European is to kill two birds with one stone . . . there remains a dead man and a free man."[41] In the Manichaean world of violence, the killer takes the place of the oppressor and the oppressor is reduced to nothing. An act of violence is revolution encapsulated; it frees both politically and psychologically. Jerry Rubin, the 1960s Yippie "revolutionary," illustrates the point: "Lee climbs to the witness stand in the Political Trial of the Century to accuse Amerika of assassinating him at birth. He screams: 'Amerika, I'm tired of wishing I were a Kennedy! I'm tired of hating what I am. I am a man!' "[42]

The Search for Identity

In many ways, Fanon's treatise, which has become the handbook of the third world revolution, is directed at the oppressed, the native, with a view to exhorting him to search out an identity. Since he must break out of that prescribed for him by the oppressor, he must create a new identity of his own. Fanon cautions against attempts to resurrect the native's dead culture of the past, but urges the forging of a new identity. What this new identity will be remains obscure, as it does in all these political ideologies. But it is clear that a major stumbling block, well recognized by Fanon, is to rise up, overthrow the oppressor, but then to avoid taking on the role or identity of the oppressor himself. It is, perhaps, ironic that many violent revolutionaries merely do what the word revolution implies: cause the power structure to simply revolve in a circle, the underdogs becoming the oppressors, and the oppressors becoming the underdogs.

The search for identity is also used as the rationalization for using violence, and this is usually bound up with historical factors relating to ethnic or national pride. The Palestinians, for example, use the argument for the necessity of a sovereign homeland—the concrete recognition of their national identity—as the sole justification for committing political violence. And this is when the majority of Palestinians have not lived in Palestine for centuries, and furthermore probably do not want to.[43] But those who *do* want to, probably a small minority, can nevertheless draw upon the sympathy that will be extended to them by expatriate Palestinians. National identity is a very powerful force, and its expression through the concrete sovereignty of a piece of land an ultimate necessity. From reports and examinations of terrorists of many different terrorist groups, but especially those of the Palestinians and more recently of the Moluccans in Holland, the search for national identity has been found to dominate the rhetoric of justification for the use of violence.

Almost word for word, what I have noted about the Palestinians may also be said in regard to the Israelis. And this leads us to our next point.

The Feuding Model

One wonders whether it is historical coincidence that the most devoted terrorists are various Arab factions whose forefathers were religiously and culturally, not so long ago (in some cases only one or two generations), devoted to the blood feud as a means of settling disputes.[44] The essential features of blood feuds are that (1) a wrong by one party against the other must be repaid by a similar reprisal (usually a killing) as a point of *honor,* and (2) the whole of the opposing party is held responsible for the wrongful act of one of its members. Therefore, it is entirely permissible to kill any member of the opposing clan as a reprisal.

The blood feud model fits very neatly into the Arab-Israeli conflict. It makes the killing of innocent civilians by terrorists entirely consistent with their cultural heritage and provides a useful political strategy as well. One might also add that the very nature of blood feuds throughout history is the continuity of their bitter hostility. Because each reprisal must be repaid by another reprisal, as a point of honor, there can be no end until one side is wiped out.

The P. L. O. has taken this model to the extreme and has added an additional twist. Not only does it argue that each act of Israeli violence must be repaid in kind, but its leaders claim that it explicitly operates upon an ideological base which is the *same* as that of the Israelis. Dr. Hacker, who reports on his discussions with the Palestinians at various refugee camps, notes:[45]

> According to the Palestinians, the success of the Zionists was due to a combination of three factors: the insistence on the realization of a dream of national independence on a certain "holy" territory; the determination to pay no attention to adverse opinions, including those of one's own people; and the unrestricted employment of all means to realize the dream of territorial independence.

The Palestinians noted that the British eventually had to give in, exhausted as they were by constant bloodletting; thus Palestinian terrorism will bring about the Arab Palestinian state in the same way. The Palestinians, of course, indulge in some distortions, and there are clear differences between the situations of the two. Terrorism was never an approved Zionist technique, martial conquest of Israel was never envisaged, and the Palestinians as a "race" have never been subjected to genocide.

It is easy to see the Manichaean perception that pervades Palestinian terrorism, to the point of using the enemy as a model for its violence. It is a justification for violence by "adoration of the enemy."

The History Game

There are many forms of this game, but they are easily identifiable as what psychoanalysts would call "intellectualization," "denial," and "rationalization," or in common language, "passing the buck." How many times has a teacher who has intervened in a classroom brawl heard, "It's not my fault, he started it!" In his discussions with terrorists Hacker found this familiar psychological defense to be used time and time again. Applied to terrorism, there are basically two forms of this history game. The first is for the terrorist to choose a particular point in immediate history to show that a particular violent act by the other side started everything. He then uses that "initial" violent act as the justification for reprisal. If one talks to the other side, of course, they will point out that there was a prior violent act so that they did not "start it."

The second form, more sophisticated, is the historical claim to sovereignty over a particular piece of territory. The most obvious and difficult example of this history game is that of Palestine, a piece of land to which several religious and cultural groups claim historical sovereign rights. And so the game goes on.

Why Not Nonviolence?

We know from the actions of Gandhi and Martin Luther King that active political protest can be launched on an ideology of nonviolence and can achieve some degree of success. Is there an important psychological factor in the choice of violence as against nonviolence as the political solution? There are two important points to this question. One is that nonviolent action, even if "unintentional," often precipitates violence. It is apparent that nonviolent action is often planned and executed with the full realization that those against whom one is protesting may be "incited" or "tempted" into doing violence. There can be no doubt that this occurred as a result of the freedom marches of the sixties and the fantastic antics of the Yippies.

The other is that nonviolence tends to be the choice made by the "liberal" intellectual, pretty much despised by right and left wing alike. The liberal has long been despised by Marxist-oriented writers for his opposition to violence. Although orthodox Marxists have generally counseled against the primary use of violence itself to bring about the revolution, it is clear from what I said earlier that violence is not *just* a by-product of revolution, as the Marxists would have us believe, but that it is essential to it. The idea of revolution without violence makes little sense.

Sorel[46], in his famous *Reflections on Violence,* insisted that violent revolution was necessary to display the humanitarian platitudes of the liberals for what they really were (i.e., middle class). He argued that the middle class uses the fear of violence as a ploy to stop the proletariat from rising up to overthrow the old order:

> There are so many legal precautions against violence and our up-bringing is directed towards so weakening our tendencies towards violence, that we are instinctively inclined to think that any act of violence is a manifestation of a return to barbarism; peace has always been considered the greatest of blessings.[47]

For the Marxist-derived theorist, violence is necessary to maintain the cleavage between the classes. Mao Tse-Tung says:

> Liberalism rejects ideological struggle and stands for unprincipled peace, thus giving rise to a decadent, philistine attitude and bringing about political degeneration.[48]

The virtuous people of the day, Sorel observes, use harsh violence to protect the existing social order and to assert the rightness of morality. And all this time the liberals preach to the left against the use of violence.

It is these liberals—the moderates, the "sensible" intellectuals—who, in preaching against violence, are the anti-heroes of the history of Western civilization. By opposing violence because it is a return to barbarity, they must put stake in a civilization whose history books are soaked with the blood of millions of people, those who were sacrificed for one "civilized" cause or another. By opposing violence they are showing faith in their Western civilization while at the same time rejecting one of its dominant cultural themes: violence. It is a strange predicament in which, by opposing violence, liberals actually help preserve the *status quo;* yet they are in fact opposing a value (violence) which the *status quo* applies for reasons of self-preservation. Yet liberals do not wish to defend the *status quo*—on the contrary, they wish to see "progressive social change." And it is at this point that they must adopt either a policy which works through the established system (e.g., lobbying, campaigning for a political candidate), or a policy of nonviolent protest. Indeed, nonviolent protest seems to offer the only way out of the liberal's dilemma—it impels him to action; it avoids the use of violence to achieve the desired ends; it does not have to work within the framework of the existing system (thus, marches on Washington have been a favorite method). Moreover, it seeks directly to change specific values and attitudes inherent in the *status quo*.

It can be seen how important to the liberal it must be for these protests to be nonviolent, regardless of who inflicts the violence—the protestors, the establishment, or both. The moment violence is involved, the liberal is placed in an impossible dilemma, unable to move in any direction. We can understand now how leaders of these liberal movements are often destroyed not only because they are despised by both right and left extremist groups, but also because they are unable to defend themselves. Thus, Martin Luther King was martyred, Ferguson and Harris (members of the extremist Revolutionary Action Movement) conspired to murder Roy Wilkins and Whitney Young, Jr. who were moderate civil rights leaders, and Malcolm X was murdered, probably by Black Muslims, just as he was beginning to liberalize his views.

The Pathology of Terror-From-Below

At the turn of the nineteenth century, when the activities of the traditional anarchists were at their height, the scientific study of human behavior was also gaining ground. There was no doubt among professionals at the time that these anarchists were stark, raving, mad fanatics.[49] Today, we are more cautious in attaching these "value labels" of mental illness, as they have come to be called.

But why are we so reticent to label terrorists as sick, when they so clearly act out the incredible contradictions that lie within their ideologies? Many of the great anarchists are characterized by historians as sweet, gentle, friendly, passive fellows. Yet all uttered the most incredible exhortations to violence, and many carried them out. Furthermore then, as now, many innocent people have been killed as a result of terrorist actions. Why should we be frightened to pass value judgments on them? If we are prepared to call them bad, why cannot we also call them sick? Surely, according to any reasonable interpretation of mental illness, the extreme acting out of a fantasy based upon so many impossible contradictions, that results in destruction often of the individual himself as well as others, warrants the label "sick" *as well as* (not instead of) bad? Or even good?

Is it not conceivable that the actions of a crazy, violent individual could constitute a violent act that was "good," yet still be a product of mental illness? An extreme example demonstrates the point: suppose a fellow in Nazi Germany was under the delusion that Hitler was Christ, and that this fellow had been ordered by the Devil to murder him. Would this not be the product of a crazed mind, but a violent act which most would applaud?

As it happens, the objects of political assassination are rarely, if ever, easily assessed as evil, or "deserving it." Rather, assassination is a facet of political violence in which the political and pathology arguments often meet head on.

Between 1865 and 1965, four American Presidents were assassinated: Lincoln, Garfield, McKinley, and Kennedy. Lincoln was the target of conspiracy, while the other three were the prey of assassins who were motivated by intense personal grievances, ideological commitments, or psychological problems. Although the Report to the Commission on Assassination and Political Violence[50] recognizes that the level of assassination of the highest officer of State is very high in the United States, another report of the Violence Commission assured us that assassination has at least not become part of the American political system itself, as it has in some Middle Eastern countries.[51] The only time when assassination became a part of the American political system appears to have been in New Mexico, from the end of the Civil War to about 1900. Many assassinations of prominent politicians of both the Democratic and Republican parties occurred during this period. Some have interpreted this outburst of assassinations as a "contagious phenomenon," when a "rash" of assassinations appears during a turbulent period, then subsides very quickly. The rash of assassinations of John F. Kennedy, Robert F. Kennedy, Martin Luther King, Jr., Medgar Evers, and Malcolm X are sometimes compared to the New Mexican period.

Space does not permit a review of all the major assassinations in United States history that would examine the motivations of the assassins or the political repercussions of their crimes. Suffice it to say that as far as the major assassinations are concerned, such as those of Lincoln, J. F. Kennedy, and Martin Luther King, there is simply no agreement on the political motives for the crimes, and there is the constantly nagging suspicion that they were the product of conspiracies of one kind or another. Undaunted, some psychiatrists have been willing to offer psychological analyses of political assassins, in attempts to show that they were suffering from severely abnormal psychological processes. Dr. Abrahamsen's assessment of Lee Harvey Oswald is a prime example.

Although acknowledging that there may be some legal doubt about whether Oswald was guilty of assassinating President John F. Kennedy, based upon an analysis of Oswald's childhood and family relationships and of apparent disturbances in his linguistic expression (spelling errors motivated by unconscious factors), Abrahamsen concluded that Oswald at the time of the assassination was probably in a world where fantasy and reality were intertwined.[52]

> During his last months Lee Oswald moved into a make-believe world where fantasy and reality were intertwined. He was functioning in accordance with what he wished the situation to be, not what it actually was. If he desired that President Kennedy, the most important man in the United States, should die, he most certainly, following his wish fulfillment, could wish that he be innocent of the crime. Protesting his innocence would have increased his sense of power, intensifying the gratification he derived from his revenge. Further, by denying the murder of the President-father, he would also be denying that he had ever had any sexual designs on his mother. Like the secret of her sexuality, he would now have a secret of his own.

Dr. Abrahamsen claims, after an analysis of the records of other American assassins, and also of a number of assassination threat cases in New York City, that there are a number of psychopathological attributes common to assassins:

1. The assassin unconsciously selects a victim who represents what he himself would like to be.
2. He experiences intense hatred, helplessness, and dependency, extreme fantasies of omnipotence, gory death wishes.
3. He always acts alone (the only possible exception to this is Lincoln's slayer, John Wilkes Booth).
4. He is always a personal failure.
5. He has extraordinary ambitions far beyond his intellectual capabilities.
6. He is incapable of establishing genuine human relationships.

It does, of course, serve the establishment well to dismiss the actions of a political assassin as those of a raving lunatic. But even if one grants the possibility that those assassins were "mad," it still remains to explain why their madness took the form that it did. After all, why not kill an overbearing wife or hostile mother, instead of a political leader? All these assassins had also developed explicit political ideologies to justify their actions. As such, their actions may quite possibly lay bare the defects of the established political order.

But when one considers the enormous machinery of violence that comes crashing down on the head of the political assassin (no matter under what political order), it is easy to understand that he would indeed have to be mad—deluded, in fact—to think that his individual act could possibly correct the injustice that he perceives in the established political order.

It is of interest that the majority of American assassins have, as far as can be established, acted alone. This is in stark contrast to the activities of modern terrorists who act in closely knit groups. I suspect that it is a somewhat easier task to diagnose as crazy an assassin who acts alone than it is to diagnose a whole group of people who act together in violence. This is not to say that this cannot, or should not be done. We have the Manson clan as clear evidence of that. In fact this question leads us to a very difficult problem concerning violence in general, and that is, if a small group can be diagnosed as suffering from some kind of mental pathology to do with violence, to how big a group can this diagnosis be applied? A whole village? A whole society? These questions are related, strangely enough, to the terror of tyrants.

THE PATHOLOGY OF TERROR-FROM-ABOVE

We find it easier to label as illness the terror that accompanies the reign of tyrants. Erich Fromm has given much attention to this question, having diagnosed such ghastly tyrants as Hitler, Goebbels, and others as necrophiliacs: persons literally in love with death, persons bent on the complete and utter destruction of everything they touch.[53]

Such reigns of terror, whether by Hitler, Stalin, Idi Amin, or Papa Doc (and I am sure there are many more—perhaps even forming a majority throughout the nations of the world), I have no difficulty in categorizing as pathological; likewise, I do not object to tracing this terror to the abnormal psychology of particular tyrants and their small groups of enforcers.

One may well ask, why are these tyrants able to get away with such unmitigated violence, often for many decades? Apart from the most obvious (and probably most important) fact that these tyrants have the monopoly on physical force, there are two other factors involved.

First, a number of theorists have concluded that Hitler, while perhaps mad, nevertheless was personifying or implementing the wishes of the mass of the German people.[54] In other words, he was merely the expression of what everyone wanted. The inevitable conclusion from this argument is that all the German people were therefore mad. Thus, the word "mad" takes on an explicit political meaning. It also loses its original meaning, since the word is usually used to refer to someone who deviates from the normal to a marked degree. Nevertheless, the argument of this essentially psychoanalytic theory is that there is a "consensual" base for the leader, but it is not a consensus of the kind I described earlier in the sense of the social contract. Rather it is an irrational, unconscious wish on the part of the masses to do violence, which the tyrannical leader expresses.

Second, there is the fact of human obedience, or what we might call obedient aggression. Psychoanalysts long ago coined the phrase "identification with the aggressor," which described the process whereby a person who is thrust into a situation of considerable political aggression and brutalized by an aggressive superior may begin to take on the attributes of that aggressor, and so brutalize those who are subordinate to him. This phenomenon was observed in concentration camps during World War II by Bruno Bettelheim,[55] and the exploitation of this psychological process has also occurred in many American prisons where particular inmates are chosen to act as guards. Inmate-guards are well known for their brutal and aggressive implementation of prison authority.

Two famous experiments, one by Zimbardo and the other by Milgram, have also demonstrated that in the confined conditions of the laboratory, subjects will obediently physically punish others to points which could be severely physically injurious to the victims.[56] However, those experiments have been severely criticized from a number of points of view, so that it is not clear whether the aggressors were aggressing because they were "obedient," rather than because they were perceptually confused by the very rare and unusual circumstances of the experiments. Nevertheless, the experiments do show that, given the right conditions, tyrants (the experimenters Zimbardo and Milgram) can get subjects to behave very aggressively.

The most serious criticism of the Zimbardo experiment has been that, by claiming to simulate prison conditions, it in fact oversimplified and distorted the prison model. Violence does, of course, occur in prisons and other confined institutions. But these cases are more complex than simply the aggressive guard-inmate relationships, as we shall see in Chapter 7.

Summary and Conclusions

1. Violence to enforce authority is used in all complex societies. The extent to which it is used will be a measure of the effectiveness of the strength of legal and consensual authority in the society.

2. Violence to challenge authority has been used by various anarchist movements and by modern terrorists. While traditional anarchists believed in the power of violence itself to destroy authority, modern terrorists use violence as a strategy to inflict terror and to invoke excessive government repression.

3. Violence to achieve power is that used by revolutionaries and many rural terrorist groups. Although revolutionary movements are based on Marxist theory, modern revolutionaries favor an "elitist" theory which requires bringing the revolution to the masses, rather than waiting for it to arise according to economic conditions.

4. Violence in the exercise of power is that used by various forms of tyranny which do not have the consensus of the population.

5. The central social-psychological processes of political violence are:
    a. A perception of the world as Manichaean
    b. The search for identity
    c. Historical claims to sovereignty over territory
    d. A feuding mentality
    e. The belief that only violence can be a radical action
    f. Both terror from above and below may be seen as psychopathological, regardless of the "political benefits" of the action.
    g. Terror from above depends upon obedient aggression.

6. The question was raised whether a whole culture can "go mad," which some say happened in Nazi Germany. The thesis implied in such a conception is that there can be a "national character" or that whole societies can be characterized as "violent." This question is of more than passing interest if we are to understand violence in the United States, for in the past two decades, America has achieved an image of being a violent society, and American scholars have done much to promote the idea that there is a thread of violence running throughout American history. The next chapter will evaluate the evidence for this claim.

Historical Violence: Continuities and Discontinuities

America's Violent Image: History Distorted

In 1970, a staff report to the National Commission on the Causes and Prevention of Violence concluded that "violence to achieve political goals is a thread which runs through the history of the United States."[1] Historians who contributed to the National Commission expressed great surprise that American scholars could have for so long ignored the importance of violence in the political history of the United States. They then went on to catalogue a great list of violent incidents beginning with the American Revolution and ending with the Vietnam War. Yet one of those historians, Charles Tilly, noted in his examination of the history of European violence, that the most salient characteristic of violence throughout history may be the incredible variety of the forms that it has taken.[2]

The truth of the matter is that there is no "thread" of violence in United States history, except under certain well defined subcultural conditions. For there to be a "thread" one must show that all varieties of violence—the Revolution, vigilantes, war against the Indians, agrarian and labor protest, to name but a few—are connected to each other by factors or forces *other than violence,* otherwise the statement about a "thread of violence" is tautological. The error all these historians have made is to assume that violence is a unitary phenomenon and that in its more extreme meaning it is a single "cultural force," or something to that effect. It may already be apparent, or if not, it will become quite clear through this book that violence is anything but a unitary phenomenon. Rather it is a catchall word that is used to refer to a wide range of often very different events and behaviors.

The thesis advanced by some of those historians about why scholars had overlooked much of America's "violent past" was that they had taken as significant only those kinds of violence which resulted in re-arrangements in the authority structure (e.g., the revolution), but had ignored history as it may be seen by "the underdog"—the ordinary, "oppressed" working man. Much of this view may have been conditioned by the climate of the times (the violent 60s) and by the then very influential shift in views of history, perhaps heralded by E. P. Thompson's classic, *The Making of the English Working Class,* towards a recounting of history "from the bottom" rather than "from the top." In any event, much of the historical and comparative work produced in the Staff Report on *The History of Violence in America* reads like an apology for the violent protests of the sixties. The thesis appeared to be, "America has always been violent, therefore, the violence of the sixties is explained by our violent past."

One final apology-explanation was presented. It was noted that Europe also has an extensive history of political violence—especially France and England—yet neither of these countries has an image of violence like that of the United States. The report went so far as to observe that the deaths resulting from the turbulent decade of the 1960s were considerably fewer in America, as compared to Europe: only 1.1 per million population compared to 2.4 per million in Europe.[3] It didn't seem to be fair. America, born the half brother to that cradle of European strife, the French Revolution; America, carrying on the traditions of violence in Western civilization, was suddenly seen as a violent country. And this image continues today, even though the levels of political violence and terrorism are vastly lower than throughout Europe.

Why? Americans have contributed a great deal to this imagery themselves. Certain aspects of historical violence, even though playing only a minor role as far as national events are concerned, have been romanticized and mythologized as national culture; the two most obvious of these are the frontier tradition and the Indian wars. Historians of the 1960s themselves contributed to this imagery by indulging in the fantasy that all violent incidents in America's history are in some way connected to produce a "culture of violence" or some other unitary phenomenon.

Let us now look at some of the forms of historical violence in the United States, which we will try to analyze from the point of view of their continuity or discontinuity in relation to other forms of violence in history. We may usefully draw upon the scheme outlined in the previous chapter: the political purposes for which violence has been used (to acquire or exercise power, to enforce or challenge authority) and the psychological processes that appear to have underlain historical violence.

Revolutionary Violence

The American Revolution may be seen as violence used at first to challenge authority and eventually to acquire power. The familiar tactics of political violence were used. In 1770, British officers and troops were goaded by patriotic roughnecks into perpetrating the so-called Boston Massacre. The old, well organized mobs of Boston were used for revolutionary purposes, and were, it seems, at the beck and call of Samuel Adams. Apart from regular military clashes, Whigs and Tories fought and ravaged each other throughout New Jersey,[4] and by 1780, guerilla bands in North and South Carolina tortured and murdered each other, no side displaying any mercy,[5] and "the most squalid sort of violence was from the very beginning . . . put to the services of revolutionary ideals. . . ."[6]

Yet it would be a mistake to analyze the violence of the American Revolution from a purely political point of view. One may also view it as a search for identity: the old, closely knit communities of New England had given way to the growth of larger towns and cities. Once, the authoritarian structure of the New England religious communities had been based upon the rule of law and of God and had provided a sense of identity and security. Now, the continued economic oppression of King George and the throb of economic life in the towns and cities forced the search for the creation of a new society, one that would guarantee basic rights and freedoms. As we are well aware, the Bill of Rights is not just a document that arose in reaction to England's oppression. Rather, it was created out of a new vision, an ideal vision of a democracy, a vision no doubt strongly conditioned by the philosophies in France which were also to lead later to the French Revolution.

In comparison to the bloody executions issuing from the French Revolution, there appears to have been little formal recrimination once the revolutionary war was won. The reasons for this were probably two. First, there was by no means a consensus among the population in the American colonies that armed rebellion against England was either justifiable or useful. The Manichaean division, about which I spoke in the previous chapter, did not occur in this Revolution as it has in most modern revolutions in the sense that there was a total division, both geographic and social, between the "good" and the "bad." It is true that guerilla forays were fought between "Whigs" and "Tories," but one needs to see this strife as strife *within* the American ranks. The Revolution was therefore not a clear fight between "the Americans" and "the British."

The second reason is that the American Revolution was, in comparison to the revolution in Europe up to that moment, fought over an incredibly vast terrain and over a long stretch of time. The sporadic guerilla fighting that had ranged from the lower Hudson, through the trackless pine barrens of New Jersey, through to North and South Carolina and Georgia, continued for much longer in these Southern states, and took on especially violent forms:

> Negro slaves were stolen back and forth, and baleful figures like the half-crazed Tory leader, Bloody Bill Cunningham, emerged from the shadows to wreak special brands of murder and massacre. Neither side showed the other any mercy. Prisoners were tortured and hanged.[7]

This guerilla strife, which lasted long after the war of independence had been brought to a conclusion, and which was isolated in the Southern states, suggests the possibility of a link to later forms of American violence. Some historians have suggested that lynch law grew out of the terrible strife that occurred in these Southern states as a result of the chaotic revolutionary guerilla wars. However, lynching, at least as an aspect of vigilante law, was in existence well before the revolutionary war. The link of violence nevertheless is there—even if viewed simply from a geographic point of view, since the cycle of violence in isolated areas of these Southern states was to continue—through the Civil War and the frontier tradition, to the violent gangsterism of the early twentieth century. We shall look more closely at these links shortly. For the moment, I want to emphasize that this is the only case for which there is any evidence for the linking between different violent events in any historical periods.

Violence and the Civil War: The Honor of the South

I am not the first to say it, and probably will not be the last, but one is simply stunned at the ghastly slaughter that was produced by the Civil War and at the deep scar that this war left upon the culture of the American South—and perhaps America as a whole. Are we able to trace a "thread" of violence from the American Revolution to the Civil War?

This is probably a silly question. The causes of each war have been analyzed by many, many scholars, and although there is little agreement concerning the dominant causes of each war, no historian in his right mind could conclude that it was "violence" or the American proclivity to violence that produced them. The historical, economic, and cultural conditions that surrounded each war were vastly different. The only similarity that one could argue for was the end result—violence.

We have noted that sporadic guerilla wars continued in the South for some time after the Revolution. Then came the expansionist war of 1812, in which Southerners fought with great gusto, followed by the Mexican War of 1846–1848. In fact, from the very beginning, it is well documented that the South established a great tradition of violence, of which she was very proud, and Southerners were quite convinced of their military superiority over the North. The reason they gave for this was frankly racial, arguing that the South was settled by cavaliers ". . . directly descended from the Norman Barons of William . . . a race distinguished for a . . . war-like and fearless character, a race . . . renowned for . . . gallantry . . . chivalry . . . gentleness, and intellect."[8] In contrast, they said, the North was settled by disaffected religionists. Furthermore, much of the back-country was settled by Scots and Scotch-Irish, a people with an incredibly warlike history. In fact, although I know of no historical documentation of it, one is inclined to see the later rise of feuding violence as a direct continuation of the tradition of clan warfare carried on for centuries in the Scottish Highlands.[9]

John Hope Franklin, in his fascinating *The Militant South,* documents the pleasure and pride with which the Southerner contemplated violence. While the North delayed in sending troops to fight the Mexican War, Southern men abandoned their homesteads en masse; Tennessee responded to the call for 3,000 men with 30,000! Governor Albert G. Brown of Mississippi was considered too slow in putting the state on a war footing. Men marched to Jackson and burned Brown in effigy, and the feelings of the men were expressed in a local paper:

> *Our Gov'ner has betrayed his trust*
> *He has disgraced our name*
> *And for his treacherous acts we have*
> *Condemned him to the flame.*
>
> *Alas! let this hereafter be*
> *A warning to the rest*
> *We love a brave and valiant man*
> *A coward we detest.*[10]

The performance of the Southerner in the Mexican War did a great deal to enhance the Southerner's belief in his military might and superiority. But there were at least two other factors that contributed to the fiercely violent atmosphere of the South. These were the "cavalier" tradition of defending one's honor—a theme that we shall run across time and again throughout this book, and the other was the social and cultural condition of slavery.

Violent defense of honor occurred in two forms: either in the formally arranged duel or in an immediate and ferocious attack by the insulted upon the insulter. Both forms were very common during the pre- and post-Civil War period:

> The Summer Sports of the South, as Major Noah calls them, have already commenced in Huntsville. On Monday last, in the Court Square, and during the session of Court, too, a man by the name of Taylor stabbed another by the name of Ware in such a shocking manner that his life is despaired of . . . this stabbing and dirking business has become so common and fashionable, that it has lost all the horror and detestation among . . . our population. . . .[11]

> In the South, the swagger of the bully was called chivalry, a swiftness to quarrel was regarded as courage. The bludgeon was adopted as a substitute for argument; and assassination was lifted to fine art.[12]

According to Franklin, this proclivity to defense of honor pervaded all levels of social life—from the most responsible churchgoers down. Furthermore, this view of violence was bred into the children:

> On one occasion a member of the grand jury went outside when he found his son of eight or nine years of age fighting with another boy. The father looked coolly on until it was ended and said, "now you little devil, if you catch him down again bite him, chaw his lip or you'll never be a man."[13]

If these observations are to be believed, then we have here one piece of evidence to support the thread of violence theory: children were explicitly taught to value the concomitants of violence with which today's sociologists have become very familiar: toughness, defense of honor, courage, hatred of cowardice, ferocity. This militant attitude of the South can be traced back well into the Revolutionary War, in which, by the way, it is now widely recognized the Southerners fought heroically and against incredible odds.

The relationship between the institution of slavery and the "martial spirit," as Franklin calls it, is also quite clear. Many view the "genteel" social structure of the South as one similar to that of classical Greece and Rome: a system of gentlemen, intelligent, aristocratic, buttressed economically and morally by an immense system of slavery. It is also apparent that apart from the obvious economic advantages of slavery, the whole culture, social structure, and psychology of the white elite depended utterly upon the maintenance of the slavery system. The strange psychological and cultural interdependence of master and slave was not to be clearly unearthed until our own time by such writers as Jean Genet, and in the works of Fanon, aspects of which I described in the previous chapter.

The important point concerning violence was that the slave was never *completely* subjugated, no matter how the whites wanted to characterize him as submissive and docile. Many outside observers who traveled through the South reported a pervasive feeling of fear on the part of the whites. There were a sufficient number of slave uprisings, some of them brutal (such as Nat Turner's bloody march) to provide justification for fear, but also for the constant vigilance over the slave, the insistance upon absolute control.[14] Judge Thomas Ruffin of the North Carolina Supreme Court noted: "The power of the master must be absolute, to render the submission of the slave perfect. . . ."[15] Brutal and savage discipline of the slave was therefore quite a logical solution to this need for perfect submission.

Another aspect of the need for eternal vigilance was the development of the patrol system, originating probably as early as 1690 in South Carolina. These patrols, at first military, but later paramilitary organizations, were empowered to enter peacefully any plantation, and forcefully any slave cabins, for the purpose of identification and regulation of slaves. Because of the fear among the white communities of runaway slaves, even among whites who were not plantation owners, the operation of these patrol systems was of great importance. In many ways it performed the functions of a special police force. It also ensured that the institution of slavery was strongly supported by the military. The patrol system was a reassurance against that ever-present nightmare, a massive slave revolt:

> Let it never be forgotten, that our Negroes are freely the JACOBINS of the country; they are the ANARCHISTS and the DOMESTIC ENEMY: the COMMON ENEMY OF CIVILIZED SOCIETY, and the BARBARIANS WHO WOULD, IF THEY COULD, BE- COME THE DESTROYERS OF OUR RACE.[16]

We see here another strange mixture often associated with violence: the Southerner was ferocious, courageous, and honorable, yet he was also susceptible to excessive fear of those to whom he insisted he was racially and civilly superior. The Manichaean psychology was at work; the Southerner unconsciously feared his own barbarity most of all—and it was this that he imputed to the black man, so that he could so vehemently repress it.

Lest it be imagined that I am suggesting that this atmosphere of Southern violence "drove" the South into war, let me hasten to add that I am not. Many books have been written about the causes of the Civil War, and it is not my intention to add to that pile of complexities. I am, however, attempting to show that there is one continuous thread in the South from the early years of colonization through to the Civil War which has been strengthened by two important facts: (1) the historical fact that there was more or less a continuous series of wars from the war of independence through to the Civil War in which, for many reasons, the South was centrally involved; and (2) a tradition of violence, or violent spirit, if you will, was consciously inculcated from one generation to the other.

Violence and the Civil War: Protest North and South

If I have given the impression so far that all of the South, to a man, rushed gung ho into the Civil War on behalf of the Southern cause, I must now correct that impression. Historians have noted that much of the Civil War violence occurred as guerilla strife which paralleled the regular military action.

Strong pockets of resistance to the Confederate government existed in the mountain regions of North Arkansas, North Alabama, and Eastern Tennessee, and even in parts of Mississippi and Texas. In North Texas, for example, a "plot" was uncovered in September of 1862, in which a number of Unionist sympathizers were said to have conspired to kill all the people in Cooke, Grayson, Wise, Denton, and Collin Counties, so that the land would have been rendered defenseless against the invading Unionist forces and the plotters would have inherited the land for themselves. This resulted in the "Great Hanging" at Gainesville in 1862 of 39 offenders. Martial law was proclaimed in the areas, and a "citizen's court" passed judgment on the accused. A contemporary account of the trial concluded that:

> . . . the guilt of the conspirators is questioned by none. That they deserved death is granted by all . . . [that] their designs would very soon have culminated in open acts of violence, bloodshed, robbery and wanton licentiousness cannot be denied.[17]

The familiar contradiction of loyalties inherent in civil war is made clear by an offender's plea for mercy from the court:

> . . . I did not think or desire an honest effort to reestablish the Union could be termed criminal. . . .[18]

The court showed no mercy, and he was hanged along with the rest of the offenders. In the North and Midwest, resistance to the war took the form of violent mass protests which culminated in the draft riots of 1863 in New York City, when for three days uncontrolled rioting took over.[19] Similar rioting occurred throughout Southern Indiana, Illinois, and Iowa, and guerilla wars broke out between Union soldiers and bands of Union deserters. The worst savagery took place along the Kansas-Missouri border, where Jim Lane and his Kansas Jayhawkers fought a guerilla war with Confederate guerilla groups that included William Quantrell, Frank and Jesse James, and the Younger boys.

The widespread use of "citizen's courts" in the northern parts of the South and in the West, are commensurate with other types of violence that continued in the South after the Civil War—vigilante violence. The uses of violence as protest during the Civil War also laid the foundations for other forms of violence after the Civil War—namely, agrarian and labor protest.

Vigilante Violence

Some historians have characterized the vigilante movements as the prototype of American violence.[20] In it we see the harsh, relentless pursuit of individuals and groups who have been defined as "bad" by the vigilante committee, which has mostly, though not always, been composed of conservative, established merchants and middle-class citizens of a town, who wished to protect their personal liberty. Furthermore, the phenomenon of vigilantism seems to be native to America, for no parallel to it can be found in European countries, even during their most violent periods.[21]

Apart from its violence, the central feature of vigilantism would appear to be its highly moralistic stance, and it is the latter, I suggest, that is more prototypically American, than is the violence per se. There is no denying that America is, and has been, since independence, and even before, a moral society in the true sense of that phrase. It was no coincidence that the great sociologist Weber chose as his model to illustrate the relationship between capitalism and puritanism, Benjamin Franklin, America's first capitalist and popular moralist.[22] With the American Revolution were born two great American preoccupations: the idea of individual liberty as a direct reaction to the yoke of colonial rule and the idea of equality, directly transported from the catch-cries that led to the French Revolution. But these two lofty goals may be inherently contradictory.[23] For within the American scene, liberty came to mean freedom to create one's own prosperity, with the concomitant emphasis upon the accumulation of property. Sociologists have come to realize what now ought to be obvious: that when equal opportunity exists in a situation of liberty which aims at prosperity for all, people do not become more equal, but in fact the gap between the haves and have-nots must inevitably increase.[24] It may certainly be that overall prosperity may increase, but it is clear now that the notion of deprivation is highly relative to what others have that one does not. We can see here that these abstract ideas are hopelessly intertwined with each other; when they are coupled with the intensity of American moralism, it is not surprising that confusion, misunderstanding, confrontation, and subsequent polarization have occurred frequently throughout the short history of the United States.

The natural outcome of this combination of contradictions and moralism is that invariably certain groups and types of people become defined as "bad," or "the enemy." In some, perhaps most, situations the question of who is "bad" is difficult to determine, which explains why so much of the action of the two great American wars was given over to chaotic guerilla violence, and also why Americans have spent so much time in identifying aliens, enemies, and heretics, especially those suspected of conspiratorial intent.

The classic definition of vigilantism is "taking the law into one's own hands." There are two factors that will produce such a radical action. First, social conditions must be such as to require radical action to preserve the very basics of order: the preservation of life and limb. Second, those who begin a radical action must hold a strong moral conviction that what they are doing is right.

Vigilantism arose around 1760 in the back country of South Carolina in response to the absence of law and order. The early phase, prior to the Civil War, dealt largely with frontier horse thieves and counterfeiters. The main thrust of vigilantism was to establish the basis for the typical American community structure: the values of property, law and order. Although the early vigilante movements commonly got out of hand and reaped more violence than the violence they claimed to be preventing,[25] by the time the nineteenth century was under way, the vigilante movement had become something of a membership club for the elite—that of San Francisco in 1856 was completely dominated by the leading merchants who aimed to stamp out crime and corruption.[26] During this era of unregulated violence, the vigilante committees were concerned with the pursuit and destruction of those whom they defined as enemies of the concrete, business-oriented values they stood for—values that could be summed up as protection of property. After the Civil War, however, the pursuit of those defined as "bad" was broadened. While the defense of property retained a great deal of attention (e.g., the anti-horse thief association which continued until World War I), a new movement grew which saw its mission as regulating poor whites and other "failures" in American society. This was the White Cap movement, which gave vent to the persecution (usually flogging) of a much broader variety of people. We can see in it an intense moralism ("loose women" were a favorite target) and the deeply symbolic function of punishing those who had failed to take advantage of the liberty to achieve prosperity that the "haves" thought everyone, if he were diligent and responsible, could attain. The victims of White Capping therefore, were "punished" because they were the unseemly evidence that the ideal of liberty, prosperity, and equality had not been achieved.

Another more notorious vigilante organization was the Ku Klux Klan. Although the first Klan arose prior to White Capping, the second Klan seems to have been closely related to White Capping, which began in the 1880s—about two decades after the first Klan, and three decades before the second.

After the Civil War, the white elite of the Old Confederacy employed violence, from beating and flogging to burning at the stake, to retain supremacy in the South. The first Ku Klux Klan lasted from 1865 to 1876, and was the principal vehicle of terror and violence in the pursuit of its fundamental objective: "the maintenance of the supremacy of the White Race in their Republic by terror and intimidation."[27]

A congressional investigation of 1871 established that the Klan was responsible for thousands of hangings, shootings, whippings, and mutilations. Why did the Klan arise? Although there were many plots and slave uprisings prior to the Civil War and these had been put down ruthlessly and effectively, it is apparent that the memory of these revolts and the psychological fears inherent in a Manichaean society, created the substance for hysterical fears by the whites of their black underlings. With the end of the Civil War, they lost many of their legal rights of domination. Furthermore, the slaves rarely were able to organize themselves into large uprisings, but tended, when they did revolt, to attack individual masters and families. Thus, the apparent randomness of these events could only serve to foster the fires of fear.

The second Ku Klux Klan sought out different victims: the Negro was only secondary, and the main targets of persecution were the "shiftless" whites—fairly clearly an extension of the White Capping movement. The congressional investigation of 1921 concluded that violence, terror, and intimidation were the dominant objectives of the Klan. By 1925, the Klan boasted four to five million members—ten times that of the first Klan—and was drawing its members from all over the United States.

Racist theories led this Klan to join with pro-Nazi movements in 1940, so that their targets of persecution were expanded to include Jews. The third Klan arose after World War II, and directed its activities towards Negroes, Jews, Catholics, and civil rights workers. Violence remained, and still remains, its central theme. We should also note that while the Ku Klux Klans have been the dominant organizations of unmitigated violence, many other organizations arose, mainly purporting to defend the moral society of America. These were often directed against immigrants from Catholic and non-Teutonic Europe. Thus, the Roman Catholics, the Irish, and the Italians bore the attacks of the Native American Party in the 1830s and 1840s, and in the 1850s from the "Anti-Popery Union" and the "know nothings" (who received their strange nickname from the instruction members were given to say, "I know nothing," when questioned about their activities). Once again, the activities of these various moralistic organizations were not confined to the South, and in fact flourished in many parts of the North and Midwest.

Protest, Reform Movements, and Violence

The two dominant classes of people that have fought violently for reform in America have been the rural farmers and the industrial laborers. It testifies to the contradictory nature of the American ideals of prosperity and equality for all, when we see what great battles these groups have had to fight to ensure that they would be given a chance to share in the landowner's or big industrialist's prosperity.

Agrarian Protest

As early as the end of the seventeenth century, there was an agrarian uprising in Virginia[28] which formed the basis of Nathaniel Bacon's movement and resulted in the burning of Jamestown. Later, violent riots and attacks on landlords occurred as a result of the activities of the New Jersey land rioters, the North Carolina Regulators, and the New York anti-rent movement, all during the eighteenth century. The Paxton Boys of Pennsylvania[29] followed their massacre of Indians with a march on Philadelphia. After the revolution of independence, there were a number of rebellions.[30] Shay's Rebellion in Massachusetts (1786–1787) broke up court sessions to delay land foreclosures; the Whiskey Rebellion in Pennsylvania (1794) and the Fries' Rebellion in Eastern Pennsylvania were revolts against taxes on liquor and land; and in the Mississippi Valley before the Civil War, the Claims Clubs arose to defend the land occupancy of the squatters.

The land reform movement in California created a night-rider league in Tulane County in 1878–1880 to resist railroad land agents. The tobacco farmer cooperative movement utilized a night-rider organization to break monopoly domination of the market by raiding Kentucky towns, destroying tobacco warehouses, and abusing uncooperative farmers. The Green Corn Rebellion organized a march on Washington which resulted in a violent confrontation with sheriffs and posses. In response to the working conditions of the agrarian depression in the 1920s and 1930s, the Farmer's Holiday Association led strikes and boycotts, roughed up opponents, and blocked roads. Professor Brown concludes along with many others in the Staff Report to the President's Commission on the Causes and Prevention of Violence: "repeatedly farmers used the higher law—the need to right insufferable wrongs, the very justification of the American Revolution—to justify the use of violence in uprising after uprising."[31]

The implication, once again, made by these historians by such a conclusion is that the "thread of violence" began with the American Revolution. Need I say again that this is a distortion of history and of the meaning of violence. There is no documented evidence that any direct relationships existed between the long string of agrarian uprisings, a small sample of which I have listed above. Rather these uprisings came about because of the unique and special economic and social conditions at particular periods in history. The mere observation that violence occurred in all of these uprisings does not justify the conclusion that they were related by a "thread of violence." To support the proposition, one would have to show, among other things, that the children of successive generations were inculcated with the value that violence is an acceptable means of righting insufferable wrongs. If anything, and the historians of the sixties even show it, children were taught the opposite—that the *only* occasion in which violence was presented as justifiable was in the War of Independence—i.e., history "written from the top."

Labor Protest

The history of the American labor movement is also one of constant battles between variously perceived "haves" and "have-nots." Along with the industrial revolution of the nineteenth century, after the Civil War America experienced an enormous industrial growth, and with it many labor organizations: the Knights of Labor, American Railway Union, American Federation of Labor, Western Federation of Miners, and Industrial Workers of the World. The strike was their major weapon, and invariably the unyielding attitude of the capitalists led to harsh confrontations, social disorganization, and violence. The great railroad strike of 1877 triggered massive riots which reached the level of insurrection in Pittsburgh, and American labor relations moved quickly towards an explosive climax. At the same time, the Molly Maguires—a secret organization of Irish miners—fought their employers with assassination and mayhem.[32]

We may identify two small threads (tiny threads) of violence transported to the coal mines from Europe. First, there was the striking similarity in social and economic conditions between the coal fields of Europe and of Pennsylvania, especially since in the case of the Molly Maguires, it was the Irish against the English. One historian has suggested that because the conditions were identical, it was inevitable that a violent secret society should arise in the United States in exact replication of the secret societies that flourished in Ireland.[33]

Second, there is some evidence that Marxist ideology had been imported at least as early as the Molly Maguires. In any event, those against whom these uprisings were directed—the wealthy industrialists—had no doubts on the matter. Franklin B. Gowan, president of the Philadelphia and Reading Railroad Company noted: ". . . a class of agitators . . . men brought here for no other purpose than to create confusion, to undermine confidence, and to stir up dissension between employer and the employed . . . advocates of the Commune and Emissaries of the International."[34] The constant involvement of Pinkerton men in the employ of the industrialists in putting down (violently and ruthlessly) many strikes was morally justified in the several self-serving novels written by Allan Pinkerton, who made a special effort to paint these strikers as "Communists and Thieves."[35]

In fact, the behavior of the Pinkerton men and the industrialists in ruthlessly putting down labor strife testifies to an important, and rather commonplace, observation: it takes two to do violence. It is one thing to "blame," as did the establishment during that time, the violence upon Irish and other immigrants. But it should not be forgotten that in their moralistic stance, the industrialists and their enforcers certainly never gave a second thought to the use of violence in maintaining their "moral" position, and this often at the expense of the lives of innocent women and children.

The period subsequent to the Molly Maguires has been termed the dynamite period in labor relations—and understandably.[36] In 1886, there was the Haymarket Riot in Chicago, in 1892 the Homestead Strike and the Coeur d'Alene, Idaho silver mining troubles, and in 1910 the dynamiting of the Los Angeles *Times* building by the McNamara brothers of the American Federation of Labor. From 1884 to 1914, Colorado experienced a "Thirty Years War" of strikes and violence, which was climaxed with the coal miners' strike against the Colorado Fuel and Iron Co. in 1913–1914. There were 38 armed skirmishes in which 18 persons were killed—with a day of horror on April 20, 1914, when after a 15 hour battle between strikers and militiamen, the miners' tent city was burnt and 2 mothers and 11 children suffocated to death in the "Black Hole of Ludlow."[37] Federal troops had to be brought in to quell the violent outbursts of the miners which followed.

Finally, the next notable period of industrial violence—though never as fierce as the 30 years spanning the turn of the century—was experienced during the 1930s when the sit-down strike movement was used in the successful campaign to unionize the automobile and other great mass-production industries.

During these times many writers, influenced by Marxist theory, tended to view all these events as evidence of what was to come—an apocalyptic class war (Jack London's *The Iron Heel,* 1907), which no doubt the Ludlow tragedy was. It is now apparent that although labor unions continue to be active and to strike, violent confrontations between strikers and their employers or other opponents do not occur so frequently today, and killings especially are less frequent. This is undoubtedly due to the recognition of the legitimacy of the union as a collective bargaining body in 1933, the setting up of the National Labor Relations Board, and the undeniable improvement in working conditions over the past 40 years.

Are we able to conclude that there is a thread of "violence for protest" running through American labor relations that dates back to the American Revolution? Again it seems silly to suggest it. The continuity, if there is any, lies in the thread of American self-righteous moralism as the justification for putting down dissent—hardly a value propagated by the American Revolution. And as for the violence of the protestors, it is likely that it was partly a direct response to insufferable economic conditions—perhaps similar in some respects to that of the rebels in the war of independence. However, it turns out that the large majority of the rebels involved in labor violence were not American at all, so that they could hardly be said to be carrying on the thread of American violence. Instead, they may have extended threads of violence from particular parts of Europe.

Urban Riots

In the sixties, it was widely believed that America was "on the verge of some sort of urban apocalypse." But only a cursory glance at American history is sufficient to tell us that the country's cities have been pretty much in a continuous state of turmoil since colonial days.[38] There were, very early, organized mobs in Boston, and maritime riots occurred there during the middle of the eighteenth century. Riotous dissent and violence broke out in most leading colonial cities as a result of the "Liberty Boy" movement in response to the Stamp Act.[39]

After the Revolution, increased industrialization and uncontrolled immigration introduced the groundwork for the now well-known urban pattern—ulcerating slums in which flourished poverty, vice, crime, and violence opened up along the five points of lower Manhattan. Ethnic and religious strife was a central problem. Between 1830 and the Civil War occurred what was probably America's greatest period of urban violence: 35 major riots took place in the four cities of Baltimore, Philadelphia, New York, and Boston.[40] These were variously labor riots, election riots, anti-abolitionist riots, anti-Negro riots, or anti-Catholic riots. During the Civil War, with the exception of antidraft violence, urban violence generally decreased. Then in 1877 the nationwide railroad strike brought on riots which left large parts of Pittsburgh in smoking ruins, a forerunner of what was to happen to Los Angeles, Chicago, Newark, Detroit, and Washington during the rash of urban violence in 1965–1968. The modern urban police system arose in response to the riots of the 1830s and 1840s, and the National Guard was developed in response to the 1877 uprisings.

The modern urban race riot had its beginnings in the period from 1900 to 1949, during which there were 33 major interracial disturbances; 22 of these occurred during 1915–1919. Major riots occurred in Atlanta (1906), Springfield, Ill. (1908), East St. Louis (1917), Chicago (1919), and Harlem (1935–1943). With the exception of the Harlem riots, whites emerged as the main aggressors, and Negroes made up most of the casualties. Not until the Watts riot of 1965 were riots the result of Negro initiative. Significantly though, in contrast to the forms of violence used by whites, typified by the massacre and torture of people, Negro-precipitated riots have concentrated upon the destruction of property—the twisted symbol of American liberty and equality. In fact, historians of political violence have noted that it is almost always property that is the object of riots, no matter what the motivation, and that violence to the person is usually the direct result of intervention by the authorities. This is, however, a very general observation. In actuality, the responsibilities for the occurrence of violence during riots may depend upon a complex set of historical and situational factors, and these we shall look at in Chapter 8.

May we conclude that urban riots represent a thread of violence in the United States? The answer is a qualified yes in the sense that there has been a lot of it, and that the ulcerating conditions of the cities have continued from pre-Revolutionary times on. But this is the only sense in which one may say they are "continuous." Urban riots have been provoked by a multiplicity of factors: racial unrest, protest against the draft, labor activity, economic depression, and many more, some of which are factors that transcend the conditions of the cities, others that are inherent in the conditions of urban life, others that are both. Although I noted earlier that some of the most violent urban riots occurred against the draft for the Civil War, it would be stretching things considerably to infer from this that this was in any way part of a thread of urban violence dating back to Revolutionary times. Rather, it had to do with a specific issue at a specific moment in history. That these riots of protest occur more often in cities is quite understandable since that is where there are more people, and it is in cities that the seats of political power reside.

Criminal Violence and the Frontier Tradition

Feuding and Crime

We have seen in the preceding chapter that feuding flourishes under conditions in which legal authority has broken down. There are other conditions which also facilitate the development and maintenance of feuding as a solution to the problem of social order, all of which I will review in Chapter 4 when we look at subculture theory. For the moment, however, two further very important conditions, apart from the lack of a legal tradition in the frontier, contributed to the rise of feuding. These were the geographic isolation of the frontier, in fact the very nature of the frontier terrain, and the scarcity of resources.

The constant feuds between cattlemen and sheepmen, cattlemen and other cattlemen; arguments over the rights to appropriate maverick cattle; contests over the legitimacy of land claims—all these and many more contributed to violence as a solution to competing claims. Without an established legal tradition, there was no other way to settle disputes, and when one considers that all this went on just prior to and following the Civil War, contact with violence in one form or another must have been an almost daily occurrence in frontier life. Finally, with the discovery of gold and the necessity for its transportation from the gold fields to the cities, stagecoach robbery became a regular trade, especially during the 1870s in California, Wyoming, Montana, and the Dakotas. Professional robbers and professional gunmen, often in the employ of various feuding factions, appeared on the scene to take advantage of the incredible disorder.

The geography of the land was such that it encouraged the application of methods learned by such persons as Jesse James during the bitter Kansas-Missouri guerilla wars: well planned sudden and violent attacks, followed by swift retreat into the vast and desolate terrain. Outlaw trails stretching from Mexico to Montana were known intimately by the outlaws who were able to "hole up" in inaccessible canyons such as Brown's Hole in Utah, Robber's Roost in Colorado, Jackson Hole in Wyoming, the Cookson Hills in North East Oklahoma, and the Osage Hills west of the Cookson Range. Professional outlaws could and did establish enduring communities in these sanctuaries where their children were raised and trained in the art of robbery.[41]

Yet it must be understood that precisely because of the pervasive feuding society of the frontier, because of the lack of an established legal authority, these professional outlaws were "criminal" only depending upon whose side one was on. Many, if not all, of these outlaws were products of deprived and bitter social conditions of the Civil War period. They most often attacked those who were perceived by many of the downtrodden homesteaders as public enemies—namely the railroads and the banks, both of which were popularly seen as cheaters and dealers. The definition, therefore, of who was "bad" and who was "good" was not at all clearly established. Frank and Jesse James, former confederate guerillas, had many Southern sympathizers no matter how many banks they robbed; and Billy the Kid was idolized by poor Mexican herdsmen and villagers of the South West. But we should not overdo this classic "social bandit" or Robin Hood conception of these violent criminals. The fact is that the people of the frontier, like those of the South that I have described earlier in this chapter, adored daring, courage, and violence.

The Adoration of Daring

A final reason for the success of these violent outlaws was the adoration of daring and violence by the ordinary people. We have already seen how entrenched was this view of violence among the people of the South. It is only to be expected that on the frontier, where violence was the main solution to everyday problems, those most proficient at it would be adored. One typical example should suffice to illustrate this point. On

September 26, 1872, at the Kansas City Fair, attended by some 10,000 people, three bandits (probably the James brothers and confederate) shot at the ticket seller, hit a small girl in the leg, and rode off with less than a thousand dollars. The Kansas City *Times* described the reckless crime thus:

> It was as though three bandits had come to us from the storied Odenwald, with the halo of medieval chivalry upon their garments and shown us how the things were done that poets sing of. Nowhere else in the United States or the civilized world, probably, could this thing have been done.

Continuity in Criminal Violence

One might ask, since these outlaws enjoyed such success, why did they disappear? The answer is twofold: first, they did not disappear until two or three generations later, and second, the reason for their demise was a simple one: violence was used to combat violence. The James brothers and those of their era were eventually dealt with by a rising body of "law and order" agents. The Texas Rangers, put on an organized fighting footing at the outbreak of the Texas Revolution in 1835, had developed into a highly effective strike force against the outlaws by 1870. The railroads and banks employed private organizations such as the Pinkerton National Detective Agency, Wells, Fargo and Co., and the Rocky Mountain Detective Association. Eventually, the capabilities of violence and surveillance brought to bear by these well organized agencies spelled the demise of the social bandit.

But the social bandit appeared on the American scene once again in the 1930s, with the exploits of the Dillinger gang and many others. These violent criminals adopted a tactic similar to that of the old bandits: a sudden or violent hit, then a speedy retreat, this time into the confusion of roads and highways. The historian of professional crime, James A. Inciardi, has noted that these criminals not only modeled their lives on such earlier criminals as the James brothers, but actually were products of the same geographical area, "forming a continuing criminal heritage and tradition handed down from generation to generation through unbroken personal connections."[42] Such criminals were Pretty Boy Floyd, who enjoyed the admiration of the sharecroppers of Eastern Oklahoma, and John Dillinger, who modeled himself on Jesse James. The crime of this period occurred mainly in a rural small town setting. It had grown from horse thievery and counterfeiting in the early frontier days to the grand and violent criminal activities of Clyde Barrow and Bonnie Parker. These criminals were, however, ruthlessly pursued by the police and authorities, and with their destruction died the tradition of the American social bandit.

Honor and Criminal Violence

The Southern tradition of violence in defense of honor has led to many documented cases of homicides which today we have no difficulty in classifying as "criminal homicide" since they are most often purposeful, willful murders. Many examples occurring in the 1920s are provided by Brearley in his classic study of homicide in the United States:[43]

> On an isolated country road in a southern state two white men, each driving a one horse wagon, met each other. One of them, Welch, gives in a sworn statement his version of what happened:
>
> "When I got right near to him he told me to stop and we both stopped the horses. Then Truett said he wanted to know the truth about what I had done about his dog. I told him I had killed the dog in my hen nest. Truett said that was a damn lie, that the dog did not suck eggs and looked like he was going to get off the wagon and I shot him twice then. He said to cut that out and started to drive on and said don't shoot any more, you have done killed me. Then I jumped off my wagon towards his wagon and shot him four more times."
>
> Both Welch and Truett were poverty-stricken young farmers, each with a wife and two small children. According to the newspaper report, "The families are said to have insufficient clothing and with one family head dead and the other in jail their condition now is worse than formerly."
>
> Welch following his confession did not seem to realize the seriousness of his offense. He asked Sheriff Gamble how much the thing would cost him. When the sheriff told him he would probably be given the death penalty if he was convicted of first degree murder, Welch broke down and cried.

*   *   *

> C. H., a Southern Highlander, fired his revolver at a distant wagon filled with Negroes and hit a woman. Later he was informed that one of his best friends had reported the facts of the case to the county sheriff who was making an investigation. C. H. sought the supposed "traitor" and shot him down without a word of warning. Then he found out that the slain man, the father of six small children, was absolutely innocent; the sheriff had learned from other sources that C. H. had done the shooting.
>
> C. H. was tried for murder and sentenced to be executed. In the courtroom he showed no sign of regret except that he had er-

roneously killed the wrong man. He expressed the wish that he could get out of jail long enough to shoot the slanderer who had caused him to slay his friend.

During his successful efforts to escape the electric chair C. H. said to the psychologist who had been sent to give him an intelligence test, "Until they brought me to G. [the county seat] I never heard anybody say it wasn't all right to shoot a man that done you wrong."

Discontinuity in Criminal Violence

The other great area of violent crime in America, of course, has been that of the cities. Crime in the cities began very early in slum areas such as Five Points and the Bowery of New York City. Murder and gang vendettas were common. At the beginning of the twentieth century, centralized criminal "syndicates" took shape under the direction of Arnold Rothstein.[44] The 1920s and 1930s saw the era of organized crime, when violence and systematic killings were used as a matter of course—as the Kefauver crime investigation highlighted in 1951.[45] There is considerable controversy in the literature[46] about whether the operations of organized crime, and especially its use of particular forms of violence, are a result of the immigration of Sicilians from the Mafia tradition. Certainly there is no evidence that I know of that is able to establish a link between organized crime violence and that of previous kinds of violence that I have described in this chapter. The thesis that the violence of organized crime represents one more point in the thread of violence in United States history is therefore not supported. It is more likely that this type of violence has arisen as a result of specific conditions (either cultural, social, or economic) prevailing at a particular time in United States history.

Conclusions and Summary

The thesis developed by United States historians of the 1960s that there is a thread of violence running throughout United States history and that some of the more revered uses of violence, such as the Revolution, provided the basis for this thread, is only partially supported. The following points should be carefully considered.

1. The identification of a series of violent events in history is not sufficient in and of itself to establish that a thread of violence exists.

2. Violence has occurred in many forms and places throughout United States history. Some of these forms, such as labor or agrarian protest,

are not the products of a continuous thread, but rather the products of specific social and economic conditions prevailing at the time.

3. The only evidence that could be said to in any way support the notion of a continuous thread of violence concerns the South and West, because of (1) the virtually continuous state of disorder and feuding in both regions from the Revolution through to the Civil War and beyond; (2) the predominance of a set of values and traditions that saw violence as equivalent to courage and necessary to the defense of honor; and (3) the evidence that these traditions were consciously transmitted from one generation to another.

4. None of the evidence examined in this chapter is sufficient to warrant the characterization of the whole of the United States as having a "violent history," or the conclusion that Americans have a national character that is deeply violent. The only other way we could support this proposition would be to show that the amount of violence in United States history has been higher compared to other similar countries, such as Europe. Historians have been unable to show that this is the case. A less convincing case might be made for the "violent Americans" thesis, if it could be shown that recent and current levels of violence are higher in the United States compared to other countries. We shall look at this in Chapter 4.

5. If anything, the material in this chapter suggests that there has been a "culture of violence" in the South, perhaps extending to the West. For this proposition to be supported, one would have to show that violence is very unevenly distributed throughout geographical areas of the United States and that the rates of violence are much higher in the South and West.

6. The next chapter will therefore look at the trends and distribution of criminal violence in the United States. However, because we do not want to foreclose the possibility that there are other factors apart from "Southernness" that may contribute to criminal violence, since criminal violence has occurred extensively in the North for other reasons noted above, we need to look at the whole range of possibilities apart from geographical area. There is a great deal of data available on criminal violence, much more than on other types of violence. An agreed-upon definition of the particular categories of criminal violence, although difficult, is also more easily obtainable, since the criminal law provides us with many well-tried definitions.

3

Criminal Violence: Patterns and Trends

Defining Criminal Violence

The kinds of violence described in Chapters 1 and 2 range over a wide area of what one might call "acceptability." Depending on the values that one holds, some of the violence described might be classified as "criminal," or if not criminal, at least "bad," and other violence perhaps even laudatory. In his review of *Violence in American History,* historian Richard Brown went so far as to classify types of violence as "negative" or "positive." Negative violence was, to him, violence that was not in a direct way "connected with any socially or historically constructive development"[1]—namely, criminal violence, feuds, lynching, racial violence, urban riots, and assassination. He classified as positive violence—police violence, revolutionary violence, the Civil War, the Indian Wars, vigilante violence, and agrarian and labor violence. Obviously, a substantial element of personal value is involved in making such classifications and in emphasizing particular forms of violence over others.

This is most certainly the case as far as criminal violence is concerned. Because of the particular values or interests which may prevail at a given time, people and governments will take notice of some types of violence but not of others. For example, as we shall see later, auto accidents are a major cause of death in America and other developed Western countries, yet the attitude towards these events is not so much that they are "wrong," but that "nothing can be done." They are accepted as a risk that is part of everyday life, even though the chances of being killed in an auto accident are far higher than of being murdered. In contrast, violence that is defined as criminal violence is seen not as something which is a normal part of everyday life, but as an "evil" which must be eradicated. The perception of criminal violence is perhaps conditioned by the Manichaean world; a world in which there is an enemy (in this case the violent criminal) who is defined according to a set of values which have a great tradition—the criminal law. Additionally, the public has become accustomed to the criminal law and the criminal justice system generally as the vehicles for implementing the moral indignation of society. In the long run, it is left to the criminal law and its various agents to define what is criminally violent and what is not.

It has become an established practice among criminologists to draw a distinction between crimes against property and crimes against the person, which has resulted in a continued tendency in Europe to characterize crimes of violence as being mostly acts against persons rather than property.[2] The growing tendency in America, however, has been to broaden the classification to include violent acts against property. This is perhaps because of the stronger value placed upon private property in the United States, but more likely because of the tendency of America to define its crime in terms of police reporting (i.e., the collection and publication of crime statistics), rather than by convictions, which is the stronger tendency in Europe. Crime defined and collected according to convictions will tend to keep to the legal definitions, whereas the American definitions are likely to respond more to either administrative or public needs. Thus, the UCR (Uniform Crime Reports) published by the FBI includes in its index of crimes of violence the crime of robbery. And the *Staff Report* of the President's Commission on Causes and Prevention of Violence defined crimes of violence as "the use or threatened use of force to secure one's own end against the will of another that results, or can result in the destruction or harm of person or property or in the deprivation of individual freedom."[3] The *Staff Report* included in that broad definition such acts as criminal homicide, forcible rape, robbery, aggravated assault, suicide, violent auto fatalities, child abuse, "other sex offenses," other assaults, disorderly conduct, burglary, arson, vandalism, individual violent acts related to gangs, and individual violent acts related to organized crime.

An important point concerning the FBI definitions of violent crime is that they are widely publicized and have frequently been used, especially when the FBI was under the direction of J. Edgar Hoover, in campaigning for more public support in the "war against crime." The FBI definitions and their accompanying statistics have become an integral part of the American perception of crime. As such, these definitions provide us with an excellent point of departure. The FBI crime reports have an added advantage in that they present the only comprehensive national statistics on crime in the United States over a long period of time.

FBI Definitions of Crimes of Violence

Since 1958, the FBI has defined a number of crimes of violence for the purposes of constructing a national index. These are criminal homicide, forcible rape, robbery, and aggravated assault.

Homicide: in the language of the criminal law, the supreme act of violence—the killing of a human being by another—is called homicide. However, according to the law, not all homicide is criminal. There are *excusable homicide,* which is the unintentional killing where no blame attaches, and *justifiable homicide,* which is the intentional killing sanctioned by law, such as execution of a legal sentence of death; or the killing of a person in legitimate self-defense; or the killing by a private citizen of a person who is committing a felony.

The types of homicide which are considered criminal are: *murder,* which is the unlawful killing of a human being with malice aforethought, deliberation, and murderous intent. This category is further classified into various degrees of murder depending upon the kind of premeditation and criminal intent present. *Voluntary manslaughter* is the killing of another person, but without premeditation, malice, or murderous intent—this category is also referred to by the FBI as *non-negligent manslaughter.* Various states differ somewhat in regard to actual definitions of the above categories, and some states have other classes of homicide, for example, *vehicular homicide,* and *felony murder,* which is the killing of a person while committing a felony.

Aggravated assault is assault with intent to kill or for the purpose of inflicting severe bodily harm. It excludes the lesser forms of assault such as battery and fighting. Attempts are included. We might note that the distinction between these acts, especially between criminal homicide and aggravated assault, may often depend to a large extent upon such factors as speed of the ambulance, competence of the surgeon, or area of the body where the weapon strikes. These factors, and probably many more, contribute to the critical difference as to whether or not the victim survives.

Forcible rape is the carnal knowledge of a female forcibly and against her will. Assaults to rape are also included in this category, but statutory rape without force is not counted.

Robbery involves the stealing or taking of anything of value from the person by use of force or threat of force. Assaults to rob and attempts are also included.

A particularly difficult problem in defining what is criminally violent is posed by the inclusion, by the criminal law, of the notion of *threat*. What is implied by the inclusion of threat is that the seriousness of "criminality" of a violent act cannot always be assessed by the injury done to the victim. Although the victim may be menaced by a robber, with a gun, provided he hands over the money, or does not call for help, he may not actually be physically injured, though of course, he may suffer fright and shock. Generally, the law has tried to solve this problem by referring to the various subjective aspects of the offender's behavior, such as his malicious intent, or the motive for the crime. Another way adopted by the law has been to identify the threat in terms of the implement of force which is used as a threat. Thus, many crimes are considered to be more serious if they are committed with the use of a firearm or other dangerous weapon, or even, in many cases, imitations of such weapons.

The Seriousness of Violent Crimes

The question of the comparative seriousness of various crimes of violence goes beyond the criminal law. The criminal law does attempt a gradation in seriousness, both in terms of its definitions and in the sentences prescribed. However, if the broader societal values are closely related to the definition of violent behavior, the comparison between the public's evaluation of serious violent behavior and that of the criminal law agencies, should be of great interest. This is especially so when it is apparent that legal penalties may often not coincide with the attitudes of the public. For example, according to many statutes, a sex offender such as an exhibitionist could receive a longer prison sentence than a person convicted of assault. With this in mind, Professors Sellin and Wolfgang[4] in 1964 asked nearly a thousand subjects to rate the seriousness of 141 offenses. The researchers specifically chose police officers, juvenile court judges, and several sets of university students who they assumed represented the middle-class value system which, they considered, dominated public attitudes towards crime. No significant differences were found between the ratings of seriousness made by these groups. Moreover, Sellin and Wolfgang argued that their results supported their hypothesis that the score values they obtained could be added together to provide a numerical score which reflected the overall seriousness of a criminal event. Table 3.1 displays a selection of seriousness scores for various

TABLE 3.1

Seriousness Scores for Selected Violent Crimes[5]

	Seriousness Score
Simple criminal homicide	26
Assault where victim is hospitalized	7
Assault where victim is treated and discharged	4
Assault where victim is mildly wounded and does not require professional care	1
Sexual intercourse by force	10
Sexual intercourse by force where victim is intimidated by a weapon	12

crimes of violence, in which it can be seen, for instance, that "simple" criminal homicide was perceived as 2½ times more serious than forcible rape, and so on.

How do these estimates compare to what the criminal law says? It is very difficult to draw direct comparisons, since the practice and theory of criminal law vary so drastically. For example, in New York State, a convicted robber may receive a sentence of anything from a conditional discharge to 15 years in prison. In a recent study comparing prison terms recommended by the public to the minimum terms handed down *in practice* in New York State, it was found that respondents generally favored more severe prison terms for violent and traditional crimes.[6]

Measuring the Extent of Criminal Violence

Considering the difficulty we have in defining precisely what is criminal and what is violent, there is naturally great difficulty in assessing the amount of criminal violence that exists in a given society over a particular period of time. Since 1958, using the four types of violent crimes previously defined (criminal homicide, aggravated assault, forcible rape, and robbery) the FBI has collected data on crimes reported to the police in an attempt to construct an index which would reflect the amount of violent crime that existed in the United States from year to year.[7] The problems in interpreting these statistics have long been recognized by criminologists.[8]

The greatest difficulty encountered in interpreting FBI and most other crime statistics is the "dark number," which refers to the gap between the amount of crime reported to the police and that which actually occurs. Some offenses have a very low reportability because they either are never discovered by the police or are concealed by the victim. Of violent crimes, forcible rape has been found to have a very low reportability. In comparison, however, criminal homicide is one of the most highly visible crimes and has both a high reporting and clearance rate.[9]

Victimization studies, in which representative samples of the population are asked whether they have been victims of various crimes or have known any victims, have demonstrated the enormous differences which may exist in the reportability of the UCR index crimes. Table 3.2 displays the differences between the incidence of violent crimes as surveyed by the victim report method and as reflected in the UCR rates. Criminal homicide is the only crime which comes anywhere near the UCR rate, but unfortunately homicide was not included in the 1973 victimization survey.

In an effort to overcome the biases and mistakes in crime reporting which creep into the administrative collection of crime statistics, academic criminologists have attempted to reanalyze police records—usually for a particular city or police district. The pioneering studies were of homicide by Harlan[10] in 1950 and Wolfgang[11] in 1958. However, there had always been the problem of whether to count the number of *offenses* or the number of *offenders,* and in 1964 Sellin and Wolfgang developed a method for the construction of an index which avoided this problem and also took into account how serious each act was in relation to middle-class values. Sellin and Wolfgang used the delinquent *event* as the pivotal concept, so that an offense might be composed of many factors, each varying in degree of seriousness. There were two "weightings" of seriousness—one derived from the assessment of middle-class attitudes as shown in Table 3–1 and the other from an assessment of whether injury, theft, or damage had occurred in the event. In this way it was possible objectively to analyze existing police records and to con-

TABLE 3.2

UCR and Victimization Rates for Violent
Crimes 1965/66 and 1973[12]
(per 100,000 population)

	Victimization Rate		UCR Rate[c]	
	1965/66[a]	*1973[b]*	*1966*	*1973*
Criminal homicide	3.0	Not measured	5.6	9.3
Forcible rape	42.5	100.0	13.2	24.4
Robbery	94.0	690.0	80.6	182.6
Aggravated assault	218.3	1040.0	119.4	198.9
Total violent crimes	357.8	1830.0	218.8	415.3

struct an index which was closer to the "true" level of violence or crime in the community. Generally, the Sellin-Wolfgang index displays greater increases in crime rates, especially for property crime, than do the UCR statistics. However, because none of the studies so far replicating the Sellin-Wolfgang method are based upon national samples, comparisons between the two are difficult. A recent study has suggested that there are no substantial differences between the two measures.[13]

Trends in Violent Crime

In the following account of trends in violent crime, I will draw heavily upon FBI data, mainly because the research statistics do not provide rates over a long period of time. They are most often conducted for a limited period and furthermore are not conducted on national samples.

Although recent victimization studies do use national samples, I will also make only limited use of that data. A victimization rate includes large numbers of "crimes" not reported to the police, and there are also probably more victims than crimes. But who is to decide what is a crime and what is not? If a victim chooses not to define his victimization as criminal by not reporting it to the police, this surely is his right, and surely it changes the quality of the "criminal" act. Victimization rates also have the tendency to inflate to fantastic proportions the rates of crime, which is clearly demonstrated in Table 3.2. Is one to believe that robbery really has increased 634% over the period reported? Without frequent annual measures, victimization data must be viewed with some suspicion. In contrast, the UCR rates do provide an adequate picture when taken over long time periods.

We can see from Figure 3.1 that there was a time when violent crime actually decreased—from 1933, when the FBI first began to collect crime statistics, to the beginning of World War II. Since we have no comparable statistics for the period prior to 1933, we cannot know what the previous "peak" was. Therefore, care should be taken not to draw conclusions that the current increase in violent crime is leading to some kind of apocalyptic disaster. We saw in Chapter 2 that there have been many violent periods in American history. Had crime statistics in the nineteenth century been collected as efficiently as they are today, perhaps the current high level of violent crime would not look so serious.

It is also clear that figures for the crimes of forcible rape and homicide are comparatively stable compared to those for the other two violent crimes of robbery and aggravated assault. This may be partly due to the fact that they are rare events, so that wide fluctuations in reporting are

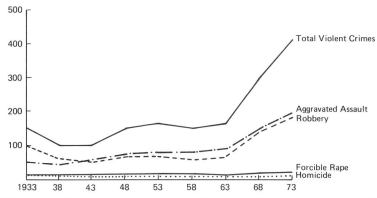

FIGURE 3.1   Variation in Reported UCR Index Offense Rates for the Four Major Violent Crimes, 1933–1973[14] (Rates per 100,000 National Population)

less likely. This appears to apply even to forcible rape, a crime that we know has a very low reportability. One might have expected that there would be a sudden increase in the incidence of reported forcible rape from 1970 to 1973 with the rise of women's liberation movements, campaigning on behalf of rape victims, and the proliferation of rape crisis centers. This is clearly not the case, even when one takes a closer look on a year-to-year basis, as in Figure 3.2. The incidence of rape displays a steady increase without any dramatic upswings.

In contrast, assault and robbery display dramatic increases compared to previous years from roughly 1963 onwards. These are the years, one may note, in which there was considerable political and racial turbulence in America. This turbulence probably reached its peak in 1968–1970, yet the strong increase has continued through to the last available statistics of 1973. However, some recent reports announced by the FBI suggest that a leveling off may be beginning in 1975–1977. Perhaps a "cooling-off" period is needed before the response of violent crime to political and racial turbulence subsides. Should the rates level off in subsequent years, it does not seem too unreasonable to conclude that the 1960s decade of political protest has been in some way reflected in the violent crime statistics.

An alternative sometimes raised to explain this sudden increase in violent crime in the sixties is that in 1958 the FBI changed its reporting system, and subsequent to that year, the reporting system has been made much more comprehensive throughout the United States and the efficiency in collection has been substantially improved. However, one could use

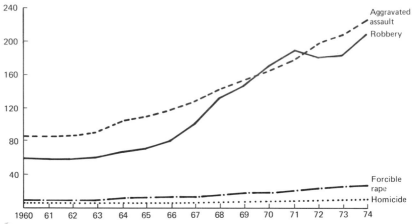

FIGURE 3.2   Variation in Reported UCR Index Offense Rates for the Four Major Violent Crimes, 1960–1974[15] (Rates per 100,000 National Population)

this observation only to explain *general* increases for all crimes, not differential increases for particular crimes, unless one argued that the reporting system was differentially efficient according to crime categories. Although this is possible, given the different legal definitions of crimes in the various states, it is unlikely, since a large part of the improvement in the crime reporting system has been dependent upon the communication to local agencies and their receptivity towards uniform definitions of the crime categories.

Incidentally, the increases in property crime as compared to violent crime are not substantially different for the period 1960–1974. The percent change over the 1960 rate for all violent crime was +186.8%; for all crime index property crimes, 154.3%. One should be careful in interpreting these percent increases since they do not mean very much without a knowledge of the rates themselves. The 1974 rate for property crime was 4,362.6 per 100,000 population, compared to only 458.8 for violent crimes. In sheer numbers, (i.e., visibility of the crimes), therefore, it is apparent that the percent increase in property crime is much more severe than that in violent crime, and this is made very clear in Figure 3.3.

The crime of robbery deserves special attention. In Figure 3–2, robbery is the only crime that displays sporadic increases and decreases. It reached a peak of 187.5 per 100,000, then actually declined in 1971 to 180.3. But in 1974 it began to pick up again. Compared to 1960, robbery has shown the greatest percent increase (+248%) compared to *all* index crimes, including property crimes.

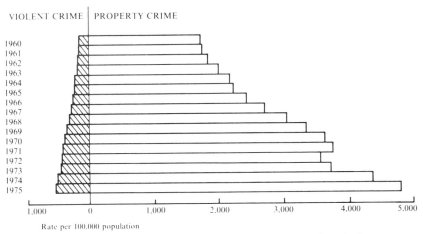

VIOLENT CRIME | PROPERTY CRIME

Rate per 100,000 population

FIGURE 3.3   Reported Violent and Property Crime, 1960–1976[16]

Violence and Age Patterns

Violent crime is most definitely a young man's game. Every separate research study conducted since 1925 and in various Western industrialized countries has demonstrated that young men between 15 and 30 are responsible for the bulk of violent crime.[17] The differences according to age can be clearly seen in Figure 3.4, where the rates of criminal homicide according to each age group are shown. For the 18 to 24 age group, the rate has increased from 10.1 per 100,000 18–24-year-olds in 1958 to 31.2 for 1974.[18] When one considers that this age group is also the one most prone to auto accidents, it indeed represents a dangerous age to live through. Also of special interest in Figure 3–3 are the clear peaks in violent crime for the 15–17 and 18–24 age groups during the 1970–1972 period. These were the years of the Kent State killings (May 4, 1970); the sniper shooting of Sacramento policemen attributed to Black Panthers (May, 9, 1970); the killing of Judge Haley in the San Rafael courthouse (August 7, 1970); the bombing of the physics building at the University of Wisconsin (August 24, 1970). In 1971, there were the May Day arrests, from May 3–5; the escalation of airplane hijackings culminating with D. B. Cooper's parachuting over Washington on November 25; the killing of George Jackson in a prison escape on August 21; the bombing of ten buses in Pontiac, Michigan on August 30; followed by the Attica riot on September 9. Then, in 1972, Gov. George Wallace was shot by Bremer on May 15; five were shot in bussing incidents in Pontiac, Michigan on November 27; two black students

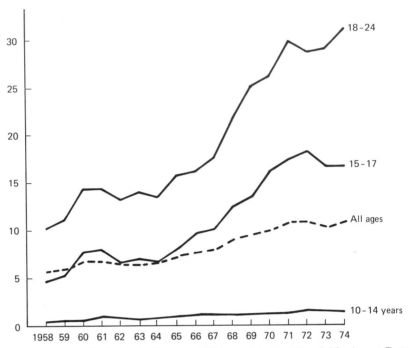

FIGURE 3.4   Variation in Reported Urban Criminal Homicide Arrest Rates by Age, 1958–1974[19] (Rates per 100,000 Age Specific Population)

were shot at Southern University, Baton Rouge, Louisiana on November 16.

That period was clearly a period of political turbulence, and the unrest involved mainly young people. The peaks in criminal homicide as shown in Figure 3.4 are strikingly similar to those in Figure 3.5, which displays a very rough measure of political bombings over that period. It should be emphasized, of course, that the statistics on bombings are not rates, but total numbers, that they are based on newspaper reports, and that the coincidence of two factors is not sufficient to warrant the conclusion of a causal relationship. The data are, however, suggestive. It may be noted that the 18–24-year-old rate began a rapid rise again in 1974. This may reflect the delayed effects of the 15–17-year-old peak of 1972. That is, the criminally violent 15–17 age group *remained* violent as it got older.

As I remarked earlier, homicide rates are the preferable measure when one is attempting to assess the differential relationships among various sociological categories and violent crime. This is especially the case when one must use arrest statistics, which are so much subject to the

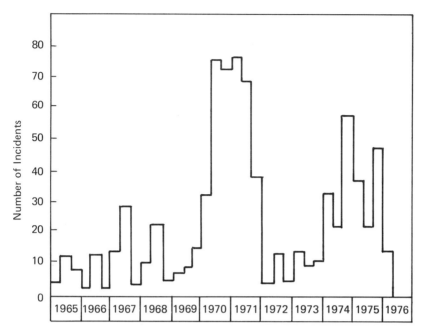

FIGURE 3.5   Number of Bombings in the United States, 1965–1976[20]

particular policies and practices of the policing agencies. Thus, when we consider the age differences for other types of violent crime, they should be interpreted cautiously.

Professor Wolfgang gives the following striking examples:[21]

> . . . very often the crude legal labels attached to many acts committed by juveniles give a false impression of the seriousness of their acts. For example, a "highway robbery" may be a $100 theft at the point of a gun and may result in the victim's being hospitalized from severe wounds. But commonly, juvenile acts that carry this label and are used for statistical compilation are more minor. Typical in the files of a recent study were cases involving two nine-year-old boys, one of whom twisted the arm of the other on the school yard to obtain 25 cents of the latter's lunch money. This act was recorded and counted as "highway robbery." In another case, a nine-year-old engaged in exploratory sexual activity with an eight-year-old girl on a playlot. The girl's mother later complained to the police, who recorded the offense as "assault with intent to ravish."

Nevertheless, most studies concerning rape, robbery, and assault have roughly demonstrated the age differences apparent for homicide statistics. In fact, for robbery, a number of researchers in addition to the UCR have shown that in the United States the crime of robbery is more concentrated in the 15–17 year age group.[22]

A recent study has suggested that the relationship between assault and age may be a little more complicated, since it was found that in social areas where there was a low rate of assault, juveniles (19 years or less) accounted for 44% of the reported incidents, but in social areas with high rates of assaults, they accounted for only 23.5%.[23] This is a surprising and perplexing finding which suggests that much more research is needed in this area.

Some have argued that the high preponderance of reported youthful criminal violence is mainly due to a widespread belief by police that the young are responsible for crime, so that the police are more likely to seek them out. This criticism is probably wrong. First, the bulk of violent crime, like all crime, is *reported* to the police, rather than sought out by them. Second, if youthful offenders were sought out, why would it be more so for robbery than for other crimes? Third, if one looks at the arrest rates of violent crimes compared to the reporting rates—i.e., the number of crimes "cleared" or "solved" by arrest—one finds that these have remained *stable* over the last 20 years. The clearance rates, regardless of even the wildest fluctuation or increases in the volume of crimes dealt with by the police have hardly varied: for robbery it has been 27–30%, for criminal homicide 80–85%, and for forcible rape 51–55%. This is especially remarkable when one considers that there has been considerably greater police activity in the form of special juvenile and gang police, which one would expect to increase the clearance rates.[24]

One may conclude from this observation that police activity as reflected in arrest statistics has a remarkable stability over time. Since the UCR data are made up of reports from several thousand different police agencies, many of which almost certainly have different policies and practices, it is doubtful whether the UCR arrest statistics express a massive, stable national discrimination against the young. And, since police activity is stable from year to year, any dramatic changes in crime rates are better explained by other factors than changes in police activity.

We may safely conclude that youthful males are responsible for roughly half of all criminal homicides, aggravated assaults, and forcible rapes. They are responsible for 75% of all robberies. These age differences have been relatively stable for the past 20 years, with a slight recent tendency for the younger age group of 15–17 years to engage increasingly in violence.

Sex and Violence

Men are the main perpetrators of violent crime, and they probably always have been.[25] Table 3.3 demonstrates very clearly that males in

TABLE 3.3

*Reported Urban Criminal Homicide Arrest Rates
by Sex (per 100,000 sex-specific population)*

	Males	*Females*
1958	9.2	2.2
1966	13.6	2.6
1974	19.8	3.3
Percent increase 1958–74	115.2	50.0

1958 committed criminal homicide at a rate four times higher than that of women, and since that year criminal homicide by men has increased at a rate twice that of women. Yet the popular view, especially since females accounted for four of the FBI's Ten Most Wanted list of 1970, is that women have been committing a disproportionately greater number of violent crimes, and that this has had something to do with the women's liberation movement.[26] However, since the increase in the crime rate for males is so much greater, it is unlikely that the small increase in the female crime rate is due to any specific conditions relating to women. The reasons for the increase are probably the same as for the males. A recent analysis of UCR data also established that there has, in fact, been no substantial increase in violent crime committed by females since 1958.[27] The area of substantial recent increases in the female crime rate was that of property and economic crime. The female rate for robbery is also much lower than the rate for other serious violent crimes, the interpretation usually being that women are less likely to deal with strangers. We might expect changes in this aspect of female crime as the role of women in society changes. But so far, there have been no substantial changes in the rate of robberies committed by females.[28]

Violence and Race

Although it must appear obvious to anyone who has lived in a large city that violent crime predominates among blacks, there has been much disagreement among criminologists about whether this is really so. This has become an issue raised especially by black criminologists who have argued that the high statistical rate of violent crime among blacks is a function of police discrimination.[29] This is an argument similar to the one I mentioned earlier concerning the high rate of violent crime for young people. Although many well designed studies[30] have demonstrated discrimination by particular police agencies against blacks in their decisions to arrest, it is nevertheless still doubtful whether such discrimination substantially affects *national* crime statistics.

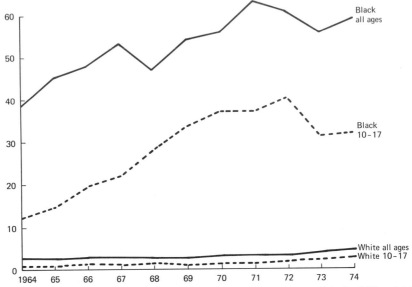

FIGURE 3.6   Variations in Reported Urban Arrests for Criminal Homicide by Race and Age, 1964–1974[31] (Rates per 100,000 Age and Race Specific Population)

For the statistically stable crime of criminal homicide and forcible rape, the proportion of total arrests accounted for each year since 1960 has varied hardly at all. Blacks accounted for 60.9% of all criminal homicide arrests in 1960 and for 61.9% in 1974. As to forcible rape, in 1960, 52.2% of those arrested for forcible rape were blacks and in 1974 the percentage was 53.6%.[32] Therefore, the urban criminal homicide arrest rates as shown in Figure 3.6 probably reflect true levels of violent crime for each race. It can be seen that the differences are vast, with the current black rate approximately 13 times higher than the white.

It is of particular interest to note in Figure 3.6 that the rate of criminal homicide of blacks has been much more unstable than that of the white. The rate for the black 10–17 age group declined substantially in 1973 and it appears that the rapid rate of increase of the sixties has come to an end—possibly for the black race in general. Perhaps this change reflects the improved economic and political conditions of blacks in the United States over the past decade.

A further check on the validity of these measures may be made by referring to the victimization statistics that were mentioned earlier. Table 3.4 demonstrates that, as measured by victim reports of violent

TABLE 3.4

Victimizations by Race for Forcible Rape,
Robbery and Aggravated Assault, 1965 and 1973[33]
(Rates per 100,000 population)

	1965		1973	
	White	Black	White	Black
Forcible rape	22	82	100	200
Robbery	58	204	600	1400
Aggravated assault	186	347	2600	3100
Total violent crimes	266	633	3300	4700

crime, the black rate continues to be higher than the white. However, the difference is clearly not anywhere nearly as great as that suggested by the UCR statistics as displayed in Figure 3.6. We may note also that the rate of increase for blacks is about *half* that for whites.

Of course, it may be argued that since there are often more victims involved in a given crime than there are offenders, the comparatively higher rate of white crime as measured by number of victimizations may be a function of blacks offending against white victims. To some extent this may be the case, since in the 1973 survey, 20% of white victims of violent crimes reported that their attackers were black, whereas only 8% of black victims perceived white offenders. The proportion of robberies and rapes which involved black offenders and white victims was much higher: 31% for rape and 41% for robbery. These percentages compare roughly to those obtained in a survey of 17 cities in 1967 except for robbery, for which 73% of white victims perceived black attackers.[34] It is difficult, therefore, to draw any definite conclusions from the victimization data.[35]

In regard to robbery and aggravated assault, crimes which display greater fluctuations, the racial differences must be interpreted with care. Police activity, as measured by proportions of arrests made of blacks of all arrests, has changed somewhat. For instance, in 1960, blacks accounted for 55.5% of robbery arrests, but in 1974 blacks accounted for 65.3%. Yet with assault, the percentage declined from 62.3% in 1960 to 45.7% in 1974. Fluctuations in these crime rates could be affected by police activity, especially if it were likely for police to arrest blacks for robbery rather than assault. In any event, the rates for blacks (especially in the 10–17 age group, for robbery) continue at an ever increasing rate without any sign of slowing down, as we saw for criminal homicide, although 1973 was a lower year. This is made clear in Figure 3.7.

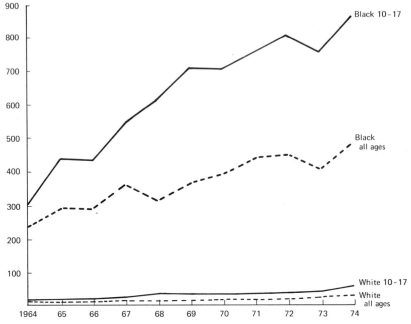

FIGURE 3.7   Variations in Reported Urban Arrests for Robbery by Race and Age, 1964–1974[36] (Rates per 100,000 Age and Race Specific population)

Yet even with these crimes, there are data that suggest that the measures we have are comparatively reliable. In the cohort study conducted by Professor Wolfgang and his colleagues,[37] which, although depending upon police records, nevertheless was able to measure events and thereby avoid the difficult definitional problems of the UCR statistics, a striking similarity was found between the arrest rates for assaultive crimes between the two measures. This is demonstrated in Table 3.5.

CONCLUSIONS: Blacks, especially young blacks, account for a substantially higher portion of violent crimes than do whites, even taking into consideration possible differentiating aspects of police activity. There are recent signs of a decline in the rate of criminal homicide for blacks, but other violent crimes continue to increase rapidly.

Regional Violence

As we saw in Chapter 2, it is a popular belief and there is some historical evidence to suggest that the South is the most violent region in the United States. Figure 3.8 shows that this has clearly been so in the

TABLE 3.5

Relationship of Black to White Arrest Rates[38]
for Four Types of Assaultive Crime
(10–17 year age group)

Offense	Number of Times Black Rate Higher Than White Rate	
	FBI *(1958–67)*	Wolfgang, et al. *(1955–63)*
Forcible rape	12	13
Robbery	20	20
Aggravated assault	8	10

past, at least since 1958. However, the 1974 increase over 1958 in criminal homicide (our most reliable statistic of criminal violence) was only 49% for the Southern states, compared to 200% for the Northeast, 183% for the North Central states, and 137% for the West. This is an interesting observation, especially when it has previously been argued by some researchers that the immigration of blacks from the South to Northern cities has contributed to the increase in violent crime rates in the North. However, at least for the past four years, blacks (and more recently whites) have been migrating to the South, yet the Northern and Western crime rates continue to increase at a high rate. The lower rate of increase for the South is quite remarkable when compared with the rest of the nation.

Reliable trend comparisons for the other three major violent crimes of rape, aggravated assault, and robbery are much more difficult to make, as was pointed out by the Violence Commission of 1969. In that report, the incidence of forcible rape was found to be higher in the West, and this continued to be the case in 1974. Although no clear differences could be assessed for robbery in 1969, for 1974, the Northeast had a significantly higher rate for this crime than the other three regions. No clear differences exist for rate of aggravated assault.[39]

As far as particular states are concerned, Figure 3.9 displays the 1974 criminal homicide rates for each state. Those states with the highest rates are Alabama, Georgia, Florida, South Carolina, and Nevada. Those with the lowest rates are Iowa, North Dakota, and South Dakota, and there are a number of states in the far Northeast and Midwest also with moderately low rates. By and large, the ranking of the states according to criminal homicide rates has not changed since 1967. Part of the reason for this regional variation may be that sociocultural differ-

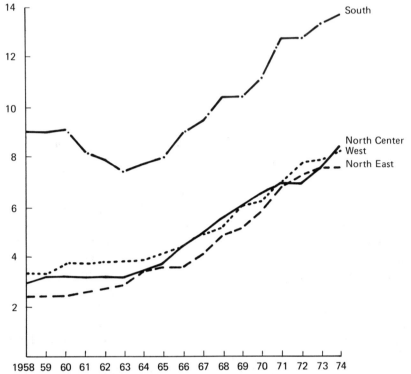

FIGURE 3.8   Variations in Reported Criminal Homicide and Non-negligent Manslaugther Offense Rates, by Region, 1958–1974[40]

ences are involved, and we will look at this possibility in the following chapter. But there is a further demographic variable—urbanization.

Urbanization and Violence

Many classic studies in criminology have identified the "urban crisis" in one form or another—the crowded slum of the inner city, the run-down industrial areas, the shifting population that lives in these areas, and the lack of recreational facilities—as being related to many forms of crime.[41]

Figure 3.10 suggests that a strong relationship exists between urbanization and criminal homicide. The middle classes are usually believed to live in the suburbs, and we can see that the suburban rate is considerably lower than the large city rate. The rate for large cities continues to increase at a rate several times higher than the rural and suburban rates.

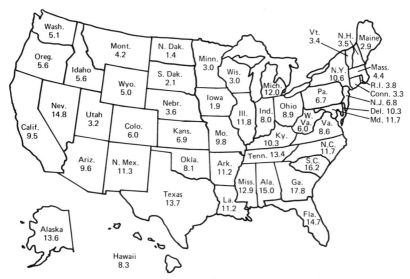

FIGURE 3.9   Variation in Reported Criminal Homicide and Non-negligent Manslaughter Offense Rates, by State, 1974[42] (Rates per 100,000 Population)

This is in spite of the fact that there has been a very large migration of people away from the cities into the suburbs and rural areas in the past ten years. Similar rates are also found for rape, assault, and robbery. It would appear that the often derided American suburb is at present the safest place in which to live in the United States, and has been for at least the past ten years.

How much of the overall increase in violent crime can be attributed to the increasing urbanization of America's population? The Violence Commission Staff estimated this for the years 1950 to 1965, by re-computing the offense rates for 1965 as though the pattern of urbanization had remained the same as it was in 1950.[43] The differences between the recomputed rates and the actual rates were calculated and it was then possible to estimate the amount of crime which had resulted from changes in the urban and rural population structure. It was found that changes in urban structure alone accounted for 8.5% of increases in all criminal homicides, 12.8% of forcible rape increases, 25.1% of robbery increases, and 13.2% of assaults. But that represented a period in United States history characterized by an extremely high rate of urbanization. Of the cities reported in the UCR there was a 99% increase in population of cities greater than 250,000 for the period 1950–1964. In

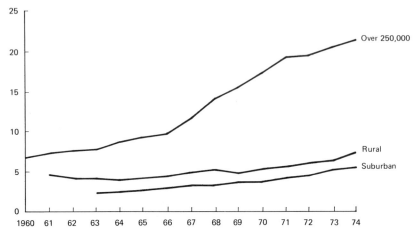

FIGURE 3.10   Variation in Reported Criminal Homicide Offense Rates by Size of City, 1960–1974[44] (Rates per 100,000 Population)

contrast, over the period 1964–1974, the population of large cities has remained quite stable, even decreasing in places, while the population of smaller cities (10,000–50,000 population) and suburbs has increased. The rural population, incidentally, has continued to decrease. Now, if we recompute the proportions of crime accounted for by shifts in the urban structure of the population for the period 1950 to 1974, a different pattern emerges. In fact, changes in the urban structure fail to account for any significant portion of violent crime increases. However, of particular interest is that the rural population has decreased dramatically since 1950. Had it remained the same, it would have accounted for roughly 25% of criminal homicides in 1974. In actual fact, it accounted for only 10% in that year.

Social areas within cities and the socioeconomic classes they represent have also been found to be related to the incidence of violent crime.[45] Many studies, in several different countries, have found that violent crime is more often an activity of the lower classes, although some have argued that the difference is less great than others have reported.[46] The only evidence against the factor of social class differences in violent crime comes from self-report studies, in which respondents are asked to identify or "confess" the crimes they think they have committed. There are many methodological difficulties with these studies, and it is probable that they are unreliable in measuring violent crime. These studies never include homicide, and rarely any serious violent crime.[47]

We may conclude that the incidence and rate of increase of violent crime is considerably higher in the large cities, especially the lower-class areas of those cities, than in the suburban or rural areas. During the period 1950–1965, a period of rapid urbanization, this fact alone was sufficient to account for one quarter of the increase in robberies—but less for other violent crimes. Since 1965, urbanization has halted and *suburbanization* has taken over, with no discernible effect upon the rate of increase in violent crime. The suburbs continue to be the safest places to live in.[48]

Violence and Age Structure

I have shown that while violent crime is basically a big city phenom-enon, changes in urbanization do not account for a significant portion of the increase in violent crime over the last decade, and did not in fact account for a great deal during the former period of rapid urbanization. Is there another factor which may explain the rapid increase in violent crime?

Since we have seen that violent crime is very much a young man's thing, perhaps changes in the age structure may explain our current high levels of violent crime. Children of the postwar baby boom of the 1950s in fact should now be at the peak age for committing violent crime. We can test this hypothesis by using a procedure similar to that used for urbanization. We can recompute the age structure of the United States population of 1974 as if it had remained the same as in 1950. Then, using the actual 1974 crime rates, we can recompute what the rates might have been in 1974 with the age structure of 1950.

We find that the effects are substantial. Twenty-three and six tenths percent (23.6%) of the 1950–1974 increase for criminal homicide is explained by the change in age structure alone; for forcible rape it is 21.6%; for robbery 18.6%; and for aggravated assault 10.4%.[49]

Suicide, Manslaughter, and Auto Fatalities

The question whether suicide is either criminal or violent behavior is difficult to answer. It would seem that it is quickly coming to be viewed as not criminal. Is deliberately taking an overdose of sleeping pills an act of violence? The meaning of the word has to be stretched somewhat to allow the inclusion of such behavior as violent. On the other hand, we might be more likely to accept the term "violent death" if the person com-mitted suicide in a more active or "aggressive" way, such as jumping off a bridge or high building. However, it might be argued that the word is used here to characterize the end result of the act rather than the act itself. The body is more obviously "violated" by these acts than it is by the act of taking sleeping pills. Thus, we have no difficulty in accepting deaths resulting from auto accidents as violent deaths and the behavior leading up to or surrounding such events as violence-related behavior.

Indeed, the relationship between auto fatalities, homicide, and suicide may be very close, and it is likely from studies reported by the Crime Commission[50] that misclassifications often occur. It is apparent that there is a definite tendency to classify suicides, especially, as accidental deaths. In fact, it has been argued that Sweden appears to have a high rate of suicide compared with many other countries mainly because suicide does not as readily incur a stigma there, so that officials are less likely to record such deaths as accidents.

There is a close relationship between auto fatalities and the type of homicide that the FBI defines as *negligent manslaughter,* a death which police investigation establishes as primarily attributable to gross negligence of some individual other than the victim. For the last ten years, 90% or more of the reported negligent manslaughters involved motor vehicle deaths. We should note that this crime is not considered sufficiently serious to be included in an index of crimes of violence in the UCR, yet it is responsible for a substantial number of deaths. For 1969, the rate per 100,000 was 4.4 (crimes of negligent manslaughter known to police) as against 7.4 for murder. In 1974 the rate was 4.5 as against 10.4 for murder, so it appears that as the rate of murder increases, manslaughter accounts for a proportionately smaller number of violent deaths.

Some researchers have also argued that suicide is a sort of "mirror image" to homicide, and in some respects the statistics support this claim.[51] We can see from Figure 3.11 that earlier in this century suicide tended to rise as homicide decreased, but this was only a very slight tendency. What is clear is that in recent years, the homicide and suicide rates have remained at roughly the same levels. As far as age distribution is concerned, suicide does appear to be a "mirror" to criminal homicide and manslaughter. For suicide, the rate increases with age, with the highest rate of 21.5 per 100,000 age-specific population in 1971. Clearly, the highest incidence is in the 45 years plus age group, and this has consistently been so for the last 20 years. As we have seen, of course, the reverse is true for criminal homicide and also for manslaughter. No difference has been found between urban and nonurban areas[52] for suicide rates. The Pacific and mountain areas display the highest rates, California being by far the highest. In contrast to criminal homicide, suicide is predominantly a cause of death for older white males (consistently close to 19 per 100,000 for the last decade). They

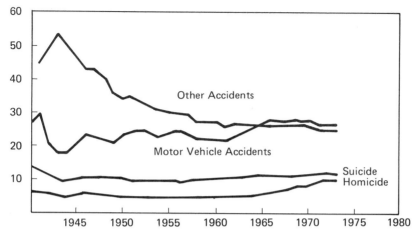

FIGURE 3.11   Loss of Life by Violent Causes, 1940–1973[53] (Rates per 100,000 Population)

are followed by nonwhite males (only 8.9 per 100,000), white females (7–8), and finally nonwhite females (2–3 per 100,000). However, there is also some evidence that young adult blacks (20–35 age group) experience a higher rate than their white peers. After 35, it appears that the rate for blacks does not increase appreciably, while that for the white race increases dramatically.[54]

The distribution of manslaughter rates over age, sex, and race categories is basically similar to that obtained for criminal homicide, although the rate for blacks is only twice that of the white race for manslaughter, whereas it is closer to four times higher for criminal homicide. We should note that these manslaughter deaths mainly involve automobiles, but that the rates only reflect roughly one in seven of all auto fatalities. Auto fatalities are the major cause of death for 18–25-year-olds; they are a far more serious "social problem" than are criminal homicides. It is also very clear from Figure 3.11 that the chances of dying a violent death, especially as the result of accidents have decreased dramatically throughout this century. Perhaps it is because of this decrease in the incidence of accidental deaths that the homicide rate becomes so large in the public mind.

The Weapons of Violence

Apart from the automobile, which as we have just seen is probably the most lethal weapon in society, other weapons are typical of various types of crimes.

For 1974, the UCR reports that 68% of all murders, 25% of aggravated assaults, and 43% of robberies were committed with firearms. From 1964 to 1969 the rate of use of the firearm in perpetrating these crimes of violence rose by 80%. From 1969 to 1974 the rate has remained stable, and the use of the gun for robberies has actually decreased. It is also of interest to note that of all police killings from 1965 to 1974, 96% have been with firearms. There is little doubt that the American perpetrator of violence prefers first a gun and then a knife, whereas the pattern in England and Wales is to use a blunt object (generally the object closest at hand) to beat the victim to death. For the 1964–1969 period in the United States, there was a much greater increase in the use of blunt objects than in the use of any other weapon,[55] but this has stabilized, and no significant changes have occurred up to 1974. Although the gun obviously plays an important role in the American violent scene and certainly comes through history as the symbol of American violence, we should avoid the too simple interpretation that therefore easy access to guns causes the high level of violence in the United States. Such a conclusion cannot be made from this kind of data, for it may equally be argued that if there were no guns, other weapons would be used in their place, and indeed are, such as the automobile. In other words, the prevalence of guns as weapons is simply a surface indication of problems which lie at a deeper level. We will look more closely at this question when we deal with cultures and subcultures of violence in the following chapter.

Summary and Conclusions

The major statistical facts of violent crime are:

1. With the exception of suicide, criminal violence is an activity most typical of young urban black males, and the violent crime in which this picture is most clearly demonstrated is that of robbery. This applies even when taking into account possible discrimination on the part of police.

2. The South continues to be the most criminally violent part of the United States, although there is some suggestion that other parts of the country are catching up. Currently, the most violent states are Alabama, Georgia, Florida, South Carolina, and Nevada.

3. Roughly 25% of the increase in violent crimes since 1950 may be explained by shifts in the age structure. That is, the post-World War II baby-boom children have hit the high crime-prone age over the last ten years, during which time the most serious increase in crime has occurred.

4. Roughly 20% of the increases in violent crime from 1950–1965

could be explained by rapid urbanization. However, since that time, the population of large cities has remained relatively stable and there has been a rapid influx of population into the suburbs. In spite of this, the rate of increase in suburban crime has not altered appreciably, and remains even lower than rural levels. The suburbs are still the safest places to live in.

5. There have been no substantial increases in violent crimes committed by females.

6. Suicides are found to occur largely among older white males, although there is some evidence to suggest a high rate for young black adults. California continues as the state with the highest suicide rate.

7. Although the use of firearms as the weapons of choice in violent crimes increased considerably from 1960–1969, the use rate has leveled out since that time at roughly 60%. In fact, their use for robbery has decreased to 43%.

8. The chances of dying a violent death have decreased remarkably throughout this century.

We now have an idea of the big picture of violence from the political, historical, and spatial perspectives. It has been clearly established on the basis of both statistical and historical data that violence is patterned consistently according to specific social and cultural categories. The following section examines these categories in detail.

Part Two

Violence
and
Culture

4

Cultures and
Subcultures of Violence

Violence and Apple Pie: American or Southern?

In Part One, an important question that I addressed was whether there is sufficient evidence to warrant the popular belief that America is a violent society. In Chapter 2, partial evidence was found for a violent tradition in the South, and Chapter 3 demonstrated that, although there is a higher level of criminal violence in the South, there are many other sociocultural categories which account for variation in criminal violence rates. A number of researchers over the past decade have examined the statistics more closely while trying to control for such factors as urbanization, median income, race, education, medical care, and level of unemployment.[1] All of these studies have still concluded that the rate of violent crime is significantly higher in the South, and more recently that this is probably linked to a higher valuation of violence by Southerners.[2]

On the basis of this research, it has been argued that the South represents a "subculture of violence," by which is usually meant two things: (1) that the South has a significantly higher rate of violent crime, and (2) that the social life of the South fosters the transmission from generation to generation of values which favor the use of violence. However, the use of the term "subculture" in referring to the South is a little misleading since the South is a vast region, enclosing an enormous amount of variety within it, and furthermore has on occasion been seen by some, especially non-Americans, as representing the true core of the American culture. It is therefore more accurate to confine the use of "subculture" to references to any small, geographically isolated community which is highly cohesive in its social organization, and is clearly separable from the dominant culture on the basis of its life styles, beliefs, and traditions. I will describe such a subculture of violence shortly.

Much of the perception of America as generally violent (as against regionally violent) is based on the belief that guns are part of the American way of life. As we saw in Chapter 3, the gun is certainly the most common murder weapon—especially if one is at hand at the same time as alcohol.[3] It has been shown in the laboratory that even the presence of a gun is sufficient to amplify aggressive actions.[4] Various researchers have assembled the following facts about guns:[5]

1. Since the year 1900, guns have been used to kill over 100,000 Americans. Total casualties exceed those from all wars from the Revolution to Vietnam.
2. Someone is shot on the average of one every 25 minutes.
3. It is estimated that there are anywhere from 100 million to 200 million privately owned guns in the United States.
4. Many more people have used guns rather than other methods to kill themselves.
5. The rate of gun homicide is 35 times higher in the United States than in England, Germany, or Denmark.

One might conclude from this evidence that the United States is "gun crazy." However, surveys have repeatedly shown that more than half of United States citizens would favor the outlawing of all handguns except those carried by police—or at least some stringent form of gun control legislation. But due to the efforts of various lobby groups (e.g., the National Rifle Association) no substantial laws have been passed. Massachusetts did pass a mandatory prison term for handgun ownership, but it has thus far failed to have any significant effect on the level of assaults or homicides with guns. It appears to be an oversimplification to lay the "blame" for high rates of criminal violence on the wide accessibility of guns, even though the United States has a much higher rate of violent crime and much more lenient gun control laws than similar countries in the West. The case of Switzerland demonstrates the point. The Swiss, because most are members of the militia, have a very high rate of gun ownership, yet the rate of violent crime is extremely low.[6] However, some would argue that it is the American's attachment to violence, rather than to guns, that is the problem. The National Rifle Association has said often enough: Guns do not kill, men do.

These arguments return us to the thesis that a pervasive "culture of violence" exists—perhaps modeled on the traditions of the South or the "frontier tradition"—and that there should be high valuations of violence throughout the United States generally. I know of only one study that has attempted to catalogue the valuation of violence by Americans,[7] but this study has come under much criticism for a number of methodological reasons. In addition, although the picture it painted of Americans was one that strongly favored the use of violence in a wide variety of situations, without comparative data for other countries there is no way of telling whether the findings of the study demonstrated excessive valuation of violence or not.

In fact, the comparative data available concerning the incidence of violence are not all that clear. As far as violent civil strife is concerned, the deaths resulting from these activities in America for the turbulent decade of the 1960s were considerably fewer than the European average: only 1.1 per million population, compared to 2.4 per million in Europe.[8] And we have seen in Chapter 1 how much less serious have been American acts of internal political violence compared with those of many other countries.

The situation regarding criminal violence is more clear-cut. In a recent survey of crime throughout 50 countries, the United Nations collected considerable data which, given certain precautions,[9] allow some general comparisons to be made. These data are presented in Table 4.1. The following observations may be made on the basis of these data:

HOMICIDE: Compared with those of 50 other countries, the United States homicide rate of 9 per 100,000 is moderately high. There are some countries with higher rates, such as Turkey, El Salvador, Costa Rica, Iraq, and Cyprus. But overall, especially compared with other industrialized countries such as the United Kingdom, France, and Denmark, the United States rate is much higher.

ASSAULT: The United States rate of 195 per 100,000 may be said to be moderate. There are many countries with excessively higher rates—unlike the ratio with regard to homicides. These include Guyana, Bahrain, Egypt, Barbados, Finland, Jamaica, Qatar, Morocco, and Sweden. Certainly, compared with those of other industrialized countries, the United States rates seem roughly similar.

ROBBERY: The United States rate of 191 per 100,000 population stands out as one of the higher rates, along with Peru, Mauritius, Argentina, and the Bahamas. Compared with those of other industrialized countries, the United States rate is certainly extremely high.

TABLE 4.1

Mean Rates (per 100,000 Unadjusted Population), 1970–1975
for Selected Violent Crimes of 50 Countries[10]

	Homicide	Assault	Robbery
Algeria	.88	5.67	.00
Argentina	6.17	74.00	230.15
Australia	1.75	18.17	13.62
Austria	2.85	424.50	10.00
Bahamas	8.95	317.67	148.70
Bahrain	1.98	737.33	18.98
Barbados	4.35	537.33	14.97
Canada	2.48	364.33	64.87
Chile	7.22	103.00	25.10
Costa Rica	15.85	. . .	. . .
Cyprus	10.43	128.33	3.78
Denmark	.63	57.67	12.78
Ecuador	.18	4.83	13.15
Egypt	3.55	355.00	106.25
El Salvador	16.85	4.50	12.42
Finland	. . .	270.00	32.95
France	.18	41.33	.60
German Federal Republic	4.30	168.00	28.38
Greece	.22	31.17	. . .
Guyana	7.03	2812.67	76.38
Indonesia	.98	7.17	2.63
Iraq	11.03	1.83	.23
Ireland	.77	25.17	16.70
Italy	2.68	54.67	.00
Jamaica	7.77	576.33	140.15
Japan	2.05	64.33	2.18
Kuwait	1.07	145.33	.00
Malaysia	1.35	13.33	15.18
Maldives	. . .	149.33	.00
Mauritius	2.72	17.67	603.02
New Zealand	.80	119.50	.00
Morocco	.73	286.33	9.78
Norway	.40	85.33	7.82
Oman	.90	. . .	.12
Pakistan	6.57	1.67	1.47
Peru	2.03	32.33	254.95
Poland	1.03	21.83	12.07
Qatar	3.37	318.00	2.20
San Marino	2.73	2.67	.00
Singapore	2.60	15.33	76.63
Spain	4.58	7.50	43.95
Sweden	3.12	221.17	23.72
Switzerland	.28	6.33	2.03
Syrian Arab Republic	5.10	1.00	18.47
Trinidad Tobago	5.37	17.00	33.75
Turkey	16.80	151.83	6.18
United Kingdom	1.08	104.83	21.42
United States	9.00	195.17	191.22
Yugoslavia	.27	110.00	2.62

We may make the tentative conclusion that for the violent crimes of robbery and homicide, the charge that the United States is a "violent society" in the sense that it is more violent than other societies either similar or dissimilar to it, is strongly supported by these statistics. The robbery statistics are especially supportive of this charge and do perhaps support the further charge that the United States has become a "predators' " society, since it is robbery that is the stranger-to-stranger crime, and it is also the crime that is more often interracial, as we shall see in Chapter 9.

However, the assault statistics do not support the idea of America as a violent culture. This is a significant exception, because it may be argued that assault statistics should provide a more appropriate base for comparison internationally. The reason for this is that when crime categories of a number of nations are compared, distortions may occur if one uses a crime category that is too legally specific (e.g., homicide), since countries vary widely in their legal definitions of homicide. Some have therefore argued that *general* crime categories may provide a more accurate basis for international comparisons. We must conclude, therefore, that the comparative data are only suggestive. Perhaps the lesson we learn is that it is an oversimplification to characterize a society as "violent." Societies may be violent in some respects and not in others.

Are we able to look into the factors that appear to affect this differential rate of violent crime across cultures? As a result of the United Nations survey, some data are available which allow us to make comparisons. Although great caution must be observed in comparing crime data cross-culturally, the United Nations survey concluded that, as very general measures, the comparisons may be valid.

We can see from Figure 4.1 that the assaultive crime rate for developing countries is consistently three times higher than that of the developed countries. The United Nations survey also found that developing countries had a higher robbery rate (70 as against 65 per 100,000 population), although this rate was increasing much more slowly than in developed countries.

Naturally, many factors contribute to these interesting findings. A significant indicator, percentage of work force in agriculture, was found to be highly negatively correlated to the violent crime rate. That is, the higher the proportion of the population engaged in agriculture, the lower the violent crime rate. This finding would suggest (since in general, developing countries were much higher in violent crime than developed countries) that another factor, most likely modernization (especially the movement of populations from the country to the city), may be

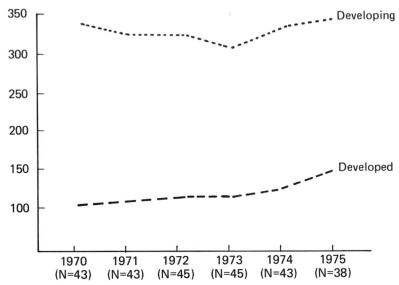

FIGURE 4.1   Reported Assaults for Developing and Developed Countries, 1970–1975[11] (Rates per 100,000 Unadjusted Population)

involved in explaining higher rates of violent crime. Urbanization has, in fact, been commonly considered a major contributor to the causes of violent crime. And it is certainly America's large cities that are often held responsible for her violent crime. The facts underlying this assertion are by no means clear.

Violence and City Life

In Chapter 3, we concluded that part of the increase in violent crime over certain periods could be attributed to the process of urbanization, simply measured by the *size* of the city. However, this does not tell us very much, since there are many kinds of urban environments. These may range from urban sprawl where the population density may be in the low thousands per square mile (e.g., Los Angeles), to Manhattan where the population density is 70 thousand per square mile. Nor is there a clear relationship between poverty or social class and urbanization as measured by population density. Many parts of Manhattan are populated by the rich. Some parts of Brooklyn that are not (comparatively) dense, are populated by the poor.

The fact is that *crowding,* per se, cannot be demonstrated to have a deleterious effect upon humans. As far as one can tell, China and India do not have excessively high violent crime rates. As Professor Freedman points out,[12] man has been living in crowded conditions for thousands of years. Only under special circumstances does crowding have deleterious effects. Most studies conducted and reported on by Professor Freedman show that, other things being equal, high population density does not appear to be related to high rates of crime—indeed the reverse is true: the higher the density, the lower the rate. This finding makes a lot of sense, since sociologists have long talked about the importance of community, and what better conditions exist for forming *group solidarity* than crowded districts where constant contact with others is possible?

Other researchers have argued the opposite: that high density living "overstimulates" individuals so that they have to withdraw or "not get involved" with too many persons at once. Hence, they have fewer social contacts. This observation has been supported (or perhaps based on) the notorious cases in New York City of serious assaultive crimes about which bystanders did nothing. When a man brutally assaulted Kitty Genovese, her cries for help were ignored by 15 bystanders. One writer argues that there is a vicious circle operating. In the urban setting, the bystander will not report a crime → therefore, criminals commit more crime → people become afraid, and so lock their doors → they become less a part of the community → thus they are less likely to report crime. . . .[13]

A more significant theory, and one that has been around for a long time, is one that points to particular areas in a city that are characterized by social disorganization, typified by a shifting population, a population that has little "stake" in the area in which it lives.[14] These areas have been identified throughout various periods in the history of most large American cities; they are areas into which immigrant groups move and establish job contacts, then move on, leaving the district to be populated by a new wave of immigrants. This process occurs all over the world. The infamous slums of Glasgow, the Gorbals, were first populated by the Irish, subsequently by West Indians. In developing countries the problem has been identified as much more serious, since young men tend to gravitate to the big cities in search of work or the excitement of modernization. The result is often the rise of "shanty towns" on the fringes of large cities in developing countries, where a high rate of violent crime is known to exist.[15]

The identification of particular areas in cities as areas of disorganization and high crime has contributed to a further hypothesis that these areas may represent "subcultures of violence."[16] One can drive through virtually any American city and locate these areas. They are identifiable, superficially at least, by any or a combination of three factors: their ethnicity, their social class, and in special cases the visibility of juvenile gangs. We shall reserve discussion of juvenile gangs for Chapter 8. Our question here is, to what extent do ethnicity and social class contribute to subcultures of violence? To answer this question, we must first understand what a subculture of violence is supposed to be.

What Is a Violent Subculture?

Wolfgang and Ferracuti, in their classic, *The Subculture of Violence,* outlined a set of seven propositions that contributed to the use of violence in subcultures. I propose to outline each of these and expand upon them in reference to what I consider to be a prototype subculture of violence, the Doukhobor Sons of Freedom in Canada. First, a little background on the Doukhobors.

The Doukhobor sect probably emerged in Russia sometime in the middle of the nineteenth century, spiritual descendants of a wide range of Christian sects such as Anabaptists, Quakers, and perhaps Raskolniks (heretics). In any event, they were called by the Russian church *Dukhobortzi*—"spirit wrestlers." They migrated as did many other religious sects from Europe in the nineteenth century to the North American continent. The first party of immigrants landed in Canada on January 20, 1899, and by the summer of that year several thousand had settled in reserves throughout Saskatchewan. Each adult male was given a 160 acre homestead. Like other similar religious sects, the Doukhobors were industrious settlers, and their community began to prosper. They were also high-principled and devoted to their religion, the basic tenets of which were: (1) rejection of any recognition of the material existence; (2) distrust of government; (3) an avowed pacifism; (4) refusal to work others (including animals) for one's own benefit; (5) devotion to community and brotherhood before one's self.[17]

The spiritual leader, Peter Veregin, issued edicts from Russia, and eventually arrived in Canada in 1902. Although there is some disagreement about it, the evidence points to the fact that this leader (and subsequent leaders who replaced him) was largely responsible for the direction that the development of this religious subculture eventually took. Veregin encouraged virtually a literal interpretation of the Doukhobor religious principles, so that the people eventually refused point blank to register their homesteads in any individual names, refused to register births or deaths, and refused to recognize the laws of the Canadian government.

In his edicts, Peter Veregin announced that clothes were evil—as a sign of the material existence—and that God's animals should not be made to do man's labor. The result was that the people sold their oxen and hitched themselves to their ploughs; and they shed their clothes, often marching miles in protest against the Canadian government, in freezing cold, with very little to eat. These protest marches were joined by hundreds and proceeded for days through many villages. The next important step came when Peter Veregin abolished all forms of private property. The effects of this edict are described in the report of a Canadian Mounted Police inspector:[18]

> These people only recognize one Ruler, Peter Verigin, whom I am told instructs them to take no notice of any laws or authority outside of those of his own making.
>
> When Peter Verigin formed the community everyone gave up their right to their own property and now when desirous of leaving this community, are not only unable to recover their property but I am informed are ill-treated in the worst way by the community Doukhobors.
>
> This ill treatment often takes the form of bodily injury. It is a well-known fact now that one-tenth of the offences committed are never brought to the notice of police. The people in the Thunder Hill region had a property dispute which ultimately ended in a fight with axes, pitchforks, etc. It is not unusual for these people to come to him [the officer in charge at Kamsack] with disfigured faces showing marks of violence.

In 1923, amidst an argument with the Canadian government over the refusal of the Doukhobors to send their children to school, Brilliant No. 1 school, the heart of Veregin's kingdom, was put to the torch. Veregin blamed the Canadian government, and two more schools were burnt down in quick succession.

Peter Veregin was bombed to death while he sat in a train on June 25, 1924. As it turns out, it is now known that his son and successor Peter Petushka engineered the assassination.[19] But the Doukhobors were told, and many possibly still believe, that the Canadian government had murdered their spiritual leader.

Peter Petushka immediately surveyed his newly acquired kingdom and set about inventing new religious principles and practices. He told the Doukhobors to "burn their consciences," which they interpreted all too literally. It became a practice every few years to burn their own as well as others' material possessions. The razing of whole villages was common. Naturally, because of those many misdemeanors and felonies, Canada's prisons started to house large numbers of Doukhobors, and it was at this time that Peter made his great prophecy of emigration:

> If we bomb, burn, fill the jails, the government will be so anxious
> to get rid of us that they will not only provide transportation for us
> and our baggage, they will even load on our outhouses for us . . .
> Doukhobors . . . [and] will shed blood on these prairies for the
> material things we are going to leave behind.[20]

And so it has gone on through subsequent generations and a new succession of leaders, reaching a crescendo of more and more violence. It may be useful to examine the Doukhobor subculture in the light of the following seven statements by Wolfgang and Ferracuti.[21]

1. "No subculture can be totally different from or totally in conflict with the society of which it is a part." It is difficult to see how this applies to the Doukhobors. They are in conflict with the very basis of Canadian society: against individualism, education, materialism, all established laws. The only common trait appears to be aspects of violence, since the Canadian government had to intervene with physical force either to apprehend arsonists and bombers or to place starving children in protective custody. This is a fascinating subculture since one can see that it began by sharing some of the dominant societal values, such as devotion to the land, but developed, out of already existing dissident religious principles, a subculture totally in conflict with the dominant culture.

2. "To establish the existence of a subculture of violence does not require that the actors sharing these basic value elements should express violence in all situations." Indeed, a number of anthropologists observed the Doukhobors and concluded that they were a highly organized and peace-loving people, devoted to a simple life of religion and the land. There are also other ways of accentuating subcultural divergence from the dominant culture. With the Doukhobors, religious nudity fulfilled this purpose very well, especially since it provoked the Canadian government into introducing a three-year prison term for public nudity.[22]

3. "The potential resort or willingness to resort to violence in a variety of situations emphasizes the penetrating and diffusive character of this culture theme." Indeed, violence became a truly penetrating theme of the Doukhobors when it was applied to the principle of wholesale destruction of one's own material possessions. As the mother of an arsonist who died by his own bomb explained:[23]

> When Harry two years, I burn house. When he five I burn house.
> Many times I burn house. Police know. I can't remember number
> times I burn house. Three times I go to jail. Harry two when I go
> to jail first time. . . . Harry see. He like I should do this. . . .
> This is Doukhobor work. For two hundred years Doukhobors burn
> churches and guns.

4. "The subcultural ethos of violence may be shared by all ages in a subsociety, but this ethos is most prominent in a limited age group, ranging from late adolescence to middle age."

Holt reports that the majority of perpetrators are young to middle-aged males, mostly beginning their career as arsonists in their early adolescence.[24] However, wives were also commonly apprehended.

5. "The counter-norm is non-violence." This is always a difficult one to uphold, mainly because, as we saw in Chapter 1, all societies depend upon a certain amount of violence to maintain order, so that it is easy for terrorists to justify their own violent acts by pointing to the violence of the dominant culture. The convoluted logic involved is well demonstrated by the following interchange between a convicted Doukhobor terrorist and his inquisitor:[25]

Q: How did your parents explain bombings and burnings—violence of any sort—was right for a person of pacifist religion?
A: . . . if the devil approaches you with force to serve him, burn his [material possessions] idol.
Q: What did you think of the fire-bombs being set under the homes of sleeping people?
A: Personally I did not like this idea. But on the other hand, I wonder how many people felt about Hiroshima dropping bombs for which they were made heroes, or how those feel that are preparing bombs. In these acts I understand caution was taken to leave doors open so no one would burn.
Q: Are not bombs and fire weapons of war?
A: No, they are means to avert war. All wars are fought for material possessions. So if wealth were burned there would be nothing to fight for.

*   *   *

Q: Did you ever wish to be like other Canadian boys with whom you grew up?
A: No I never wished to be a transgressor of God and his laws. To me it was the feeling of being a murderer.

6. "The development of favorable attitudes toward, and the use of, violence in a subculture usually involve learned behavior and a process of differential learning, association, or identification." This process was clearly at work among the Doukhobors. Apart from the fact of the constant visibility of violence, considerable training was involved, and in addition considerable group "coercion:"[26]

Q: Were you actually forced into this work? Did you fear reprisals if you did not do it?
A: That is right. We are forced into these acts otherwise we cannot

remain Sons of Freedom. I would have no place in the group if I refused to obey orders.

Q. Who are the trainers of bombers?

A: Those who have been at it for years. These acts are always done only under a command from the higher officials.

Q: Do the older men train the youngsters, working young-old teams?

A: That is right. It is forwarded—passed on.

Q: What is paid in expenses for bombings? Does the Fraternal Council actually pay?

A: Generally gas, watches and other supplies that have to be bought are expenses covered by the Fraternal Council.

Q: Who are the "Big Bombers"?

A: Those who have been at it for years.

Q: Who are considered the best bombers?

A: The youth because they are young.

Q: Are the bombers paid?

A: No. It is their duty.

Q. Who are the actual organizers?

A: The Fraternal Council and other elders who were at it at the time of Peter Chistiakoff.

Q: You say you are ready to give your life in this work. Would you be happier if you did not live in this self-imposed danger?

A: No, because it is a sacred duty of each Doukhobor.

7. "The use of violence in a subculture is not necessarily viewed as illicit conduct and the users therefore do not have to deal with feelings of guilt about their aggression." This point is clearly apparent from the examples I have already given. Not only do the Doukhobors think their actions are justified, but they believe they are doing God's work as well:[27]

Q: You love your children very much. Can you really believe that the happiness you want for them can come from a life of bombing, burning, nudism, and fighting government?

A: Yes. We love our children. That is why we want them this way. If we did not love our children we would be like a pig which will eat her small ones if they are not taken away in time. We do believe that happiness is not far away.

Q: Could you not see any happiness in careers, say as lawyers, writers, nurses, doctors, who serve humanity?

A: We would never allow our children to be educated to be criminals and partakers in mass murder. All the above mentioned are only riding on the back of the working people and sooner or later the working man will be overburdened and then watch out, because he too knows better. All should work for a living.

Teenage Doukhobors commonly admit: "I don't know what it was; something said I must go out and make some excitement, do the Doukhobor work. . . ."[28] Clearly, these Doukhobors would be guilty if they *did not* use violence.

A point that was not discussed by Wolfgang and Ferracuti, but which seems to be relevant to the Doukhobors, is that subcultural values, traditions, and life styles may not be enough on their own to generate violent action. It takes a central figure or figures to fire the imagination of the people—to interpret their traditions and incite them to action. The series of weird—and some would say, criminal—leaders of the Doukhobors makes this point very clear.

One should also point out that not even among the Doukhobors was the violent tradition all-pervasive in the sense that all, or even a majority of the Doukhobors bombed and burned. The main violent element was a small sect, the Sons of Freedom. Many Doukhobors became assimilated or partly assimilated into Canadian society.

I have discussed an extreme example of a subculture of violence. This is, however, only one form of a violent subculture, and it is apparent that there are many different varieties—some more and some less violent, some more and some less organized, some more and some less different from the dominant culture.[29] It is our task now, however, to look at the more pertinent aspects of American "subcultures" and to assess (1) the evidence that they actually *are* subcultures, and (2) the extent to which violence is part of these subcultures.

Ethnic Subcultures

The Biological Basis of Ethnicity

We shall see in the following chapter that even where we have two reasonably biologically distinct population groups (e.g., males and females) it is very difficult to conclude that their different rates of violent crime are due specifically, or only, to their biological differences. When we come to consider race as a biological category (i.e., a transcultural category), the task becomes well nigh impossible. Yet, it is very clear from the United States data presented in Chapter 3 that American blacks as a group display considerably higher rates of violent crime. The difficulties associated with interpreting and explaining such statistical facts using a biological definition of race are considerable.

The early studies by the physical anthropologists at the end of the nineteenth century concentrated on the morphological differences between races, which were described according to exterior characteristics (e.g., skin color, language, geographic location). Hooton defined race as "a great division of mankind, the members of which, though individually varying, are characterized as a group by a certain combination of morphological and metric features, principally non-adaptive, which have been derived from their common descent."[30] Although it need not have done so, this conception of race contributed to the idea of a race as a separate or clearly differentiated group. Of course, this was not so, even from Hooton's work, but the insistence by Hooton (who later changed his mind) on the nonadaptive features of racial morphology led to this stereotyped understanding of race.

Today the physical study of the classification of race concentrates not on morphological characteristics, but on gene structure. Races are now defined as "populations which differ in the frequency of some genes,"[31] although this approach has also recently come under attack.[32] It certainly raises difficult problems for the study of American blacks as a biologically distinct category, for it turns out that probably 30% of the American black gene pool is of Caucasian origin.[33] This makes it difficult, if not impossible, to make valid inferences concerning the biological bases of observed differences in violent crime between the two races.

Nevertheless, there are certain diseases that are well established as race-specific as well as inherited through a specific gene. Sickle-cell anemia in blacks is an excellent example. When black parents both have the sickle-cell trait, they have a 25% chance of producing offspring with the disease; yet, researchers have shown that this trait had its origins in particular environmental and cultural conditions several hundred years ago (the slash and burn method of agriculture in regions of Africa) and that its evolution has been considerably influenced by cultural and environmental conditions.[34] This observation has led Professor Katz to suggest that, not only should improved environmental conditions help eliminate or at least modify the evolutionary pattern of sickle-cell anemia, but also that genetic counseling—in the form of strongly urging parents, when both have the trait, to forego having children—should help eliminate it. (The gene, of course, will not be eliminated, but the trait will.)[35]

What about criminal violence? Unlike sickle-cell anemia, no single gene has ever been identified with a "disease" anywhere near resembling any of the forms of criminal violence. Even if we take "intervening variables," such as low intelligence, which are sometimes argued to be related to crime (and with lesser success to violent crime),[36] no single gene characteristic (except the rare Huntington's chorea and microcephaly) has been found to affect the central nervous system.[37] The controversial work of Jensen and others has argued that intelligence is largely inherited and that since blacks score consistently lower on IQ

tests than do whites (even controlling for social class), they are therefore innately less intelligent.[38] Many criticisms have been made of these
findings, all of which we need not go into here. But the general weight
of opinion is that valid comparisons cannot be made across populations
concerning the heritability of IQ (1) because of the enormous and
varying effects of environment (e.g., a lower class white boy is still different from a lower class black boy), and (2) because intelligence is
treated as a continuous trait for which, because it probably involves
many gene characteristics, there is no valid solid genetic basis for
comparison.[39]

All of these studies, and all of the data reported in Chapter 3, rely
upon a social definition of race. That is, they depend on the perception
either by the victim or the arresting officer of the offender as "black" and
on the recording of this perception in official records. This means that
these categorizations are made not only according to perceived skin
color, but also according to dress, language, physical styles, and other
ethnic cultural identifiers.[40] In many cases, if not all, the offender also
perceives himself as "black" or as representative of the race to which
he is attached. It also is well known that those of similar ethnic background also tend to live in the same geographical areas. These observations have led some researchers to consider the possibility that the
subcultural way of life of some ethnic groups may in itself contribute to
violence. This has led to the study of ethnic subcultures.

Ethnic Subcultures as Feuding Subcultures

When we are dealing with explanations of the relationship between
crime and subcultures, we are confronted with two difficult problems.
First, many ethnic subcultures in the United States and many other
countries, whether indigenous minorities (e.g., the small subcultures of
violence in Sardinia) or immigrant minorities (e.g., Koreans in Japan)
also tend to be very poor, or, one might say, lower-class subcultures as
well as ethnic subcultures. Because there are special problems attached
to the analysis of lower-class subcultures, we shall reserve discussion of
this aspect of ethnic subcultures until later in this chapter. For the
moment, we want to concentrate upon the *ethnicity* of violent subcultures. The second and related problem is that not all ethnic minority
subcultures are violent, even though many are and have been discriminated against by the dominant culture (e.g., the Japanese and Jews in
the United States).

An ethnic subculture may be defined as a segment of the larger culture which is functionally isolated from the dominant culture according to geography, language, particular customs such as dress and cuisine, and history. The earlier historical forms of these subcultures which tended towards violence are what we call *feuding subcultures,* of which there are many in existence throughout the world. These ethnic subcultures tend towards violence as a traditional method of solving problems of conflict between individuals or groups. The violence of vengeance is used instead of the usual mechanisms of formal criminal or civil law as we know it.

We should make it clear that not all feuding subcultures are violent, nor have they been historically.[41] However, most feuding subcultures today do resort to violence as a means of the informal regulation of social conduct.

It should also be clear that not all violent ethnic subcultures are necessarily poor, nor are all poor subcultures ethnic, although they may be "closed" in the sense that there is little marriage outside the subculture. There are many variations on this theme. For example, Japan has a very low crime rate, and Japanese immigrants to the United States also have a very low rate of crime. On the other hand, Sardinians have a very high violent crime rate, yet when they migrate to Genoa, their rate of violent crime decreases dramatically. Puerto Ricans have a comparatively low crime rate in Puerto Rico, but Puerto Ricans in New York City have excessively high rates of violent crime. The differential and/or universal effects of migration and culture have yet to be studied in any detail.

To further complicate matters, unlike traditional feuding subcultures which tend to remain the same, some subcultures in the United States tend to undergo considerable transformation. For example, one would hardly call the Italian organized crime families identified by Professor Ianni[42] as "lower-class," although undoubtedly that was their origin. Puzo's *The Godfather* is in many ways a study of the modernization of a traditional feuding subculture.

Although the study of feuding subcultures is in its infancy, it appears that they arise as a result of the following conditions:

COLLECTIVE RESPONSIBILITY. Historically, blood feuds have probably existed since men began to organize themselves. One theory suggests that they arose during a period in history when collective responsibility was not distinguished from individual responsibility. The transition to individualistic concepts occurred relatively late in both Western and Eastern cultures. In the West it occurred some time during the Middle Ages,[43] and in the East with the introduction of Islamic thought.[44] The most significant characteristic of historical feuding subcultures is their resilience. In the face of wars, occupations by foreign invaders, and all manner of incursions, they remain. This is true today of such subcultures in Albania, in much of the Middle East, and in Sicily and Sardinia. In the United States, some still continue in the mountain country of the deep South, although those subcultures are comparatively young compared to those of Europe.

SCARCITY. Some anthropologists have referred to the concept of "total scarcity" as "the moral, institutional, and material pressure of a certain type of society in which everything felt by the people themselves to be relevant to human life is regarded by those people as existing in absolutely inadequate quantities."[45] The feud performs important functions under such conditions. It ensures collective responsibility, so that the subculture has a greater chance of survival. It also introduces an abstract dimension into the subculture: the idea of honor. In a subculture where material goods are so scarce that social status simply cannot be defined in such terms, the anthropologist argues that honor becomes such a commodity that feuding subcultures develop a highly organized and rigid social hierarchy based upon the ideals of prestige and honor.[46]

NONVIOLENT VALUES, BUT VIOLENT SOLUTIONS. Because of the confusion between lower-class subcultures and ethnic subcultures, some researchers have been led to suggest that in violent ethnic subcultures children are trained to value violence as a solution to interpersonal problems. This claim is as yet unproven. A number of studies have failed to show differences in the valuation of violence between samples from supposedly violent subcultures and those from "nonviolent" cultures.[47] But these studies did not define "subculture" very clearly, nor were they careful in measuring the valuation of violence. However, one study of Sardinians did argue that it was not so much the valuation of violence itself, as the valuation of the conditions under which violence was accepted as a solution to social conflict, that was the crucial differentiating variable.[48]

FEAR. Many of these "violent" subcultures are permeated by fear— fear of starvation and fear of attack from the dominant culture. The result is that kinship patterns tend to be highly cohesive and there is heavy reliance on families themselves to solve social or individual problems.[49] Thus, in defense against the dominant culture which often sends in "national" police and government agents, the ethnic subculture develops its own system of social control which parallels and often bypasses the formal system of criminal law established by the dominant culture. The forms of these informal systems of social control may range from highly ritualized Mafia organizations to the activities of juvenile gangs in urban ghettos which defend the territory of all the inhabitants of the ghetto. Such informal and highly ritualized systems have been reported in Sicily, Sardinia, Yugoslavia and Albania, the Middle East, Mexico, Colombia, Texas, and many other places.[50]

HONOR AND MACHISMO. We have already observed the nearly universal role of honor and shame in feuding subcultures. Honor and shame are central to small, exclusive subcultures where intimate face-to-face contact occurs often.[51] The concept of honor is central to the social hierarchy of a feuding subculture and is also of lasting historical significance, especially because of its origins in physical power and physical redress. "La lessive de l'honneur ne se coule qu' au sang" (the laundry of honor is only bleached by blood).[52] In many feuding subcultures, the concept of honor, because it is so closely attached to physical prowess, is often referred to as "machismo," since it is almost always sought and defended by males of the subculture. Children are brought up to recognize that honor must be defended and sought after at all costs. As Hobsbawm has noted, in an economically homogeneous society, a man's prestige is the only quality that he possesses which differentiates him from other members of the same society.[53] Machismo is often seen by researchers as typical of lower-class violent subcultures. But middle- and lower-class males also display macho values and traits (otherwise, why the fancy cars, dress, sports, frequent accusations of chauvinism, etc.?). The crucial factor appears to be the combination of macho values, especially honor, with an ethnic subculture in which there is severe material scarcity.

How does all of the above apply to the explanation of high rates of violent crime among United States blacks and other minorities? There are a number of direct applications.

1. Contrary to popular stereotypes, the kinship ties (especially of extended kinship) among black ethnic subcultures tend to be very close. Commonly, extended families live together under the one roof. There is, in fact, considerable cohesiveness in black ghetto subcultures; it amounts virtually to a mutual aid system, and this is well described and documented by Elmer and Joanne Martin in *The Black Extended Family*. Family cohesiveness is probably even greater among Latin subcultures in the United States.

2. The language, style, and customs are historically well-defined, and geographical isolation, although changing in particular areas over the past 200 years, has nevertheless tended toward clear separation and isolation. Once again, these tend towards the internal cohesiveness and closed nature of the black ethnic subculture.

3. Juvenile gangs with a long history have arisen in most black urban communities. These gangs may be conceived of as feuding gangs which have arisen in response to the situation of severe material scarcity, real threats by police, the Ku Klux Klan, and others of the dominant culture. They have therefore developed a highly ritualistic defense of the isolated geography of the ethnic subculture, along with the development of a highly organized social hierarchy based on honor and prestige. At least one study has documented the importance of honor in relation to violence in Chicano gangs.[54]

4. Following from the above, the tendency in some places has been to develop informal systems of self-help and enforcement of "laws." But it must be said that this has been minimal and that blacks have not resisted the enforcement of the law upon them by the dominant culture. This is about as far as our exploration of feuding as a factor in the high black crime rate can go, mainly because there are further complicating factors.

Relationships Between the Subculture and the Dominant Culture

Most feuding subcultures throughout the world have occurred in isolated geographic regions where it was possible to keep the influence of the dominant culture at bay. But this is not the case with ethnic subcultures in the United States. Instead, because of their historical origins, ethnic subcultures tend to be heavily interwoven with the dominant culture, and this applies especially to black subcultures. It is this factor that has produced a level of disorganization in the black subcultures that is not typical of other feuding subcultures.

In the isolated peasant subculture, such as Sardinia, the subcultural ethos may be seen as having largely developed separately, or at least in antagonism to the dominant culture. In contrast, the history of American blacks is closely intertwined with the history of the whites. The black subculture is, after all, one that has arisen from slavery, an institution that presupposes a deep interdependence between master and slave. The factor of economic exploitation is, of course, obvious, and we will shortly go into it more deeply. For the moment we are more concerned with understanding the ethos of the black subculture.

Dr. Frantz Fanon has clearly outlined the process in his moving *The Wretched of the Earth.* The black man exists for the white man not only to satisfy his material needs, but his psychological needs. The black man is stereotyped as having all the "bad" traits a white man likes to think he does not have; yet at the same time would deeply like to have—incredible animal strength, excessive sexual prowess. The subcultural black man is just that: he is *sub*-cultural. A product of the disgusting recesses of the white man's unconscious.[55] The black man is seen as brutal, lazy, deceitful, lying, and all the other traits of the wicked. This goes on for so long under slavery that the black man comes to see himself in the same way. Worse, after slavery and especially in modern times, the white man's culture becomes excessively seductive in a truly material sense: the media of the twentieth century provide the ideal image for the black man. He should try to be more like the white man—straighten his hair, work hard, buy many material possessions, dress beautifully. This is the image he should develop! There is much evidence to suggest that the black child of the first half of the twentieth century saw the image of the white man as the identity for which he should strive.[56] It was, of course, a clearly impossible task. The result was the black man's (especially *man's,* because of the male-dominated white culture) hatred of himself as black—and, logically, his hatred of other black men. This may well explain why it is that blacks kill and assault each other, rather than attack the more obvious source of their distorted identity—the whites.

This explanation is all very well. Unfortunately, in the face of a rapid improvement in the economic and social condition of black people over the last decade and the largely successful efforts of black power ideologists to correct the distorted self-image of the blacks, black crime continues to stay at roughly the same excessive levels as a decade ago. Why? It is probable that the reason still lies in economic conditions, to which we must now turn.

Social Class and Violence

There are many theories to explain the relationship between social class and violence.

Lower-Class Subcultures

By lower-class subculture I mean a geographically isolated segment of a larger culture that is typified by its own set of values, life styles, customs, dress, and cuisine that are not ethnic in origin. In the United

States, this probably means that there are not many, depending on whether one excluded Irish, Polish, and Italians as "ethnic." In any event, it is apparent from recent United States history that the Irish, Polish, Russian, Jewish, and Italian immigrants have each gone through a period of poverty. Many, or even most, have become assimilated into the American way of life, and have left their original isolated ghettoes. But many have remained, or have congregated in new areas of ethnic identity. Such areas can still be found in most major American cities. Some have argued, however, that there is a subcultural ethos that transcends these ethnic identities and that there is a set of values and life styles typical of the lower class, which has evolved over many generations.[57] This is a somewhat unpopular view of lower-class culture, since it appears to imply that the lower class has evolved from the successive "failures" who have filtered down from other classes and that the lower-class culture has tended to propagate itself independently. This image of the lower class goes against the popular American belief in endless mobility—the "anyone can become President" syndrome. Some would argue that mobility out of the lower class is achieved by only a few. In fact, Professor Miller argues that the majority of lower-class individuals have absolutely no aspirations to gravitate upwards. Their lives, instead, are dominated by six "focal concerns" which are special to the "lower class milieu":[58]

1. Trouble—law-violating behavior
2. Toughness—physical prowess, skill; masculinity, fearlessness, bravery, daring
3. Smartness—ability to gain money by "wits," "dupe," "con"
4. Excitement—thrill, risk, danger
5. Fate—favored by fortune, being "lucky"
6. Autonomy—freedom from external constraint; independence

One can readily identify a number of the violence-related themes already identified in early chapters: toughness, macho, daring. Although it need not be, Miller's characterization of the lower class comes close to the view of the poor as the "dangerous classes" held on and off in Europe since the eighteenth century, when the lower classes were characterized as a violent, lustful, belligerent mob.[59]

The Lumpenproletariat

A similar view of the "dangerous classes" as the most feckless of all is the Marxist concept of the *lumpenproletariat:* the class Marx saw as existing *below* the lower class, incapable of reaching class consciousness, existing *parasitically* through criminal endeavor and pathological unemployment. It was from these ranks that the most violent criminals were seen to come. Although Marx and his followers have viewed this criminal proletariat as possibly useful during the revolution, they were quite clear that there was no hope for this group. It would never learn its role in history.[60]

Class War

Variations on the Marxist theory of the conflict between the proletariat ("lower class") and the bourgeoisie ("middle class") have been put forward to *explain* violence, (in contrast to *justifying* violence—a perspective we considered in Chapter 1). Starting with the work of Wilhelm Bonger in 1916, Marxist theorists argued that it was the economic oppression of the working class that predisposed it towards crime.[61] A difficulty with early Marxist criminological theory was that it could only explain lower-class crime in a general sense. The capitalist system emphasizes "egoism" and private property, with the result that there is a great deal of property crime by the lower class, since it has less property. In addition, although the propertied classes have property, egoism motivates them to want more and more. Since they make and enforce the laws, they are able to exploit the lower classes with impunity. This does not, however, adequately explain the higher incidence of lower-class violent crime as against the clearly lower level of violent crime of the upper class.

Modern Marxist theorists have tended to make two rather contradictory arguments in reply to this criticism. First, they point out that crimes of violence are crimes legislated purely by the ruling class. Hence, the lower class is differentially selected by biased capitalist laws.[62] It can be seen that this is a circular argument, since it does not explain how lower-class violence began in the first place.

The only way out of this difficulty is for the Marxist to argue that all lower-class violent crime is an "act-of-revolution" in the sense that it is an expression of defiance of the capitalist order. Since most of lower-class criminal violence is perpetrated against others of the lower class, and not against the ruling class, it is hard to see how this violent behavior is a reaction against oppressive capitalist laws. To get out of this bind, some Marxists have recently begun to hint that all acts of criminal violence by the lower class are *unconscious* acts of rebellion.[63] Certainly Fanon's analysis would support this view. But this means that these theorists would be led into a psychological analysis of the relationship between the classes, not a purely politico-economic one, as has been the trend so far by Marxist theorists in criminology. Although the political and economic relationship between the classes is no doubt of great significance for understanding society as a whole, it is difficult to make a class-caused link between these observations and the high rate of lower-class violent crime. Other researchers have examined different aspects of the relationship between the classes and crime.

Opportunity Theory

In all of criminological theory, this hypothesis is probably the one most often repeated. Professor Merton, back in 1938, developed the thesis that society (in the United States) was structured in such a way that all people pursued a common goal, such as success or financial acquisition. This is seen as a *legitimized* goal for everyone to aspire to. Unfortunately, not everyone has access to the means (e.g., education, jobs, skills, cultural background) of achieving these goals; hence certain sociological adaptations result. One of the adaptations is rebellion—especially when individuals, fed up with trying to achieve the goal when they lack the means to do it, reject both the means and the goal: "When the institutional system is regarded as the barrier to the satisfaction of legitimized goals, the stage is set for rebellion as the adaptive response."[64] This theory was intended to explain *group* adaptations, essentially the rise of revolutions. In a later variation on this theory, Professors Cloward and Ohlin, tried to explain individual violence more fully. This theory argued that a crucial factor in the choice of criminal activity when faced with rejection of goals and means to those goals, was the availability of illegitimate opportunity. Should it be available, then this illegitimate means will be pursued toward the legitimate goal. Thus, a Sicilian immigrant unable to get a good job may turn to organized crime as a means of achieving financial success.[65]

But these "barrier" theories do not explain why it is that criminal violence occurs in the lower class rather than other classes. A theory must be advanced which explains why it is that the blocking of opportunity instigates violence in the lower class, rather than, say, despair and submission. The only hypothesis that seems relevant to this question is frustration-aggression theory, in which it is argued that aggression is the natural outcome of frustration.[66] Though on the psychological level, much research has been conducted on this model, with inconclusive results (see Chapter 11), some sociological investigations have supported the idea. One cross-cultural study showed that political instability was related to various measures of what one might call "national frustration" (e.g., number of radios, average diet, etc.).[67] Another study of suicide and homicide tried to show that Southern blacks were more extrapunitively aggressive because they were more frustrated.[68]

Yes and No

Another explanation of lower-class violence has been advanced by Professor Cohen,[69] who observed that a very common explanation that delinquents gave to explain their own destructive behavior was "we are just plain mean," "just ornery." Cohen interpreted these statements as symptomatic of the nonutilitarian, malicious, and negativistic aspects of lower-class culture (largely seen as synonymous with "lower-class gang"). The source of this maliciousness, he argued, was the problem posed to these delinquents because of the fact that they belonged to the lower class. For example, they were unable to measure up to the standards of behavior required of them in school because the school was based upon middle-class standards—delay of gratification; the virtues of ambition, rationality, individual responsibility, respect for property, etc. In contrast, growing up in a lower-class culture teaches short-run hedonism, defiance of taboos, and physical aggression.

So far, we see that there is not altogether much difference between this characterization of the lower class and Miller's. (It certainly sounds like a dangerous bunch if ever there was one!) The extra twist that Cohen gives to the theory, however, is that the extent to which the lower-class boy sees the middle-class life style, or values (whatever one wishes to call them) as worthwhile—the extent to which he may even have internalized those values—will determine the seriousness of his problem of adjustment, since his lower-class upbringing does not equip him to cope with life according to the middle-class measuring rod. The result is an expressive, malicious rejection of middle-class values. In short, lower-class destructiveness depends upon the extent to which the delinquent at first says yes to the middle-class values, and then no to them when he finds that there is no way of fulfilling them.

There are many variations on these five themes. One of the most difficult aspects of these theories is that they mainly purport, to some degree or other, that lower-class individuals have a different value structure from that of the middle and upper classes, especially in relation to crime. In general, the more recent evidence is against this view: there appears to be an across-the-board consensus concerning the perceived seriousness, punitiveness, and other perceptual aspects of crime and its control as far as social class is concerned.[70] There is, however, considerable difficulty in interpreting these studies since they are mostly of a general nature and do not attempt to relate values to actual behavior. With the possible exception of Miller's theory, there is the further difficulty that the theories also argue for some degree of similarity between lower-class values and the values of the wider society. This applies especially to Cohen and to Wolfgang and Ferracuti, whose first proposition, we saw, was that no subculture may be entirely separate from the dominant culture.

Class Theory, Age and Sex

A number of books of the 1970s have attempted to picture the broad dimensions of age or sex as a "class-in-itself," in the Marxist sense. This has especially been the case in the deschooling movement and the women's liberation movement of the seventies. Although Marx's original analysis of society saw it broken up basically into two factions—the proletariat and the bourgeoisie, modern liberationists have applied his analysis wholesale to other groups which they have perceived as oppressed minorities. Cries have come for the liberation of children from the "prisons" of nursery schools, day-care centers and ordinary school.[71] In criminology, one researcher went so far as to argue that age was *the* factor in the separation of society into conflicting groups,[72] and the following chapter will indeed look at this inherent conflict between the generations. But the important point of these "conflict theorists" is that not only is violence explained by class theory, but it is also, to a large extent, justified by it. The oppressed minority is encouraged to become conscious of itself as a class.

For children, consciousness as a "class-for-itself" is not likely to be totally achieved, for reasons that will become apparent in the following chapter. Certainly attempts have been made to "ideologize" children, with sometimes violent results. The publication of "The Little Red Book" in England and Australia, a book which "demystified" the authority of teachers—telling children how to deal with it—created considerable controversy and was banned in many places. From time to time, rebellions have occurred and do occur among schoolchildren when they act collectively—in Marxist terminology, as a "class-for-itself."[73]

As far as women are concerned, many Marxist-oriented books have been published, and there is a great deal of talk about "consciousness raising." Of the books, Susan Brownmiller's *Against Our Will* is perhaps the most pertinent to criminology, since it deals with the violent crime of rape. The argument, briefly, when used to explain the high level of the crime of rape (and the low level of reportability of this crime, as we saw in Chapter 3), is that it is a crime committed by men who are basically predators in search of sexual prey. Although one may develop various psychological explanations for the male's attitude toward rape, the essential political analysis is that men own women as property. Women are therefore "bought" and "sold" into the slavery of the family, where they are required to be absolutely faithful, in contrast to men, whose extramarital affairs are tolerated. Worse, women are seen by men as *material objects* of pleasure, an observation supported by the mass communications media, advertising, etc. which present the stereotyped "dumb blonde" as the ideal type. Because they have all the powerful positions in society, men may rape women with impunity. If the victim does report the crime, she is treated suspiciously by all concerned, including her husband. The law requires that the rape be "without consent" of the victim. Men prefer to believe that "all women really want it."

Whether or not one would classify the writings and activities of women's liberationists over the past several years as "consciousness raising," it is clear that a great deal has been achieved by this movement. Although some would argue that the consciousness of women as a "class-for-itself" has brought with it added responsibilities, which include more crime,[74] it may nonetheless be said that the establishment of rape crisis centers and the media publicity given to the criminal justice processing of rape victims have had enormous effects. A judge was only recently voted out of office for remarking, when setting a rape offender on probation, that the offender was probably influenced by the seductive dress of the victim. The effects of consciousness-raising on the reportability of rape are difficult to gauge. As we saw in Chapter 3, the annual increase in the incidence of rape appears to have remained fairly stable over the past five years.

Summary

1. Comparative crime statistics provide some support to the hypothesis that America is a "violent society" when contrasted to other countries of similar social and economic development. However, the fact remains that violent crime is predominantly the typical crime of developing countries.

2. The question of the extent to which the tradition of Southern and frontier violence has pervaded the whole of the United States remains

unanswered, but it is probable that the image that America has is that of the Southern culture. On the other hand, the evidence for a Southern culture of violence continues strong.

3. Subcultures of violence exist in many places throughout the world and are characterized by geographical isolation, by marked differences in life style, tastes, customs, and traditions (as compared with the dominant culture), by highly organized and cohesive social structure, and by the excessive use of violence which is taught to children at an early age.

4. Three types of subcultures of violence were discussed: a religious subculture (the Doukhobors), ethnic subcultures as feuding subcultures, and lower-class subculture. Although the extent and use of violence by the Doukhobors has been well documented, the extent to which violence is used in ethnic and lower-class subcultures still remains a big question. All we know is that the rates of violent crime for these subcultures are much higher than those of the dominant culture, but we do *not* know how much of this crime is due to subcultural themes as against other factors.

5. Two such factors that clearly dominate the differential rates of violent crime are age and sex. Together, these categories provide the biological basis of culture, which we may now examine.

Violence and the Roots of Culture: Age and Sex

From a cultural point of view, there are three aspects of violence to be considered. It should be borne in mind that: (1) violence can occur as a result of certain conditions specific to a particular culture; (2) some conditions related to violence exist in all cultures (these may be termed "transcultural factors"); and (3) violence can occur as a result of intercultural conflict.

In this chapter we will deal with two elements of culture which are universal across cultures and even species: age and sex differentiation. We are more interested in this chapter in contrasting universalistic explanations, which are often biologically based, with culturally specific explanations.

There are at least two universal facts concerning crime. These are that (1) the bulk of crime, especially violent crime, is committed by the young persons of any culture, and (2) by far the greater portion of violent crime is committed by the males of any culture.[1] There is no country for which there are official crime statistics where the male rate, and the youth rate, of violent crime is not inordinately large. It would, therefore, be a distortion to begin an explanation of the differences between males and females, young and old, on the basis of culturally specific theories. We must instead look for explanations that may apply universally—across all cultures.

Age and Violence

Transcultural Factors

We may consider the significance of the age factor in relation to violence from two perspectives. The first is that of age in relation to dominance hierarchies, the second is that of violence in relation to the process of growing up.

AGE AND SOCIAL DOMINANCE. Ethologists have observed that "pecking orders," or set hierarchies of who bosses whom, tend to be established very early in a wide variety of species, from chaffinches, wolves, wasps, and turtles, to baboons, dairy cattle, and electric fish. In general, but not always, it is usually the strongest and biggest that dominates the group.[2] There may, however, be many exceptions, and certainly the ethologist Eibl-Eibesfeldt has insisted that, in the majority of cases, the particular animal which becomes dominant must show consideration for the weaker animals, or it will not be accepted.[3] The question, however, as to whether age is closely related to dominance in animals is difficult to answer. It appears that experience is an important factor in the leadership of some groups of wild animals (e.g., baboons, macaques) where defense against predators is necessary. In general, ethologists have found that it is the stronger, older males that become dominant, and it is the younger "adolescent" males who try to "rebel" and attempt from time to time to usurp the position of the older leader.[4] By and large, dominance hierarchies among animal species, once established, tend to be very stable and enduring structures, and the experience of the older members seems very important.[5]

Among humans, the question is even more complicated today. Traditionally, age has been equated with wisdom, especially in traditional, close-knit cultures with extended kinship systems, or in social organizations which revolved around the "council of elders." In such cultures, the older men have traditionally been the most dominant. But it is also apparent that they reach this position, not because of aggression as such, but because they are *experienced,* or worldly. In traditional societies the authority of the elders is accepted by the younger members without question. Yet we also see the eagerness with which the young rush to embrace the promises of "modernity" in traditional societies that undergo massive social development.[6] One of the promises of modernization is very often a weakening of strict kinship systems, a weakening of the authority of the aged.

It is very likely, therefore, that the young, even in the most traditional societies, harbor deep feelings of wanting to rise up and free themselves from the authority of their fathers.[7] We should be surprised, therefore, if there were any societies in which aggression was more marked among the old as against the young. By the same token, we should also expect the proportion of violent crime accounted for by the young to increase as modernization increases. Again, the crime statistics available to us support this hypothesis.[8]

GROWING UP. Apart from the universal social structural aspects of age, the growing up process may also be seen from a universalistic point of view. This is not to say that growing up is the "same" in every culture. Of course, different cultures place different interpretations and socializing emphases on growing up. But there are some general theoretical propositions that have some claims to universality. These may be listed as follows:

1. *Physiological Maturation at Adolescence.* Although there is some argument about it among anthropologists, all children of all cultures go through substantial physical changes when they reach maturity. Although the particular age at which physical maturity is reached may differ from culture to culture, and the way in which each culture reacts to these changes may differ, there is little doubt that the onset of physical maturity—"adolescence," if you will—is accompanied almost universally by *Sturm und Drang,* "storm and stress," as the early child psychologists used to call it.[9] This period is often accompanied by rebelliousness, intense increase in sex drive, moodiness, and general aggressivity, and may last, depending on the culture or the individual, from a year to several years.

The oldest theory to explain this surge of aggression at adolescence was that proposed by G. Stanley Hall—called the recapitulatory theory.[10] According to Dr. Hall, the stages of an individual's development reproduce or recapitulate the evolutionary stages of the whole of man's culture. Thus, the early years, from birth to four, correspond to the cultural period of self-preservation; the period from four to eight years corresponds to primitive man's adventures in hunting and fishing and use of weapons; and that from eight to twelve years to the "humdrum of savagery." The period of adolescence, the years of storm and stress, is roughly equivalent to that described by Goethe, who wrote of the "pact with the devil" and other stressful temptations; and lastly, adulthood is equivalent to "civilization." This theory has largely been discounted, although we can see that it has quite considerable implications. It would have to be argued, for example, that those societies that are considered "primitive societies" would be populated by childlike individuals, since by definition they could not have reached the stage of civilized adulthood. The theory, therefore, as it is stated, is heavily culturally biased. But there are other theories that argue for universal stages in development.

2. *Moral Development.* The great Swiss psychologist Piaget, and

others after him, have argued that there are universal stages in the intellectual development of children.[11] Once again, however, we must be aware that these stages, although claimed to be universal, may nevertheless be passed through at different ages by particular individuals, and in particular cultures.[12] There is some evidence that poor intellectual development may be related to delinquency,[13] and some researchers have suggested that the reason for this finding is that intellectual development is directly related to moral development.[14] The theory argues, parallel to Piaget's theory, that moral development proceeds through stages, each stage depending on successful development through the previous stage, and each stage becoming more and more cognitively complex. Professor Kohlberg and his associates have produced some evidence to demonstrate the possible universal application of this theory.[15]

The implications of this theory are also quite considerable. It means that, similar to Hall's recapitulatory theory, one is forced to make assessments of the moral development of particular cultures. One would have to predict that some cultures (especially primitive ones) which have generally defective moral development will have a high rate of crime. In fact, it turns out that this is not the case for property crime (economically well developed countries have much higher property crime rates), but there certainly is the possibility that less developed countries, as a whole, do have more violent crime.[16] We can see that the Kohlberg theory is immediately open to the charge of cultural bias: one might argue that it is modern society, with its materialistic values and commercial enterprise, that is morally defective, and that this is why it has high property crime rates; yet Kohlberg's test of moral judgment may not produce such a conclusion.

It must be said that much of this is largely speculative, for research data to test these hypotheses are simply not available. Certainly there is no study that directly links defective moral development to violent behavior, except a few clinical case studies of psychopaths (who by definition are morally deficient). (See Chapter 11.)[17]

Hard evidence that aggression corresponds to these developmental stages is difficult to come by. One study that developed measures of aggressive acts on the basis of observation of children in normal daily activities (play, school, etc.), produced some fascinating results.[18] The researchers found that roughly ten percent of a child's outdoors behavior was aggressive. They also found that although the level of aggression remained the same throughout all of childhood, its form changed considerably. Up until the third year, the child was extremely aggressive physically, but after that, physical aggression declined and was replaced by a more subtle form which required more cognitive skills, such as analyzing the motives of the provocateur. This finding held across all six (very different) cultures studied. Unfortunately, the researchers did not assess the level of aggression of adolescents, who, as we saw in Chapter 3, account for an inordinately high level of violent crime.

Culturally Specific Factors and Age

Each culture has its own way of dealing with the growing up process. There is a long and involved history of the way in which Western society has looked upon childhood. Although there is some argument about it, it is clear that children up until very recently were the defenseless objects of sexual and aggressive abuse.[19] We shall have more to say about this in the following chapter when we look at the problem of battered children. For the moment, we are interested in the broader cultural features relating youth to aggression. I am able to list roughly five important facets of Western culture that might conceivably lead youths to criminal violence.

THE "GENERATION GAP." This is a hackneyed phrase, I know, but there is some truth to it, at least if we see this concept historically. The extended family unit (i.e., a household of nuclear family, extended family, servants, slaves, nannies, lodgers, etc.) has been the central unit of social organization in Western culture at least since Roman times. Historians of childhood have shown that the distinctions between childhood and adulthood were not clearly drawn until very recently—perhaps the past 200 years.[20] This distinction arose at a period when the family became more a nuclear family, owing to the break-up of family industry and crafts, the rise of wage labor, and the rise of schooling systems which more and more separated children into age and ability groups. Thus, the tendency today is to keep the child a "child" much longer, and to deny him the "freedoms" (e.g., work, sex) of adulthood for much longer than was the case 200 years ago. In an important historical way, then, the "gap" between the generations is structured into modern society.

This structured separation produces a number of important societal problems:

1. It forces children to be with other children more than with adults, especially parents. Thus, children naturally develop their own form of social organization, and juvenile gangs arise.

2. The difference between what juveniles and adults are allowed to do (e.g., sex) and to have (e.g., automobiles, money) becomes considerable and accentuated. The feeling of juveniles of an unmitigating oppression by adults is therefore inevitable.[21]

3. Following from (2), the adolescent, as his analytical and cognitive skills develop, finds that the adults have a separate set of rules for children (including the adolescent) and a separate set of rules for themselves. It may be reasonably argued, of course, that this double standard is essential in dealing with children (and maybe even with adults). But the fact of (2) makes this point seem to the adolescent a very serious breach of faith.

4. The conspicuous nature of adult freedoms and possessions in Western cultures, especially the automobile, clothes, and other symbols of material wealth, accentuate even more the adolescent's situation of oppression; especially when he is kept at school for so long—or, in recent times, when he is unable to find employment.

The inference is that, given a situation of such oppression, violent rebellion is a natural product.

Is there any hard evidence for this general theory? Yes. A number of studies have identified the delinquent's lack of attachment to society—whether to home, school, or even his own juvenile gang—to be related to delinquent behavior.[22]

Some researchers, of course, argue that there is no "gap" between generations in the sense that delinquents have been found to share values similar to those of the general public. But this finding adds to the gap problem.[23] The juvenile does not want to be separate, he wants to be a "free adult," so it is perfectly understandable that he will espouse values similar to those of the adult world.

CULTURAL MODELING. The communications media consistently bombard the public with news and dramatic presentations involving violence, although the media people commonly insist that they are "giving people what they want." The mass media influence is highlighted by the recent case of 15-year-old Ronny Zamora, who was charged with the brutal murder of 82-year-old Elinor Haggart. The defense was that the killer was "under the influence" of the television program "Kojak." At the trial (ironically it, too, was televised), the boy complained that he was not allowed to do anything, had nowhere to go, and so had to stay inside and watch television.

Many studies have shown that children will model their behavior on the basis of aggressive models they see on television, whether or not the models on TV are rewarded. That is, children learn aggressive behavior patterns and the justifications for them. They will also, in the laboratory setting, display more aggressive behavior after watching aggressive models.

However, the conditions under which children both learn aggression and perform aggressively vary somewhat, and the explanations of these conditions also differ considerably. The greatest part of research has been conducted by learning theorists, whose theories differ widely from each other. From the work of Professor Berkowitz, for example, it appears that a viewer will display aggressive behavior only if (1) the viewer is angered by the person against whom he will be allowed to aggress, and (2) the film provides a clear justification for aggression.[24]

A study by Professor Walters and his associates (whose work we will look at more closely in Chapter 6) is of considerable interest. The media reported a murder which was apparently carried out by a boy after watching a knife-fight scene from the film *Rebel Without a Cause*. Professor Walters tried to measure, in an experimental design, the effects, shown in subsequent aggression of children, of watching this film. He found that it did indeed increase their aggressive actions. Many other studies using different methods have found general support for the hypothesis that TV violence begets violence in the viewers.[25] There are, however, many contradictions among the studies and they have all been conducted under artificial laboratory conditions. Certainly there is no research (beyond the occasional sensational cases), that can demonstrate a direct link between the watching of TV violence and subsequent criminal violence. A few naturalistic studies have failed to demonstrate this relationship.[26]

From a cultural point of view, one can see how a culture which constantly bombards itself with the drama of violence must unavoidably appear to place a premium on it in the eyes of an oppressed mass of juveniles who only want to be like adults. Thus, if the adult world is characterized as violent, it stands to reason that juveniles will see violence as at least a solidly justifiable way of dealing with life's problems. If this is the case, we would expect that juvenile violence may be considerable among juveniles, rather than between juveniles and adults. We saw in Chapter 3 that the crime statistics we have available show this generally to be the case. But there are other reasons why aggression is largely contained within juvenile groups rather than against adults. This seems to be a puzzle, since I have suggested that it is the adults who are partially the source of adolescents' oppression.

JUVENILE PECKING ORDERS. Although Piaget has argued that children's moral judgment develops as much or more out of cooperation than out of competition, he failed to take into account the dominance factor of the age structure of the children's world, or the cultural premium placed upon competition in Western society. Children develop a very clear pecking order at school according to age, experience, friendship groups, popularity, academic ability, and sports ability. Because the United States culture is based upon competitive individualism, these dominance orders are established on the basis of fierce competition and may be established as early as kindergarten. The modern schooling process is, of course, based almost entirely upon the assumption of competitive individualism.[27]

It has been found in animal societies that dominance and subordination have a "filtering down" effect. That is, the more the boss pecks his next in line, the more the next in line pecks his subordinate, and so on down the line. Some research has suggested that this phenomenon also occurs among children (we have, of course, always known that it occurs among adults!), who, as they grow older, learn where it is "safest" to be aggressive. And, of course, it is safer in the children's world if you choose someone younger and smaller upon whom to aggress![28] A recent variation on this phenomenon is the increase in attacks on the elderly by juvenile muggers and gang members. We see here the effects of a society in which respect for the natural authority of the old has disappeared, so that they remain largely at the mercy of youthful predatory gangs.

It also appears that different types of competition occur at different age levels throughout childhood, although the intensity of competition is highest at adolescence, the period in which academic success is necessary to obtain occupational placement, sports success is especially important, and "good looks" are essential. Many have argued that aggression is a natural consequence of intense competition.[29]

OPEN REBELLION. Since the protest and civil unrest related to America's involvement in the Vietnam War, we tend to regard student protest that may lead to violence as something only very modern. It is widely believed today that we have a crisis of violence in the schools. This belief was propagated by the release in April, 1975 of the Preliminary Report of the Subcommittee to Investigate Juvenile Delinquency, by its Chairman Senator Birch Bayh. Five hundred sixteen (516) school districts were surveyed, covering 10,000 pupil enrollments. Senator Bayh estimated that there were approximately 70,000 serious physical assaults on teachers each year. The assaults ranged from the shooting death of an elementary school principal in Chicago to the beating of a high school mathematics teacher.

> The survey shows literally hundreds of thousands of assaults on students including more than 100 students murdered in 1973 . . . and confiscation of 250 weapons in one urban school district in one year.

But it is not at all clear that juvenile violence has increased to such frightening astronomical proportions. The most horrendous reports of particular crimes invariably come from inner-city rundown slum areas, where inadequate school systems and other factors related to inner-city decay are in evidence, and have been in evidence for a long time. The terrible violence of mugging and gang warfare have existed in such areas for at least a hundred years and probably more.[30] In addition, in another survey conducted among teachers who were sampled from suburban as well as urban school districts, teachers reported that violence of their students was *not* a serious problem. Vandalism was the major concern.[31]

A historical survey of violence in the schools also demonstrates that it is unlikely that school violence has increased as substantially as is popularly believed. Although it is difficult to make historical comparisons, since records have never been kept prior to 1970 of the *number* of violent incidents in schools, it is sufficient to note that there are plenty of descriptions available of students, at least 150 years ago, attacking their teachers, often with guns and knives, and marching in protest over a wide variety of issues to the point where militia were brought in to quell the riots. And this behavior commonly occurred in England's most prestigious private schools.[32] It is more than likely that today's sudden "crisis" of violence in the schools is largely an artifact created by the reporting system. It does, of course, still remain a serious problem in ghetto schools, but this is a result of factors other than age itself.

It is also now possible to view the years of protest during the Vietnam period with a little more calm. The fact is that very little violence was perpetrated by the protestors themselves. Rather, when violence developed, it was very often a function of interpersonal situations and confrontations between the protestors and the "establishment" (police). The violence related to such situations may more easily be explained by social factors which we will consider in Chapter 7.

An important observation to be made at this point is that violent protest among the young has a long history. And that once again, as far as universities go, those institutions that have experienced the most violent protest in the United States have by and large been the most prestigious.[33] Since I have argued that the young have been separated from adults for about 150 years, this observation supports the view that student protest is related to the structured differentiation between the generations, rather than to something that is merely of contemporary significance. The Vietnam War provided a focus for rebellion, but the propensity for youth to rebel in Western society has been there for 150 years.

IDENTITY CRISIS. Erik Erikson[34] has reinterpreted the psychoanalytic approach into a theory that is broadly culturally relative. He downplayed the "fixed" aspects of psychoanalysis (e.g., instincts: see Chapter 10), and instead emphasized the role of culture in the individual's development. Building upon Freud's various stages of psychosexual development, Erikson identified a number of crisis periods through which all people pass in the process of growing from childhood to old age. For Erikson, adolescence is a crucial period not only because of the abrupt sexual changes that occur, but because of the abrupt challenge to the adolescent to become adult. The problem becomes one of maintaining continuity in one's development—facing up to planning one's future. If one reaches this stage without having clearly resolved the crises of earlier stages, a problem of "role diffusion" arises: a serious identity crisis in which the adolescent is unable to decide whether to play a role of grown-up, juvenile, boy or girl. Deviance and delinquency result.

Unfortunately, there is no research to tell us just what form the delinquency will take; certainly nothing to tell us specifically whether aggression will follow. From the descriptions of identity crisis given by Erickson, it is more likely that the kind of delinquencies which would accompany role diffusion would be retreatist behavior—such as taking drugs, running away from home, leading an uncommitted "hippie" life, heavy solitary drinking. Or, another major alternative may be that the adolescent will seek his identity in the primitive "culture" of the juvenile gang, some of which may become violent. We shall have more to say about violent gangs shortly. For the moment, it is sufficient to note that some theorists have suggested that the juvenile gang provides an important ego-molding function during the period of adolescent crisis, since it satisfies two conflicting needs of the youth: the need to be told what to do according to a rigid set of values (what his parents used to do), and the need to feel free of the perceived totalitarian family situation. It can be seen that, if a youth were to stay with such a gang, he might never grow up, because it provides the perfect situation for him to avoid facing up to the responsibilities of planning his future life.

The theory of identity crisis is a particularly useful theory, and it is a pity that there is so little research bearing directly on it in relation to violence. It certainly would explain, for example, a rather well established fact about crime, especially violent crime—namely, that many juveniles commit a number of offenses prior to marriage, but after they are married, the incidence of offenses diminishes considerably, and becomes non-existent for most.[35] These days, though, some might argue that this abrupt decline in violent offenses after marriage is only reflected in official statistics, and that these young men go on being aggressive against their wives, an activity that is largely not detectable by the police, and even when it is, is rarely recorded as a crime. Chapter 6 will examine this problem in more detail.

Sex Differences and Violence

Transcultural Factors

Men are aggressive, women are passive. That is the popular belief. And as a general observation, it is also supported by scientific research. As one prominent psychobiologist concluded, "from mouse to man, with few exceptions, the male of the species is more aggressive than the female and the most frequent target of hostility."[36] But the reasons for this vast difference between the sexes in the level and intensity of aggressive behavior are more difficult to isolate. The question is especially confused today, since various platforms of the women's liberation movement find ideologically unacceptable the idea that women are "by nature" passive. They see this as a convenient rationalization fostered by a culture dominated by males to keep women in a lesser status—a self-perception by women that they cannot "reach for the top" in the social hierarchy. The term "by nature" of course implies an unchanging quality or trait, typified by Freud's now infamous observation (borrowed from Napoleon) "anatomy is destiny."

We saw in the previous chapter that the differences between males and females in committing violent crimes are indeed striking, and that even in the face of the supposedly widespread influence of women's liberation, violent behavior of females has not significantly increased (although there are some researchers who deny this).[37] But the difference between the sexes is certainly universal according to all available crime data, and according to a wide range of studies conducted in this century.[38] Since cultures vary enormously in tradition, social structure, role of women in the economy, and many other factors, we would expect considerable variation in differences between males and females in the commission of violent crime, according to different cultures. In fact, there is little variation.[39] We are forced to conclude, therefore, that the differences between males and females in committing violent crime are related to factors that are transcultural. The argument then hinges on the innate physiological differences between male and female. This is referred to as sexual dimorphism. To understand how sexual dimorphism is related to aggression, we must ask three questions. First, what are the physiological differences between male and female, and have any of these differences been directly related to aggression or passivity? Second, how unchanging or fixed are the physiological factors? Third, what roles do learning and experience play in the development of sex differentiation in aggression?

Physiology of Sex Differences and Aggression

THE EXTENT OF THE DIFFERENCE. In most animal species, the male tends to be more active, more aggressive, and physically larger and stronger, and to have brighter coloring or plumage. This observation holds for species as wide apart as fighting fish and grizzly bears.[40] Male domestic dogs are on the average 10–20% larger than their female counterparts,[41] and in some species of seals, the male may be up to 10 times larger.[42]

There are some notable exceptions. Female bees are the ones with the sting; the female wasp and praying mantis are the larger and more aggressive; and female spiders eat their male lovers.[43] In some species sexual dimorphism is not marked (i.e., the outward sex-distinguishing characteristics are not present), so that often the male-female difference in aggression is not apparent. This is the case for howler monkeys and gibbons.[44] There are also a number of species which change their sex under certain environmental conditions. Some researchers have observed, for example, that among cleaner fish, if the only male is killed, the most dominant and largest female will assume the role of the male (i.e., defending territory) and within a few days changes its sex to male.[45] Rapid sex reversals have been found in a number of other species, which has led researchers to hypothesize that hormonal changes are central to the process.[46] In fact, hormones are now seen as the central intervening factor in explaining the differences in male and female aggression levels. After all, it is one thing to observe that males are always bigger than females, but why should the physically larger be more aggressive? Why shouldn't he be more altruistic because he is secure in his physical safety?

Clearly there must be a further factor involved, and that factor has quite definitely been identified as hormonal.

AGGRESSION AND HORMONES. Androgen is the generic term given to all substances (usually hormones, such as testosterone) that stimulate the activity and growth of male sex organs and male sex characteristics.

Estrogen is the generic term given to all substances that stimulate the activity and growth of the female sex organs and secondary female sex characteristics.

All persons (both male and female) produce some of each. Males, of course, have much higher levels of androgen, and females much higher levels of estrogens. Between the ages of 10 and 15, the increase in androgen is tenfold in adolescent boys, whereas the average rate in older men (30 years +) is about half that of the younger (17–28) age group.[47]

Can the presence of androgens be shown to be directly related to aggression? Yes. One study has shown a relationship between testicular activity and feelings of hostility and anger.[48] Incarcerated criminals who had committed violent crimes during adolescence had higher testosterone plasma than incarcerated criminals with nonviolent records. However, when this inmate sample was divided according to other definitions of "aggression," no differences were found.[49] Many clinical studies have reported direct effects on levels of aggression in males when treated with an estrogen.[50]

Another way to test the effects of hormonal factors on aggression in males is to castrate them. This practice was first begun in 1894 by Dr. Pilcher of the State Training School of Winfield, Kansas, as treatment for sexual perverts. It has been used in many different countries since, in Nazi Germany in 1933, Norway in 1934, Finland in 1935, Iceland in 1938, and Sweden in 1944. The practice became most famous at the Danish prison for extremely violent offenders, Herstedvester. A number of studies have been conducted to follow up the effects of this procedure, and all have concluded that the procedure drastically reduced subsequent aggressive and perverted sexual activity.[51] However, in spite of the apparent successes of this treatment procedure, the practice has been abolished at Herstedvester. The reason appears to be on moral grounds rather than because of lack of effectiveness.[52]

The effects of castration and tampering with hormone levels in animals have been extensively researched. It would appear that the earlier the hormone level is changed, the more extensive will be the effect. Among mice, for example, castration before 10 days of age results in considerable reduction in later fighting. But castration after 10 days has little effect.[53] However, other researchers have reported that injection of baby chicks with testosterone will result in the early development of male secondary sexual characteristics. An interesting additional finding was that testosterone-injected chicks not only pecked their way to the top of the pecking order, but stayed at the top even when the injections were stopped.[54]

A further interesting finding has been that females do not respond in the same way to injections of male hormones as do males, nor do they respond in the same way to removal of their ovaries (the biological equivalent to male castration). For example, female hamsters which tend to be highly aggressive, are not made less aggressive by removal of their ovaries. Administration of estrogen to females may make them more aggressive. Yet, administered to *males* it makes them less aggressive. These puzzling findings have led researchers to hypothesize that males and females have different neural systems in the brain which react differently to the hormonal stimulation. There is some evidence for this in the case of animals.[55] But it must also be kept in mind that very early administration of hormones can have a lasting effect. It is therefore likely that, during critical periods of neural development, it is sex hormones that organize the brain tissue, and not the other way around.

We are able to conclude, as does one expert in the field, that "overall there are fairly consistent data indicating that vertebrate male aggression is organized by the early influence of androgens and is triggered post pubertally by androgens."[56]

Genetics and Sex Differences in Aggression

Some researchers have suggested that there are other genetic factors besides hormonal differences that may be responsible for higher aggression in males. These may be summarized as follows:

GENETIC FACTORS. Chromosomal studies have looked at the relationship between physique, chemistry, and aggression. Turner's syndrome, for example, has been identified among males in whom only one sex chromosome is present (the female X chromosome). Such persons are characterized by "short female stature and exaggerated female interests."[57] In Klinefelter's syndrome, the person has the XXY chromosome (i.e., extra female X chromosome), has male sexual organs that are extremely small, and is sterile. The extra Y chromosome (XYY syndrome) has been recently studied in detail, on the hypothesis that it is related to a particular body type (mesomorph) which in turn is related to aggressive behavior. Many studies have also tried to show the link between the XYY syndrome and a higher testosterone level. However, there has been much controversy over the interpretation of many of these studies. It appears that there are more XYY individuals who are incarcerated than would be expected in comparison to the normal population. But in general, we must conclude that the results are inconclusive as to whether presence of an extra male chromosome is related to aggression. There is growing evidence that body type may be related to aggression, so that it is logical that, since body type of males is clearly different from that of females, there may be some indirect relationship between body type and aggression. What do we mean by "indirect relationship"? One meaning is that body type is related to hormonal activity, hence to aggression. But another mediating link between male body type and aggression may be the fact of dominance and genetics.[58]

SEXUAL MONOPOLIES. Earlier in this chapter we saw how many animals establish dominance structures based largely upon age and physical size. Since males are larger than females, we would expect them to be dominant, and, as we have seen, this tends to be almost universally the case. But apparently because of the high testosterone levels in all males, males fight among themselves a great deal. A dominance pattern among males in many vertebrate species is sexual monopoly. Battles over who will receive the favors of the opposite sex are very common, occurring in such species as camels, the American chameleon, wolves, deer, and monkeys in captivity.[59] Professor Johnson reports that of the Pacific Coast elephant lions, 85% of the females are inseminated by only 4% of the males. As he notes, "this certainly gives the other 96% something to fight about." In the laboratory, it is the dominant mice or rats which end up impregnating the females.[60] Thus, constant fighting among males is in a way "forced upon them" because of the genetic propagation of aggression-related genes (i.e., only the aggressive get to have children) and higher levels of testosterone. We are left with a picture of a constant battle for the attention of the sexes. Does this occur in humans? Probably, but it is related more to other factors such as cultural mores, traditions, and socialization, which we shall look at shortly.

Ritual Male Aggression

A number of ethologists have pointed to an interesting and baffling feature of inter-male aggression, and that is its amazing similarity to the courtship routines that males perform when trying to "woo" the opposite sex. In numerous species, from fish to giraffes, intense inter-male fighting occurs, with some coincidental wounding of each other, but these fights are never fights to the death. Each animal adopts stereotyped poses as an attacker or as a defender. This is especially pronounced when it is a stranger that approaches. In this case it has been observed (as it was by Darwin) that the physical posturing of greeting when meeting a stranger is the exact opposite of an offensive posture. In the one there are clear postures of submission (e.g., crouching low, tail down) in the other, hair is bristling, tail is raised, lips are tight—postures of attack. It has been argued by some[61] that the ritualism in fighting acts as an inhibitor against the urge to kill the other, and that postures of submission (very often the presentation of the hindquarters) immediately inhibit aggressive behavior on the part of the attacker.

Konrad Lorenz argues that the reason why these aggressive behavior patterns are so stereotyped and so similar to courtship routines is that the "bond" between individuals—the lasting force of mutual attachment that even overrides basic drives of hunger, thirst, sex, or aggression—intervenes to prevent the male from killing his mate. Thus, the lead-up to copulation between male and female has evolved over the centuries from an original urge of the male to kill the female. Inhibited by the bond of mutual attachment, these behaviors have been attenuated to form rituals, and the aggression is *displaced* onto another object, very often a nearby male who would be more than willing to replace the suitor. According to Lorenz, this analysis explains why there is often such a potential for intense hatred for a loved one—the familiar Freudian ambivalence between love and hate. As Lorenz states: "There is no love without aggression, but there is no hate without love!"

Could this analysis apply to humans? There are some striking similarities. When men are getting ready for battle, they dress in all kinds of uniforms and insignia. The ambivalence between love and hate has been well documented by the Freudians. The stereotyped nature of barroom brawls, the importance of "saving face" (the duels to preserve honor are not so long past), the defense of the "macho" image, the preoccupation of men with aggressive competitive sports, all suggest a ritualism of aggressive behavior. The essential difference, though, between humans and the rest of the animal species, Lorenz argues, is that the inhibitory behaviors (i.e., the postures of submission) do not seem to work so well, since the human species is the only species that fights to the death. This is, however, a controversial conclusion, which has been questioned by ethologists and anthropologists alike, who insist that there are many animal species that do fight to the death, and that love is a separate force in and of itself, with a function beyond that of merely inhibiting aggression.[62] Nevertheless, the absence of these aggression inhibitors in man, Lorenz argues, is the reason why man has developed a variety of moral codes and norms (laws and customs) to prevent the wholesale destruction of the human race by itself.

Culture and Sex Differences

All of the features concerning sex differences that I have so far outlined may be seen virtually as universals, in the sense that they are factors which transcend cultures and very often species. This is not to say, of course, that they do not vary according to cultural conditions. There is every chance that, within limits, they may do so. They are factors which are, given basic conditions of life, largely unchanging, or which at least change only very slowly over time, unless interfered with artificially. However, it has been argued for some time that sex differences in behavior patterns are largely (if not wholly) due to cultural factors: the early training and experience that the children receive. In short, children are "sex-typed" from the day they are born. There are a few variations on this theme which we will now consider. Some ignore completely the fact of sexual dimorphism. Others start from that fact.

PSYCHOANALYTIC THEORY.[63] Freud's dictum "anatomy is destiny" was meant to refer not so much to hormonal and other such differences between the sexes, but to the inevitable psychodynamic effects of the fact of sexual dimorphism. Freud's theory of the derivation of passivity in the girl rests upon his concept of penis envy. He postulates that children must try to explain why boys have a penis and girls do not. The boys observe this fact in girls and infer that the girls have been castrated. Thus, they themselves suffer castration anxiety. There are many other factors involved, but the short story is that the boys, to overcome this castration anxiety, "compensate" by being more aggressive, to prove to themselves that they are men. For the girl, it is too late. She suffers considerable guilt because she thinks she must have done something terrible to have her penis cut off. She sees herself as "deserving punishment," especially since she longs to have a penis, or, to be "more like daddy." But here is the irony. Boys, through the resolution of the Oedipal complex (i.e., the wish to sleep with the mother and kill the father), "join forces" with the father in a kind of identification with the aggressor—a syndrome that we will return to later in the book. They are able to do this because they have penises. But the girl also goes over to the father—not because of identification with the father, but as his love object. The girl cannot identify with her mother because the mother, she discovers, has no penis either. Thus, she develops the identical sex-role of her mother, only it is patterned not directly on her mother's behavior (as the boy's is on his father's) but rather as a dependent role with regard to the father. In other words, the girl in fact may not fully resolve her Oedipal complex. Thus, Freud logically develops the description of the female as emotional, passive, more personal, and dependent, and the description of the male as active, aggressive, impersonal, and independent. The argument, then, as far as aggressive crime is concerned, is that since females have developed passive personalities, they are incapable of committing the aggressive crimes of men.

The Freudian theory of the origins of sex-roles has been seriously criticized from a number of quarters, especially by recent women's liberation theorists. The existence of penis envy has been denied.[64] Many have argued that while Freud's theory may have described middle-class Vienese people of the late 1800s, it has little relevance today.[65] The central issue now is whether the fact of anatomical difference must necessarily lead to different psychological perceptions and development of the two sexes. Some would argue that Freud began with the cultural differences and explained them away by pointing to anatomical differences. He mistook a "cultural fact" for a scientific fact. Some have pretty much accused him of blatant sexism: ". . . the effect of Freud's work was to rationalize the invidious relationship between the sexes, to ratify traditional roles, and to validate temperamental differences."[66] In short, the theory, it is claimed, rests on the assumption of male superiority. Freud's retort would be that this is indeed the case, since (1) males are larger physically, (2) their sex organs are "superior" anatomically in the sense that they are more "noticeable" or "intrinsically fascinating" to the very young observer, so that it is only natural that the child's attention should be drawn to them, and (3) it is a cultural fact that males are the dominant persons in the family, so that the male sex organs take on great importance. And I think Freud would say that the chances of any truly fundamental change in the father's dominant familial role are slim. The differences between the sexes will therefore perpetuate themselves, as they have for 2,500 years.

It might be added that some Freudians would see the development of sex roles, as I have just outlined it, essentially as a universal process, since the anatomy of males and females is the same all over the world. However, this is probably extreme, since although most cultures have familial organizations based upon the authority of the father as a dominant male figure, there are sufficient cultural variations to throw the dynamics of the relationship between anatomy and culture into some doubt. But within cultures, the fact of deep and substantial sex differences in aggression in a wide variety of situations cannot be doubted.

Of 47 studies reviewed by Maccoby,[67] which included studies using experimental designs, observation studies, rating studies, projective tests, self-reports, and fantasy aggression in doll play, and including subjects ranging in age from 2 years to college age, males were found in almost all studies to display more aggression. In a similar review of dependency studies, females were found to be almost always more dependent than males. The contrary interpretation of these findings is, of course, that they are the result of sex-typing processes that are specific to all, or most, cultures.

SEX-TYPING AND EARLY EXPERIENCE. Social learning theorists have argued that sex-role behaviors are virtually entirely learned. "In social learning theory, *sex-typed behaviors* may be defined as behaviors that typically elicit different rewards for one sex than for the other."[68] Thus, children from a very early age learn "how to behave" as boys or girls according to the established mechanisms of learning—through simply imitating live or symbolic models (parents and storybook characters),[69] especially if these models are nurturant or rewarding; from direct rewarding by parents of desired sex-role behavior; from the mere presence of many factors, such as the different decorating styles for children's bedrooms according to sex. The social learning approach argues that as a result of this incessant and early sex-typing, children develop fluid concepts of themselves as "a boy" or "a girl," and that there is considerable plasticity in cognitive and value styles of boys and girls.[70] Of course, this position is argued because of the assumptions social learning theorists make about the malleable nature of man—who has no truly *fixed* traits, or at least irreversible traits. This opinion is in contrast to the developmental view held by Freudians and cognitive theorists such as Professor Kohlberg, who insist that once the self-concept of "boy" or "girl" is developed (usually at a comparatively early age) it is irreversible.[71] Kohlberg argues that the child first learns his sex, then chooses the appropriate sex-role behavior. Others argue that the child first learns the sex-role behaviors, and only then learns his sex.

In any event, the logic of the social learning approach is clear. If its proponents are able to show that there is an initial plasticity in the intellectual, emotional, and social behavior of the sexes, but that there later appear deep and substantial differences, then they have a strong case. In general, there is substantial research to support their view.[72] Perhaps the strongest support comes from the many studies that have demonstrated very clear sex differences in child training in relation to aggression. Boys are permitted to display more aggression to parents (sometimes they are even encouraged to do so); also, they may be more often physically chastised by their fathers, which results in their copying this form of aggression from their male parents.[73] These differences apply both at home and in the school. Many studies have shown that dependency in girls is also rewarded in the same way that aggression is rewarded in boys. However, there is less support for this process from field studies.[74] Finally, many studies have found that as sex-typing develops, children will seek out and imitate those of their own sex. Thus, because of the differential association of the sexes at an early age, they tend to mutually reinforce their separate sex-typed roles.

PSYCHOPATHOLOGY AND AGGRESSION. It is well established both from studies of clinical records of mental hospitals and from self-report surveys, that women exhibit a much higher rate of neurotic disorders than men.[75] Although it is possible that women are more willing to admit personal distress, the weight of the literature still supports the fact that there is a higher incidence of neurosis among women. There is also some research which suggests that marriage is a more stress-invoking factor for women, in that married women appear to suffer more mental illness than matched unmarried women. On the other hand, married men appear to benefit from marriage, since they display a lower rate of mental illness than unmarried men (and these results take into account the selection factor).[76]

It appears, however, that in psychopathology it is difficult to conclude whether or not there are any sex differences. Rather, the differences appear to be specific to the type of disorder. Thus, men have been found to be overrepresented in the ranks of the "psychopaths;" psychopathological studies of children have shown boys to display much greater antisocial behavior; as measured by hospital admissions, male alcoholism is roughly five times higher than the female rate and the rate of drug addiction double the female level.[77] Although the rates vary among cultures and subcultures, the general finding on suicide is that although women make more attempts, a greater proportion of men actually commit suicide. In general, the hypothesis that male psychopathology is more destructive in form than female psychopathology is upheld.[78]

CONCLUSION ON SEX DIFFERENCES AND AGGRESSION. Some writers have noted recently that each culture tends to establish myths about the attributes and roles of each sex.[79] Some see these myths as having a definite basis in the basic anatomical, reproductive, and physiological functions of each sex. Others see these differences as essentially cultural in nature and therefore, presumably, plastic and changeable. The myths of sex roles are taken by some of these people, especially women's liberationists, as rationalizations on the part of a male-dominated world to excuse what men do, not only to women, but to the world as a whole. The difficulty these liberators face is the eradication of these myths. If they are truly based on the fact of sexual dimorphism, then there would appear to be no hope. If they are based purely on culture, then it appears that nothing short of a total conversion of culture is necessary to shatter these myths, since they are born and propagated within a paternalistic family structure and represent the accretions of 2,500 (or more) years of male domination.

But even the question of which is the "stronger" sex is difficult. This is why I have used "dominant" rather than "stronger." Although men are almost universally more dominant all over the world, and win more fights with their women, the fact is that there is extensive evidence from research to show that men do not live as long as women and that they are considerably more apt to contract most physical diseases (although there are many exceptions).[80]

Conclusions and Summary

1. There are substantial differences between male and female, old and young, in aggressive behavior, and there are biological, cultural, and social reasons for these differences, none of which may be said to be sufficient on its own to explain the wide range of aggressive behaviors.

2. There is little doubt that males, especially young males, always have been, and probably will be for a long time to come, the dominant aggressors in society.

3. Many of the psychological theories concerning the origins of sex or age differences in aggression have focused upon the family as the kind of microcosm within which aggression is developed and formed.

4. The family is, indeed, the logical place to look for the origins and forms of aggression, since it is the cultural unit within which the two great biological differentiators of culture intersect. The following chapter examines the dynamics of this microcosm in more detail.

6

Recycling Violence: The Family

The paradox of interpersonal violence is that it reaches its greatest intensity at two opposite extremes: in conditions of close intimacy and in cold, impersonal, stranger-to-stranger situations. There is a close correlation between intimacy and form of violent crime. Robbery and rape appear as the crimes of strangers. Homicide and assault occur among friends and intimates. Many studies have attested to the markedly intragroup nature of assault and homicide—whether within sex, race, class, age group, or family.[1]

Although we have seen in previous chapters that there are many cultural conditions that make for the intra-group nature of assaultive crime, we must take a closer look at the way in which these cultural conditions are translated into everyday life. In order to do this, we must understand both the dynamics of intimate social life and the paradox around which social violence revolves: the unhappy relationship between sex and aggression. In this chapter we will consider these two issues as they relate to the intimate forms of violence, those of the family.

Sex and Aggression: An Unhappy Marriage

Sigmund Freud first clearly identified the deep relationship between sex and aggression. He saw that it was both a physiological and cultural paradox. The *physiological paradox* was that "love," the ideal expression of a sexual relationship, nevertheless rarely occurred without the male act of domination and the necessity of the female to submit passively. Many case histories of sexual sadists and masochists since Freud's time have displayed in extreme and horrifying form the terrible implications of this unhappy relationship between sex and aggression.[2]

Some have criticized the use of evidence from abnormal persons to support the idea that sex and aggression have a common physiological base. Yet it is clear that in a wide range of species,[3] the male displays considerable dominant aggression to his mate, sometimes to the point of causing considerable physical injury.[4] But the difference between the sex-related aggression of animal species and that of man is that, most commonly, extreme acts of sexual aggression by men are against *total strangers,* not their mates. Although, as we shall see, men are probably also extremely aggressive towards their mates, the tendency towards sadistic murder is more common against strangers of the opposite sex, as we shall see in Chapter 11. This is in contrast to the animal species, in which aggression against strangers is almost always against *male* strangers.

Further evidence for the sex-aggression relationship comes from (1) studies of brain damage that has resulted in the reduction of both sex and aggressive drives; (2) the observed close proximity of areas that can be stimulated by implanted electrodes which will produce both sexual and aggressive responses; and (3) studies of castration, which brings about a considerable decrease in aggressive activity.[5]

A number of experimental studies have tried to provoke aggression in the subjects and then measure their sexual fantasies—compared to the sexual fantasies of those not provoked. In general, it was found that the two were related. However, attempts to accomplish this the other way around (i.e., to show that sexual arousal is accompanied by aggression) have produced inconclusive results.[6] In this regard, the role of pornography in provoking aggression has been extensively studied. Although the issue continues to be debated, the general conclusion reached by the President's Commission on Obscenity and Pornography probably still holds:

> In sum, the empirical research has found no evidence to date that exposure to explicit sexual materials plays a significant role in the causation of delinquent or criminal behavior among youths and adults. The Commission cannot conclude that exposure to erotic materials is a factor in the causation of sex crimes or sex delinquency.[7]

The *cultural paradox* to which Freud referred was his poignant observation that love *divides* as well as unites. His view of sex (the libido) was that it was finite—that is, individuals do not have enough to go around for everyone. Freud made fun of the "golden rules" of Western society of "love thy neighbor" and "love thine enemies." Love forms alliances, but it also sets people against each other.[8] And, as if to add salt to the wound, Freud saw that culture—that is, Western civilization—has created further woes for the individual, since it requires that he live in enclosed, monogamous families: an incredible repression of the libido. Thus, the final paradox is that the family, that bastion of the social order of virtually all civilized societies, is also the source of great social and inner conflict for man. It is little wonder, therefore, that recent studies of violence have begun to concentrate more and more on *family violence*.

The Social Life of Intimates

The phrase "social life" has come to mean many different things to many psychologists and sociologists. In general, these different meanings have been embraced within a general set of principles, based upon observation and experimentation, which go together to make up what is generally called *social learning theory*. In criminology, many of the principles of social learning theory have been dominant for several decades, although known by another name, "differential association." The major principles of this very general theory, simplified and adapted to the explanation of aggression are:

1. There are generally two kinds of learning. One depends upon reinforcement (i.e., the giving of rewards for an act performed), the other upon *imitation* (i.e., the "copying" of an act performed before the learning).[9] The latter form of learning has been recognized for a long time in criminology—since the work of Gabriel Tarde early in this century.[10] In psychology, it is sometimes called "one trial learning," or "vicarious learning," or "self-reinforcement." There is considerable controversy about whether this kind of learning involves rewards or not (in which case it would be a form of reinforcement learning), but the general opinion at present is that it does not necessarily involve rewards,[11] although in most human interactions rewards are probably involved. I should emphasize that I have considerably oversimplified these two "types" of learning. There are countless variations of them and many instances of combinations of the two types of learning.

2. It is generally argued that reinforcement theory is unable to explain the acquisition of a new response, except by saying that it will be learned if "accidentally" reinforced. Imitation, on the other hand, easily explains this phenomenon since all it requires is for the act to be "observed" in a "model" and thus copied.[12]

3. A basic distinction has been made between *learning* and *perform-ance*.[13] For example, a child may observe his parent regularly act aggres-sively over a considerable period of time. He may "learn" those aggres-sive behaviors and the situations they are used to solve, but he may not necessarily *perform* them, either immediately or even much later. In other words, he may "store up" this information. He learns how to act aggressively, but may not actually perform aggressive acts until much later (when he is an adult or perhaps never), depending on many other factors which may intervene, such as the specific situations that arise, his perception of situations which may be similar to those of his parents, and many other similar instances. In any event, the main thrust of the learning-performance distinction is that there is a cumulative process at work in which the learner stores up and processes the responses that he has learned.[14]

4. "Modeling"[15] refers to, generally, behavior of a "significant other" which is used as a model by the observer, upon which to "style" his behavior. This concept was around long before social learning theory, in the form of such concepts as "identification," which grew out of Freudian theory. There are two essential features of modeling.

a. If models are rewarded and punished as in any learning experiment, the observer will learn just as though he himself had been rewarded or punished.

b. The most effective models are those who have a close relationship (usually of authority) with the observer. Thus, the natural models for the child are his parents, and perhaps older siblings. Or in criminology, according to differential association theory, the neophyte pickpocket will model his behavior on the professional; or in gang theory, the new recruit will model his behavior on his peers or the gang leader. However, care should be taken to see that this is not *necessarily* so. We know that chil-dren often reject the ways of their parents; we know that children can acquire new response repertoires from strangers, by way of television. Obviously, many, many, other factors may impinge upon this general rule.[16]

5. Although early social learning theorists, because of their strong experimental bias, used to look upon learning as limited to a series of "trials" or "runs," it is now clearly recognized that:

a. There is an important perceptual or cognitive aspect in which the observer must perceive or interpret the model's behavior. This may depend upon many other things apart from the specific rewards or pun-ishments applied to the model at a particular time. Among these factors is the concept of prior experience.

In fact, Bandura and Walters have long argued for the importance and necessity of such cognitive factors as *attention,* which the observer must first pay to the model, and the discrimination that the observer uses in defining the situation of the model's behavior. Children are often told by parents, "Do as I say, not as I do." But according to Bandura and his associates, this is double-edged instruction:[17]

> Indeed, parental modeling behavior may often counteract the effects of their direct training. When a parent punishes his child physically for having aggressed toward peers, for example, the intended outcome of this training is that the child should refrain from hitting others. The child, however, is also learning from parental demonstration how to aggress physically and this imitative learning may provide the direction for the child's behavior when he is similarly frustrated in subsequent social interactions.

It is argued that as children grow older, they learn a highly complex set of discriminations concerning the *cultural* approval of aggression (e.g., war; violence in games or against criminals), but a highly specific set of prohibitions against aggression (e.g., murder, hitting one's teacher, etc.).[18]

The notion of continuity in the learning process advanced by the social learning theorists also leads them to reject the notion that adolescence is an abrupt or "separate" stage in human development. Rather, they see the aggression of adolescence simply as the product of faulty early socialization, insisting that only about 20% (if that) of adolescents actually behave according to the "aggressive adolescent" stereotype. A number of studies have been conducted which generally support this view. Aggressive boys (compared to nonaggressive boys) have been found to have parents who actively encouraged aggression, permissive fathers, inconsistent enforcement of rules, more physical (as compared to verbal) punishment, and disruption in identification with the father.[19]

b. "Experience" is seen as an important processing factor, in the sense that the interactions of both parties (the model and observer) are mostly (in families at least) ongoing ones which do not occur in an experiential vacuum. This is important even when the two parties are face-to-face strangers, as we shall see in Part 3 of this book. Each brings with him certain notions of what to expect from the other.

c. There may be an important element that is situation-specific to many aggressive encounters, in which modeling occurs. However, it must be said that considerable experimentation has shown that standard principles of generalization of learning (i.e., transfer of learning from one situation to another similar, though different, situation) apply to the learning from models.[20]

We should also be aware, though, that while the parent is the model to the child, there is also the possibility that the child in many ways is a "model" to the parent! By this I mean that the way in which the parent disciplines, punishes, or rewards the child may depend on the way in which the child reacts or responds to the parent's "teaching." To assume that it is "all one way," i.e., from parent to child, is to assume that the child begins with a *tabula rasa,* and that all his behaviors are totally learned from others. Many hold this extreme view. Of course, it is entirely antagonistic to the instinct theories that I have reviewed in various parts of this book, especially Chapter 10. If we are less extreme, however, we readily see that some of what the parent does with his child may depend at least to some extent on the child's "natural" behavior patterns.

The Violence of Relatives

The general principles that I have outlined above may be used to explain sex-typing, or sex-appropriate behavior, as well as aggression and many other aspects of intimate social life. Let us look to the constellation of these factors: how social learning, sex, and aggression produce enduring and specific kinds of violence, those within the family. Research in this area has rapidly expanded in only the last three years. Although much of it is interrelated, we may usefully divide this topic into a number of sub-areas: battered wives, battered children, and children who kill (mainly their parents).

Battered Wives

It is perhaps symptomatic of social movements in general that they are led by those who are more "liberated," compared to the group whose rights are being fought for.[21] The women's movement of the 1970s is no exception, and its focus upon rape as the symbol of male oppression is therefore even more understandable.[22] Led largely by women who were either unmarried or no longer married, the women's movement concentrated upon rape as the apparently most shocking of crimes against women. In their view, the attacking by men on women who were strangers to them was the expression of a kind of male power sickness.

Not until recently have those women who should, according to the women's liberation movement, be seen as the truly oppressed group— the housewives—raised their voices and directed attention to another hideous activity of men: the battering of their wives. Although we have seen that in many species the males indulge in physical aggression towards their mates as a part of the courtship ritual, the batterings which wives have begun to report are hardly similar to lovemaking. We find here the classic picture of the family as a political tyranny in which the father has virtually the power of life and death over all members. In this closed authoritarian setting, the political oppression of women in society is played out in face-to-face everyday life. Because of the contradiction involved in monogamous conjugal living that we have referred to above—the ambivalence of love and hate—which is coupled with the authoritarian structure of the family[23] (to which Freud gave too little weight), we can see very easily not only why men are constantly tempted to bash their wives, but also why women have passively and secretly put up with it: it is a role they have fulfilled for more than 2,000 years.

Only now is the "truth coming out," although the evidence has been available in social history all along. Here are some excerpts from a letter of a battered wife:

> I have been kicked in the abdomen when I was visibly pregnant. I have been kicked off the bed and hit while lying on the floor— again, while I was pregnant. I have been whipped, kicked and thrown . . . punched and kicked in the head, chest, face and abdomen more times than I can count. . . . I have been threatened when I wouldn't do something he told me to do. . . . After each beating my husband has left the house and remained away for days. . . . Everyone I have gone to for help has somehow wanted to blame me and vindicate my husband. . . .[24]

How extensive is it? There are no definitive figures. However, we do know that about 30% of all homicides occur within the family. Husband-wife killings amount generally to half of these, and it is also probable that the majority of wife-husband slayings are the result of the wife's acting in self-defense.[25] Take, for example, the following news item:

> **Woman Denied Acquital In Killing of Ex-Husband**
> LANSING, MICH., Oct. 13 (UPI)—A mother of four lost a bid today for a directed acquittal verdict in a murder trial that feminists hope will result in a landmark ruling on a woman's right to defend herself from domestic abuse.
> Aryon Greydanus, the defense lawyer, said the prosecution had failed to show that Francine Hughes, 30 years old, was guilty of premeditated murder in the death of her former husband, James.
> Mr. Hughes, who allegedly beat, choked and threatened his former wife for many years, died of smoke inhalation March 9. Accompanied by three of her children, Mrs. Hughes surrendered to sheriff's deputies minutes later and admitted she had set fire to the room where he was sleeping.

"We feel there has not been adequate evidence shown to present the case to the jury on the charge of first-degree murder," Mr. Greydanus said in asking Judge Ray C. Hotchkiss of Circuit Court for a directed verdict.

Judge Hotchkiss, in rejecting the motion, said it would be "grievous error for the judge to take the case from the jury, unless the prosecution presented no evidence."

Four policemen and one former officer testified that Mr. Hughes was known to them as a troublemaker and they had been called to the family home on several occasions over the past few years. Although the couple were divorced in 1971, they resumed living together after Mr. Hughes was involved in a near-fatal auto accident.

Mrs. Hughes was, in fact, acquitted in a later trial. Generally, in police departments around the country, 60 to 70% of police night calls are for domestic disputes. Usually three-quarters of the complainants are women.[26] In New York, 14,167 wife-abuse complaints were filed in 1972–1973.[27]

A number of researchers have found that physical violence between spouses is accepted as routine. In one study, Richard Gelles[28] found that in his "control group" of nonviolent families, 37% had experienced at least one incident of violence. Other surveys have shown a surprising approval of wife beating. In one national survey conducted in 1968 (Harris poll), 20% approved of the slapping of a spouse on "appropriate" occasions.[29] Other studies have generally supported this finding.[30] Most striking are the findings that approval of marital violence appears to increase with education and income, and that there appear to be no clear differences among blacks, whites, and Latin Americans.[31] These findings seem to support the view that oppression of women is virtually universal.

The role of women in the home is also depicted by various studies of homicide and assault that have located the rooms in which violence is most likely to occur. Gelles found that the kitchen was the most likely location of violence.[32] Studies of homicide found that this was the room in which a wife was more likely to kill her husband. And it is in the bedroom, of course, that the husband is most likely to kill his wife.[33]

I should add that all of these statistical details, heaped one upon the other, tend to give the impression of a rapidly rising crisis in wife beating. But as I have already suggested, this has been going on for centuries. Furthermore, it is abundantly clear that wives are not subject to the fierce, wholesale abuse that they once suffered. Women are not now pursued as witches; they are not presumed legally guilty if they bring forth stillborn babies, as they once were in England; they are not subject to being fitted with bridles and braces as "scolds" for talking too much.[34] They are treated much less savagely today, at least as far as their official treatment is concerned. One might also validly argue that their less brutal treatment is a part of a general tendency towards more humane treatment of all those of minority status (from animals and children to criminals), and not a function of any claimed "liberation."[35]

Are battering husbands embattled husbands? There is very little research on this matter. The difficulty is that this kind of violence is so little reported, since it occurs within the fortress of the home, that the subjects are hard to come by. Because the law is uncertain just how much it will allow husbands to physically manhandle their wives, only cases of very serious assault and battery are processed. Furthermore, complainants very often are reticent in pressing charges.

Del Martin characterizes batterers as "losers," though there is no research to back her up. Based upon the scant evidence available, I would hypothesize that the following conditions are probably related to wife beating:

1. The presence of alcohol. Alcohol, as we have seen in other parts of this book, is often closely tied to aggression. At least one study has uncovered the suggestion of alcohol's role in evoking aggression from an otherwise docile husband.[36]

2. Hostile-dependency. Husbands may appear mostly docile and passive, yet may be prone to sudden outbursts of rage. This may also be related to sexual inadequacy (for whatever reason). One researcher has suggested that the husband is in many ways childish, in that he transfers the dependency he had on his mother to his wife. He then resents his dependency on his wife, who, after all, according to our cultural roles, is the one who should be dependent on him.[37]

3. The mechanism by which rage is released appears to be extensive brooding on the part of the husband, who becomes obsessed with the shortcomings of his wife. Thus, he may "suddenly" erupt, often while the wife lies sleeping, or he may perhaps be provoked in a verbal argument. Even a minor thing like a wife's idiosyncrasies may be sufficient to provoke aggression. For example, one wife was beaten because she wore her hair in a ponytail.[38]

4. Because society condones in a general way the physical abuse of wives, the extensive brooding on the part of the husband is facilitated by ready-made rationalizations to justify his violent acts. In at least one case the husband could not accept it as reasonable that his wife should have left him for the sole reason that he beat her.[39]

5. The wife may become the object for aggression as a result of frustrations experienced by the husband in his work or other activities.[40] This view, the "socioeconomic" theory, would lead one to suspect that the incidence of wife battering would be higher in the lower socioeconomic class. But so far, the available data do not clearly support this position.[41] For example, one wife was beaten because her husband's driver's license was suspended. The pressure that men are under to "succeed," to be the "provider," is very strong and occurs at all levels. The wife is the obvious target for aggression which may be released by the frustrations of the man's cultural role.

6. Battering occurs as a sudden or abrupt onslaught. One study found that only in 23% of cases were beatings administered after a verbal dispute. This is further evidence for the theory of brooding and rising anger that erupts suddenly.[42] The clear tendency is, however, for men to blame their women for provoking the aggression.[43]

7. A number of studies have reported a much higher incidence of wife beatings among members of the military, and that husbands who beat have more often been in the military than those who do not. The explanation for this finding is not altogether clear, beyond the more facile one that "men learn violence in the military."[44] The problem appears to be more serious for wives of husbands currently in the military. A rough hypothesis: life within a family is enclosed as it is; in the military it is even more enclosed because of the separation of the military base from the rest of society. This may occur especially in overseas bases. My guess is that the high incidence of aggression has much to do simply with the fact that, as one researcher has noted, the participants are in each other's presence a lot.[45]

8. Current studies also suggest that a large proportion (close to one-half) of battering husbands have criminal records. However, since the cases studied are those that are prosecuted in the courts, one might expect prior records simply because these are the persons most likely to be in constant contact with the police. There may be, therefore, a considerable selectivity factor.[46]

9. Apart from all of these factors, we know from research concerning other aspects of family violence that the chances are that battering husbands were also battered children themselves.

10. *Characteristics of the victim:* In his excellent study, Gayford[47] found that of his 100 battered wives, close to half tried to commit suicide, although 19 of those said they used the "suicidal gesture" to attract attention to their plight. Very few fought back when attacked. Many had put up with beatings for 25 years. Close to one-third had left home more

than 4 times, only to return when the husband promised to reform, or because of feelings of sorrow, or because he threatened more violence, or there was nowhere else to go. But soon after return, the cycle of violence began all over again. Some might interpret this finding as indicating that "the wives want to be beaten." However, Gayford studied essentially those wives who had returned at least once, and others have insisted that many wives do or would leave and never go back. There is little doubt—given the passive role that women are forced into today, the difficulty in obtaining employment, and a whole host of other difficulties that the women's liberation movement has so clearly brought to light—that the reason of "nowhere else to go" is a very real one.

A final point of Gayford's, and of other findings generally concerning violent families, is that the initial marriages are often described as "disastrous." In Gayford's study, 45 women were pregnant by the husband before living with him, and 15 were pregnant by another man. Most of the women had come from large families and saw that getting married and having children was the "thing to do." With no alternative, they married their "strong males" (25 of whom had even battered them before marriage) and were then trapped in violent marriages. The feelings (and reality) of being trapped are helplessness and, worst of all, fear.[48] The deeply cultural nature of the "trap," of course, is the determined role in which the wife finds herself: she cannot leave, because it is her responsibility to "keep the family together."[49]

A common finding for battered wives and battering husbands is that both very often experienced physical violence in their homes when they themselves were children. It is to this horrifying subject that we now turn.

Battered Children

The range, type, and extent of child abuse is very difficult to identify. On the one hand, surveys show that probably upwards of 90% of all parents have at some time or other physically chastised their children as a punishment. It does not appear that there are any distinct class differences in the use of punishment (although blacks tend to use physical punishment more than whites), nor that its use has significantly decreased during this century.[50]

As with women, children have also been subject to considerable abuse for many, many centuries.[51] In antiquity they most often held a rank below that of slaves. During the industrial revolution they were virtually used as slave labor. They have been the subject throughout early history of systematic infanticide, especially the girls. The historian of childhood,

Lloyd Demause[52] has shown that parents, especially during the Victorian period of the nineteenth century, played out elaborate death wishes onto their children, largely as a result of the repression of sex and the idea that children were conceived in sin. Until the late nineteenth century, the sight of dead, cast-off children on the dung heaps of London was very common. It is even still permissible for teachers in most English-speaking countries to physically chastise their pupils—this, when it is not permitted to corporally punish criminals. The defenseless position of children—corresponding to their low status in society—although less desperate today than it was, is still one that virtually invites the aggression of tyrants. Worse off than wives, children are trapped at the bottom level of the household tyranny, most often with *both* parents to beat them.

Since the physical punishment of children is so widespread as to be "normal," a problem arises as to what is "really abuse" and what is not. This is not to say, of course, that the widespread approval and use of physical punishment is defensible—although its very existence provides a ready-made rationalization for its use in more serious situations. In the newspapers we tend to read of the more serious cases:

> A woman who is eight-and-a-half months' pregnant was under arrest on a murder charge at Fordham Hospital today after the death of her battered two-and-a-half-year-old daughter. . . . The child had multiple lacerations and many scars and bruises. [*New York Post,* March 29, 1974.]

> A crippled seven-year-old child, whose abuse apparently included having the words "I cry" burned into his back with a cigarette, was wheeled into a Harris County (Texas) courtroom in a crib today. . . . The boy, described by one witness as "bright, but a loner" prior to his injuries, had suffered a ruptured colon from something inserted into his anus, and the ensuing infection resulted in brain damage. [*Washington Post,* May 5, 1977.]

> Linda Fay Burchfield [has been] charged with imprisoning her daughter Patti in a closet for four years. . . . Last July 5th, police burst into the home and found Patti. She weighed 23 pounds and was less than three feet tall, about half the normal size of a nine-year-old. On the same day, Patti's sister Donna, then 13, was having an abortion. . . . Mrs. Burchfield's husband has been charged with raping Donna. [*Washington Star,* March 17, 1977.]

> A young southeast Washington couple were found guilty of involuntary manslaughter yesterday in the death by starvation of their infant son. [*Washington Post,* March 17, 1977.]

A Cleveland, Tennessee, couple were indicted yesterday on a first-degree murder charge for the torture death of a four-year-old girl. [*Washington Star,* October 23, 1976.]

EXTENT OF THE PROBLEM. A number of estimates have been made of the incidence of child abuse. Before it became a publicized problem, as it now is, the reporting of child abuse by physicians was not legally required.[53] To make matters worse, parents cover up for each other, and physicians are often hesitant about reporting suspected child abuse cases for fear of infringing on the "privacy" of families—to a large extent an inalienable right. Certainly, parents have the legal right to physically chastise their children.

In 1963, it was estimated that 183,000 children were affected by neglect, abuse, or exploitation on any one day in the United States.[54] In 1966, it was estimated that 200,000–250,000 children were in need of protective services each year and of these, 30,000 needed protection against serious physical abuse.[55] However, in 1967, as the result of a national survey, 3% of adults over 21 reported having knowledge of an incident of child abuse. Eventually, these researchers estimated the incidence of 2.5–4.1 million cases a year.[56] And in a national survey conducted in 1975 by Doctors Gelles, Strauss, and Steinmetz, more than 3 million children reported having been kicked, hit, or punched by their parents at some time in their lives. More than 46,000 were threatened by their parents with a gun or a knife; 460–750,000 were beaten to the point of injury.[57]

The Staff Report to the President's Commission on Causes and Prevention of Violence concluded in 1967 that child abuse did not "constitute a major social problem at least in relative terms, tragic as every single incident may be."[58] But in a study conducted in New York City by Doctors Lash and Sigal, it was estimated that the incidence of the reporting of child abuse had risen 1026% between 1964 and 1974. Although much of this increase may be due to greater public awareness of the problem, nevertheless, the U. S. Department of Health, Education and Welfare stated: "An epidemic of child abuse is occurring in this country."[59]

TYPES AND CAUSES OF CHILD ABUSE. Professor Gil in a national survey found that 58.3% of respondents thought that "almost anybody could at some time injure a child in his care."[60] There are two implications to this finding. It may mean that we are most of us capable or even half willing to physically injure a child. But it might also mean that people by and large recognize that children create demands upon adults which are often difficult and sometimes impossible to meet. Therefore, it may just as well be the case that the children ("innocent" as they may well be) may contribute to the frustration of their parents, which may in turn release aggression. Findings, such as they are, concerning the causes and patterning of child abuse may be summarized thus:

1. *Age of the victim:* children who are abused tend to be less than 5 years old (41% in one study).[61]

2. In child killing, mothers are generally the murderers, which is understandable when one considers that they are more often with the children and are under considerable strain in "coping" with them. There are studies which support this explanation.[62] Strangers, such as babysitters, or even close relatives, are rarely involved in the slaying of young children in the home.[63]

3. A number of clinical studies have identified psychoses in the mother which may take the form of "child-centered obsessional depression," in which the parent suffers from a feeling of inability to care for the child. Suicidal tendencies are also common.[64]

4. There is some disagreement about the socioeconomic background of offenders. The popular press tends to sensationalize cases when they occur in middle- and upper-class families, but at least two studies have not found social class differences.[65] However, at least six studies have identified the lower-class family as being more likely to produce the serious child abuser.[66] These "hard core" families are characterized by unemployment, apathy, drunkenness, prostitution, vascillating attitudes towards power, remorseful overprotectiveness and emotional explosiveness, and drug addiction.[67]

5. *Family structure and relationships:* Two studies have found that the family of the battered child is intact in 60% of the cases. The average ages of the parents are 26 for the mother and 30 for the father.[68] However, it seems likely that conflict between the mother and father is closely related to abuse of the child, some researchers suggesting that the parents displace hostility onto their children.[69]

6. *Infanticide:* This crime tends to be distinguished from child abuse and child murder because the parent is often motivated for humanitarian or "honor" reasons. Some researchers have also identified these "humanitarian killings" as a form of obsessional mental disorder.[70]

7. *Sexual abuse.* Sexual abuse of children may be seen as a special type of child abuse. Once again, reliable figures are difficult to come by. One estimate made in 1967 was that there were probably nationally

360,000 cases a year.[71] In general, offenders are usually closely related to the victim, between 35–40 years of age, and out of work. Unlike child murderers, these offenders are almost always men.[72]

8. *Parental ignorance:* A number of studies have noted that parents have little knowledge of what behavior is appropriate for children at each stage of development, and often have unrealistic expectations of them—especially very young children. Thus, tiny children's failure to "do what they are told" is often interpreted as willful naughtiness. As a result, the parent becomes more and more frustrated, and stress gradually accumulates, until finally the child is beaten. And once a parent has beaten a child, it seems that it is easy to do it a second time.[73]

9. *The Generational effect:* Our brief review of the dynamics of social learning and aggression at the beginning of this chapter would lead us to expect that battering parents had battering parents themselves, since children learn aggression from aggressive role models. Indeed this is now a well established fact, and a number of studies have traced back the battering syndrome through at least five generations.[74] It has also been found that some mothers who beat their children not only had been battered children themselves, but also had been beaten by their husbands a few weeks before they attacked their own children.[75]

10. *Lack of bonding:* In one study it was found that it is rare for all children in one family to suffer the same amount of child abuse by parents.[76] It appears that particular children are "singled out" by parents because of a number of factors which probably signify a lack of bonding between parent and child. Many of the children identified in these studies suffered defects of one kind or another—usually noticeable physical or mental defects—so that it is suggested that parents were unable to accept these children as they did others in their family. These studies lead us to look at a question that has perhaps been ignored in child abuse studies, and that is the extent to which the child contributes to the problem. We do, after all, know from the many studies of homicide already reviewed in this book that the victim commonly plays an unmistakable role in an assault—often precipitating the incident.

Violent Children in the Home

Fortunately, the number of young children who kill either other children or their parents is statistically very small. Psychologists have observed, however, that most young children are capable of (or usually display at some time) the most violent rage—certainly enough to kill another small child if one is unlucky enough to be in range.[77] Other cases appear to be direct examples of the social learning theory:

> A young Cleveland woman, baby-sitting with her four-month-old niece, rushed to investigate the child's frantic screams. She passed her two-year-old son running from the bedroom, saying, "Hit the baby, Mommy! Baby bad girl!" The infant died a short while later, bludgeoned by the boy with a heavy metal toy.[78]

Other clinicians have presented cases which suggest that in the case of sibling killings, the parents played a subtle part in conveying "commands" to one of the siblings to do the other in.[79]

Parent killings by children are also fortunately very rare (about 700 a year) although it is surprising that they do not occur more often. These murders are most often performed by adolescents, almost always by a son, and more often against a mother. Parent killings account for about 6% of family killings.[80] In general, children prefer to kill parents rather than other children.[81]

The reasons are probably many, and there have been very few studies, most published material being descriptions of clinical cases.

Some have suggested that the child is encouraged by one of the parents to aggress against the other.[82] In other cases there is a history of parental brutality.[83] But it seems likely that a major cause is the building up over a number of years of a "neurotic relationship" between the victim and the adolescent—usually involving a son who gets into trouble, is overdisciplined by his parent, gets into more trouble, and so on. The case of John, a 17-year-old, illustrates the point.[84] John was raised in a rural area, and attended school in a nearby town. He had a history of rebelliousness at school and had been suspended. As punishment, his mother had constantly restricted him to his room—virtually for three years on end—before the shooting:

> On the day of the shooting he returned home early on suspension from school. His mother scolded him, and threatened him, and said she would not care if his father killed him when he came home. He saw his father's gun on the shelf and the shells nearby. Without saying anything he picked up the gun, loaded it, and began firing at his mother, who was standing at the top of the stairs. He next recalled finding himself outside with the gun in his hands and hearing his mother screaming. He hurried up the stairs to see her lying in a pool of blood. . . . His immediate reaction was one of relief, with no guilt or remorse. . . .

Another pattern, which appears on the face of it to contradict social learning theory, is that a number of cases have turned up in which the child appears to have been a very well-behaved child, and that the murder appeared to erupt suddenly, provoked by a very trivial circumstance.[85] But other investigations have suggested that these children may have been excessively attached to their mothers, and may have fought against the impulse to kill for some time.[86] The sudden eruption of the deed, as observed in many cases,[87] would support the theory advanced earlier to explain wife beating: the killer broods and harbors resentment which builds up over a long period of time, until the "trivial" circumstance is enough to "break the camel's back."[88]

Summary

1. The family, being an enclosed, socially intimate group, provides the forum in which is played out the paradoxical relationship between sex and aggression. The result is that there is probably extensive battering of wives by men, and of children by parents, much of it unreported.

2. The factors involved in the appearance of family violence go beyond the problems of sex and aggression in the Freudian sense. A process of social learning, the learning of aggression from parental models, the learning of sex-appropriate behavior, and many other processes all contribute to a generational effect, in which patterns of familial aggression are transmitted from one generation to the other.

3. A breakdown in the social bond, whether between husband and wife or between parent and child, appears to be a crucial precipitating factor, especially for husbands or teenage children who brood during long periods of resentment, then suddenly erupt into violence.

4. For all participants in family violence, the family appears to be a kind of trap. The victims have nowhere else to go, and the perpetrators seem to be caught up in the cycle itself, often unaware of the extent of the damage they are doing.

5. In many ways, the family may be seen as a particular context in which violence occurs. It is, of course, a special kind of context, since it is one of the basic units of our culture. There are many other contexts in which violence appears, and it is to those that we turn in the following chapters.

Part Three

Violence in Context

Violence: An Occupational Hazard

We have seen how violence is reflected in the social life of family members. Another major area of social life is that of work, so that we should expect violence to be reflected in different ways, depending upon the players and the vocation. The names of some vocations immediately conjure up images of violence (the Marines, the Green Berets, "cops," robbers, convicts, guards, prizefighters, and many more). Depending upon the situation and the vocation, the use of violence may be seen as a special act of valor, or a mean, evil necessity. There are many *justifications,* as we saw in Chapter 1.

Virtually by definition, of course, the use of violence is hazardous, so that one cannot clearly distinguish between violence as an incidental aspect to a vocation (e.g., police) and violence as a stock-in-trade. The vocation which perhaps personifies this ambiguity most clearly is that of the American policeman, dramatized in its more extreme forms on television and in children's games.

Cops and Criminals

New Brunswick, N. J. (UPI)—Two state policemen were shot and seriously wounded early Sunday when they stopped a car with South Carolina license plates for a routine check. A short time later one suspect was killed and two others captured at a nearby girls' school. [November 28, 1971]

The Police Department's Civilian Complaint Review Board is investigating charges that a Brooklyn policeman shot and critically wounded an auto-theft suspect Sunday afternoon out of personal dislike. [November 9, 1972]

> Detroit, Jan. 16—A man shot and killed two police officers and wounded two others today during a gun battle that began shortly after the police responded to a call about a domestic quarrel. [January 17, 1974]

> Dallas (UPI)—Three sheriff's deputies, their hands tied behind their backs, were shot and killed Monday as they fled across the Trinity River bottomland from two burglary suspects who had disarmed them. [February 2, 1971]

> Dallas, July 24 (AP)—A 12-year-old boy, handcuffed and seated next to a policeman in the front seat of a squad car, was shot to death today by an officer seated behind him, the police said. [July 25, 1973]

These are reports of extreme acts. Probably, if the truth were known, 80 percent of policemen have never used their guns, except on the practice range. But these examples are enough to demonstrate that violence is a real risk to both the policeman and the criminal.

What *are* the statistical realities? We cannot be sure. We do know that proportionately more nonwhite civilians are killed by police violence: evidence, some say, of direct racial discrimination. Nationally, 60% of persons shot by officers are nonwhite.[1] However, the claim of prejudice cannot readily be clearly substantiated since it is also established that most persons are shot by police during the commission of a serious offense.[2] Furthermore, black policemen (who are, incidentally, more likely to be assigned to high crime areas) tend to be disproportionately responsible for fatalities involving black suspects.[3]

Do cops fare as badly as criminals? No, fortunately, they do not. Only 10% of police killings are the result of "ambush" or premeditation. The majority die either from involvement in domestic disputes or from serious road accidents. It is very clear, however, that very few cop killers get away with it. For the period 1964–1973, 1,238 known persons were involved in the killing of 872 officers. Of these suspects, 1,038 were arrested and charged.[4]

In contrast, one study reports that of 1,500 incidents in which police killed citizens, only 3 ever resulted in prosecution.[5]

Information on other forms of violence used by police officers has been collected through interviews with police (especially "violence-prone" police), from records of civilian complaints, and from civilian observation of police behavior.

Several studies have identified a number of major factors relating to police violence. These may be summarized as follows:

1. Although they are very few, there are nevertheless some police officers who are "violence-prone," who are most clearly identifiable by violence itself—that is, they have histories of repeated and excessive use of violence.[6]

2. There is considerable variation in the amount of deadly force used by police according to social areas and the different states of the United States. For example, for the decade 1961–1970, Georgia experienced a rate of homicides caused by police 12.8 times that of New Hampshire. One study has suggested that police will adapt their modes of operation to the cultural styles of the local public. If the area is one in which violence is little used, then police will show restraint. If the area is one in which much violence is used, then police will use less restraint.[7]

3. Much of the routine use of violence by police officers is explainable by the respective roles into which the police and the "public" seem to be forced, by way of the adversary nature of our criminal law process. The cop is seen by the public as the one who interferes, "a symbol of brass and blue, irritating, a personal challenge, imminent defeat and punishment."[8] And the police see the public as "whining, uncooperative, self-concerned and unjust."[9]

4. Routine use of violence is supported by a "locker room support system."[10] The rookie learns that "you can't do it by the book," that "you keep your mouth shut, never squeal on a fellow officer." Violence may be used directly by the officer to solve quickly a complicated situation—or the other extreme may occur, where a cynical officer allows violence to occur by "letting well enough alone."[11]

5. The informal socialization of police officers appears to be a self-differentiating one, in that some rookies may become socialized into being "hard-nosed," others into a "service oriented" disposition, with the result that different "kinds" of cops emerge and are often assigned to the appropriate aspects of police work. The "hard-nosed" may end up on the beat in a tough neighborhood. The "soft-nose" may end up behind a desk, or directing traffic.[12]

6. Cops are no more authoritarian or punitive, according to test scores, upon entering the force, than any other similar working class groups. It appears, however, that the socialization process of the force can bring about radical changes. This change is towards the belief that an officer must accept the challenge to fight, or the public will think it "can get away with anything," or will "push the police around."

7. Violence-prone police use violence mainly in response to what they see as an affront to their authority, a lack of respect, or loss of self-

esteem. This is especially salient when one considers that many abuses directed at police, with their resultant retaliation, often occur in front of a crowd of witnesses.[13]

It should be emphasized, however, that these situations involve at least two opposing factions (the cop and the criminal), each of which contributes in varying ways to the eventual eruption of violence. In other words, "it takes two to tango." Professor Toch[14] has identified a number of "perceived causes" of violence from the point of view of the person who assaults the police officer:

- Assault in defense of personal autonomy
- Assault as an expression of contempt for the cop
- Assault in an effort to escape
- Assault in an effort to prevent being "moved on"
- Assault to protest captivity
- Assault as extension of other violence
- Assault in defense of others

These are, however, largely situational determinants related to the "role" of the criminal. Professor Toch also identifies a number of traits of the violence-prone person (who may be either policeman or criminal). These may be divided into two dimensions. The first of these is one in which the person feels he must use violence to promote his self-image—the cop may see himself as the defender of authority, the enforcer of the rules—his objective is to protect himself against the physical danger threatened by others, or to remove pressures from a situation with which he feels unable to deal. Here is a description of one such "self-image" promoter:[15]

> We have an awfully powerful young man here who conceives of himself as something of a human tank—who feels that he is undamageable and that anyone who tackles him is going to go out of commission. Picking on him means several things, depending on the mood he is in. If he is angry or tense or depressed, it takes very little to pick on him. In other instances, he may give the person an awful lot of latitude, particularly if he defines the person as the sort of individual he feels it is beneath his dignity to clobber, such as a diagnosed sex pervert.
>
> He attacks when he feels that some aspersion that counts is being cast on him as a person and as a tough person. This happens, for instance, where after his arriving at a prison (while relatively young) he is whistled at in the yard. Following this encounter, he goes and broods for awhile and then comes out seeking the people who whistled at him, making them confess that they are sorry, and then beating them up.

In various incidents that he tells us about he is quite specific about the fact that he just doesn't teach people a lesson—he puts them out of commission. He doesn't just vindicate himself—he destroys people. Even in one case where somebody comes and stabs him in the arm, he is very proud of the fact that with his bare fists he reduced this person to a condition where he had to be carried away in a stretcher. In several instances where someone foolishly tried to hurt him, he tells us that he immediately turned around and broke the person's jaw.

It sounds like a broken record, "I turned it off, and broke his jaw." There isn't much time wasted here on verbal discussion. By and large the sequences are, "somebody says something to offend me; I provide the person the opportunity to challenge me to a duel and then I make mincemeat out of him." In other words, he puts the other person in a position where he can justify viciously attacking him. He very seldom feels sorry for what he has done, including killing his father's common-law wife in an argument or beating and knifing his father. He feels no remorse because he has already decided to his own satisfaction that violence is not only justifiable but necessary.

One statement he makes, which might tell something about what goes on in his mind as he approaches these situations, is the statement that he has "never lost a fight." It is obviously quite important to him not to come out at the bottom, and he starts his fights knowing that he will come out on top. He is apparently compensating physically—where he knows that he can come out on top—for any encounter where there is some question about his being the victor.

The other group of traits may be described as those that are related to seeing others as objects, merely there to satisfy one's own needs. There may be four aspects to this: *bullying,* by which pleasure is obtained from exercising terror against individuals; *exploitation,* by which others are manipulated as tools of one's pleasure, and violence is used against them if they react against one; *self-indulgence,* based on the assumption that others exist to satisfy one's needs; and *catharsis,* the use of violence to discharge accumulated pressure. Here is the description of a classic bully type:[16]

> Without making a value judgment, we think it would be fair to say that this man is a consistent, unmitigated, low-level heel, who has never had what one could describe as a fair fight. The pattern in a variety of situations (starting with a few boyhood escapades, and terminating with adult felony assaults) involves his taking advantage, unfairly, of somebody who is in a weakened position. As a second step, he will, when the other person gives some indication of weakness (begs for mercy or asks him to stop), accelerate his violence, and he here describes himself as becoming angry. And

at this point he resorts to walking over the person's chest, or stomping on his face, or doing any number of other things that are obviously extremely cruel.

One consistent pattern with him is that he will do almost anything to create a situation in which the other person is at a disadvantage before he strikes. He will use deception; he will maneuver the situation physically. And as soon as he has achieved the objective of being able to surprise the other party, or being able to place a blow which creates an immediate advantage for him, he proceeds—but not before. He will also use people other than his victims. There is one classic instance of this in which he makes a pact with a girl to fight a person who is hunting for him, and then leaves the girl to do all his fighting. This episode not only illustrates his tendency to use people, but also exemplifies his outlook toward the female sex, where we even have two or three instances in which he shows no hesitation about fighting girls. And he assesses them pretty much like he does his male opponents.

The general way in which violence occurs with him is that he evaluates instantaneously a situation in which it becomes possible. It even occurs in instances in which the other person involved, the potential victim, is in the process of complying with demands, or is in a conflict with him in which he had previously obtained the upper hand, but now somehow the tables can be turned, and advantage can be taken of this. And this second type of situation is important in that before the fight starts he might have experienced fear, and part of the reaction may be against his own fear. As a matter of fact, fear is a kind of theme that runs through the sequences in a variety of ways. It occurs very directly in any situation in which the other person does, objectively speaking, have the advantage, and he can't do anything about it. Then he has no compunction whatsoever about running, about giving up. It occurs in that he initially fights, as we have indicated, when he himself has experienced fear, and it occurs very blatantly in a situation in which the other person shows fear; that is, in which there is the request for mercy, or some other indication that the other person is afraid of him; and then he becomes extremely furious, and he shows no mercy whatsoever. And what one might infer from this is that in all of these situations what he's really doing with his violence is handling his own fear. That is, he is a bully in the classic sense—a person who acts extremely unmercifully toward others because of the fact that he himself (as he introspects) feels terribly small and disadvantaged.

Needless to say, these types may occur in the form of both criminals and cops. That is, their violence is not *caused* by their vocation. But there is little doubt that the vocation provides an excellent opportunity for its expression.

8. None of the factors so far outlined are complete determinants of

violence. There are many ways of maintaining "face" and not using violence. This depends upon a tacit understanding between police officer and suspect. This point is well demonstrated in the words of one delinquent:

> If you . . . and say, "Yes Sir, No Sir," and all that jazz, then they'll let you go. If you don't say that, then they gonna take you in. And if you say it funny, they gonna take you in. Like, "Yes, Sir! No, Sir!" But if you stand up and say it straight, like "Yes, Sir" and "No, Sir" and all that, you cool. . . .[17]

9. *Fear.* Professor Toch has found a rich and common thread throughout his study of police and criminal violence. Among those who are consistently involved in violence, there is a pervasive feeling of danger, an obsession with fear of the police on one side, and fear of the public or criminal subculture "getting out of hand" on the other.

Criminal Violence as a "Profession"

We know very little about persons who see violence as a "professional" tool, and much of what we do know is probably clouded by the imagery of the fictional and television portrayal of "hit men" and Mafia "enforcers." Violence as an aspect of a criminal vocation may be seen as providing two possible avenues for work. These I call the instrumental use of violence to achieve the ends of specific criminal activities (e.g., a bank job) and the use of violence as a means of enforcing discipline within a criminal organization.

CRIMINAL VIOLENCE AS AN INSTRUMENT. Violence of this type is used mainly by the professional robbers described in Chapter 9. Such persons will use violence coldly and methodically to achieve the ends of a specific crime, whether it is robbing a bank, or mugging a rich-looking man. In these cases, there appears to be a complete lack of interest in the victims themselves. They are objects to be overcome or bypassed by whatever means necessary.

Another very common use of violence in achieving criminal ends is extortion, in which violence and the threat of violence are used as the central feature of the crime. There are many variations of this type of violence, such as protection rackets, and these have a long and varied history. The most recent historical prototypes of some forms of extortion rackets were those of the "Black Hand" used by Sicilian immigrants towards the end of the nineteenth century. The Black Hand worked by sending anonymous letters to individuals which delivered veiled threats of death or destruction to loved ones of the victim, unless he paid a certain amount of money. If he did not, the threats of the letter were carried out.[18] Today, there are many variations on this theme.

CRIMINAL VIOLENCE AS DISCIPLINE. There is much controversial literature on the purposes and uses of violence within organized crime in America and elsewhere. Although the Mafia is depicted as a bloody terror that maintains a brittle discipline within its own ranks only by ruthless enforcement of a "code of honor" (i.e., breaking the code means certain death by "hit men," "soldiers," or "enforcers"),[19] other researchers on organized crime have emphasized the more traditional, self-disciplinary nature of Mafia families, in which the mafiosi obey the rules of the criminal organization not only out of fear, but also out of respect. One such study would suggest, for example, that a modern Mafia family, although it may have originated four generations ago with the aid of the ruthless violence of its founder (who did command fear from his workers because of those original violent acts), nevertheless, has evolved into a semilegitimate family business. Four generations later the family members venerate the old founder of the family, so that today the use of violence appears minimal or nonexistent in maintaining family discipline, largely because of the virtually unquestioned recognition of the designated head of the family and loyalty to the family tradition. While "fear" may play a part in the maintaining of discipline, it is fear, not of violence, but of loss of approval by other family members.[20] The initial use of violence in an organized crime family may therefore have far-reaching, nonviolent effects.

But that is only one picture. The other picture is of warring "crime families" which periodically conduct violent "wars" against each other over the control of various rackets or crime areas. These wars are well documented and their dreadful violence is well known to all (e.g., the Valentine's Day Massacre). Furthermore, some would argue that many crime families have been unable to establish a peaceful method of transferring leadership, so that internal feuding and violence very often erupt. Once again, these instances have also received wide publicity and are clearly documented, especially in New York City.[21]

The major concern over violence as a criminal profession is that there may be a national "conspiracy" of organized crime cartels which, while moving more and more into legitimate enterprise, nevertheless has an unfair advantage over legitimate business, in that it will use violence to achieve its ends.[22] It must be said, however, that there is virtually no agreement on this hypothesis. Law enforcers tend to believe it. Academic criminologists tend not to. These days, the argument is made rather difficult, since it is very hard to make a clear distinction between "legitimate" and "illegitimate" enterprise—because it is believed that much of the profits from the "rackets" is invested widely in legitimate businesses.

The Keepers and the Caught

There are some limited parallels between the violence of guards and inmates in prison and that of police and criminals. However, because of the highly controlled and regimental setting of the prison, the guards usually have much less experience than police in dealing with challenges to their personal decisions.[23] The chances are, therefore, that affronts to the guard will be dealt with less judiciously, and will be perceived more often as "politically motivated."

It is also important to realize that a filtering process of "decarceration" has begun in recent years, so that prisons generally have a much greater proportion of recidivist, tough, and violent offenders. Jails and prisons are sunk in a "climate of violence." The threat of violence hangs over every prison like a stormy sky. Horrifying tales of brutality are used to "initiate" new arrivals.[24] When prisons are calm, it is always an uneasy calm. The reason is obvious. The inmates outnumber the guards to an incredible degree. It may be prestigious to an inmate to be punished. Inmates hate guards. The power of the staff, it has long been known, is largely illusory. Yet, it is an amazing fact that custodial attacks on inmates and inmate attacks on guards are comparatively few. By far the major portion of prison violence is accounted for by inmate attacks on fellow inmates.

The facts, such as they are, of prison violence, are as follows:

1. The number of inmates killed annually in prison is probably between 100–150, which in itself is a very small number,[25] when one considers that the population of prisons was roughly 200,000 at the time. But when compared to the murder rate outside of prison, it is about 7 times higher.[26]

2. It is probable that because of the close supervision of inmates in prisons, stabbings and other severe assaults that would have led to the death of the victim are often quickly dealt with medically, so that the rate of inmate killings may be seen as just the tip of the iceberg of extensive violence.

3. Violence in prisons is estimated as extremely high. One study estimated that in California in 1970 an inmate had one chance in a hundred of being hurt seriously, and that in 1974 the probability had increased fourfold.[27]

4. Some prisons and jails are much more violent than others. In Philadelphia, it was estimated that one out of every 30 jail inmates was forcibly raped. And in 1974 alone, 12 men died in San Quentin[28] as a result of violence.

5. The incidence of staff violence against inmates is low, although statistics are very hard to come by. In 1973, 386 incidents were reported in New York State involving 547 inmates (out of a total prison population of 15,000 and 1,288 employees). In one third of these incidents no one suffered injuries.[29]

Explanations of Inmate Violence

VIOLENCE-PRONE PERSONS. Early explanations of inmate violence centered around the personal histories of particular prisoners, the identification of violent persons. These inmates were seen as "standing out" against the rest of the inmate population. However, the filtering process of decarceration, the fact that prisons now hold a much greater proportion of men who have extensive violent histories, has led to a focus on violence itself in the prison setting. Certainly, this disproportionate makeup of the prison population seems the simplest explanation of the very recent rapid increase in prison violence.[30] Here is a description of an inmate who is violence-prone, perhaps an extreme case of the "bully" described earlier:[31]

> The coldest instance of instrumental violence in this interview is one in which our man wants to be transferred, picks himself another inmate almost at random and assaults him—and as a result gets transferred. In several of the incidents the inmate reinforces his role. This occurs, for instance, where our friend learns that a new inmate has informed on his brother and everybody is telling him to murder this man, in retaliation. He does end up stabbing the man—not with the intent to kill him but to bruise him. A couple of incidents are minor, but this doesn't deprive them of information value. For instance, it turns out that our man cannot just walk away from a situation in which somebody sat down on his chair in the television room; he has to use violence, he feels, because otherwise people may have contempt for him. He definitely feels that when he is standing as a look-out for a friend who is collecting debts it is his obligation to intercept and fight the victim when he flees.
>
> It appears that with him violence seems necessary and proper. We have here a man who uses every opportunity for violence provided him. And he not only strikes first, but he is extra careful to be systematic in the preparation and execution of his violence.

SUBCULTURAL SEDIMENT. As we have noted, some prisons are more violent than others. There is every chance that violence in San Quentin may derive from the violence of the Mexican street gangs from which many of the inmates have come. The proportion of prison aggressors in California who are Latin has risen from a steady 26 percent in 1963 to 40 percent in 1973. The violence of New York's prisons may mirror the ghetto norms of Harlem.[32] Although violence may be an "expression" of the intimate nature of the subculture, it may also be the result of the clash between two subcultures (usually defined in terms of race), as Professor Toch reports:[33]

> During a period of racial tension, a clique of white prisoners had issued an ultimatum to blacks, prohibiting them from entering the T.V. room. Black inmate T resolved to "lead his people" (against everyone's advice) by watching television. T and C enter the T.V. room, and are immediately assaulted with some homemade black-jacks by a group of whites. Staff prevents the murder of the two men.
> While walking along a corridor, Inmate M (a "Mexican") is knocked unconscious by a black inmate. The next evening, several inmates of Mexican origin push a black as the latter leaves the T.V. room. "This causes the races to group and arm themselves." Chairs are thrown, and men are hit with socks containing soap. The battle is averted by the staff.

We have seen throughout this book that the traditions and processes of subcultures are in large part self-perpetuating, so that it is entirely understandable that they should reproduce themselves in prison. One can see how incredibly complicated the "inmate subculture" must be: it not only develops special styles, values, and beliefs having to do with prison life itself, but it incorporates and reflects the many subcultural traditions which the inmates bring with them from the outside. Thus, if there is a strong feuding element in any of the subcultures (e.g., Latin versus black), we would expect extensive and bitter violence to ensue in prison. And we know from our study of family violence that its intensity may reach severe proportions when violence occurs within closed personal groups.

YOUTH AND SEX. We know that male youths are responsible for the largest proportion of violent crime. It comes as no surprise, therefore, that they should be centrally involved in prison too. If we accept Professor Toch's all too obvious assertion—that violence begets violence—we should not be surprised that by throwing together young, violent men, more violence will be kindled. The logical and ridiculous extreme is to do what many prisons have unfortunately done in reaction to prison violence: they introduce disciplinary segregation. Of course, it has been found that disciplinary segregation also enhances violence, sometimes running out of control.[34]

Youth is especially important from a sexual point of view. In a mono-sexual society, it is only to be expected that certain psychological and sexual adjustments will be made. And in a subculture where violence and terror are the pervading stuff of social life, it is only to be expected that homosexual rape will take on a specially violent form; ". . . prison rapists seem to regard terror as more essential to creating a climate of submission in men than in women." Professor Toch provides us with another excellent sketch of such a situation:[35]

> Inmate A sits in C's cell listening to C play his guitar; four other inmates enter. The situation looks sufficiently unpromising for A to attempt an exit, but he is stopped as he tries to leave. He gets a beating from C (which fractures his jaw). Following this beating, A is forced to lie down on the floor, where C performs sodomy on him. After lunch, A is "escorted" back to A's cell, where another inmate (M) rapes him.

The young white first offender especially is seen as weak, fearful, and therefore *unmanly*. There is much argument about the reasons for the patterned way in which prison rapes occur. Some argue that it is because of the emasculating impact of prison.[36] But this seems unlikely since the prison, if anything, is *too masculine*. Another argument is that it is the reflection of subcultural values that the inmate has brought with him into prison.[37] Certainly the aggressors have a clear and unshakable image of the nonmanliness of their victims. This stereotype is probably a function of both outside subcultural values (manliness/nonmanliness is a value that we have come across again and again in this book) and the enduring nature of the inmate subcultural norms themselves.

A general profile of prison rape has been summarized in the Davis study of Philadelphia rapes, as follows:[38]

- Victims tend to be white
- Victims tend to be younger and smaller than aggressors
- Most victims are afraid to report their aggressors to the authorities
- Virtually every person having the characteristics of a potential victim is approached sexually by aggressors
- Aggressors tend to be black

- Aggressors tend to be guilty of more serious and more assaultive felonies than victims
- Both aggressors and victims tend to be younger than other prison inmates

Criminal Behavior

EXTORTION: A setting where the threat of violence is the rule provides a virtually perfect home for extortion. But the setting is also such that the kinds of things that can be extorted seem extremely minor to the outside observer, which creates the impression that the violence used in such settings as an extreme overreaction:[39]

> Inmate A has made a name for himself as "dumb hillbilly," and this is viewed as an invitation to extort cigarettes from him. One inmate approaches him and informs him that if he does not deliver two cartons of cigarettes "we'll get the ———." A replies that he owes no cigarettes, and has no objection if this should lead to a fight. The next day he is stabbed in the back while on his way to his cell.

VENGEANCE: The following sketch, again from Professor Toch, is self-explanatory:[40]

> CA is in debt to CH, and CH requests at least partial repayment. CA replies by becoming abusive, and CH tells him to "forget about it," and follows CH to the bathroom, where he subjects him to "vile names." CH administers one blow to CA, which knocks the latter unconscious. CA is only 4'11" tall, is very conscious of his size, and is known as "Toughy" among friends. When several inmates make remarks to him about the bathroom incident, he is unable to cope with these, and decides to take "revenge." The next day, he approaches CH, who is seated at a table, and stabs him twice.

One must emphasize, however, that these actions only appear to us, the outsiders, as overreactions. Within prison, where cigarettes and other small commodities that most of us take for granted become the central medium of exchange of the informal "inmate economy," the payment of debts assumes massive importance. Given the distorted economic and cultural situation in prisons, the inmates' violent solutions to these problems of social and economic relations may be seen as a natural outcome of their predicament.

Inmate Suicides

"The most frequent victims of violence in prison are self-mutilators whose plight—except for completed suicides—draws no sympathy."[41]

The prison subculture views such acts as unmanly. There are many factors related to inmate self-inflicted violence, and they are only just coming under study. Important factors seem to be crises of self-doubt, hopelessness, fear, abandonment, which themselves may be provoked by a wide range of social factors both inside and outside prison.[42]

Crowding

Although we saw in Chapter 4 that crowding both in the laboratory and in cities has not been found consistently to contribute to violent behavior, one study by Professor Megargee has suggested that prison may be an exception to this rule. Professor Megargee found that the reduction of space was closely related to increases in violence in prison, and he concluded by suggesting that the phenomena of dominance hierarchies and territoriality in relation to crowding in prison could be productive areas of further research.[43]

Teachers and Pupils

There has been much public concern in the 1970s concerning violence in the schools. While we have long known—and it is made clear time and again in this book—that violence is primarily an activity of the youthful, little attention has been paid to this as it relates to schools themselves. Rather, whenever youthful violence has been studied, it has traditionally been looked at as an activity of the street, not of the school.

Why this shift in focus? One reason may be that gangs themselves have become less violent, and we shall look at this proposition in the following chapter. But another more likely reason is that schools have been under attack during this decade from all quarters. They have been criticized for promoting segregationist policies; for failing to provide special facilities for minorities and the handicapped; and, worst of all, for allowing permissiveness to pervade the schoolroom.

In the early 1970s, teachers began to complain that they were being attacked by their students. Principals complained that their school buildings were being vandalized. In short, there was a "crisis in the schools." In 1973, the National Schools Public Relations Association reported startling increases in school violence.[44] In Detroit, for example, it was reported that an average of 25 assaults on teachers were reported every month. Eventually, Senator Birch Bayh headed a subcommittee to investigate the problem. This committee reported a number of disturbing findings:[45]

- From 1970 to 1973, homicides in schools had increased 18.5%
- Assaults on students by 85.3%
- Assaults on teachers by 77.4%
- Rapes and attempted rapes by 40.1%
- 75,000 teachers are injured badly enough each year to require medical attention
- The problem of violence was largely one of large urban secondary schools.

As if to heighten the atmosphere of crisis, the Committee Report offered a graphic portrait of the "crisis of discipline."

Teachers find that if they report to the principal an assault, the principal who feels that his own reputation or her reputation or the school's reputation is at stake here, will very frequently turn around and start harassing the teacher by saying, "Well, if you had these assaults, how come you are the one always complaining. You must have more observation or better planning or this or that." So the teacher soon finds out that bringing the reports to the attention of the principal is something that is not wanted and tends to suppress the information.[46]

It isn't only in the school or school yard that students are likely to be exposed to violence. School buses . . . are frequently a terrifying experience for children who are captive passengers. They are the scene of rip-offs for lunch money, physical violence and pressure to indulge in the illegal use of drugs . . . Students who are normally nonviolent have started carrying guns and knives and lengths of bicycle chains for protection on campus . . .[47]

A teacher in a North Central junior high school comments:

It's just a sick place to be in. It's so chaotic, it's not like teaching at all. Sometimes I have to spend 40 to 50 minutes of class time just getting the students to sit down. I'm hoarse from shouting when I leave school. I know I could lose my job for saying this, but who minds losing a bad job?[48]

These graphic descriptions, presented along with the statistics reported here, do indeed suggest not just a crisis, but a catastrophe. Fortunately, they represent a considerable overstatement. The statistics were collected partly on the basis of questionnaires answered by school districts; some also depended upon student reports of victimizations. We know from Chapter 3 that if we take rates of victimization on the basis of questionnaires as a "true" measure of crime, the rates do indeed appear alarming. Furthermore, the Committee's sample of districts was most incomplete; in fact, it sampled mostly large urban schools—the very schools suspected in advance of being those with the most violence.

A recent study has reviewed the levels of violence in schools from a broad historical perspective, and has observed that violence—of both pupils and teachers—has been a common thread throughout the history of the school. The public schools in England during the eighteenth century were characterized by constant mutinies, strikes, and violence, sometimes so severe that the teachers had to call upon the military for assistance.[49] The American schools of the nineteenth century were characterized as "chaotic places, with teachers attempting unsuccessfully to maintain control over unmotivated, bored, unruly and unmanageable children by disciplinary methods which were often novel, and were often brutal. Schools at this time were violent places, at least for the pupils."[50]

A historical overview of the schooling process also reveals a gradual change in the ideology of school discipline. In the eighteenth and nineteenth centuries, the brutal and violent use of force was seen as the only sensible way to quell the violence of the pupils. This was especially so, since American pupils were seen as truly "sons and daughters of the revolution" who simply refused to recognize authority:

> What difficulty has not an American teacher to maintain order amongst a dozen unruly little urchins; while a German rules over 200 pupils with all the ease of tranquility of an eastern monarch. There is little disposition on the part of American children to obey the uncontrollable will of their masters as on the part of their fathers to submit to the mandates of Kings.[51]

The only educated solution was: "A boy has a back. When you hit it, he understands."

But Dewey heralded the shift in disciplinary ideology. He wrote that the role of education was to free minds, not to force upon them a body of preexisting knowledge. The notion of "permissiveness" thus gradually crept into the schools. Or at least the public belief in it did. The use of the paddle continued and still continues to this day, supported by a recent Supreme Court ruling.[52]

The current situation is that the tables have been turned somewhat. Instead of arguing that it is because of the violence of pupils that violent discipline must be used, it is argued that the excessive use of discipline is responsible for much of the violence of pupils. Senator Bayh's committee reported:

> . . . hundreds of thousands of students are removed from schools each year by short-term, long-term or indefinite expulsions or suspensions . . . far in excess of those who must be removed as a means of maintaining order.[53]
> The misuse of discipline . . . often occurs because racial, cultural and generation differences cloud the judgment and actions of teachers and administrators alike.[54]

Viewed historically, however, the problem is overblown. The fact is that inner-city schools have a long history of chaos, rebellion, and brutality. Senator Bayh's committee reports that urban gangs are an extremely serious problem: "Although the number of gang members, in proportion to the overall student population in most schools is minimal, the trouble they cause is at times cataclysmic. Students are robbed, intimidated, raped, bludgeoned and sometimes fatally wounded. Teachers and other adults in the schools are threatened and on occasion, physically assaulted. . . . In some schools, gang activity is so intense that it is necessary for the school security officers and the local police to escort one gang through the territory of a rival gang at dismissal time."[55]

New York City has a 100 year history (and probably more) of gang violence and school disturbance.[56] Another report, less often quoted, of the National School Public Relations Association, based on a survey of 258 school districts in 1975, found that only 3.2 percent of teachers said that school violence was a major problem (and only 20 percent said that it was a minor problem). Furthermore, it appears that the violence was seen as a problem almost exclusively by teachers from large urban school districts.[57]

There is no clear evidence that there is today a crisis of school violence that is any more special than any that has occurred at other times. Nor is there any clear evidence that it is the disciplinary practice of the schools that is itself a "cause" of school violence: whether because it is "too permissive" or "too punitive." The extent of school violence has probably remained pretty much constant, regardless of the disciplinary ideology in vogue.

Violence-Prone School Children

If we exclude the problem of violent gangs, which I will consider in the following chapter, we are left with the question of why there are children who are violence-prone, and whether the explanation of their social behavior requires further explanation beyond that given in reference to police and prisoners. In some ways, their situation is similar. They are "imprisoned" compulsorily in an institution (the school). The teachers are the concrete image of authority, with close to absolute power over the children for 6 to 8 hours a day. But we have to ask, why are not *all* children therefore aggressive?

There is very little research in this area. In fact none that centers specifically on the school and classroom. There is one classic study, however, of aggressive children who were dealt with specially in a residential institution. This is as close as we can get to the analogue of the school. This study was conducted by Professor Redl and his associates, and we may outline his findings as follows:[58]

1. The most serious forms of aggressivity in children are those which stem from two "sicknesses": a defective ego and a defective superego.

2. The defective ego of the aggressive child is in fact a hypertrophied ego: one that is *over*developed so that the child can defend himself against the world and himself. Professors Redl and Wineman describe the cunning defenses or "alibis" of the delinquent ego: aggressive children put on a front of unconcern about their aggression. In fact, underneath they almost always "feel bad" about what they have done. This is a form of "denial."

- Repression of own intent: aggressive children like to be punished for delinquencies as such (e.g., stealing) because it allows them to repress the fact that they did something mean to somebody else. Thus, the punishment allows them to avoid guilt.
- "He did it first." If one saw someone else do something wrong, one can repeat this behavior without feeling guilty, since the "justification" is already established.
- "Everybody else does such things anyway." A boy will complain that "there isn't a single boy in my neighborhood who doesn't steal."
- "We were all in on it." The boy complains, "why pick on me?"
- "Somebody else did the same thing to me before."
- "He had it coming to him."
- "I had to do it or I would have lost face."
- "But I made up with him afterwards."
- "He is a no good so-and-so himself."
- "They are all against me, nobody likes me, they are always picking on me."
- "I couldn't have gotten it any other way."

3. The aggressive delinquent will also adopt other ploys to support his activities:

- He will seek out the "wrong" friends, especially a willing masochistic partner.
- He can size up a group situation with uncanny accuracy to tell if it will support his delinquency.
- He can seek out situations which will tempt his own impulsivity.
- He can exploit his own *moods*: "I can't help it once I am in this state."
- Rebel for somebody else's cause.[59]

4. These adaptations of the delinquent ego become firmly entrenched in the personalities of violence-prone children to the extent that they resist all efforts to change them.

5. There are many other facets and techniques of ego and superego functioning in the aggressive child. However, although these patterns of acting and reacting are deeply embedded in the childrens' lives, Professors Redl and Wineman use their knowledge of these tactics when they give advice on the handling and treatment of such children. Although it is not clear what "causes" such children to become aggressive in the first place (there may be a host of factors, as we shall see in Chapter 10), Redl and Wineman provide the teacher or parent—the person who must deal with aggressive children on a day-to-day basis—an understanding of "what is going on" during confrontations, and some ways of defusing violent situations.

Sports

Assaultive behavior has increased on all fronts quite drastically over the last 10 years, and this includes professional sports. There are many old and well-worn explanations of the function of violence in sports, most of which have a certain amount of plausibility. But before we look at these explanations, we should first define a few terms.

SPORTS AND PLAY. Many, perhaps most, people "play" some kind of sport or game as a part of leisure activity. We are interested not only in those who play sports as a way of earning an income—i.e., their "play" is their "work;" but also in those who play various violent sports as a leisure time activity. Although the two players are perhaps playing for different reasons, there is sufficient evidence to suggest that the long histories and traditions of many sports may produce very similar forms of violence, whether the game is played by amateurs or professionals.

TYPES OF SPORTS VIOLENCE. Sports may be divided into a number of different classes according to the differing degrees of physical force that are required and the object to which this physical force is directed:

1. "Loner" sports such as running, high-jumping, and other athletics very often require considerable physical force (e.g., throwing the shot-put). They are competitive, but the physical force is applied to objects or expressions of individual stamina, and could not be called "violent" in the proper sense of the word.

2. One-on-one sports in which the force of physical contact between two players is the central focus: e.g., boxing, wrestling. Although some

would argue that it is *skill* that is essential in these sports, nevertheless the focus of the game is explicitly on violent physical contact. Such sports have very ancient origins (at least as far back as the ancient Greeks) and have varied during different historical periods in the extent of violence either favored or allowed. The ancient Olympics placed emphasis on skill, and fights to the death were never allowed. But fights to the death in the Roman Colosseum were the order of the day.

3. Violent team games. In these games, although their main focus is on skill, team play, and winning (naturally), violent physical contact is a traditional and often essential aspect of the game. Included in this category are American football, rugby, Irish football, Australian football, and ice hockey.

4. Nonviolent team games. These include games in which the use of violent physical contact is either minimal or nonexistent, and is rarely tolerated as a way of playing the game. These include cricket, baseball, and soccer. Of course, there are ways of "getting" an opponent in all of these games, but the point is that such acts are comparatively rare compared to the violent team games.

MASS-SPECTATOR SPORTS. Team games that are played professionally are also mass-spectator sports; some of these have in the last 10 years seen a considerable increase in the violence of their spectators. Paradoxically, it does not seem to be the violent team games that have been related to the most violence in the spectators, since very serious riots and "hooliganism" have been mostly attached to soccer.

Very little research has been conducted on the causes or functions of violence in sports. However, there is sufficient evidence to allow us to make a few suggestions.

Professional Boxing

The paucity of research into this aspect of violence is to be lamented. I have located only two studies of any import, and both of these concern the sociocultural aspects of prizefighting. In their classic study in 1952, Weinberg and Arond[60] made it very clear that the social background of professional boxers reflected changes in the ethnic composition of the lower class urban slums. The Irish predominated in the early part of this century; by 1928 Jewish fighters had succeeded them, only to be replaced in 1936 by Italians. Since 1948, blacks have dominated the ring, and pretty much continue to do so.

Why does professional boxing draw upon the "lowest of the low?"

There are a number of reasons.[61] Many black prizefighters claim that they saw professional boxing as the quickest way out of their oppressive conditions of poverty and that their experience in street fights helped prepare them. But others suggest that there is definitely an element of racial hostility involved; prizefighting perhaps provides a symbolic way for the oppressed black man to defend himself against the white oppressor. Certainly there is considerable evidence for the pleasure both fighters and spectators have drawn from interracial prize fights. Prestige is also another important factor—in fact, it becomes *the* factor, after the fighter has "made it."

But most of this is mythical. The cold facts are that 80 percent or more of professional boxers never remain out of poverty for long. In fact many who were followed up in one study, were found to have sunk back into worse conditions.[62] Furthermore, it turns out that the *managers* of professional boxers have, until recently, been of upper-lower-class or middle-class origin. Certainly, up until the sixties, the majority of black prizefighters had white managers. It is therefore difficult to escape the impression of a rather brutal system operating in which all spectators enjoy the violence of battle; the whites can feel pleased that at least one black man has "made it," and he becomes something of an adored mascot; and the blacks can feel that they are "getting their own back," while all along, it was the whites who made most of the money.

Violent Team Sports

The historical traditions and the camaraderie of these sports would seem to have much to do with their high expression of violence.[63] In one fascinating study of rugby, it was hypothesized that a detailed ritual "subculture" had arisen around the Rugby Club and game.[64] The rituals relating to this subculture were characterized by the deliberate (and tolerated) mocking of dominant middle-class values. Those activities included public nudity, lewd initiation ceremonies (covering the genitals with shoe polish), singing obscene songs mainly concerning the defilement of women, excessive beer drinking, public vandalism (also tolerated), and preoccupation with homosexuality: its denial by excessive "macho" behavior. Most important was the demonstration of one's male "toughness" by violent physical contact in the game. Yet many of the obscene songs of the subculture are concerned with homosexuality:

> *For we're all queers together,*
> *Excuse us while we go upstairs,*
> *For we're all queers together,*
> *That's why we go around in pairs.*

Symptomatic of this song is that it was sung to the Eton Boating Song. The game has its origins (and continues) in middle- and upper-class public schools in England, and the authors of this study argue that the game reached its zenith during the second half of the nineteenth century when the cultural repression of middle-class males was most dominant. In fact, they argue that a "culture of bachelors" arose during that time. Others have also suggested the strong tendency (some have even argued that it is a biological "instinct")[65] for males to establish a male bond, and that this can best be done through violent (male) team games.

In a study of perhaps one of the most violent of team games, ice hockey, it was found that the longer the player has been playing, the more likely he was to use violence, and this was explained simply by the fact that he had a longer exposure to norms and values favoring violence. The tendency was for new players to choose role models who were violent, and the influence on the newer players to do this was felt not only because of the inherent traditions of violence of the sport itself as evidenced by the older team players, but also because of the expectations of the team players' nonplaying peers. With younger players, parents had minimal influence.[66]

It would seem, therefore, that a process of "locker room socialization" occurs with ice hockey players, probably in a manner very similar to that described earlier in this chapter in relation to the socialization of police recruits. A similar process of "bachelor socialization" has been observed among Irish drinkers.[67]

Team Games and Spectator Violence

The most serious spectator violence has occurred in soccer. Serious riots have occurred in South America and Italy where many have been killed. In England "soccer hooliganism" has become a "social problem."

Soccer hooliganism has been studied by Ian Taylor, who argues that soccer has traditionally been attached to various forms of violence for a long time, and especially has been an activity of the lower class. One of his arguments is that the game has been more and more appropriated by the middle classes, in the sense that the soccer stadiums have been re-designed to have more seats, and so therefore less room for people to stand. Thus, conflict has arisen when some have been unable to gain admission to the stadium. A few nasty incidents occurred, the media publicized them, the courts introduced stiffer sentences for those who committed assaults at the soccer match, and thus "soccer hooliganism" was created as a social problem.[68]

But this tells only part of the story. There is also a long tradition of drinking for a couple of hours at the local pub before going to see the game. There is also some evidence to suggest that juvenile gangs, who formerly (in the fifties at least) found their "rumbles" at the Dance Hall (which has largely disappeared), now find a ready "market" for their violence: they have taken up soccer (as somebody else's cause, one might say) and used it as a forum for gang activity. This is especially significant as these gangs make no attempt to go to the game, but rather indulge in violent conflict with receptive local defenders (who have had enough drinks to get up the courage) in the streets surrounding the stadium.[69] We can see that, under both theories, violence occurs not so much among the spectators as among those who either cannot or will not become spectators.

Violence may also occur as a result of deep subcultural commitment to a particular team. Once when I arrived in Glasgow to live for a time, the first warning I received was not to go to the Celts vs. Rangers game. The reason, of course, is that the fans are fanatically committed along religious lines: the Irish Catholics to the Celts, and the Protestants to the Rangers. Serious bloodshed almost always accompanies these games. In similar fashion, national pride may be related to riots that have occurred in international soccer matches played in South America, Italy, and other parts of Europe. The incredibly violence-charged atmosphere at football games is eloquently captured by Davies:[70]

> The police let them stay where they were, but as the Coventry supporters slowly grew in number, the Coventry songs and shouts got louder, beginning to equal the volume of the Spurs songs. It became a dialogue, with each side of the thin blue line taking it in turns to sing insults at the other.
>
> "IF YOU ALL HATE CITY, CLAP YOUR HANDS," sang Spurs, and the claps that followed shook the ground.
>
> "MAN-CHESTER CITY, MAN-CHESTER CITY," shouted Coventry in reply, very nastily, getting in one below the belt. It had been Manchester City who'd hammered Spurs earlier in the season, 4–0. When they'd finished this chant, they continued with shouts CITY, CITY, this time meaning their own club. The Spurs boys punctuated it by shouting SHIT after each shout.
>
> For an hour, they kept up the songs, solidly and without ceasing, one leading to another. I couldn't understand a lot of them. Many of the chants had actions with them, like "We hate Arsenal," where you punch one fist in the air in front of you, like a Nazi salute. My ears were numb, being right in amongst them. There was a definite feeling of power and excitement, but we were deafening ourselves more than anyone else.

There are many functions of violence in sport, most of which have well-worn explanations. These may be summarized thus:[71]

CATHARSIS: People have built up a high amount of aggression, and they must be able to "let off steam." They can do this by indulging directly in violent sport, or indirectly by watching it. There is much difficulty with this catharsis theory of aggression, as we shall see in Chapter 11.

J. P. Scott has pointed out that most team games have the specific function of building up tension and anxiety before the game, just so that it can be relieved afterwards. In other words, the steam has to be "built up" before it can be "let off."[72]

FRUSTRATION: This is a popular theory, perhaps best stated by Thorstein Veblen in relation to sports. Veblen saw sports as an outlet for the frustrations brought on by an exploitative society, created especially by the "emulative magnetism" of the leisure class.[73]

SEXUAL IDENTITY: Some have suggested that by watching extreme forms of "maleness" (e.g., wrestling, boxing) both males and females are more easily able to establish their own sexual identity.[74]

ANONYMITY OF THE CROWD: Many have written on the anonymity of the crowd. Some suggest that the situation of mass spectator sports allows for persons to "let themselves go," and that the situation is always potentially explosive, verging on rioting. In fact, the similarity between riots and playing has been noted by at least one writer.[75]

EXCITEMENT: Harrington,[76] in his review of soccer hooliganism concluded that excitement may account for a large part of the attraction and violence of soccer hooliganism. Excitement was generated through fanatical attachment to a team and the pervasiveness of "rumours" concerning mistreatment of one's own team. Violence was precipitated, however, not as a result of a large mob suddenly "turning angry," but by specific violent acts of a few individuals. We shall come across this phenomenon again when we look at riot behavior in the following chapter.

Summary

POLICE VIOLENCE: Statistical data on police violence are difficult to obtain because such police activities are poorly reported. A violence-prone type of police officer has been identified, but there are very few actual examples. The routine use of violence by police may depend on the way they are treated by the public and on the "locker room" socialization process; violence may be precipitated by an affront to the police officer's self-esteem.

CRIMINAL VIOLENCE: Two types of criminal violence were identified: violence used to assist in other crime, such as robbery, and violence used to enforce discipline both within and between organized crime "families."

PRISON VIOLENCE: The rate of homicide in prisons is roughly seven times higher than for the noninstitutionalized population; the incidence of staff violence to inmates is probably comparatively low.

INMATE VIOLENCE: Inmate violence may be related to the preponderance of violence-prone persons in prison; subcultural sediment; youth and sex; criminal behavior such as extortion and vengeance; psychological factors relating to suicide; crowding.

SCHOOLS: Serious violence remains a problem of inner-city ghetto schools; school violence is no worse today than it has been at other times in history; there is no clear evidence that the disciplinary practices of schools correlate with levels of violence.

SPORTS: Assaultive behavior of both participants and spectators has increased dramatically over the last decade; the violence of team games may be mediated by a "locker room" socialization process similar to that of police and other bachelor groups; spectator violence is a function of fanaticism and the quest for excitement, and is often precipitated by the violent acts of one or two individuals. The dynamics of these aspects of *collective* violence are the subject of the following chapter.

Mobs, Riots and Gangs

Mobs and Riots

There are many different kinds of riots, and their causes are certainly many and varied. The literature on riots has moved between two extreme images. The early image, made more famous by such writers as Le Bon,[1] saw the crowd as potentially violent and destructive, creating a milieu where herd instincts took over and civilized men became anonymous beasts. Crowds were seen as intrinsically irrational, fickle, suggestible. The opposite image (and the more recent one) advanced by Professor Neil Smelser[2] is the view of the crowd as purposeful and goal directed— which leads to the idea of riots as a rational response to identifiable conditions (e.g., political and economic oppression). The latter image of the crowd has certainly been the most popular during the sixties, the period of political turbulence in America. In 1968, the President's Commission on Civil Disorders[3] identified five catalysts of riots, all of which fall within Professor Smelser's imagery of the crowd: (1) frustrated hope in relation to the civil rights struggle; (2) a climate of approval and encouragement of violence; (3) feelings of powerlessness to change the system; (4) a new mood among the young seeking self-esteem and racial pride; and (5) the perception of police as the symbol of white oppression.

Professor Gary Marx[4] has sought to correct this imbalance by suggesting that there may be many different kinds of riots: some charged with the "beastly" emotions imagined by Le Bon; some very purposeful, but others somewhere in between. Marx suggests that riots may be simply classified in terms of (1) the extent to which there is a generalized belief

182

among the participants (close, but not exactly, to the Le Bon image of the "like-mindedness" of the crowd), and (2) the degree to which "riot actions" themselves are instrumental in collectively solving a group's problems. These two dimensions combine to give the following four types of riots:

TYPE I RIOTS: Focused riots of well established dissident groups who know what they want. Similar to terrorist groups described in Chapter 1. Targets are often those in powerful positions.

TYPE II RIOTS: Targets will more likely be ethnic minorities. Violence is more *expressive* of generalized belief, less instrumental—except in the sense that scapegoating may be instrumental.

TYPE III RIOTS: These are more of a transitional type, where a crowd may "run amuck" with a purpose. The best examples of these riots are (1) the crowd at a mass spectator sport that rushes onto the ground to grab pieces of turf or a player's clothing and (2) the lynching of a hated criminal.

TYPE IV RIOTS: Issueless riots. These are more spontaneous and occur when traditional social controls suddenly are lifted. The 1977 New York riot that erupted while there was a total energy failure fits easily into this category.

There can be little doubt that the worst riots in terms of the amount of destruction of persons and property are race riots, although once again, their severity may be mitigated by particular political or economic conditions. The prototypes of severe race riots are those that have occurred throughout India for many years, possibly reaching their worst peak prior to separation in 1948.[5] Indian riots are significant for the incredible number of persons involved and often killed or injured, and for the fact that there is a very long history of such riots. Mahatma Gandhi, the great exponent of nonviolent protest, probably understood the dynamics of mass behavior, including riots, better than most. Gandhi identified several causal factors in riots, which, while they were expounded with the specific conditions of India in mind, have broad application:[6]

FEAR AND COWARDICE. "The Musalman as a rule is a bully, and the Hindu as a rule is a coward."[7] Gandhi exhorted the Hindus to stand their ground, since bullies are only to be found where there are cowards. His logic was that since it is the bully who creates the quarrel, if one stands up to him, there can be no bully, thus no quarrel. We can see that Gandhi clearly understood the role of stereotyping, and tried to use the process itself to break down the stereotype of the "bully Musalman" and "coward Hindu." The importance of stereotyping in facilitating violence has been extensively studied by social psychologists.[8]

ATMOSPHERE OF HATRED: "The fact is that when blood boils, prejudice reigns supreme; man, whether he labels himself a Hindu, Musalman, Christian or what not, becomes a beast and acts as such."[9] Again, Gandhi observed that if persons held a set of fixed attitudes and beliefs about another group (i.e., the Hindus vs. the Muslims), hatred may develop to such a pitch that individuals will feel justified in killing and butchering even innocent people such as women and children, just for the reason that they are "on the other side." We see here the operation of the familiar Manichaean division.[10]

WEARINESS OF NONVIOLENCE: Groups that have for so long nonviolently protested against the authorities, and see that they are getting nowhere, that nonviolence is having no apparent effect, eventually, in frustration and anger, lose patience and demand concrete action. Thus, they turn to violence.

DISTRUST: Gandhi noted that each side distrusted the stated motives and actions of the other. The Musalman distrusted the Hindu's notion of "fair play." The Hindus are convinced that the Musalman is dishonest. Gandhi was referring to what we call selective perception: persons disposed to violence may selectively perceive the actions of antagonists to suit their situation. A white cop who arrests a violently drunk individual with every good reason may be selectively perceived in a black ghetto as a symbol of white oppression. A quick movement by an antagonist may be selectively perceived as an act of aggression. The causes, intentions, and emotions of the opponent's behavior may be selectively perceived according to the situational, personal, and cultural conditions of the participants.[11]

PROPAGANDA: "The newspaper man has become a walking plague. He spreads the contagion of lies and calumnies."[12] Gandhi saw the press as a central factor in fanning the flames of hatred, especially in inciting hatred of the Hindu. Propaganda put out by both sides served to increase the Manichaean division in Indian society.

How Do Riots Begin?

Although Gandhi was able to isolate the main causal factors in riots, the fact is that a number of the nonviolent protests that he led ended up in violence. As one Indian researcher on riots has observed: "Violence . . . is potentially present in all mass movements: its actual use is irrelevant and in practice it is difficult—almost impossible—to say whether violence will be used or not."[13]

The conclusion that we come to, then, is that while there are certain cultural and societal conditions that provide the arena in which riots can occur, it nevertheless takes *individuals* to start them. Riots do not occur as abruptly as the flocking of birds. A number of writers have shown that riots are precipitated by a series of situations and personal factors.

Professor Toch's account of the Watts Riot of August 11, 1965 shows that many of the cultural and social motivating factors that we have already outlined were in operation: generalized belief in police brutality, retaliation against white exploitation, unemployment, hopelessness, feelings of anonymity, lack of identity. Nevertheless it took particular incidents and particular persons to precipitate the riot. Professor Toch's account of these incidents and the final, precipitating act cannot be improved upon. Here it is in full:[14]

> The events that triggered the Watts riot began with the arrest, on a drunk driving charge, of a young Negro named Marquette Frye. There were spectators to the arrest; their mood was one of amusement. If anything, their sympathies extended to the officer, who was clearly justified in making his case. Everything went lightheartedly until the trooper and his partner tried to place Frye into physical custody. The young man reacted with panic. Robert Conot reports that as the officers started toward Frye, he broke down completely:
>
>> As he spoke to his mother, his voice broke. He was almost crying. Spotting the officers, he started backing away, his feet shuffling, his arms waving.
>> "Come on, Marquette, you're coming with us." [Officer] Minikus reached toward him.
>> Marquette slapped his hand away. "I'm not going to no sonofabitching jail!" he cried out. "I haven't did anything to be taken to jail."
>
> As Frye's fear increased, so did his awareness that he was exposed in the eyes of his neighbors. Shame produced resentment, and resentment brought memories of past humiliations: "What right had they to treat him like this? 'You motherfucking white cops, you're not taking me anywhere!' he screamed, whipping his body about as if he were half boxer, half dancer."

The incident had been converted into a tense, violent confrontation, and it was acquiring connotations susceptible to more general interpretations. Conot reports that the witnessing crowd—now including mostly persons who had only just arrived on the scene—became sympathetic to Frye. Frye's situation seemed to be that of a victim, and his fate mobilized feelings of indignation grounded in a common underprivileged past:

> The officers were white; they were outsiders; and most of all, they were police. Years of reciprocal distrust, reciprocal contempt, and reciprocal insults had created a situation in which the residents assumed every officer to be in the wrong until he had proven himself right, just as the officers assumed every Negro guilty until he had proven his innocence. The people began to close in on the three highway patrolmen.

As the situation degenerated (Marquette's brother, Ronald, had become engaged in the dispute), another police officer arrived. This officer, like Frye, was a man susceptible to panic—a person who seemed prone to precipitantly aggressive action. Conot describes his entrance into the sequence in the following terms:

> Officer Wilson, as he arrived on the scene, riot baton in hand even before he had the kickstand of the motorcycle down, was confronted by an image of blurred chaos . . . he went into action with no more opportunity to assess the situation than those Negro spectators who had arrived late and assumed from what they saw that there was violent conflict between Marquette and the officers . . .
>
> Rushing toward Ronald and Lewis, and without speaking to either, Wilson jabbed the riot baton into the pit of Ronald's stomach. As Ronald doubled over, he jabbed again. Ronald rolled to the ground.
>
> With one adversary dispatched, it was but a half dozen steps to where Marquette was fending off Minikus. Wilson swung the baton. He caught Marquette with a glancing blow to the forehead, above the left eye. As Marquette turned instinctively to meet him, Wilson jabbed him hard in the stomach. Marquette doubled over.[42]

At this juncture, Ronald's mother, seeing her sons painfully beaten, indignantly intervened. As a result, the crowd was treated to the spectacle of an old lady forcibly pushed into a patrol car. One member of the crowd later declared: "When that happened, all the people standing around got mad." Conot reports that there were isolated shouts of: "Come on, let's get them!" "Leave the old lady alone!" "We've got no rights at all—it's just like Selma!" "Those white motherfuckers got no cause to do that!"

The situation degenerated even further after one officer complained that a young lady in the crowd had spit at him. Several other officers converged on the girl, and they apprehended her after considerable resistance. The picture of the girl's helpless struggle against overwhelming odds symbolized, for many in the crowd, the hopelessness of their own fate: This feeling, and the resulting impotent rage, is vividly described by Conot:

> In the manner with which the police had handled the girl the people saw, or thought they saw, the contempt of the white man for the Negro. They felt, collectively, his heel grinding in their faces. They were stricken once more by the sting of his power.
>
> "Goddam!" a woman cried out. "Goddam! They'd never treat a white woman like that!"
>
> "What kind of men are you, anyways?" another challenged. "What kind of men are you, anyways, to let them do that to our people?"
>
> "It's a shame! It's a pitiful, crying shame!"
>
> "Blue-eyed white devils! We is going to get you! Oh, shit! We is going to get you!"
>
> "Motherfuckers!" It came from all sides of the crowd. "Motherfuckers!"

The Riot Commission's "cumulative chain" had reached its last link. An incident had been generated which symbolized for those present every ounce of humiliation, every nuance of hopelessness, every hurt to pride, self-esteem, and loyalty possible. The fruits of second-class citizenship had taken shape: they had become sensitivities which turned private conflict into public issue, which converted disputants into Oppressors and Oppressed; which metamorphosed a minor exercise into a morality play that promised intolerable victory to unspeakable evil.

To be sure, the transformation was not inevitable: some actors played their parts too well; some pawns proved ambitious, and hastened the plot. Frye's fear impelled him to present himself as a frenzied martyr; Wilson's pugnaciousness converted him into a caricature of arbitrarily exercised power. Tragedy might have been averted if one impulsive girl had been permitted to escape into the crowd. And there might have been no riot if one man had not felt more humiliated, more resentful, more excited, more impotent, more shamed, more desperate, more angry, and more compelled to act than his neighbors. It took one man, feeling what others felt and converting these feelings into action, to generate the last interpretation, the ultimate connotation, the irreversible inference—the crucial conclusion that violence was in order:

> Without conscious thought of his action he darted into the street and hurled the empty pop bottle in his hand toward the last of the departing black-and-white cars. Striking the rear fender of Sgt. Rankin's car, it shattered. And it was as if in that shattering the thousand people lining the street found their own release. It was as if in one violent contortion the bonds of restraint were

snapped. Rocks, bottles, pieces of wood and iron—whatever missiles came to hand—were projected against the sides and windows of the bus and automobiles that, halted for the past 20 minutes by the jammed street, unwittingly started through the gauntlet. The people had not been able to overcome the power of the police. But they could, and would, vent their fury on other white people. The white people who used the police to keep them from asserting their rights.

It was 7:45 p.m. Amidst the rending sounds of tearing metal, splintering glass, cries of bewilderment and shouts of triumph, the Los Angeles uprising had begun.

Once collective action has been initiated, it acquires a momentum of its own; even if people did not suffer from grievances, riots would attract and recruit participants. They would do so because they appeal to boredom, anger, frustration, desire for adventure; because they provide a ready-made opportunity to discharge feelings: because they furnish festive activity with the sanction of peers and under the aegis of principle.

As violent crowds form, bystanders are invited to join; if not, they find it natural to fill gaps in the ranks. Streets become an arena for heroism, a proving ground for bravery, a stage for protest. Boys can achieve manhood heaving rocks or defying police officers; men can acquire purpose through guerrilla warfare; groups can gain meaning through riot-connected projects. Benefits are provided to so many persons that there are few left to disapprove. At some point, nonviolence calls for special explanation and requires special motives. Violence becomes, temporarily, a way of life.

Friends and Enemies: Violent Gangs

TERROR IN BROOKLYN: YOUTH GANG TAKES OVER AN APARTMENT HOUSE

By Dena Kleinman

A neighborhood gang has seized a six-story apartment house in the Williamsburg section of Brooklyn, terrorizing the more than 100 tenants by ripping out the building's pipes, punching out its windows and smashing its furnishings. Only two tenants remain, and the gang has boasted of plans to burn the house down.

The building, at 396 South Fourth Street, is in a neighborhood where gangs seeking plunder, clubhouses and turf have seized tens of other buildings, robbing some of the tenants not only of their possessions but of their very homes. The residents have been forced like refugees to flee from building to building. The gang follows.

"The gangs are messing up everybody's life," said Israel Melendez, who grew up in the neighborhood and has since got out. "People have no place left to move," he said.

The South Side of Williamsburg—a 30-block stretch between

Grant Avenue and Broadway—used to be a stable neighborhood of prospering businesses, children playing stickball in the street and friendly neighbors who welcomed newcomers. Gradually, however, restless local youths, turning to violence, have taken over.

Marauders armed with machetes, baseball bats, guns and chains have terrorized the community, battling in the middle of busy inter-sections, vandalizing cars and apartments, mugging elderly couples and finally invading entire buildings and forcing the tenants out.

There are many stories of individual suffering. Some people have spent weeks searching for other apartments. Finding none, they have had to leave behind furniture, clothing and other possessions. Several families had to split up. An elderly couple cleared out of the apartment they had lived in for more than 20 years.

Gang members who have cannibalized the area do not perceive themselves as criminals. They contend they are "protecting" the building and say that the pipes, stoves and sinks they steal give them a chance to earn some money. They say they don't know why the tenants feel forced to leave.

"We help them," said one gang leader, who called himself Clark. "They help us." [New York Times, October 26, 1977]

The violent activities of youth gangs have been a perennial concern in most developed countries of the world. England and Scotland have a long tradition of violent gangs in most of their large cities—the Teddy Boys, Skinheads, and many others.[15] In the United States, gangs have existed in Philadelphia, Chicago, New York, and San Francisco for at least a century or more. They maintain considerable continuity, defending specific areas of "turf" against outside groups.[16]

In some cases, police have "given up" trying to control such areas, and often the juvenile gangs see themselves as maintaining the social control of the area, protecting all of its inhabitants from outside threats. As the gang leader says in the news item above, "We help them." It is possible that they do, but it is also possible that when youths gain power, the kind of social control they will wield may be close to terror.

We saw in Chapter 4 that there are many factors that enhance the use of violence in subcultures. Time and again we find these same themes among violent gangs: the importance of honor, toughness, trouble, "macho image," and survival to juvenile gangs which are indigenous to a particular community cannot be underestimated.

Of course, not all juvenile gangs are violent. In fact, most, according to a recent survey, are not.[17] Nor are all violent gangs highly organized, with leaders, rep defenders, etc. Some have suggested, in fact, that many juvenile gangs are very loosely-knit "organizations," with perhaps two or three central figures and a large number of "members" who may occasionally come together for some "action," then drift away again.[18]

Patterning of Gang Violence

A recent survey of gangs[19] in twelve major cities* of the United States has produced a great deal of interesting information which may be summarized as follows:

EXTENT OF THE PROBLEM. Of the 12 cities surveyed, 6 were identified as being "gang-problem" cities. It is extremely difficult to get reliable information, largely because of the difficulty involved in coming up with a consistent and agreed-upon definition of "gang." However, Table 8.1 displays the very rough estimates gained mostly from police departments by Professor Miller on the number of gangs and their membership.

The extent to which these gangs are violent gangs is even more difficult to establish. It would appear to vary according to each city. Table 8.2 tries to get at this problem.

We can see that the proportion of criminal violence accounted for by gang members—whether measured by arrests for violent crimes in general, or for homicides—works out to, on the average 1 in 4, with a wide range among the cities. When one considers that many juvenile arrests are for "status" offenses (i.e., running away from home), rather than specific crimes, we must conclude from these two tables that the part played by violent gangs is considerable in the generation of criminal violence.

AGE, SEX, AND ETHNICITY. In general, the ages of gang members were found to be remarkably similar in all six problem cities. The ages ranged

TABLE 8.1

*Rough Estimates of Number of Gangs and Gang Members, 1973–1975 in Six Gang-Problem Cities**

City	Number of Gangs	Number of Members
New York	315–473	8,000–40,000
Chicago	700–220	3,000–10,000
Los Angeles	160–1,000	12,000–15,000
Philadelphia	88–400	4,700–15,000
Detroit	30–110	500– 1,250
San Francisco	20	250

* From Miller, W., *Violence by Youth Gangs*, 1975, p. 17.

* These cities were New York, Los Angeles-Long Beach, Chicago, Philadelphia, Detroit, San Francisco-Oakland, Washington, D.C., St. Louis, Cleveland, and Houston.

TABLE 8.2

Gang Member Violence as Proportion of
*Juvenile Violence, 1973–1974**

	Gang Member Arrests for Violent Crimes as % of All Juvenile Arrests		Gang-Related Killings as % of Juvenile Homicides (arrests)	
		N		N
New York	31.4	23,600	15.0	268
Chicago	25.7	65,166	10.0	188
Los Angeles	44.5	35,593	42.0	92
San Francisco	Not available		72.0	18
Philadelphia	Not available		30.0	127

* From Miller, *Violence by Youth Gangs,* 1975, pp. 31–32

roughly between 10 and 22 years, with a "peak" age of 17.[20] Of course, gang activity was found to be largely an activity of males. Although some female gangs exist as "auxiliaries" to male gangs (e.g., Crips, Cripettes; Disciples, Lady Disciples), autonomous female gangs were found to be very rare. It was estimated, for example, that in the Bronx and Queens area, there were six autonomous female gangs. No data suggested that there had been any increase in female gang activity, which would have been expected according to the women's liberation thesis outlined earlier, in Chapter 5.

The social areas of gang activities continued predominantly to be in the inner-city slum areas. There was, however, some evidence that some cities had developed "slums" in suburban areas, and that gang activity was flourishing.

Ethnic background continues according to a well established pattern. In past periods, Professor Miller notes that most gangs were white. Today, approximately half of the gang members of the six problem cities were found to be black, one sixth Hispanic, and one tenth Asian. But each city varied considerably: 90% of gangs in Philadelphia are black, compared to only 5% in San Francisco. A number of gangs were also found to be racially mixed, but this was comparatively rare. The rise in Asian gangs was seen as a sudden and marked departure from the past. The old ethnic gangs of the past: the Irish, Italians, Jews, and Slavs of the 1880–1920 period; and the Germans, British, and Scandinavians of the 1820–1860 period, appear to have diminished considerably, if not disappeared altogether. In many cases, the same geographical areas continue to be gang-ridden, but the ethnic composition has changed according to the changing patterns of migration and social mobility.

Do Gangs Seek Out Violence? The prototype of gang violence is the gang "rumble," a kind of warfare between gangs from one territory against gangs of another. The "causes" of these rumbles may again vary considerably according to situational conditions, honor and shame, defense of territory, and so on. All problem cities reported that a wide range of rumbles occurred between gangs in their cities. These included:

- planned rumble—a prearranged encounter between sizable rival groups
- warfare—continuing pattern of retaliating engagements by members of rival groups (similar to feuding)
- "foray"—smaller bands engage rival bands
- "hit"—smaller bands attack one or two gang rivals
- "fair fight" or "execution": a single gang member engages a single rival
- "punitive assault": gang members assault or kill present or potential members of their own gang

The Objects of Gang Violence. There is a widespread feeling, demonstrated and propagated by news items like the one on page 188, which is that the victims of gang violence are becoming more and more those who are "innocent" in the sense that they are non-gang members. Table 8.3 presents data on this question; it can be seen that (a) roughly 60% of victims of gang violence in 1970–1973 were in fact gang members, (b) 40% were non-gang members, and (c) these proportions are very similar to those found in a study of gangs in 1955–1957. It appears, therefore, that predatory gang activity against non-gang members has not drastically increased during this decade.

TABLE 8.3

Gang Member and Non-Gang Member Victims,
1955–1957 and 1973–1975*

Type of Victim	301 press-reported incidents, four cities 1973–1975 %	77 field Recorded incidents, Boston, 1955–1957** %
Gang-member	60.5	57.1
Non-gang child or adult	27.6	22.0
Non-gang peer	11.9	20.8
Three categories	100.0	99.9

* From: Miller, *Violence by Youth,* p. 40.
** Figures do not add to 100% because of rounding.

WEAPONS. The image we have of gang rumbles is one of knife fights, bicycle chains, brass knuckles, and homemade "zip" guns. Although these were still reported by all cities, it appears that guns have now become the predominant weapon. The Bronx Division of New York City's Gang Intelligence Unit records weapons according to 25 categories, 17 of which use gunpowder in one form or another. There were commonly found among juveniles: rifles and shotguns of all calibers; homemade mortars; homemade bazookas; Molotov cocktails; pipe bombs. The "Saturday night special" (a cheap short-barrelled .22) was surprisingly rarely cited. Professor Miller observes that the press has propagated a theory that there has been a basic change in the personality of the gang member, that he has become "sociopathic," lacking the moral capacity to see the wrongness in killing. He suggests, however, that it is more likely that the wide availability of handguns and a variety of other weaponry to youth (and indeed clearly used by youth) may account for any increase in the lethal violence of gangs. For, as Professor Miller concludes, there has indeed been a drastic increase:

> In sum, taking into account tendencies to exaggerate the scope and seriousness of gang violence, and to represent the "gang of today," as far more violent than its predecessors, evidence currently available indicates with considerable clarity that the amount of lethal violence currently directed by youth gangs in major cities both against one another and against the general public is without precedent.[21]

MATERIALISM. Whereas the classic gang literature refers to the quest for status within the gang, and argues that violence is one of the best means to establish one's "rep," Professor Miller suggests that, while this may still play an important part with many gangs, especially those that are indigenous gangs, nevertheless, there appears to be a strong materialistic element.[22] Gangs will attack and rob and steal for the *material* gains, as much as for the "honor" of having had the courage to do it. This recent aspect of gang activity is perhaps clearly demonstrated by the Brooklyn gang described in the news item earlier. This kind of activity is most commonly perpetrated upon *strangers* rather than gang members.

Summary

1. There are many different types of riots, which may range from the heated, unfocused, angry behavior of a "mob gone wild," to a narrowly focused, well organized violent demonstration.

2. Gandhi has identified several causes of riots, which are: fear and cowardice, an atmosphere of hatred, weariness of nonviolence, distrust, and the use of propaganda.

3. The study of riots in India, however, has concluded that even when these ingredients are present, it is never possible to predict whether violence will occur in a mass protest or not.

4. Riots may be touched off by a few specific incidents, apparently minor, but which are perceived in a distorted way because of the operation of many of the factors identified by Gandhi.

5. The conclusion is that it takes the actions of a few individuals to precipitate a riot.

6. Violent juvenile gangs exhibit many of the same themes identified in Chapter 4 concerning subcultures of violence: machismo, defense of honor, a survival orientation.

7. Gang members account for roughly one in four of all violent juvenile crimes, as measured by arrests.

8. Gang violence remains mostly directed against other gang members, not against the wider community as is popularly supposed. The level of gang violence appears however to be at the highest level in some decades, so that the public is currently very concerned about being victimized in the street—being robbed or mugged by these juvenile gangs. In fact, it is the predatory, cold-blooded violence that people seem to fear most: the violent crimes in which the assailants seek out strangers as their victims. Chapter 9 analyzes these crimes.

The Violence of Strangers: Rape and Robbery

Rape: That Special Non-Relationship

Rape statistics are probably the most difficult of all crime statistics to interpret with any degree of confidence. We have known for a long time that rape is the most under-reported of personal crimes.[1] There are many reasons for this, the main ones being that women feel ashamed, guilty, or afraid to report the offense.[2] Although much evidence has come to light concerning the under-reporting of rape as a result of victimization surveys, it is likely that even in these interviews, victims would still be reluctant to report the crime. There are a number of controversial or contested aspects of rape statistics, which I will now list and try to resolve as far as possible.

BLACK ON WHITE? We are all well aware of the racial stereotype held of blacks for many years, which I referred to in earlier chapters. The men are seen as oversexed beasts longing to rape white women. Black women are seen as "loose," "hot," natural prey for white men. Are these stereotypes borne out by the "facts"?

The first basic statistical research on rape was conducted in Philadelphia by Professor Amir some 20 years ago and involved the study of 646 rape events that had occurred in that city over the period 1958 to 1960.[3] Many of the results of this study have been seriously questioned since that time. But many have also stood the test of replication. We can see from Table 9.1 that the Philadelphia study found a minimal amount of black on white rapes, and minimal white on black rapes. In

TABLE 9.1

Forcible rape by races of victim and offender
(In percentages)

Data Source and Year[4]	Total cases	Black on black	White on white	Black on white	White on black
Police *Data*					
Philadelphia[a], 1958–60	646	76.9	16.3	3.3	3.3
Washington, D. C.[b], 1966	151	78.8	8.6	12.5	0.0
17 Cities[c], 1967	465	59.6	29.6	10.5	0.3
Metropolitan Cities[d], 1967	459	82.2	12.0	5.0	.8
Oakland, Ca.[e], 1971	192	40.0	19.0	33.6	2.0
Hospital Data					
Washington, D. C.[f], 1971	1,243	76.0	3.0	21.0	0.4
Victimization Data					
National Sample[g], 1974	130,550	19.9	59.7	15.5	2.9

fact, the clear finding was that most rapes were *intraracial*. We can see, however, that recent victimization data convey a different picture. There are a number of ways in which these data may be interpreted.

First, we should note that those studies showing the higher intraracial proportions are those of big cities and that at least three of those have a much higher proportion of blacks in the population than does the nation as a whole. We should therefore expect national surveys to turn up much lower proportions of within-black rapes and higher proportions of within-white rapes.

Second, there is a strong possibility that the women's liberation movement, largely one of middle-class white females, has had a considerable effect upon rape victims who, although they may have been reticent about reporting their victimizations to the police, have been willing to do so to an interviewer. This is only a hunch, admittedly, but it suggests that one needs much more information on the differential responsiveness to interviews of this kind between blacks and whites.

Third, the explanation of the official data has usually been that of a "subculture of violence" in which blacks (especially) prey on each other. This was the explanation provided by Amir, which has subsequently been criticized.[5] However, the data of the NCP survey would be consistent with this explanation insofar as it makes clear that, proportionally, whites are preying on each other to the same extent as are blacks. One might note that Philadelphia, the location of Amir's study, is perhaps a special case, because it has many well entrenched subcultures of

TABLE 9.2

Percentage of rapes between strangers

Data source and Year[6]	Total cases	% Stranger
Philadelphia[a], 1958–1960	646	42.3
Washington, D. C.[b], 1966	151	33.0
17 Cities[c], 1967	465	52.8
Washington, D. C.[i], 1965–1966	1,243	42.1
Oakland, Ca.[e], 1971	63	90.4†
(MacDonald)[j], 1971	200	60.0
New York City[k], 1973	389	58.0
National Sample[h], 1974	130,550	73.0

† This excessively high rate is for interracial rapes. However, although the researchers do not give figures for intraracial rapes, they say that the prior relationship found between victim and offender was "at most slight."

black, Jewish, Italian, and other ethnic origin. The subcultural explanation may therefore be appropriate to the city, but not necessarily the whole nation.

Fourth, the black on white column makes it quite clear that there are proportionally a large number of black on white rapes, but the data are not strong enough to warrant the general conclusion that rape is an *interracial* crime. One must still conclude that it is basically a within-race phenomenon. However, the data are strongly suggestive of a substantial increase in interracial rape in the 1970s.

STRANGERS OR INTIMATES? Amir concluded incorrectly from his study that rape was not a crime of strangers, yet he says that two thirds of his cases *were* between strangers. This has been a very controversial issue, because many use this finding that rape victims previously knew the rapist to infer that, because there was a "relationship" between them, there was some basis for "consent" by the victim. That is, it is suspected that on many occasions the victim "seduces" or "goes along with" the rapist, but then changes her mind at the last minute (or after it is over). The data of Table 9.2 show that rape is much more a crime among strangers. Although the data reported by the two earlier sources suggest roughly a half-and-half breakdown, the recent victimization and official data are sufficient to weight opinion towards the conclusion that rape is now committed predominantly by strangers. A number of recent writings also support this view, especially that seduction of the rapist is very rare.[7]

If these data represent an increase (or if, indeed, rape by strangers has always been more common), they then provide support for the currently popular women's liberation view of rape as a "terror tactic" which not only expresses male tyranny but also serves to keep women frightened and to reinforce their feelings of powerlessness.[8] The data may also support some studies that have identified particular attributes in the offenders, which we will review shortly.

Other research does suggest, however, that in a sizable minority of cases, the victims are of "doubtful reputation." In Amir's study, 20% of victims had previous police records (a figure somewhat lower than that for victims of other assaultive crimes), and 20% were regarded by police as having "bad reputations" in the neighborhood.[9]

The question of resisting the attacker has also been researched. The Philadelphia study found that over 50% of the victims failed to resist in any way at all.[10] But this statistic must be interpreted with caution, since the definition of "resist" is somewhat difficult. Some would argue that from the rapist's point of view, intimidation of the victim is a prerequisite for rape. Thus, rapists may intimidate the victim in order to eliminate any possibility of resistance. But it must be said that most research does not support this view. It is more likely that women submit without strong resistance because of their fatalistic feelings of powerlessness.[11]

Another type of rape situation (but probably rare) in which resistance is often questioned is "rape by fraud."[12] This type of rape occurs when the offender in some way "tricks" the victim into thinking that she must have sexual intercourse with him. The extremes of rape by fraud are illustrated by the many jokes that revolve around a doctor convincing an innocent patient that having intercourse with him is part of the treatment. A number of complicated cases have arisen in this decade as the result of the use of sexual intercourse as a part of "sex therapy." But there are many cases in between where seduction is virtually indistinguishable from "rape by fraud."[13]

It has also been suggested that girls who hitchhike are placing themselves in a position that makes them more liable to be raped. While this has been shown statistically to be probably correct, it is another thing to infer from this statistic that girls who hitchhike "want" to be raped. A study in California estimated that 20% of rapes were perpetrated against hitchhikers, and that most of these victims were students whose appearance was probably perceived by the offenders as indicative of "loose morals."[14]

ONE ON ONE? Various estimates have been made of the extent to which rape is a "gang" activity as against that of a lone offender. The Philadelphia study concluded that 43% of rape victims were victims of multiple rapes,[15] but estimates in other studies have been higher—up to 70%.[16] However, data from the NCP survey suggest that only 25% of rapes (including attempted rapes) are committed by multiple offenders.[17] Some have suggested that gang rape is increasing dramatically because the women's movement is challenging the macho values of young men. But others attribute the cause of group rape to the dynamics of the juvenile gang, especially the tendency to "follow the leader," who is always the first to violate the victim.[18]

THE VIGOR OF YOUTH? The NCP survey for 1974 indicated that 82% of offenders were perceived by their victims as being over 21. This statistic can be compared with roughly similar percentages reported by the FBI on the ages of offenders arrested for rape (82.7% are reported to be over 18 years of age) and Amir's study which found that 56.7% of offenders were above 19 years of age. The majority were, however, between 15 and 24 years of age.

ALCOHOL? Evidence that the offender and victim both spent time drinking alcohol together has on occasion been taken as evidence that the victim "consented" to the rape.[19] The Philadelphia study did not find that the presence of alcohol was a major precipitating factor in rape. It was, however, significantly related to the form the rape took, being most often accompanied by excessive violence and sexual humiliation by various perversities. One other study has found from an analysis of the autobiographies of convicted rapists, that 35% were alcoholics and another 50% had been drinking at the time of the offense.[20] As with other assaultive crimes, it is likely that alcohol plays a central, though complicated, role in this offense.

THE VIOLENCE OF RAPE? Only in 15% of Amir's cases was no physical force used at all. Twenty percent (20%) involved brutal beatings, 15% chokings. Severe violence was especially apparent in the cases of black on white rape, and in gang rapes.[21] The Violence Commission report in 1967 estimated that 90% of victims were injured.[22] Thus, it appears that injury is highly likely in most rape cases. However, Amir also found that there was a strong correlation between the amount of resistance displayed by the victim and the amount of physical force used by the attacker. The crucial question, of course, is which one comes first? Does a violent attacker invoke violent resistance? Or does a violent resister invoke violent attack? So far, there is no research to answer this question.[23]

EVIL INTENT? The popular belief has been that rape is an "explosive" crime in the sense that the male, overendowed with sex drive, succumbs to the temptation of the moment. Amir's study found that 71% of the rapes he studied in Philadelphia were planned by the attacker. The form of the planning was as follows:

1. Get the victim drinking alcohol (23% of the cases).
2. Find a suitable victim either at a party, park, or bar, or give a hitchhiker a ride.
3. Get your gang behind you.

There is some difficulty in interpreting these findings. First, at least one other study has shown that 60% were "explosive" rapes.[24] Furthermore, Amir also found that the planned rapes tended to be *intra*racial, whereas explosive rapes were interracial.[25] Since we have seen that his study seems to have underestimated the incidence of interracial rape, we might infer that explosive rape is more common than he suggests. Some of these statistical findings also require the imputation of motives to the offender, without inquiring about the motives of the victim. For example, we have seen that hitchhikers have a greater than average chance of being raped. Is the correct interpretation that girls "choose" to take the higher risk? Or is it that intending rapists plan to take advantage of a situation in which they can virtually hold a girl "captive"?

IMMORAL COMMUNITY? Some have suggested that the general "social climate" of a community or city is likely to affect the incidence of rape. One study compared two American cities (Los Angeles and Boston) according to "permissiveness" of the sexual and social climate and the incidence of rape. It was found that the more permissive city (Los Angeles) had a higher rape rate, and this relationship held even when the policies and procedures of the police were taken into account.[26] There were, however, many uncontrolled variables in this study, and, since its results fly in the face of other research, they should be accepted, for the moment, as only suggestive. Other studies have looked at the effects of pornography (a sign of "permissiveness," one may presume) and have found little evidence that its ready availability is related to higher levels of sex crime, including rape.[27]

THE RAPIST AS "SICK"? The modern view, fostered by women's liberation ideology, goes something like this: All men are sick because they crave power, domination, the violation of women. Therefore those who commit rape are sick, because they are men. But although there may be some truth to these claims, as seen from the point of view of our culture, as I have in fact suggested in Chapters 5 and 6, this answer is not really very helpful in telling us why it is that not *all* men commit rape. Some liberationists would, of course, claim that they *do*—against their wives. But this is a bit extreme, and tends to abuse the definition of the word "rape."

The opposite extreme is the kind of clinical study that concludes, after the analysis of a few cases, that the rapist's sex aggressive drive becomes transferred into destructive aggression instead of the normal sexual response.[28] In fact, there are extremely few studies specifically of the characteristics of rapists. However, we may get a rough picture of the extent to which there is, perhaps, "normal" rape, as against "abnormal" rape, from the studies of habitual, repeating rapists.

One study[29] conducted in England in 1957 concluded that only 9.1% of convicted rapists or attempted rapists had any previous convictions for sex offenses. Most recidivists (60%) had first been convicted of a sex offense between the ages of 21 and 40. At least half of all offenders did have previous convictions for other crimes.

The persistent sex offender (offender with three or more prior convictions for sex offenses) accounted for only 3 percent of the entire sample of sex offenders studied. There was no evidence that those who repeated had begun with a less serious offense and "progressed" to more severe sex offenses. Repetitions appeared to be strikingly similar in type.

For those offenders convicted for the first time, it was found that more than one in six in fact admitted to having committed a number of other offenses prior to conviction. Almost double the proportion of heterosexual offenders as against homosexual offenders had previous convictions of breaking and entering. This finding supports other research that has suggested that many rapes may be "spur-of-the-moment" rapes, committed by a burglar who is tempted by the utter helplessness of the victim. This has come to be termed "felony-rape" in the United States (i.e., a rape committed during the course of a felony).[30]

The major psychological study of rapists is that by Gebhard, et al., conducted during the 1940s and 1950s.[31] On the basis of extensive interviewing of convicted rapists, these researchers reached the following conclusions:

1. *Early life*—a strong preference for the mother as opposed to the father; 60% come from broken homes; more prepubertal sex play; 10% have been sexually approached as children by adult females.

2. *Sex dreams*—strong heterosexual dreams and more sadistic dreams than other sex offender groups studied; sadistic fantasies during masturbation.

3. *Marriage*—estimated that one fourth were married at the time of the offense; there was a definite tendency to marry more than once, as

well as a high frequency of marital coitus; 25% had anal intercourse with their wives; offenders assessed their wives as reaching
orgasm rarely.

4. *Criminal record*—22% had previous convictions, many for serious
crimes. A number had also committed other sex offenses (exhibitionism
and peeping—40%).

5. *Varieties of offenders*—Gebhard, et al. found a number of special
categories and characteristics of offenders, including the following:

> *Sadists*—those who are unable to obtain sexual satisfaction without
> accompanying physical violence. These men usually have a past
> history of violence and have strong hostility to females.[32]
>
> *Amoral delinquents*—these offenders are simply "egocentric
> hedonists." They are not hostile to females; in fact, females seem in
> some ways "irrelevant" to them, so long as they submit and satisfy
> the rapist's desire. Used to brushes with the law, the offender will
> use force to get what he wants.
>
> *Drunken variety*—these cases may range from drunks who delude
> themselves into thinking that a female is trying to seduce them, to
> the more extreme cases of alcoholic aggression, where serious in-
> jury is inflicted on the victim.
>
> *Explosive* (about 10%)—the apparently inexplicable, sudden
> attack by an otherwise "upright" citizen. Disturbed family back-
> ground usually underlies the behavior of these offenders.
>
> *Double standard*—these offenders divide females into "good"
> females who deserve respect, and "bad" females who are not en-
> titled to consideration if they become obstinate. Thus, they rational-
> ize the use of brutal force, if necessary, on "bad" girls: "Man, these
> drunk broads don't know what they want. They get you worked up
> and then try to chicken out. You let'em get away with stuff like that
> and the next thing you know they will be walking all over you."

Other studies of rapists have produced further findings, some a little
puzzling. One study, on the basis of psychological testing, concluded
that, compared with normal males, rapists were less aggressive, less self-
assured, and less dominant.[33] It is difficult to interpret these findings
when one recognizes that the central element of rape is aggression, unless one adheres to the "explosion" theory of frustrations that build up
over a long period of time. This may be true, since one other study has
suggested that rapists who are married tend to have dominant wives,
who are better educated. Paradoxically, these researchers found that the
husband's offense tended to reinforce the wife's moral and social
strength.[34]

Robbery

TYPES OF ROBBERY INCIDENTS. That robbery is a crime perpetrated on strangers there can be little doubt. Seventy-eight percent (78%) of the robberies studied by the Crime Commission in 1968 were against strangers.[35] The NCP data for 1974 show that the proportion is as high as 90% for male victims (for females a little lower—74% for white female victims and only 57% for black female victims).[36] Other studies also provide evidence in support of these findings. One study conducted in Philadelphia and another in London used similar classification systems to identify types of robberies. The comparative results of these studies may be seen in Table 9.3. We can see that if we collapse the first two categories and consider them as crimes against "strangers," then the proportions are very similar to those mentioned above.

BLACK ON WHITE? Table 9.4 presents the results of several studies that have collected data on interracial robberies. They are from differing sorts of data, so there are naturally some discrepancies. However, it is clear that robbery is less "subcultural" and more interracial. The very high black on black percentage in the Philadelphia study compares also to the very high proportion found in Amir's rape study in Philadelphia.

TABLE 9.3

*Types of robbery incidents
in London and Philadelphia*[37]
(In percentages)*

Robbery Group	London[a] (N = 749)	Philadelphia[b] (N = 1,732)
Robbery of persons who, as part of their employment, were in charge of money or goods	35.9	25.8
Robbery in the open following sudden attack	36.0	52.2
Robbery on private premises	10.0	7.3
Robbery after preliminary association of short duration between victim and offender	14.3	10.2
Robbery in cases of previous association of some duration between victim and offender	3.7	4.5
TOTAL	100.0	100.0

* Figures may not add to 100% because of rounding.

TABLE 9.4

Robberies by races of victim and offender[38]
(In percentages)

Data Source and Year	Total cases	Black on black	White on white	Black on white	White on black
Police data					
Philadelphia[a], 1960–66	1,722	63.0	13.0	23.0	1.0
17 Cities[b], 1967	269	38.4	13.2	46.7	1.7
Metropolitan cities[c], 1967	1,786	58.0	13.0	28.0	1.0
Westchester County[d], 1970	265	14.0	15.0	69.0	3.0
Victimization data					
N.C.P.[e]	476,880	17.1	37.7	36.7	2.6

It may be that black-black crime is a product of the specific characteristics of the black ghettoes of Philadelphia. Another discrepancy which
requires explanation is the high white-white proportion found by the
NCP study. Since this study is the only one of those presented in Table
9.4 which uses victimization data, it seems reasonable to conclude that
the disparity with the other studies relates to the victimization survey
method itself. It may be that the national probability sampling used in
the NCP survey takes into account a wider variety of contexts than do
the other studies which on the whole have sampled only cities. Another
explanation may be that victims perceive the race of their attackers
differently (or recall it differently when interviewed) compared with the
way the race of offenders is perceived through the recording process in
official police procedures.[39] The latter explanation is weak, though, since
research on racial prejudice has shown that whites, when threatened by
an attacker, are more likely to perceive the attacker as black.[40] Clearly,
more work is needed to investigate the differential responsiveness of
whites and blacks to official interviews of the victim survey type. With
this difficult exception, our conclusion is that robbery is basically an interracial crime.

A CRIME OF THE STREET? More data that support the view that robbery is largely a crime of anonymity come from an analysis of where the
crimes mostly occur. Table 9.5 clearly demonstrates the findings of six
separate studies: robberies are predominantly performed on the street—
unlike rape, which although also performed often in the street, is also

TABLE 9.5

Location of robberies in London, Philadelphia,[41] Boston, and Westchester County

(In percentages)

Location	London[a] (N = 749)	Philadelphia[b] (N = 1,722)	Boston[c] (N = 1,240)	Westchester County[d] (N = 407)	17 Cities[e] (N = 3,789)	NCP[f] (N = 975,630)
Street	54.3	55.8	49.0	49.1	50.7	60.0
Establishment	25.7	17.8	23.7	27.4	9.2	15.0
Vehicle (car, taxi, bus)	1.4	4.3	16.1	6.3	5.4	10.0
Residence	16.7	7.0	7.4	8.9	16.4	15.0
Other places	1.9	16.1	4.0	8.3	18.3	
Total	100.0	100.0	100.0	100.0	100.0	100.0

TABLE 9.6

Means of force or intimidation used in robberies[43]
(Percentages)

	Philadelphia[b]	Westchester[d] County	NCP[f] (1974)	UCR[c] (1975)	London[a] (1957)
Firearms	32.4	22.5	15.0	44.8	7.8
Knife (sharp instrument)		19.4	20.0	12.4	1.9
Blunt instrument	18.4	NA	11.0	7.8	20.1
				(other weapon)	
Bodily force	37.5	20.3	NA	NA	50.6

often performed in the victim's house. This is not the case with robbery. Consistently, less than 20% of robberies occur in the home. We should also note, however, that there are considerable variations according to the environmental features of particular areas. Those areas which have high-rise apartments are more likely to have robberies occur in these buildings, whereas those with suburban sprawl are more likely to have them occur in the street.

A CRIME OF THE GUN? Although the gun is used commonly for roughly 20 to 40% of robberies, it is by no means the dominant method of inflicting injury, as can be seen in Table 9.6. It is of some significance that in the Philadelphia study, the cases where injury was most common to the victim were those in which bodily force was used. These results were also supported by the Crime Commission study in 1967, and it has been found generally that the victim has a much greater chance of being injured if the robber has no weapon. We can see, therefore, that guns are not the sole source of concern in robbery. The comparison with the London data is also suggestive of the established finding that the gun is the more popular weapon in the United States and blunt instruments are preferred in England.[42]

ONE ON ONE? The majority of robberies are committed by multiple offenders, as can be seen clearly from Table 9.7. This is, of course, quite logical, since many against one stand a better chance of success in intimidating a victim.

KINDS OF ROBBERS. Professor Conklin,[44] on the basis of interviews with 67 convicted robbers and interviews with 90 victims, described four types of robbers:

TABLE 9.7

Proportion of robberies committed by multiple offenders[45]

	N	%
London (1957)[a]	462	60
Westchester[b]	376	59.1
NCP[c]	1,173,980	57.0

1. *The professional robber,* who carefully plans his job, carries loaded firearms, is most often white—between 20–30 years old, and from middle to working-class background. He has a "long-term commitment" to crime.

2. *Opportunists,* who make seemingly random attacks upon victims who are, nevertheless, clearly vulnerable targets. These offenders are more often black and in their teens and have much lower criminal aspirations, in the sense that they steal only small amounts of money. These are probably the most common types of robbers. We saw in the previous chapter that Professor Miller identified a drastic increase in this type of activity in some inner-city areas among youth gangs, but that it was still not the most typical form of gang violence. There are no statistics available on the proportion of robberies accounted for by youth gangs, but it is probably quite high.

3. *Addict robbers,* who rob primarily to support a very expensive habit. Some degree of planning is involved, but a weapon is not commonly used, with the result that there is a greater chance that physical force will be used.

4. *Alcoholic robbers,* who exhibit some of the characteristics of the addict and of the opportunist. They rob only to get money for an extra drink, or if the opportunity presents itself (e.g., another drinker encountered in the bathroom).

It is difficult to estimate which types are predominant. In terms of monetary loss, it is clear that the major loss occurs as a result of large robberies, probably by professionals. But in terms of actual physical harm to victims, it is probably the opportunists who are most prevalent. No studies have so far managed to analyze this aspect of robbery.

Summary

1. Rape is essentially an intraracial crime, although the black on white rape rate is much higher than the white on black rate; it is pre-

dominantly a stranger-to-stranger crime; alcohol is often involved on the part of both victim and offender; there is no clear relationship between the amount the victim resists and the degree of injury.

2. Rape is chiefly a planned rather than an explosive crime, although explosive kinds do occur.

3. Only a small proportion of convicted rapists have prior sex offense records, although a substantial number do have previous convictions for other crimes.

4. There are no psychological studies of rapists per se, so that it is open to question whether some or all rapists are "mentally ill."

5. Robbery is essentially an interracial, stranger-to-stranger crime, committed mostly on the streets by small groups of youths.

6. Weapons are an important aspect of robbery. Although the gun is the weapon most commonly used, it is also apparent that the victim is much more likely to be injured if the robber has no gun or other weapon.

7. Types of robbers that have been identified are: the professional, the opportunist, the addict, and the alcoholic. Once again, no psychological study has ever been conducted on robbery offenders, so we have no way of knowing the motivations, reasons, etc., associated with the robber's violence.

8. More than any others, these crimes of stranger-to-stranger, especially those of robbery in which persons are often either killed or seriously injured for trifling amounts of money, stimulate us to ask, "Why do people do such things?" We have seen throughout this book that there are many social and cultural reasons. One question that we have not so far addressed is: does the explanation for violence perhaps lie within each individual? The following section will try to answer this challenging question.

Part Four

Violence
from
Within

Born to Kill?

To simplify the task of explaining aggression at the individual level, one may view the problem of aggression in psychology as bedevilled by the classic inner/outer problem. At one extreme, aggression may be conceived of as some kind of internal state or process, whether chemical, physiological, or psychological, which exists as a kind of *disposition* regardless of the surrounding environmental factors. At the other extreme, it may be seen as a set of external, observable behaviors, which the researcher classifies as aggressive responses patterned in a consistent way, to particular stimuli that arise in the environment. The great challenge is to find a middle ground, to link the two together. In this chapter we shall look at mainly the inner process theories. In the following chapter we shall examine theories that have concentrated on external behavior patterns and those that have searched for a middle ground.

The Instinct of Aggression

An instinct may be defined as a set of behavior patterns which are innate, transmitted from one generation to the next, and usually elicited by some triggering mechanism in the environment or maturation factor within the particular animal. The word itself is very difficult to define, and there is today much disagreement about whether any instincts as such exist at all. Certainly psychologists in the 1950s preferred to refer to "drives" rather than "instincts," and today it must be said that many psychologists have discarded even these terms as not helpful in explaining human behavior. Probably the main reason for this has been the failure to isolate in the experimental laboratory specific drives in relation to specific behaviors. But, what is more important is that psychologists have more and more come to rely on cognitive aspects of man's behavior as the key to explaining his actions, rather than on the vague postulated drives or "inner states" that are so difficult to measure.

The modern trend in psychology towards explanations in terms of cognition is thrown up in stark contrast to the resurrection of the concept of instinct by the comparatively new discipline of ethology: the study of animal behavior in its natural habitat. The tension has further been exacerbated by the inclination of psychoanalysts to incorporate much of the thesis of ethology, and of ethologists to incorporate much of the thesis of psychoanalysis, since both have assumed the all-pervasiveness of two instincts: sex and aggression.[1]

The idea that man is naturally aggressive is perhaps the oldest characterization that man has made of himself over the ages. If one peruses the documents of most religions, one finds that they are full of exhortations to "love thy neighbor." None assume that man *naturally* loves his neighbor. It is a state of affairs that must be striven for. The conclusion that one must reach, therefore, is that since time immemorial, man has *believed* that he is *homo homini lupus*—a wolf to other men.

Whether in fact he has really been hostile throughout history we discussed in Chapter 2—and found partial support for the theory. But we may certainly ask the question, whether man is more aggressive than the lower animals. This is the question that the ethologists have addressed themselves to, and also, recently, the sociobiologists. The question is asked seriously, on the assumption that man has evolved through the lower species. Therefore, the argument is that by studying the aggressive behaviors of the lower species, one may make certain inferences about the functions of aggression in man. Much of the ethologists' argument therefore revolves around the close observation of similarities and differences between aggressive behavior in men as against that in animals.[2]

The general conclusion (but by no means agreed upon) by ethologists is that both man and animal possess the two instincts of "love" and of aggression, but that whereas in the lower species these instincts are expressed as innate behavior patterns that are largely unchangeable (although they do adapt and modify according to changing conditions over time, i.e., many generations), they are highly modifiable in man. Man's instinct to "love" is sometimes seen as merely an inhibitor to the instinct of aggression,[3] although some ethologists have insisted that the instinct to love is strong (or stronger) in its own right.[4] As evidence of this, they point to the many close community and family ties that man develops.

The argument continues to rage over whether aggression is the dominating drive in man, or whether it is love. Freud was the first to see clearly the symbiotic tension between love and hate. The dominance of the argument in the ethological literature about which is more dominant, seems to support Freud's thesis.

Another argument put forward by the ethologists is that, in contrast to the lower animals, man has no built-in inhibition to aggression against his own species. The ethologists point out that among animals, within-species aggression is rarely carried through to the point of destruction (but is, rather, ritualistic), whereas in man, killing other men appears to present no serious problem. The only animal species which appears similar to man in this case is the rat, which lives in close-knit families and tribes and will ferociously murder any strangers.[5]

The conclusion made by these ethologists is that it is the role of culture to provide inhibitory mechanisms against aggression. We have seen in Chapter 4 that it is by no means clear whether culture has inhibited aggression throughout the ages, or whether we in fact live in a culture disposed toward violence.

Aggressive Instinct and Survival

Because of the evolutionary perspective that ethologists maintain, they necessarily assume that instinctual behavior is behavior that is programmed for survival of the species, and, by implication, of the individual. The question arises: since aggression is by definition destructive, and since there are no natural inhibitions to aggression in man, what is the "good" of aggression, especially since it appears that man is capable of completely destroying his own species? Surely this aggressive instinct cannot be for survival?

The ethologists have given two answers to this question. One is to say that the direction in which man's aggressive instinct has evolved is an evolutionary "blind alley." There are many cases on record in which a particular species has not adapted to the changing conditions of the environment, and so has died out. Therefore, it may be, in the evolutionary plan, that man is not destined to survive.

The other answer is that it is precisely because of man's greater adaptiveness, his ability to initiate change, that he gets out of step with culture. That is, in the case of dinosaurs, the environment changed as a result of many factors, none of them of the dinosaur's making. In contrast, it is *man* who directly influences the environment, so that it follows that he has a greater chance of adapting, since he himself has made the changes to which he must adapt. The inference that can be made from this argument is that those who develop the inhibitory aspects of aggression are more likely to survive than those who do not.[6] This is a direct contradiction to the theory that it is only the more aggressive who survive, since they are more dominant.

Survival of the Fittest

Aldous Huxley popularized this extreme interpretation of Darwin, and people have hence developed the rationale that those born in the lower positions in life were meant to be so, and that those who were the toughest and meanest were those meant to survive. This allowed, at the turn of the nineteenth century, for a moral justification for a lack of consideration for the weak, since it was the latter's destiny not to survive.

Many experiments on animals (especially mice) have shown that it is indeed the more aggressive mice who are more likely to have more "wives," bear more children, and so produce more children who are aggressive and thus become more dominant. Certainly it is possible to breed mice and other animals so as to enhance their aggressiveness.[7] But these experiments are carried on in laboratory settings. If taken literally, the thesis would have to mean that in any natural "culture" of mice, because the more aggressive are more dominant (and responsible for more offspring who will be more aggressive), we would have to end up with a culture of incredibly aggressive mice, since those less aggressive would be naturally bred out. Of course, this does not occur. It assumes that aggression is a unidimensional trait passed on in particular genes. There is no evidence that ordinary (nonlaboratory) mice are becoming increasingly aggressive. Nor, for that matter, are any other animals. Nor is there any evidence that this applies to man. It is true that he is now able to destroy more with less effort (by pushing a button). But if anything, since there is less effort involved, one might conclude that man is no more aggressive than he was 200 years ago, maybe even substantially less so.

Finally, the evidence from breeding aggressive animals when applied to humans is hardly convincing, since it is the very nature of our society that it does not allow rule by the brute force of an individual. Technology and intelligence are able to transcend brute force. Dominance by aggression (as defined by brute force) in a society is typical of a primitive society, not a modern, complex society such as ours. Aggression is not easily seen as an adaptive mechanism for survival in modern society.

Can We Observe an Aggressive Instinct?

The model of aggression as instinct is not unlike that of electricity. One does not "see" electricity. Yet we know that it flows along wires, can be switched on and off, and can be stored. And we certainly know it if we touch it! In much the same way, the theorists of instinct have viewed aggression as a kind of "fluid" that gets dammed up and has to be released. Thus, Freudians and Lorenzians will talk of such mechanisms as displacement, when a person or animal wishes to strike a love object, is inhibited from doing so, and instead will strike a close observer. The aggression has been displaced away from the truly desired object, onto a "scapegoat."[8]

What, precisely is it that is being "dammed up" inside? What precisely is it that must be released through socially acceptable channels such as violent sports? Can we open up the brain and find out where this aggression is?

To some extent we can. But when we do, instead of finding something called aggression, we find chemicals, molecules, electrical impulses, and cells. Professor Moyer has reviewed in great detail the neurological basis of aggression, and it is to that evidence that we must shortly turn.[9] But we may say at the outset that, although Professor Moyer concludes that some of the neurological evidence does support the idea of a building up of an "excitatory state" in various parts of the brain, which may precede aggressive behavior, he has found no evidence that this excitatory state *must* be released by aggression in order that it may be dissipated. The idea of its "damming up" therefore, is not supported biologically. But the idea that certain neural states which might be termed "drive states" occur within the brain, which might impel the individual to action, is supported.

The conclusion is that we cannot observe an instinct of aggression, because the concept of instinct is an abstraction, perhaps even a reification of an abstraction! But we can observe particular formations and functions of the brain as they relate to aggressive behavior.

Aggression and the Brain

It seems obvious that somewhere, somehow, the brain has to be the source of aggression, and of all other behavior for that matter. Scientists have studied the anatomy and physiology of the brain for a long time, so that we are now in a position to know generally what areas of the brain are related to what functions, including emotions such as fear and anger. The trouble is, we only know generally; and we do not know specifically how whatever goes on in the brain is related to the eventual expression of aggression.

We do know that it is definitely a physiological process. As one great psychologist, William James, said, emotion is the feeling of bodily change. We feel angry, and this makes us want to fight. Or we feel frustrated, so we want to hit out. These feelings are distinctly physiological in nature: butterflies in the stomach, rapid pulse, sweating, etc. It follows that if we want to "observe" anger or fear or pain, the supposed emotional sources of aggression, we should open up the brain and have a look.

There are generally three ways in which we can "observe" what goes on in the brain: (1) we can make lesions (by cutting various parts of the brain) and see what effects this has on behavior; (2) we can directly stimulate the brain using implanted electrodes; and (3) we can indirectly observe what goes on in the brain by means of looking at "brain waves," as measured by the electroencephalograph. All three methods are now widely used.

DIRECT STIMULATION BY ELECTRODES. This technique has been developed since 1952 and is now very widely used. There are patients who have as many as 125 electrodes implanted in the brain. The importance of this procedure is that the electrodes are very tiny, so that their location in the brain can be more precisely determined than is the case with lesions, which tend comparatively to be gross. We should be clear, however, that the electrical impulses imparted to the brain by this method are quite different from the natural electrical impulses in the brain itself. Furthermore, little is known of the way in which the various locations of the brain are interconnected, so that stimulating the electrode may well be like throwing a brick in a pond so that the waves affect a distant lily pad.[10] Be that as it may, some striking results have been obtained. Many experimenters have been able to evoke a wide variety of emotional states in patients: fear, terror, rage, "drunken euphoria," restlessness, sadness, depression, and orgiastic responses. One of the more interesting findings has been that both fear and anger can be evoked by stimulation of the same area of the brain. Thus far, it has been possible to locate general areas relating to fear, anger, and pain.[11]

It has also been possible to evoke aggressive reactions that appeared to be unmixed with other emotional reactions. A colorful case is described by Professor Moyer:[12]

Julia was a 22-year-old girl with a history of brain disease that evidently began with an attack of encephalitis before she was 2 years old. She had seizures with brief losses of consciousness, staring, lip smacking and chewing, frequently ending in a state of fugue in which she would find herself in a strange neighborhood alone and confused. Between seizures she showed severe temper tantrums, which were usually followed by intense remorse. On 12 different occasions Julia seriously assaulted people without apparent provocation. These included a near-fatal stabbing of a girl in the heart and an attack on a nurse in which she plunged scissors into the woman's lung. Julia had received extensive treatment, including psychotherapy, antiseizure medication, and a variety of other drugs. Finally, she was subjected to a course of 60 electroshock treatments. None of these treatments resulted in any improvement in either her seizure pattern or her assaultive behavior. An array of 20 electrodes was chronically implanted in each temporal lobe, and over a period of time each electrode was stimulated in an attempt to duplicate her seizure pattern so that the appropriate area could be lesioned. These stimulations were carried out in the laboratory setting while her electrodes were connected to recording and stimulating equipment. In this situation she showed neither seizure activity nor hostile behavior. Only a "racing, restless" feeling was produced, which was typical of her preseizure response.

Later, however, Julia's electrodes were connected to a stimulo-receiver that could be activated remotely without attached wires. It was then possible to stimulate in the depths of the temporal lobe as well as record from it without connecting wires and in a natural setting. In one instance stimulation of the hippocampus, while she was talking to her psychiatrist, resulted in gradually increasing EEG and clinical abnormalities. Over a period of several seconds after the termination of the stimulation, she lost responsiveness to the examiner and suddenly began furiously to attack the wall with her fist. The attack coincided with bursts of high-voltage, spikelike EEG tracings from the right hippocampus and amygdala. In another instance stimulation was applied to the amygdala while she was playing a guitar and singing for her psychiatrist. Again, after a buildup lasting a few seconds, she lost contact, stared ahead blankly, and was unable to answer questions. Then, during a storm of sub-cortical electrical activity, she swung her guitar just past the head of the psychiatrist and smashed it against the wall.

BRAIN LESIONS. The most impressive evidence for the relationship of particular "goings-on" in the brain and aggression come from a number of cases (and subsequent extensive research) of persons who were extremely assaultive, and were later, under autopsy, found to have brain tumors or malformations in various parts of the brain. The most famous case of this kind was that of Charles Whitman, the maniac who shot and killed 14 innocent people from the Texas University Tower. From his own report, it appears that Charles Whitman was "driven" to kill by impulses or thoughts that he could not control. The neurologist would say that he suffered from "excessive activation of the neural systems of hostility."[13]

Autopsy revealed that Whitman had a malignant infiltrating tumor (glioblastoma multiforme), probably in the temporal lobe region. However, because of extensive damage by gunshot wounds, it was difficult to make any truly firm conclusions, and indeed some have insisted that it could not have been the tumor that caused Whitman's aggression, since he planned his killings so carefully. But it is again pointed out that Whitman's behavior was one of gradual change as the tumor progressed. There are many cases on record where excessive aggressivity has been relieved by excision of tumors from various parts of the brain. It is therefore difficult to escape the conclusion that aggression can be activated by an internal physiological process, and that there are specific neurological mechanisms that control aggression. Professor Delgado has demonstrated the latter possibility by implanting electrodes in the brain of a bull, so that when it was in the middle of a charge, he was able to stop it abruptly in its tracks by stimulation through the implanted electrodes. There are a few human cases in which stimulation of some areas of the brain has inhibited aggression. Delgado and his associates report one case of a man whose physical attacks on other members of his family were considerably reduced by repeated stimulation of the amygdaloid nucleus.[14]

There are also a number of diseases, either of the brain or indirectly affecting the brain, that cause brain damage which appears to result in higher aggressivity. These are rabies, certain types of encephalitis, the Lesch-Nyham syndrome (very rare, only 100 identified cases in the whole world), and certain limited types of epilepsy.

ABNORMAL EEG (ELECTROENCEPHALOGRAM) AND AGGRESSION. A number of studies have found that some persons diagnosed as "psychopaths" have abnormal EEG patterns compared with the normal population. In one study of 64 English murderers, 73% of those who murdered without apparent motive showed EEG abnormalities. However, just what an abnormal EEG signifies is another question. It has been shown to be related to pressure caused by brain lesions and tumors,[15] but by no means always, or even often. The fact is, we know too little. The abnormal patterns could mean that there is direct damage to the neural systems related to aggression. But it might also mean damage to the systems that inhibit aggression. Or, it might be evidence of a generally lowered level of neurological competence.

We may make a number of definite conclusions, however.

1. There are neural systems in the brain which are related to or which mediate aggressive behavior.

2. There are neural systems in the brain which also inhibit aggressive behavior.

3. Certain types of uncontrollable aggression can be and have been eliminated by certain lesions in the brain.

4. Aggression can result from internal physiological causes largely unrelated to the outside stimulus situation. This is mainly linked to the presence of tumors and other diseases that directly affect brain physiology.

It is apparent, however, that there is another source of aggression that, one might say, is "inside the body"; this is the chemical basis of behavior—for instance, blood chemistry and glandular changes.

The Chemical Basis of Aggression

In Chapter 5 we considered briefly the biological basis of the differences in aggression between males and females, the role that estrogens and androgens play. These observations have to do with different classes of persons (i.e., males as against females); they do not primarily attempt to assess the individual aspects of aggression, unless of course, it is found that an aggressor is abnormally high in androgen.

The important factor to be considered here, however, is that drastic changes in drug levels in the person's bloodstream change each person's subjective experience. Thus, different individuals will interpret their internal drug changes differently according to their experience. This is why taking drugs (whether alcohol, nicotine, LSD, or marijuana) requires a period of learning and adaptation.[16]

AGGRESSION AND ALCOHOL. The most obvious drug that is widely believed to be related to aggression is alcohol. Indeed, in a well known Philadelphia study of homicide, 64% of cases involved alcohol.[17] And in a study of rape, one third of both victims and offenders had been drinking.[18] But the way in which alcohol is related to aggression is difficult to interpret; especially since many studies have shown that drinking alcohol brings on increases in happiness, self-satisfaction and relaxation, and makes people less irritable.[19]

However, there have also been studies in which it was noted that subjects went through an early stage of low aggression, but, after six drinks (86-proof alcoholic beverage), displayed increased aggression. There was wide individual variability in all three studies, but the general finding was that greater consumption of alcohol produced correspondingly stronger hostile feelings.[20]

It must be realized, of course, that the taking of alcohol is heavily embedded in cultural mores concerning its appropriateness. There may be a view in some subcultures that an individual is not responsible for his actions if drunk, so that the social barriers against "freaking out" may be much less. Physiological aspects may also combine with social factors. Assaults between family members or drinking companions may more easily erupt if the inhibitions against saying nasty things to each other are lifted by alcohol. And laboratory studies have shown that alcohol decreases inhibitions.

Pathological intoxication may also be a factor in aggression. It appears that some individuals have a pathological reaction to alcohol, resulting in maniacal outbursts and extreme aggression:[21]

> A 27-year-old male had been perfectly normal until the age of twenty-three years, when a craniocerebral injury resulted in a right temporal skull fracture and an associated period of unconsciousness. Subsequently, following the ingestion of even a minor amount of alcohol he became belligerent, confused, and destructive. On one occasion, the patient had two cocktails five minutes before he walked into a liquor store to purchase additional liquor. On being refused the sale of the liquor he went into a rage, and the salesman attempted to subdue him. The patient picked up a knife from the counter and stabbed the salesman several times. He was overcome by several bystanders before the police arrived. The salesman was dead on arrival of the ambulance. An alcohol-activation electroencephalogram was requested by the public defender. The routine study showed generalized instability and isolated short spikes in the right anterior temporal area (region of the skull fracture). Following alcohol-activation, profuse spikes were recorded in the right anterior temporal area with spreading to the right parietal and temporal areas.

DRUGS AND AGGRESSION. Amphetamines and their various derivatives are widely used as stimulants to the nervous system. These drugs have the paradoxical effect of reducing aggression in children, yet when given in large doses to adults they may precipitate violent aggressive rages. This effect is especially heightened if the drug is taken intravenously. Upon injection, the person feels the "rush" of euphoria, but over several hours the feeling dissipates into anxiety and irritability. If this procedure is continued over a number of days, the "downer" which follows may be severe and may be accompanied by extreme aggression. Some have suggested that the subculture of methamphetamine users ("speed freaks") is a violent subculture because of this fact. The question of just how violent drug subcultures are, however, is one that is raising considerable debate right now. Certainly, violence would occur more readily, since another side effect of methamphetamines is paranoid panic. A case was reported in 1971, for example, of a 27-year-old truck driver who believed his boss was trying to kill him with poisonous gas. He shot his boss dead, and it was subsequently discovered that the truck driver had been on an amphetamine run for a 20-hour period in an effort to complete a 1,600 mile trip nonstop.[22]

AGGRESSIVE ALLERGY. Specific allergens may bring on aggressive episodes. The case described by Professor Moyer is perhaps similar to pathological intoxication in its abruptness of onset:[23]

> You wouldn't believe bananas. Within twenty minutes of eating a banana this child would be in the worst temper tantrum—no seizures—you have ever seen. I tried this five times because I couldn't believe my own eyes. He reacted with behavior to all sugars except maple sugar. We went to California the Christmas of 1962 to be with my parents. Robbie's Christmas treats were all made from maple sugar. He was asking for some other candy. My mother wanted him to have it and I told her allright if she wanted to take care of the tantrum. Of course, she didn't believe me but predictably within thirty minutes she had her hands full with Robbie in a tantrum. It made a believer of her. These discussions did not take place in front of the child if you're wondering about the power of suggestion.
> If you go into this food reaction thing it will make you feel so sorry for people you can't stand it. After bad behavior from food, Robbie would cry and say he couldn't help it and feel so badly about it. You won't be able to read of a Crime of Violence without wondering if a chemical reaction controlled the aggressor—in fact, you'll be unable to condemn anyone for anything. . . .

Although there are few documented cases as serious as that of the banana boy, there are certainly many clinical reports of reactions of irritability, combativeness, anger, violent temper, paranoia, peevishness, and many others occurring in response to particular allergens. Some have suggested that these allergic reactions may be related to minimal brain damage or malfunction, probably temporary swelling in particular parts of the brain. But it must be said that the evidence for the relationship between extreme allergies and aggression consists largely of case studies, and that no experimentally controlled studies have yet been conducted to demonstrate the causal connection.

AGGRESSION AND LOW BLOOD SUGAR. Unlike other organs of the body, the brain is unable to convert glycogen to glucose when the need arises. It is therefore completely dependent on the blood stream for its glucose supply. Thus, if the blood sugar level decreases, there may be brain malfunction, which may lead to aggressive behavior. Low blood sugar is accompanied by faintness, fatigue, dizziness, and irritability. Some have estimated that there are 10–30 million persons in the United States suffering from low blood sugar.[24] The hypothesis is that increased irritability makes it easier for individuals to get into fights.

The "illness" may be caused by tumors in the pancreas or abnormal endocrine secretions which result in excessively high levels of insulin secretion. In this case (as may happen with diabetics who must manually maintain the level of blood sugar by injecting themselves with insulin) the person may become excessively or uncontrollably aggressive. However, this type of aggression can easily be controlled by feeding the person a little sugar.[25]

Summary

1. The work of ethologists argues that man is "driven" by an instinct of aggression in the same way as are most animal species. However, since it is man's culture that provides the inhibitions against aggression, it follows that the more "cultured" man will survive, rather than the most aggressive.

2. Although in animals, the most aggressive tends to be the most dominant, and it is possible to breed aggressive strains of mice, there is nevertheless no conclusive evidence to support the idea that from an evolutionary point of view, only the aggressive survive.

3. There is no physiological evidence for a general instinct of aggression, but there is evidence that specific "excitatory states" occur which might impel an individual to action.

4. It is conclusively established that some forms of aggression may be either elicited or inhibited by direct stimulation of the brain either through implanted electrodes or lesions.

5. It is likely that some forms of aggression (how much, we do not know) may originate from internal physiological causes largely unrelated to outside stimuli.

6. There is probably a chemical basis for some forms of aggression, especially where alcohol is involved, but the relationship is as yet unclear.

7. *Born Killers:* It stands to reason that, if it can be shown that there are specific neural systems (i.e., brain cells interconnected in patterns and processes as yet not understood), just as there are specific physical attributes such as eye color, height, skin color, and so on, it is quite likely that the physiological bases for these neural processes may also be inherited. We are quite certain that many, many, physical attributes are inherited through the genes. Why not brain cells too?

Until recently, the view of criminologists was quite definite that personality characteristics such as aggression were *not* inherited, but learned. It has long been accepted in American criminology that all criminal behavior is learned. This seems a bit farfetched to me, and it is simplistic as well. There are two main reasons for my view. The first is that intelligence—an attribute of the mind—has quite definitely been shown to be at least partly inherited; to what extent we do not know, and it probably does not make much sense to make such an estimate.* In any event, there is a good chance that at least some attributes of the mind are inherited. Further, other work has recently suggested that some forms of schizophrenia may also be partly inherited.[26] Certainly, if we view mental illness as based upon physiological and anatomical structures of the body, there appears to be no alternative to accepting the possibility that some people may be born with a physiology that is likely to predispose them (or even in some rare cases determine them) to become killers.

8. *A Word of Caution:* It should be emphasized that although we have reviewed so far many physiological factors that appear to be related in one way to aggression, the ways in which they are related remain, basically, mysterious. They are most often (including even the cases of direct brain stimulation) mediated in some way by environmental factors, or by factors of the person's prior experience. The results are highly variable among individuals (and among animals too). They should therefore be accepted for what they are. That there is a relationship between physiology and aggression is clear, but the nature of the relationship is largely speculative. Nevertheless, Professor Moyer, after an exhaustive review of the research in this area, feels confident in con-

* I make this argument in spite of the fact that this view has been damaged by the scandal over Cyril Burt's apparently fraudulent twin studies. The case can be, and has been, made just as well without Burt's data.

cluding that "the general weight of the evidence seems to indicate that man, for all his encephalization, has not escaped from the biological determinants of his hostility."[27]

Of course, it is not that simple either. You can't be "born" a particular anything. We know very well from many research studies that physiology, especially neural functioning, does not reach its full potential unless there are certain environmental conditions that will allow its development. It is upon this developmental aspect of human behaviors that psychiatrists depend heavily to explain "what goes on in the mind" and subsequently to explain why a person aggresses, or does not aggress. It is to this that we must now turn.

The Dynamics of Violence

The Mind and Early Experience

Theorists who adhere to a *maturational* view of psychological development argue that the blueprint for particular developmental stages is laid down genetically and no amount of environmental training will affect it. Thus, many experiments have been conducted in which one group of young children has received, say, training in walking skills, and a control group has not. Those without previous training walk just as soon as those with training.[1]

Experiments have also shown that extreme deprivation at an early age (whether of sustenance, "love," or even painful stimuli) may have far-reaching effects: to the extent that lasting neurological damage occurs.[2] Some very striking examples of the importance of environmental conditions for the proper development of genetic blueprints are seen in the "wolf" boys (feral children) who, through some accident of circumstance, have been reared completely apart from humans by animals.[3] One child, discovered when he was around ten years old, (the wild boy of Aveyron) never learned to do even the simplest of human tasks, and learned only a few words in a human tongue, in spite of attempts at intense individual instruction.[4]

Thus, although enhancing the environment of a young child may not necessarily improve or overcome any inherent genetic predisposition, severely limiting his environment may have deleterious and lasting effects. Therefore, we should expect that those persons found to be severely aggressive may also have early histories of severe deprivation.

A number of studies suggest that this may be so for some, but they are inconclusive.[5] Certainly, in the case of murderers statistics show that the proportion of those who were reared in institutions (commonly assumed to be equivalent to severe deprivation) is higher than that of the normal population.

Psychiatrists who are psychoanalytically inclined, when writing about killers or violent individuals invariably place great importance upon early childhood experience. It is thought that the mind of the murderer is a product of what has happened to him or to her as a child, and this of course, involves his or her parents and siblings. Though we have looked at the various family dynamics that are said to be related to aggression in Chapter 6, we have said very little so far about that central concept in psychoanalysis through which all past experience is mediated and in which it is stored—the unconscious.

Very briefly, the psychoanalytic argument runs as follows. Our lives are dominated by two drives—sex and aggression—which, although naturally closely related or even indistinguishable in the young child, become gradually differentiated in the adult. The growing person, through experience of rewards and punishments from the external world, learns to channel and control his drives for sex and aggression in ways acceptable to society. Because these drives are so strong, it requires a great deal of "mental effort" to deal with their never ceasing demands.

This mental effort is both enhanced and challenged at particular crisis periods during the individual's development. The child by the age of three or so, has developed an attachment to his or her parents which the Freudians see as essentially sexual. He or she also develops strong aggressive urges against whoever competes with him or her for the attachment to the particular parental object. Thus, conflict arises, and the urge to kill one's parent is extremely great, but is so devastating a solution that the child "represses" it—i.e., "forgets" these urges. They remain in the unconscious. This repression is made possible by the child's incorporating, or introjecting, the attributes of the parent (usually the one with whom he or she competes) so that societal values as displayed by the parent become a part of the child's mind. These become largely unconscious and make up what we call the conscience. This is the basis of guilt.

Conflict is very great at this stage, and since the urges of sex and aggression are so strong, the chances of something going wrong with this whole process are considerable. If the parents either wittingly or unwittingly act in an extreme way—e.g., have sexual intercourse in front of the young child; unmercifully beat the child; fail at the other extreme to discipline the child; and a host of other possibly disturbing things—

the child's mind will become confused, its development possibly arrested (it may even return to an earlier stage of development), and the all-demanding urges of sex and aggression may bubble up to the surface.

Although I have oversimplified the theory, because of pressure of space, the bare bones of it remain. The result, if anything goes wrong with psychological development, is confusion, irresistible impulses, low regard for the self (i.e., poor self-esteem), lack of identity ("Half the time I don't know who I am, or what I'm supposed to be like"), and many more. Dr. Abrahamsen has concluded after his many years of practice as a psychoanalytic psychiatrist with severely assaultive patients that the most common characteristics of a murderer are:[6]

1. Extreme feelings of revenge and fantasies of grandiose accomplishments which may result in the acting out of hateful impulses.
2. Loneliness, withdrawal, feelings of distrust, helplessness, fears, insignificance, loss of self-esteem, caused by early (pre-Oedipal) childhood experiences.
3. Sexually overstimulating family situation because of primal-scene experiences.
4. Errors of spelling or speech related to emotional disturbances in early (pre-Oedipal) childhood.
5. Tendency toward transforming identification. Blurred self-image; suggestibility, impressionableness.
6. Inability to withstand frustration and to find sufficient gratification by expressing hostile aggressive feelings through constructive outlets.
7. Inability to change persistent egocentricity, self-centeredness (primitive narcissism) into elements of healthy ideals and conscience (ego ideals and superego elements), resulting in dependency on and contempt for authority.
8. Suicidal tendencies, with depression.
9. Seeing the victim as the composite picture of murderer's self-image.
10. History of previous antisocial or criminal act associated with threatening or committing murder.

The trouble with all of this, and Abrahamsen admits it too, is that these attributes, and the experiences outlined above, may be common to many, many people most of whom do *not* become aggressive or kill people. In fact, Abrahamsen and most other psychoanalysts argue that we *all* feel urges to kill at times, yet only a very few "give in" to this urge.

The fact that aggression is an observable behavioral phenomenon in *all* persons has led psychologists to seek general explanations of aggression by studying normal individuals. An enormous amount of research material has accumulated in just two decades, so I will present in what follows only the essential elements of the various approaches.

Aggression and Emotion

People who from time to time cry at the slightest provocation or who smash things when annoyed are often characterized as "emotional" people. It is clear that there is a close relationship between the emotions and aggression. It is, however, entirely unclear which emotions are more related to aggression than others, nor is it clear whether they precede or follow aggressive behavior. Emotions such as anxiety, fear, and rage may all act differentially in aggression.[7]

Anxiety may occur *after* a person has committed a violent act, or it may be because of an intolerable state of anxiety that a person finally "freaks out." Also unclear is the extent to which the emotions are "triggered" by some kind of external stimulus (e.g., like a "red flag to a bull") or whether in fact a person must consciously work on his emotions (e.g., "whip himself into a rage"). It is likely that both conditions operate from time to time. But the differential conditions under which emotions lead to or follow aggression have not yet been well defined, although as we shall see below, considerable research has been conducted in this area.

It is probably fair to say that, whereas it used to be held that either the emotions "automatically" erupted to produce aggression—usually as the result of external stimuli or as a function of a particular personality trait (e.g., the person with a "terrible temper")—it is now conceded that external stimuli (and internal stimuli for that matter) are cognitively processed by the individual. That is, he must first interpret the situation around him as "threatening" or as some other condition, before his emotions are aroused, and he must also interpret his internal state (i.e., his emotions) before he proceeds to express aggressive behavior on the basis of his emotions.

But we have gotten ahead of ourselves. The first comprehensive theory of aggression to be developed and tested, almost ad nauseam, was frustration-aggression theory, which derived many of its basic postulates from Freudian theory. First stated in a classic monograph in 1939, by Dollard, et al.,[8] this theory has been, and perhaps even continues to be, the most dominant psychological theory of aggression.

Frustration and Aggression

The original definition of frustration was: "an interference with the occurrence of an instigated goal-response at its proper time in a behavior sequence."[9] Translated, this means that frustration occurs when something or someone intervenes just as one has begun to reach for what one wants. The early formulation, derived from Freud, would have said that one had a "drive" which directed one's behavior to a specific goal with the result that the drive would be consummated. Depending upon one's learning theory model, it could be the goal that "instigated" the drive. In any event, frustration-aggression theory depends entirely on the idea that behavior is directed towards a particular end, and the observable behaviors which achieve this particular end are called a "behavior sequence." An interference with this behavior sequence "at the proper time"—that is, at a significant point when one is presumably almost at the point of reaching the goal, is a frustration. The following example based on Dollard, et al. illustrates the theory clearly: Johnny hears the bell of an ice-cream vendor, which *instigates* all kinds of behaviors relating to the delights of ice cream. He runs to his mother, pulling her to the door, asking her to buy him an ice-cream cone. These are goal-directed behavior sequences. Johnny gets as far as the door, sees the cart, his mother says "No," the vendor drives off, Johnny gets angry and hits his mother. In this case, the source of frustration was *external;* the mother said "No."

The source of frustration may also be internal. Suppose instead that the boy runs to his piggy bank to get the money, shakes it out, gets as far as the door, but remembers that he is saving up for a new baseball glove and that he should save his money. He sees the vendor drive off, says, "Oh shucks!" and kicks the dog. The frustration was the interference of a different goal-directed activity (i.e., wanting a baseball glove), and was essentially internal, or "self-instigated." Some would term the latter example a situation of "conflict" and indeed some theorists have argued that there is no essential difference between conflict and frustration. Two such theorists, Brown and Farber, defined four frustrating conditions as follows:[10]

1. Physical barriers
2. Delays between initiation and completion of a response sequence
3. Omission or reduction of a customary reward
4. Eliciting of a response tendency that is incompatible with the ongoing one

Are we to take these as definitions of frustration or as definitions of conditions that lead to frustration? Although the above theorists preferred to define frustration as an hypothesized internal state, we can see very easily that if one wished to be a "conservative" theorist, not depending on hypothetical internal states of the mind or body, one could simply define this condition in terms of situations of frustration and leave it at that. One then simply studies the relationships between these conditions, behavior sequences, and subsequent reactions to these conditions. We see here the old problem of "inner versus outer" that psychology has faced for many years, and it is not our place to attempt a solution to this conceptual puzzle.

But the distinction is important, according to the most ardent revisionist of frustration-aggression theory, Leonard Berkowitz,[11] because, as he points out, Dollard's work claimed that aggression will always be directed towards the source of the frustration. This idea opens up all sorts of complications but also some possible interesting explanations.

If we return to Fanon's Manichaean psychology, for example, it may explain why, initially, the natives fight amongst themselves rather than against the external source of frustration, the colonialists. One might reformulate the theory in this way. The goal for the black man is to be free of oppression by the colonialist. But he cannot achieve the goal because (1) the colonialist has the command of physical force and so thwarts any attempt to break free—he is the external source of frustration; and (2) the black man has been taught that he is incapable of rising up on his own behalf, that he is lazy and stupid. The problem, as Marxists would say, is one of "consciousness," and the internal source of frustration is the black man's self image as incapable. One would therefore expect either one or both reactions to frustration: either mass suicide on the part of the blacks because of the self-hatred generated by the internal source of frustration; or mass slaughter carried out against the colonialist because he is the external source of frustration. But rising up against the colonialist is simply not a possible response since it is totally thwarted by the monopoly on force held by the colonialist and by the black man's lack of consciousness of himself as a human being. Why not mass suicide? The facts in the United States, as we saw in Chapter 4, are that whites have a generally higher suicide rate than blacks, but that blacks have a much higher homicide rate. Yet most black homicides are committed against other blacks, not against whites whom frustration-aggression theorists would identify as the external source of frustration. How to solve the puzzle?

There are two interrelated solutions. One is that aggression against the self may be *displaced* onto objects most similar to one's self, such as other blacks. The process of displacement of aggression, also of psychoanalytic origin, has been researched extensively and is a commonly observed phenomenon. And it has been especially the psychoanalytic argument that aggression cannot be released against a potentially dangerous object. The second, and this is actually very similar to the first solution, is that since in the Manichaean world each native is stereotyped into having exactly the same identity as every other native, self-hatred becomes hatred of one's cultural group. Thus, aggression against other blacks is simply the cultural expression of aggression against the self.[12]

There are many, many variations of frustration-aggression theory, but those that I have outlined do, I think, illustrate its essential ingredients. The major changes that it has undergone are these:

1. In the original Freudian conception it was believed that the relationship between frustration and aggression was innate.[13]

2. Subsequent laboratory experiments supported this conception because it was claimed that aggression was always the consequence of frustration.[14]

3. Many studies conducted on fish, rats, other animals, and children then showed that a wide variety of responses may result from frustration (such as regression) and that aggression was *not* the only response.[15]

4. The theory was reformulated to recognize that aggression may be a *learned* response to frustration, so that the relationship was not innate.[16]

5. The further conclusion was made that although frustration may lead to more vigorous responding by the individual, vigor was not necessarily translated by the individual into aggressive behavior.[17]

The many reformulations to which the frustration-aggression theory has been subjected have led to the suspicion that perhaps it is trying to explain too much. Certainly, much of the criticism of frustration-aggression theory has to do with disagreements over what is frustration and what is not, and what it is that is being frustrated.

For example, in his well-known criticism of the theory, Karl Menninger argued that the theory was "nonsensical" because, he said, "anyone who has had his toe stepped on, which is certainly not a frustration, knows how inadequate such a formula is."[18] Berkowitz replied to this criticism by trying to show how having one's toe stepped on was an interference with goal-directed activity.[19] Menninger's definition of frustration, according to Berkowitz, was too narrow. One suspects, however, that it may be that Berkowitz's is too broad.

The recognition that aggression may be a *learned* response and that it was not automatic to frustration, led to research aimed at identifying aggression that may be not only learned, but also specifically chosen to achieve a particular goal. This was called instrumental aggression.

Instrumental Aggression

The fine line between instrumental aggression and aggression in response to frustration is difficult to draw. A child may have been promised a lollipop for being good at the dentist's. He is not given the candy, so he throws a tantrum and lashes out at his mother. Mother is embarrassed, so gives the child a lollipop. The frustration-aggression hypothesis would say that the child has become aggressive as a result of frustration. But the instrumental theory would say that the child has learned that by using aggression he can get what he wants. Much laboratory research on both animals and humans has demonstrated conclusively that aggression is closely related to instrumental behavior,[20] and, as usual, there are many, many variations on the theme, many of which are incorporated into the body of research called social learning theory, which I outlined in Chapters 6 and 7.

One type of instrumental aggression, however, is suggested by Berkowitz which represents, perhaps, the prototype of the "cold-blooded calculated murder." He describes the behavior of airmen during World War II as instrumental aggression in the sense that "many airmen had not the slightest anger toward their civilian victims," so that "aggression was carried out coldly and deliberately as a matter of policy. It was *instrumental aggression* in the sense that the behavior was oriented toward the attainment of some goal other than doing injury (such as winning the war)."[21] By this formulation, we can easily see that the aggression of most of the terrorists that I described in Chapter 1 would be classified as instrumental. On the other hand, killing one's wife because she burned the dinner would be more easily explained by frustration-aggression theory. Killing one's husband's mistress might be a mixture of both.

In any event, the problem that faces us here is the extent to which conscious choice or reason is involved in aggression, as against the more expressive aspects of behavior such as the emotions of anger, hate, and rage. There are a number of ways in which researchers have suggested that aggression may be a "rational response."

Aggression and Rationality

Dr. Seymour Halleck has argued that aggression (and crime generally) may be viewed as an adaptive response.[22] Aggression may be a rational "choice" of behavior, given the situation (both within and external to the individual) in which the person finds himself. This type of aggression is a little different from that described above as instrumental aggression, since it emphasizes aggression as a solution to prevailing situational conditions, and is not directed towards a specific goal. It is, rather, an *adaptation.*

Briefly, the theory first clearly articulated by Karl Menninger[23] argues that the body (which for most psychiatrists includes physical as well as mental processes) must maintain a consistent, ongoing state of equilibrium which it does through the process of *homeostasis.* There are many variations of this theory, but the general point is that man must maintain a "vital balance" among the various psychological, chemical, and physical attributes within himself, as well as between these inner aspects and the external world. The simplest example of the inner-outer balance is that of putting on an extra sweater if a room suddenly becomes cold. If there were no extra sweater available one might attempt to adapt internally by imagining one is in a desert. The extent to which one is unable to make this adaptation is a measure of the stress that one is feeling. The aim of adaptation is to eliminate stress.[24]

We can see that, in part, this model is not unlike the frustration-aggression theory, with the essential difference that whereas the frustration-aggression theorists posit a drive as the basis of goal-directed behavior which is interfered with, the adaptation theorist posits the goal to be one of homeostasis, or balance. Both the theories, it seems to me, see aggression as an attempt to "make up for" an excitation that occurs because a customary way of behaving has been interfered with. For the adaptation theorist, "stress" is the hypothetical internal state variable; for the frustration-aggression theorist, "frustration" is the hypothetical internal state variable. And both schools of research, it turns out, have had similar arguments about whether their respective terms "stress" or "frustration" are "internal" or "external."[25]

A further difference between the two theories is that the concepts of homeostasis and adaptation, although originating with concepts of physiological stress, have been extended by psychiatrists to apply equally to psychological stress, and because of the somewhat abstract and vague meaning of these words, it has been easy enough to introduce a heavy cognitive element into the theory—namely, that persons who feel stress will purposefully choose certain behaviors that will help them to adapt.[26] Once again, we should recognize that the frustration-aggression theory can be and has been reformulated to take cognitive aspects into account (especially in relation to perception of sources of aggression, selection of targets of aggression) but it must be said that the general emphasis of the theory has been more on aggression as an emotional or expressive response to frustration.[27]

As used by Dr. Halleck, stress theory as it relates to aggression as adaptation posits a more cognitive way of solving imbalance. Dr. Halleck observes that there are a number of sources of stress which may be solved by criminal or aggressive behavior, especially in the sense that aggressive behavior has a very direct effect on the environment, so that it may very quickly correct imbalance. He recounts six main sources of stress and their concomitant criminal adaptations:[28]

1. Stress arises from external oppression—the criminal's feelings of powerlessness. The planning and carrying out of a crime offers immediate hope, a moment of autonomy. Thus, an aggressive act (what more autonomous act could there be than the killing of another person?—it is in a way the ultimate in personal power) is an adaptation to the feeling of powerlessness.

2. Stress occurs as the result of boredom. Juvenile delinquents especially have been observed to suffer this supposed cultural malaise. Crime offers excitement. A serious malaise may be corrected by a serious act of aggression done "for kicks." One is reminded of the occasional newspaper headlines one sees: YOUTHS DRENCH WOMAN WITH GASOLINE, TORCH HER TO DEATH.[29]

3. Stress occurs if one's conscience becomes too heavy a burden. Persons with such consciences seem to suffer excessively under what most would consider to be ordinary conditions. They are sometimes termed "over-controlled" personalities. Professor Megargee[30] has reviewed and researched this type of aggressor, and, although it is apparent that this type is in the minority as far as aggressors go, it at least explains the often baffling reports of a "gentle, easygoing, good-natured young man who suddenly kills, for no ostensible reason, three unarmed victims during a bank robbery," or a "mild and loving person" who shoots his twin sister. The inhibition of aggression builds up so long that finally it erupts. This model is closest to the frustration-aggression model, which asserts that aggression, if not released, "dams up" over time. The aggressive act, therefore, is an adaptive response to extreme internal stress.

4. Stress may occur if the aggressor comes to think "there is something wrong with me." By directing hostility outwards, especially through violent behavior, the external environment will usually react in no uncertain terms. Thus, the individual is provided with an external source for his trouble: "It's them, not me."

5. Aggression may offer a good rationalization for inadequacy. "If only I didn't have such a bad temper, I would have kept my job."

There are many other ways in which aggression can be used as a "defense." These have been described by Dr. Fritz Redl in his fascinating work with children who hate, described in Chapter 8.[31] Dr. Redl combines psychoanalysis with just plain shrewdness to penetrate the unnerving behavior of extremely aggressive children. He postulates that these individuals often have extremely well developed egos, in the sense that they know how to use aggression to manipulate the external environment (especially to get grown-ups mad to the point of physically punishing them), and also to get the sort of responses out of those with whom they deal that will reinforce their perception of the world. For example, if a child throws a terrible tantrum, destroying furniture, physically hurting an adult supervisor, the adult responds aggressively (naturally enough) either verbally or physically, so that the child then says, "There you are, you see; I knew you didn't love me."

The manipulative and adaptive uses of aggression are countless, especially when used by an intelligent and perceptive individual. The self-perpetuating paradox of this situation, though, is well demonstrated.

Does Aggression Make Us Feel Good?

Usually this question is asked in order to learn whether aggression in and of itself is satisfying. The implication here is that aggression may be similar to other "needs" or "instincts" such as hunger, thirst, or sex, which make physiological (and psychological) demands upon us to the extent that they must be satisfied, or we suffer considerably, even perish. We saw in the previous chapter that the evidence thus far advanced to support the notion of an aggressive instinct is inconclusive, and what evidence there is derives largely from animal studies by the ethologists. However, we may also conceive of aggression's making us feel good, in terms of the theories just discussed, because the implication of these theories is that aggression is seen as a kind of "solution" or "resolution" of a situation. Aggression is seen as "satisfying" or "releasing" or neutralizing frustration, or simply as "giving vent" to strong emotional feelings, or as eliminating stress. In any event, the implication is that it is aggression that "solves" this state of affairs. The further implication is that this is a desirable state to be in—i.e., one in which stress or strong emotions are not dominant.

For instrumental aggression there is the same implication. Aggression is the instrument by which a desired goal is obtained. Therefore, it follows that aggression, if it is closely linked to the attainment of the goal, will "make us feel good" too. There is some research evidence that supports this view.[32]

Aggression and Personality

Many psychiatrists and psychologists would argue that there is no such thing as an "aggressive person."[33] People are simply not aggressive all the time, or even most of the time. Murdering someone, after all, only requires the time and effort it takes to pull the trigger of a gun. And with murders that are planned for weeks or even months (very rare types of murder) one could hardly term the behavior of *planning* aggressive. In fact it is just the opposite.

Psychiatrists, from their clinical experience, however, probably have formed an idea of what constitutes excessive aggressive behavior, in the sense of counting or taking note of past incidents of temper tantrums, fights, and so on. But no one has ever thought to research this question. How many aggressive encounters per year constitute an abnormally high level of aggression? Could we develop norms for the levels of aggressive behavior—in other species as well as humans? There is considerable disagreement about the comparative levels of aggression in men and animals.[34] Using the techniques of self-report studies in delinquency, this kind of research could perhaps develop estimates of levels of aggressive behavior that could be considered "normal" in humans.

In a way, personality tests try to do something similar. But they do not depend upon the individual's reporting his past behavior. Instead they rely on various projective techniques or the individual's responses to attitudinal or "belief" types of items. Some attempts have been made to establish or isolate the "aggressive personality," but it must be said that they lack any definitiveness. The general opinion at present, it is probably fair to say, is that aggression is not a single personality trait (or even a single neural process), but the result of a variety of different neural processes, drives, and personality attributes.

The work that comes closest to identifying an aggressive personality is one which has identified certain traits which, taken together, are said to be those of the "psychopath." This concept has a long and rather sordid history in the world of psychiatry and criminal justice, and has these days fallen into considerable disfavor among criminologists who are sociologically inclined. The main reasons for this disfavor are that the term has been used arbitrarily and vaguely, so that it has assumed a host of "multiple meanings,"[35] and, worse, it has been used punitively, to refer to the "pure criminal," the incorrigible, the one whom we should "lock up and throw away the key." The result was that some states for a time passed laws specifically identifying this type of criminal, so that he or she could indeed be locked up without a trial, or, if there was a trial, would be tried not so much for the crime that he or she had committed, but for being a particular type of person. The dangers to civil liberties inherent in such a procedure are quite obvious.[36]

But from a scientific point of view, I see no reason why we should throw out this concept, simply because legislatures and the criminal justice system are sometimes insensitive to issues of civil liberties. There is considerable consistency in the description of persons characterized as "psychopaths," since the early use of the term. The description of the type has, in my opinion, hardly changed; what has changed is the label: from "psychopath," to "ideopath" to "sociopath" to "antisocial personality"—as well as many other variations.

In 1930, the psychoanalyst Franz Alexander described the "pure criminal" as one who completely lacked guilt.[37] Prior to that time, persons who appeared to repeatedly and aimlessly break laws were seen as morally insane, Pinel himself suggesting that they were mentally ill. In 1956, McCord and McCord defined the psychopath as follows: "He is an anti-social, aggressive, highly impulsive person who feels little or no guilt and who is unable to form lasting bonds of affection with other human beings."[38]

I could recount many other descriptions that are basically similar to this one. The difficulties that have arisen are that in practice, those persons labelled as psychopaths turn out to be an amazingly variable lot—certainly not all or even mostly criminal, and certainly not all or even mostly mentally ill. But this is only a problem in practice. As a theoretical concept we can speak of the ideal "pure psychopath" whom we will probably never find in reality; psychopathy should be considered, according to Dr. Halleck, "to be a state which theoretically exists at one end of a continuum of behavior and personality traits."[39]

Now, if we put aside our concerns, for the moment, about whether psychopaths are mad or whether they are criminal, we can turn to further important evidence which supports Dr. Halleck's thesis of a continuum of psychopathy, for, if he is correct, we should be able to find aspects of this type in a large number of people that we would easily classify as "normal." It is here that the work of Professor Eysenck is of considerable relevance, both concerning the scientific assessment of personality and in linking personality traits to antisocial behavior.

Professor Eysenck begins by arguing that the human personality has two basic dimensions: neuroticism and introversion-extraversion. His argument is based on two solid pieces of evidence: that (1) historically (that is, at least as far back as the medieval period) students of personality have tended to divide the personality up into these traits, and (2) most of the empirical research (using personality tests) of the twentieth century has corroborated this basic typology. This typology produces four personality types, one of which is described as the "unstable extravert," who is characterized as "touchy, restless, aggressive, excitable, changeable, impulsive, optimistic, and active." And the pure extravert, as described by Eysenck:[40]

> needs to have people to talk to, and does not like reading or studying by himself. He craves excitement, takes chances, acts on the spur of the moment, and is generally an impulsive individual. He is fond of practical jokes, always has a ready answer, and generally likes change; he is carefree, easygoing, optimistic, and likes to "laugh and be merry". He prefers to keep moving and doing things, tends to be aggressive and loses his temper quickly; his feelings are not kept under tight control and he is not always a reliable person.

Having developed this typology of personality types, Eysenck then shows that extraverts are less easily conditionable than introverts, so that they do not learn from experience, are impulsive, and so on—just as his description of them suggests. He also points to the similarity of the description of his unstable extravert to that developed independently by Professor Harrison Gough, as part of his well-known work on personality assessment. The psychopath is described by Professor Harrison Gough as:[41]

> characterised by an over-evaluation of the immediate goals as opposed to remote or deferred ones; unconcern over the rights and privileges of others when recognising that they could interfere with personal satisfaction in any way; impulsive behavior, or apparent incongruity between the strength of the stimulus and the magnitude of the behavioural response; inability to form deep or persistent attachments to other persons or to identify in inter-personal relationships; poor judgment and planning in attaining defined goals; apparent lack of anxiety and distress over social maladjustment and unwillingness or inability to consider maladjustment as such; a tendency to project blame onto others and to take no responsibility for failures; meaningless prevarication, often about trivial matters in situations where detection is inevitable; almost complete lack of dependability and of willingness to assume responsibility; and finally, emotional poverty.

It is to be noted that Professor Eysenck's theory has come under attack from a number of quarters: some deny that there is any such type as "psychopathic personality"; many modern psychologists deny that there are any enduring personality traits in any one person—rather most people display aspects of traits at different times, depending on situational factors; and they maintain that there is certainly no such thing as an "aggressive personality" (by which we probably mean extraversion). The fact is that Professor Eysenck has not developed his theory upon the basis of clinical observations of psychopaths—a practice long criticized for its lack of experimental controls and bias in the clinician. Rather, he has marshalled a great deal of scientific evidence to support his contention that:

1. People are born with different neural systems, ranging from those that are easily conditionable to those not easily conditionable.
2. "Conscience" is the result of a long period of "combination and culmination of conditioning."
3. Those less easily conditionable are unstable extraverts.
4. Therefore, unstable extraverts (psychopaths) have weak consciences.
5. Psychopaths commit more crime (especially aggressive) than other personality types.

Professor Eysenck does not indulge in the often criticized practice of clinicians of looking at the internal dynamics of the mind (with the exception of his speculations regarding the function of neural systems in the brain). He bases his entire argument upon observations of consistencies and inconsistencies of observable behaviors—in the situation of pencil and paper personality tests, or in the laboratory conditions of learning experiments. Among other things, this means that Eysenck also must (and does) take into account the effects of the differential application of learning experience on the growing child. He does *not* deny the importance of environmental factors, but rather tries to show how they are related to the basic biological factors of personality. In this way, he is able to explain what many sociologists cannot: why it is that *most* children who grow up under the worst environmental conditions do not turn into criminals or aggressors. Eysenck posits the intervening variable of differentials in neural systems.

Many studies have been conducted which lend support to Eysenck's observations (which therefore strengthens his theory, although it does not directly test it). Studies applying the Rorschach and other personality tests to known murderers have generally concurred that the murderer, when compared with normal subjects, is characterized by "egocentrism and a lack of emotional control . . . explosive, immature, hyper-thymic . . . unable to establish social contact . . . deficit of conscious control . . . strong need for immediate gratification of impulses."[42]

However, it must be said that the question, whether the "aggressive personality" of those subjects caused their murdering behavior, is moot: none of the studies, obviously, administered their tests prior to the act of murder. We do not know, therefore, whether the syndrome of psycho-pathic personality is a cause or a result of the murderous act. Further-more, there have been many criticisms of the methodology involved, since only in a very few studies had the Rorschach tests been conducted "blind." That is, the analysis of the test has been done by people who already knew that the subject was a murderer.

Eysenck's work is nowadays characterized as a kind of extremist posi-tion. With respect to his approach to psychology, there may be some validity to this accusation. But in his approach to psychopathy, we can see that his work dovetails with Halleck's more cautious approach of postulating psychopathy as one end of a continuum of personality traits, which is a clear recognition that there is no hard and fast division be-tween "psychopaths" and "us."

Violence and Madness

Are the mentally ill violent? Are violent criminals mentally sick? The popular image of the mentally ill is indeed that they are "dangerous," and it is often thought best to keep them locked up. Indeed, some at-tempts to deinstitutionalize communities have met considerable public opposition.[43] The belief is based partly on fact, but it cannot be said to be true either. Nor can it be clearly demonstrated that violent criminals are mentally ill. There are some severe difficulties associated with re-searching this problem, the main one being that aggressive behavior itself is commonly used by psychiatrists as a diagnostic sign for particular types of mental illness. There have been six types of research into this problem.

1. The analysis of clinical case material of persons convicted of violent crimes, and the subsequent estimation of the proportion of these crim-inals displaying various forms of mental illness. By and large, these studies tend to show that the proportion of mental illness in violent criminals is higher than the known incidence in the total criminal popu-lation. The criticism is that because of lack of controls, clinicians invari-ably overdiagnose mental illness in known criminals. The general estimate is that about 20 to 30% of convicted murderers have diagnosable psychia-

tric disorders. There are, however, some who believe *all* offenders to be mentally ill. In addition, whereas in the United States only 3 to 5% of homicide offenders are adjudicated as legally insane, in England one-third to a half are so classified.[44]

2. Analysis of homicide offenders committed to a maximum security hospital. The estimate is generally that among such patients roughly 60% have records of multiple prior arrests for violent crime. Comparison of this population (i.e., those murderers found "not guilty by reason of insanity") with regular homicide offenders produced little difference as measured by recidivism rates, subsequent crimes, and psychiatric prognoses. Murderers deemed insane were, however, quite different from mentally ill patients without criminal records.

3. Analysis of arrest records of mentally ill patients. In general, it has been found that these patients have been arrested for violent offenses at a rate similar to and often less than that expected in the general population.[45] Only one study has shown a positive correlation of mental illness to arrests for violent crime—and these were the illnesses of alcoholism, addiction, anxiety neurosis, and sociopathy. However, this research concluded generally that, ". . . taking all the information available into consideration, the prevalence of individual psychiatric disorders and the recidivism rates, it would appear that psychiatric illness plays only a limited role in determining criminal recidivism once a man has been convicted of a felony."[46]

4. The experimental comparison of murderers or other aggressive offenders with "controls." Sometimes the control group has been from the normal population, and at other times the group has been matched. In one study, for example, murderers were compared to their brothers.[47] Among the incarcerated murdering population, murderers have been found to display a significantly higher incidence than control groups of epilepsy, severe measles, poorer reading ability, more phobias and compulsions, stuttering, sleepwalking, nightmares (these are all prior to the homicidal act); also slightly lower IQ, higher egocentrism, and a variety of other personality differences.[48]

5. Comparison of criminals who have committed violent crimes with property offenders. The differences found have been inconclusive, although it appears that murderers display more sadistic-hostile responses in projective tests than do other offenders.[49]

6. Comparison of violent mental patients with nonviolent mental patients according to diagnostic labels and personality tests. Here again, there appears to be no clear diagnostic syndrome that separates violent mental patients from nonviolent mental patients.[50]

It is clear that some differences have been found between violent and nonviolent offenders, according to a number of psychiatric and psychometric measures. Yet there still persists a reluctance to accept the possibility that these persons *are* different from the rest of us. After a detailed review of the evidence concerning the psychological differences between violent criminals and nonviolent criminals, which showed that there consistently *were* differences, Wolfgang and Ferracuti concluded only that:

> The collected evidence for a consistent personality pattern of the homicidal offender is scarce and unreliable. The several studies examined here confirm that the diagnosis remains a matter for the ability of the individual clinician.[51]

If diagnosis is indeed individualistic, one would surely not expect the general agreement of most studies reviewed by Wolfgang and Ferracuti (many were conducted in different parts of the world, and in different cultures).

Yet, if Wolfgang and Ferracuti are right, then the only definite factor which separates violent offenders or persons from nonviolent persons, is violence itself. It follows, therefore, that there *are* certain people whose personalities may be described as being typified by the use of violence. Hence it is *this* that makes them different. This has led to the notion that it is the hard-core, habitual (repeated) violent offender who is truly "different," and the recent move has been to single out such "hard-core" criminals for special treatment. Is there such a "thing" as a hard-core, violent offender?

The Repeated Violent Offender

Of course there is. The well designed cohort study by Marvin Wolfgang and his associates at the University of Pennsylvania showed that 18% of offenders accounted for 51% of all crimes.[52] The President's Commission on Crimes of Violence concluded that habitually aggressive persons were responsible for an inordinately large number of violent crimes.[53] The trouble is, of course, that these findings tend to be to some extent tautologous. It is interesting to discover that a small group of offenders are probably responsible for a large portion of violent crime. But this observation does not tell us anything more about these violent offenders except that they are habitually violent. The tendency has been to define these persons as "dangerous" and then try to isolate those violent offenders who it is expected will be dangerous if released.

However, it is one thing to predict violence without making a mistake, and another to observe that there are some relationships between habitual violence and some other criteria.

In general, most studies purporting to have found specific factors related to habitual violence have been clinical studies, which means that there was no control group. These studies have suggested that as a group, habitually violent offenders have abnormal EEG patterns,[54] histories of numerous accidents in which they were injured in some way—with a very high incidence of self-destructive behavior, concussions, and loss of consciousness during childhood[55]—and various personality traits as outlined in the above section.

The extensive work conducted by Dr. Steadman and his associates has produced the conclusion that, although one may be able to predict dangerousness with an accuracy rate of roughly 80%, the attempt is simply not worth the costs in loss of liberty for the remaining offenders who would be misdiagnosed.[56] The main factors these workers have found to be related to subsequent violent behavior upon release from incarceration have been: presence of juvenile record, number of previous arrests, presence of convictions of violent crimes, severity of the original offense that precipitated incarceration, and age under 50 years. We can see from this that we are really no further ahead than when we started: since the violent criminal behavior is "explained" by violent and criminal behavior.

It must be stressed that although future violence cannot be predicted with much accuracy, it cannot be assumed that there is therefore no relationship between the factors just cited and the commission of violence. Clearly these factors suggest, perhaps tautologically, that there is a special type of person called "the habitual violent offender" whose significant *personality* trait is that he repeatedly commits crimes of a violent nature. In this sense, these persons certainly are, as a group, different from most of us.[57] This conclusion has nothing to do with the question of whether we can predict which individual will be violent, and when.[58] This is asking too much.

Violence in the Extreme

Two points emerge from the previous discussion of violence, madness, and psychopathy. First, if we take a continuum view of psychopathy, we should expect that those on the extreme end of the scale, the "pure psychopaths" would be extremely aggressive persons. Second, if we take the observation that there are repeated violent criminals, some of whom use violence in the extreme, but who are not psychopaths, we might ask, do they suffer from any other mental illness? I am speaking here not of psychopaths as a group, but rather of those rare cases of criminals who use violence in such an extreme and bizarre way that we wonder "what makes them do it?" Extreme cases such as those that I am about to describe occur very rarely. But they are important to the study of violence because they receive much wider coverage in the communications media, which often gives the impression that they are not rare, but typical cases.

The Psychopathic Killer

Though Eysenck and many psychiatrists would all hastily point out that there are many psychopaths who are not criminal, and vice versa, there nevertheless has been a continuing, long-standing interest in the psychopathic criminal, especially the psychopathic killer who appears to commit crimes truly "in cold blood"[59]—without a shred of emotion or concern for his victims either before, during, or after the deed. Most psychiatrists have been prepared to describe this type of killer and make a few suggestions about the possible causes, such as a deep disturbance in family relationships early in life, but generally there appears to be some recognition that the explanation for this disorder remains a mystery.

The despair that even psychiatrists have come to in regard to this type of criminal is well demonstrated by the case of Herman Duker reported by Doctors McCord and McCord in their classic *The Psychopath*. Duker, in the course of a robbery on April 30, 1931, shot and killed the victim. In court, he displayed a "brazen guiltless defiance." Five psychiatrists testified as to his psychopathic state. The judge summed up the case as follows:[60]

> Duker's twenty-two years of life unfold types and degrees of activity that indicate a grossly distorted personality. He is not merely a youthful delinquent who has achieved a precocious maturity in crime. As a small child he exhibited an appalling and inhuman cruelty to animals which persisted for many years. The full record of his robberies and like crimes will never be known. He confesses many for which he was never apprehended; and says that after committing them he experienced an unusual sense of peace and satisfaction—almost of exaltation—a release from his nervous restlessness. This is certainly not the common experience of normal criminals. He has for years suffered from serious abnormalities in the sex sphere. None of these peculiarities is at all obvious to superficial examination. On the witness stand he presents the picture of an alert, courageous and peculiarly plausible individual. His

apparent normality, coupled with his abnormal career, is itself an evidence of his pathological condition.

What is that condition? With a degree of unanimity that reflects credit upon every medical witness in this case, the Court is assured that Duker is a "psychopathic personality." This is the conclusion reached by the present and former medical officers of the Supreme Bench, whose freedom from bias was to be presumed. It is the conclusion reached in 1928 by Doctor Partridge, then psychiatrist of the Maryland School for Boys, and in 1930 by Doctor Christian and the late Doctor Harding, Superintendent and Psychiatrist, respectively, of Elmira Reformatory—long before the murder had been committed. It is the same conclusion reached by Doctor Truitt, employed by the defense, and by Doctor Tanyhill and Doctor Gillis, employed by the State, for the purposes of this hearing. The "battle of experts," so often and so properly denounced as characteristic of American criminal trials, did not occur in this case.

The jury found Duker guilty of first degree murder, for which the judge could choose between only two sentences: death or life imprisonment. It is of great significance that every psychiatrist who was a witness testified to the peril of imprisoning Duker: [61]

> Doctor Guttmacher says of Duker that he is potentially one of the most dangerous types of individuals that society knows; that in a penal institution he would not be amenable to authority, and would be among the leaders in rebellion against it. Doctor Truitt, interrogated by the Court specifically as to how he thinks Duker would respond to the discipline of imprisonment for life in the Maryland Penitentiary replied that "the outlook would be unfavorable." The court had, then, to decide between life imprisonment and hanging for a man who is legally sane, medically of abnormal psychology, and socially extremely dangerous. Moreover, he is socially dangerous and a menace to the life of others whether he be at large or confined in prison. And it must not be forgotten that prison guards are human beings—and that administration of law "for the protection of society" applies to them as well as to other citizens

Judge Ulman, understandably, sentenced Duker to be hanged by the neck until dead. Said Ulman, "This action is a confession of social and legal failure."

Paranoid Schizophrenia

According to Dr. Lunde, a forensic psychiatrist with extensive experience with mass murderers, this is the most common form of mental illness suffered by those murderers who are mentally ill.[62] Typical of this condition are gross disturbances in perception and thinking processes, usually coupled with delusions of considerable grandiosity. Very often, the paranoid schizophrenic will identify persons who are the source or objects of his delusions, and these are those whom he may murder. Paranoid schizophrenia is distinguished from the more common term paranoia, in that the paranoid has usually developed logical and specific theories concerning who is persecuting him, and his delusions may be less severe. In contrast, the paranoid schizophrenic may have multiple delusions, and he is less highly systematized, changeable, illogical, and bizarre.[63]

There are many famous cases in this category. In fact, they are probably the most colorful crimes, and, since they are the most publicized, provide the public with a distorted image of "the murderer." In fact, as we have seen in previous chapters, those who murder as a result of a deranged, lunatic, "evil" mind as presented in the movies are very few. But when such persons do kill, it is often with a flair, and often mass murders result.

Most of these murderers have developed fantastic (delusional) beliefs about the world and their place in it. The case of John Frazier is an excellent example. On October 19, 1970, he killed a prominent eye surgeon, his wife, their two young sons, and the doctor's secretary. Frazier blindfolded, bound, and shot each one and threw the bodies into the swimming pool of the doctor's home. Under the windshield of the doctor's red Rolls-Royce was this note:[64]

> halloween....1970
> today world war 3 will begin as brought to you by the pepole of the free universe.
> From this day forward any one and ?/or company of persons who missuses the natural environment or destroys same will suffer the penelty of death by the people of the free universe.
> I and my comrads from this day forth will fight until death or freedom, against anything or anyone who dose not support natural life on this planet, materalisum must die or man-kind will.
> KNIGHT OF WANDS
> KNIGHT OF CUPS
> KNIGHT OF PENTICLES
> KNIGHT OF SWORDS

Frazier was convinced that the last book of the Bible, Revelations, was addressed specifically to him, and that he was carrying out God's divine mission to save the earth from materialism.

Another famous case was that of Herbert Mullin, who between October 13, 1972 and February 13, 1973 killed 13 people. Mullin had collected an enormous amount of demographic data and other information on earthquakes. The conclusion he reached from his studies was that: "We human beings . . . have found murder decreases the natural disasters and extent of the devastation of these disasters; therefore, we will always murder."

Mullin was even convinced that his victims were asking to be killed. He tried to explain this to the jury:[65]

> I, Herb Mullin, born April 18, 1947, was chosen as the designated leader of my generation by Professor Dr. Albert Einstein on April 18, 1955. . . . His hope probably was that the April 18th people would use his designation and its resulting power and social influence to guide, protect, or perfect the resources of our planet and universe. . . . *One man consenting to be murdered protects the millions of other human beings living in the cataclysmic earthquake/ tidal area.* For this reason, the designated hero/leader and associates have the responsibilities of getting enough people to commit suicide and/or consent to being murdered every day.

Once again, however, it should be pointed out that many (probably most) paranoid schizophrenics never become violent. The reason why particular paranoid schizophrenics become murderous depends, more than likely, upon the form that the delusion takes.

Depression

There are many different types of depression varying from mild forms of personality disturbance (the "blues") to severely chronic and acute depressive states. There are many environmental factors that seem to bring on or invoke severe depression, but it must be said that the true cause of this condition is unknown. The severely depressed person is usually described as one who sees himself as completely worthless and his situation (as well as that of his loved ones and the world around him) as "hopelessly lost." One occasionally reads newspaper reports of a father killing his whole family and then himself. Commonly, such a parent is around 30 years old and struggling to "make it."

Psychoanalytic thinkers have suggested that suicide is a displaced form of murder, or, more correctly, is murder of the self, which results from the repression of murderous feelings towards others. Some researchers have noted, for example, that murders decrease in time of war.[66] The inference is that "murder and suicide are complementary phenomena: the total amount of available destructiveness is discharged in two psychologically similar, socially distinct *Gestalten*."[67]

Others have tried to show that suicide and homicide are "mirrors" of each other in the way that they are related to the business cycle. Henry and Short[68] concluded that as business prosperity increased, there was less suicide and more homicide. And the reverse was the case with a depressed business cycle. Henry and Short conducted their study within a frustration-aggression model, hence they postulated that the increase in the homicide rate in times of prosperity occurred largely among the lower classes—who would feel more frustrated because they were relatively worse off—and that suicide rates went up among the upper classes during periods of economic decline. However, the interpretation of much of the Henry and Short data is very controversial, and a number of researchers have claimed that the correlations between these variables are in fact opposite to those claimed by Henry and Short.[69]

Very often, cases of murder followed by suicide are explained by the displacement of suicidal feelings onto the unfortunate victim. Once the act is completed, the murderer "realizes" what he has done, and later commits suicide. Dr. Abrahamsen describes the painful case of *Tiger,* who murdered the girl he loved and subsequently committed suicide by throwing himself under an oncoming car.[70]

The relationship between victim and assaulter is, of course, complex. We have seen in Chapters 7, 8, and 9 that victims may precipitate crimes. Such indirect suicides have been known to reach epidemic proportions. In the seventeenth and eighteenth centuries in Norway and Denmark, people were committing murder so as to receive the death penalty. Because of depression, they wanted to commit suicide, but their religious values prevented them from doing so.[71] Similar cases have occurred recently in the United States, when convicted murderers have refused appeals to have their death sentences commuted and have instead pleaded for the death penalty. The execution of Gary Gilmore in 1976 by firing squad was a notorious example. Many opposed his execution on the ground that the State was assisting him in his suicide, especially since he had made two attempts with drug overdoses.

Sexual Sadists

Dr. Lunde suggests that all mass or multiple murderers are probably mentally ill. He distinguishes between mass murders and serial murders. Mass murders are those in which the murderer kills several people in one single killing spree. Serial murders are those in which the murderer kills a number of people over a considerable period of time. A paranoid schizophrenic is most commonly the multiple murderer, usually of the serial type. A sexual sadist is generally the mass murderer, and his condition is a "deviation characterized by torture and/or killing and mutilation of other persons in order to achieve sexual gratification."[72] There is not much more that we can say about this type of murderer. We are all well acquainted with the details of such crimes—ranging from Jack the Ripper, to the Boston Strangler and to Richard Speck, who killed eight nurses in Chicago in 1966. The only explanation offered for such behavior is the psychoanalytic one that the murderer has undergone a fusion of his sex and aggressive drives, so that he cannot obtain satisfaction of one without the other.

In his description of Edmund Kemper, who killed and mutilated eight women between May 7, 1972 and April 21, 1973, Dr. Lunde shows how Kemper had fantasies very early in life of cutting off limbs, attempting sexual intercourse with corpses, and indulging in acts of cannibalism. Indeed, he first tortured and killed animals (the first victim was the family cat), and at the same time he had extensive fantasies of killing his mother. His first six victims were hitchhikers, the last two were his mother and her friend. He cut out his mother's larynx and put it down the garbage disposal. "This seemed appropriate," he said, "as much as she'd bitched and screamed and yelled at me over the years."[73] In his murders, Kemper carried out all of his infantile fantasies.

Panic

Dr. Halleck identified a type of homicide that may occur when normal persons who are ordinarily quiet and law-abiding are thrust into a situation which is overwhelmingly stressful, with the result that deep internal conflicts erupt. He describes one syndrome, homosexual panic, as a typical example which he says occurs among personnel of the armed services, merchant seamen, prisoners, or any group denied contacts with the opposite sex. Dr. Halleck describes one such case:[74]

> The patient was a nineteen-year-old youth who had recently joined the United States Coast Guard. He had never been away from home before, and he immediately encountered great difficulty in adjusting to the service. An essentially shy and unsophisticated person, he was embarrassed by the intimacy of barracks life. He could not accustom himself to open nudity, shared toilet facilities or any kind of earthy or vulgar masculine behavior. For two weeks prior to the offense he had been experiencing strange and disturbing feelings. These began when he was assigned to a bunk next to a man who made frequent suggestive remarks about the patient's attractiveness. The patient felt vague, erotic stirrings which in turn made him feel extremely guilty. One night, a week before the offense, the patient dreamed that he was kissing this man and awoke

to find that he was sexually excited. After this he became even more withdrawn and kept to himself as much as possible. He began to experience feelings of uneasiness which he could not relate to any concrete problem in his daily life. Each night he had nightmares in which animals were chasing him. Two days before the offense he thought that he had heard a soft voice from somewhere behind him calling him a "queer." When he turned, no one was present. The next two days were characterized by extreme anxiety. Although he managed to continue working, he felt that people were making derogatory remarks about him and believed they could detect that his body was becoming more feminine.

On the night of the offense the patient was feeling distraught and nervous. He readily accepted an invitation to spend a weekend leave on a proposed drinking spree with some of his acquaintances. This group included the man who had made suggestive proposals. After several hours of heavy drinking this man suggested to the patient that they find a hotel room and spend the night together. The patient felt both temptation and guilt and almost in a dazed condition accepted this proposal. When they were settled in the hotel room, the friend began to embrace him in an erotic manner. At this point the patient "went berserk." He grabbed a heavy lamp and bludgeoned his companion to death. Several hours later the patient was found by the police wandering along a city street in a confused state. When they tried to question him, he became assaultive. Several officers were required to subdue him. He seemed both terrified and enraged and continually shouted that he wasn't going to let anyone "f—k" him. At the jail he shouted and insisted that his life was in great danger. He accused the police of ridiculing him and had to be forcibly restrained. The patient was taken to a prison hospital, where he remained in a disorganized state for another twenty-four hours. As he gradually calmed down, he was able to relate some of the details of his offense. Most of the above information was not obtained, however, until many months of pretrial hospitalization had passed.

Summary

1. Frustration-aggression theory continues to be a dominant explanation of aggression. It is now conceded that it is not an innate response, and that many other factors are involved in determining whether aggression will follow frustration. It is, nevertheless, largely an emotive theory.

2. Aggression may be used instrumentally to obtain a certain goal— e.g., a child hitting his mother to get what he wants or an airman bombing civilians with a view to winning the war.

3. Aggression may be a rational response to conditions that are stressful to the individual. Aggression is seen as adaptive in such situa-

tions since it has a direct effect upon the source of stress and thus may restore an individual's "vital balance."

4. At the cultural level, the application of these psychological theories is very complicated, but may be achieved as illustrated by the interpretation of the Manichaean world in terms of frustration and aggression.

5. An "aggressive personality" has so far not been isolated. The personality type closest to this is the "psychopath," and, though it is contended that such a personality type probably exists, the extent to which it is related to aggressive behavior, especially criminally violent behavior, cannot be determined.

6. Similarly, whereas many tests, both clinical and psychometric, have demonstrated differences between murderers and nonmurderers, many have not, so that there is still considerable disagreement in the literature about whether murderers, as a group, are substantially different from the normal population.

7. It is clear that there is a group of persons who are most easily identified as repeated (habitual) violent offenders. Once again, however, the extent to which this group differs from the normal population according to other psychological measures remains in question.

8. There is no evidence that the mentally ill, as a group, are more violent than the normal population.

9. The extreme use of violence is observed in persons suffering from particular kinds of madness: the psychopathic killer, the paranoid schizophrenic, the severely depressed, the sexual sadist, and the "normal" who suffers from sudden situational panic.

Conclusions

I did not want to end with the usual note "Toward an Integrated Theory . . .", or "Toward the Control of . . .".

It would be absurd to suggest an "integrated theory of violence" since I have clearly shown throughout this book that violence involves such diverse phenomena, contexts, conditions, etc., that there cannot be a unitary explanation. Yet, I think that many of the conclusions I shall state in this chapter could not have been reached without a survey of the "big picture," an idea of the breadth and diversity of the research and theory that have contributed to our understanding of violence. Without it, one cannot make a balanced assessment of the direction which future research on violence should take.

It would also be absurd to take each theory of violence that I have reviewed and infer policies for the practical control of violence for each —the reason being that many of these theories assume that violence is a unitary phenomenon. I have, therefore, confined myself to very brief suggestions concerning the kind of "violence control" programs that might be worth pursuing, but even these suggestions I have tied very closely to the extent to which such programs may be directly related to the particular contexts of violence.

In this brief conclusion, I intend to reconsider a few of the dominant themes that have emerged from the material, assess their validity or merit, and then try to suggest what new questions should be asked and what research might be most fruitful.

Violence as a Cultural Force

In his later works, Freud spoke of two great forces in culture, Eros and Thanatos, Love and Death. The neo-Freudians of the 1940s and

252

1950s severely criticized this part of his theory because they preferred his earlier formulation in which he saw aggression as part of the libido, which only later became a quasi-independent drive as a result of various phases in psychosexual development. I think it also possible that his later writings on culture may have been misunderstood, in the sense that his conception of Eros and Thanatos was not so much one of "instincts" as one of "forces." There is, indeed, some question as to whether even his use of the word *trieb* in German has been correctly translated into English as "instinct."[1] Certainly modern psychologists prefer the term "drive," and this is probably a more appropriate translation.

As a theorist of culture, I prefer the word "force" in relation to Freud's later writings because he was speaking of culture in very general terms and not addressing himself as much to individual psychology, although the genius of his essays, especially *Civilization and Its Discontents,* was that he managed so successfully to blend the two. I understand the word "force" in this context to mean something like the "forces of nature": the elements of wind, rain, ice, sun, fire, earth. These are the elements out of which over millions of years humankind has developed a civilization, a way of both interpreting and structuring human existence.

The question that Freud finally found himself asking was, are the "small" drives that he had so often identified within his patients—those drives of sex and aggression which seemed to be at the bottom of so much trouble for individuals—of such importance as to rate with the other great forces of nature? His answer was a tentative yes, and the results were his brooding, pessimistic essays on the origins and achievements of civilization and the psychological costs of those achievements. Much of this pessimism arose from his conception of the death instinct, the drive to destruction, the apparent logical extension of the "smaller" instinct of aggression.

From the point of view of a theory of culture, therefore, the notion of violence (or aggression, or destruction) as a force of nature must be taken seriously, so I propose to review, in the light of the material and conclusions reached in this book, some of the ways in which violence may be conceived of as either a force of nature in and of itself, or as a direct expression of a number of nature's elements. One should add that the use of the word "force" here is also distinct from its use as part of the basic definition of violence given in the Introduction: "physical force or injury." Violence as a force of nature here means that violence is elevated to the position of an object of our lives. It lies at the source of our existence. The opposite to this would be to regard it as a product of our existence (a view which we shall also discuss shortly).

Violence as a Creative Force

If we look to nature as our model, we find indeed that the violence of the elements is creative. Often out of destruction grows new life. For example, the raging bush fires that occur so frequently throughout Australia's eucalypt forests are needed for regeneration of the forest, because without intense heat the eucalypt nuts, which house new seed, cannot open. And we are well aware of the beneficial effects of glaciers, flooded river flats, and other forms of violence in nature. We have seen that terrorists-from-below implicitly use the model of "violence as creative," to justify assassination and the destruction of an existing order. But lest we go over too easily to their ideology we should also remember that the same model has been used by terrorists-from-above. It was by complete extermination of the Jews that Hitler hoped to create a pure Aryan master race.

Historians have also argued for the "positive" aspects of violence: for example, the American War of Independence out of which was created the United States, or the Civil War, because it was instrumental in freeing the slaves.[2] I am sure that many other instances could be recounted of wars and violence that "created" a better world.

I suggest, however, that there are none that fit the model of violence as one of nature's creative forces, the reasons being (1) that there is no way of telling whether the changes that have occurred after political violence would not have occurred without it, and (2) that there is no conclusive way of assessing whether what it is claimed was created out of violence was "new," i.e., "creative." In many cases, "new" political orders turn out to be simply replications of the old ones, except that the actors have changed. Some might even argue that because of political violence, some political orders revert to older and less defensible forms of order, in which case one might argue that political violence produces a *reactionary* product, which is hardly creative.

All of these views of violence see it as creative in the long term. In contrast, the immediate products of violence are destruction. Of that there can be no doubt; it is part of the definition of the term; it is part of its practical application. But whereas many of nature's elements produce destructive first effects, they also provide immediate beneficent results: rain for the germination of seeds, wind for pollination, sun for photosynthesis, and so on. These elements have readily apparent and immediate creative effects. So we see that although it might be argued that over long periods of history, the violence of nature—like glaciers, floods, and forest fires—might have creative value, the case for immediate creative effects of human violence is more difficult to prove than it is for nature's other elements.

A further important distinction should be drawn between violence as a possible "force" and death as a "force." The distinction has been blurred for some time because Freud, it is now clear, wrongly equated death with destruction.[3]

There are many interpretations of death as creative, many of them expressed in various forms of Western religion. The most common has been to view death as a kind of rebirth, with various visions of people going to heaven. The difficulties of this view of death as creative have been discussed in many places, and are not entirely relevant here. Suffice it to say however, that this fundamentalist Christian view of death as creative contradicts the notion of death as a natural force, and rather sees it as *super*-natural. As a force of nature, death is absolutely necessary for creation, because it makes it possible for successive generations to renew each other. The idea of everyone living forever is at bottom anticreative. Recent theorists of death have made impassioned pleas for a return to the conception of death-as-part-of-life.[4] The point of all this is that violence should not be construed in any way as a death instinct, for although both can be seen to bring about destruction, Thanatos must be seen as having an important creative element.[5]

It seems to me that it is very difficult to find any hard evidence to support the notion that violence in itself is a force that creates anything worthwhile. This is *not* to say that violence can never be justified, that all wars are unjust, and so on. Many wars may indeed be justifiable on other grounds. I have here simply shown that violence is not justifiable on the grounds of its being a creative force.

Violence as a Destructive Force

The vision of apocalyptic doom, that humankind is destined to end in the bloody fire and destruction of hell on earth has been a major preoccupation of Western man for many hundreds of years. In this century, each generation exudes this tragic sense of life; and since the atomic bomb, each generation wonders whether it will be the last. Freud's *Civilization and Its Discontents* expressed much of this foreboding. But we have seen that for all that Freud saw death as a totally destructive force, it is not. It is *violence* that is destructive, not death, and it is a serious distortion to link the two together.

It remains for us now to ask the question whether violence is *such* a destructive force that it warrants pride of place among one of nature's forces. I have the choice of two answers to this question (since this is the way I set it up!). I could give a summary of Gibbon's *Decline and Fall of the Roman Empire* or an outline of Toynbee's *A Study of History* and conclude that, yes, indeed, violence is *the* central feature of history—that history is simply the story of so many wars, revolutions, and massacres. "There has never been a period in history when the whole of the world was at peace," or something to that effect.

Or, I could say that civilization has indeed made progress, that there have been many faltering steps and much violence, but, in sum, we have overcome violence to a large degree, or at least we have not allowed it to interfere with the civilizing process. I could point to the great strides in medical care, technology, nutrition, and welfare and to the many wars that could have been fought and were not. Is it a matter of an "optimistic" as against a "pessimistic" interpretation of history or of "human nature" in general? We have seen in Part 4 that humans have not been conclusively demonstrated to be "innately" disposed to violence, to any seriously high level, or compared with other animal species—so that rules out the proposition that "human nature" is the cause of violence.

Must the answer lie in history? We saw in Chapter 2 that it is very difficult to demonstrate an overall relationship between particular violent events in history. Sometimes we can trace direct relationships, but at other times violence occurs in situations remarkably different, isolated from other historically violent events, so that the only similarities one can posit between them are (1) violence and (2) the fact that people are involved. The first is redundant to the point and the second we have already rejected when we rejected human nature as a possible explanation.

We must search for a middle ground, and to this end I would suggest that the partial answer to this difficult question lies in a recognition of the peculiarity of the human condition—a peculiarity in relation to history. It is here that much work needs to be done. I have in various parts of this book sketched in the thread of continuity in the use of violence that runs through various historical periods. There is undoubtedly continuity in the use of violence in the South dating at least from the War of Independence and possibly before. It is a continuity dependent upon a number of factors: the tradition of the defense of honor, the martial spirit of the cavaliers, economic scarcity, political disorder, geographical isolation, and others. These combined to ensure that violence would continue as an acceptable part of life. But one can only speculate on the patterning of this violence: why it continues in some parts of the South and not others; how it becomes transformed (if it is) into criminal violence of a less honorable nature—there are many other questions that could be asked. What we must note here is that historical events, combined with other conditions, may *determine* subsequent events, may increase the likelihood that violence will continue down through many generations, perhaps hundreds of years. Of course, it may be that violence itself *is* historically regenerative in the sense that once it has been used as a solution to a problem, it is "hard to give up." But I think the evidence so far suggests that for violence to be continuous, it must occur under quite specific historical and cultural conditions that will facilitate its transmission.

Another continuous thread in history is the persistent phenomenon of objects of violence. One can easily enough document the almost un-broken record of the use of Jews as objects of violence from the begin-ning of history until the present. Wilhelm Reich explained why it is that Jews are selected as targets of aggression, and why it is that people im-pute to target groups beastliness, savagery, filthiness—all that civilization is not supposed to be, all that civilization has repressed. The conclusion seems to be that at times we cannot stand the constraints of civilization, and that the destruction of the Jews and other target groups keeps us "sane." They are, to put it bluntly, the rear end of our "civilized" culture.

The process of consigning human beings to the scrap heap continues all over the world. In some cases they are disposed of violently (cur-rently in Uganda and Cambodia), in other cases the method used is systematic moral-economic discrimination (the untouchables in India), and in still others abject neglect (the old and the insane in many Western cultures). This is indeed a universal and continuous process. But I must point out that there is more than violence involved; in fact violence may be involved in only the minority of cases (neglect is *not* violence, as we saw in the definitions presented in the Introduction). My guess is that there is a universal force at work here, which may well be destructive, of which violence is but one small expression. I do not know what that "force" is. It may not be a force at all, but simply a symptom of the contradictions that exist between men's minds and the societies that they build.

Our conclusion: violence in itself is not a force in the sense of its being a universal and continuous impetus throughout history. Where evidence for its continuity is found, the continuity depends not so much on violence itself, but on the specific historical, cultural, and economic conditions necessary to promote it. One very clear thread that ties some instances of violence together throughout history is the recurrent selection of target groups as objects of aggression, the prime example in Western culture being the Jews. However, it is quite clear that target groups can be and are destroyed without the use of violence. Thus, violence may possibly be a small part of a broader destructive force, but it is not a destructive force in itself.

Violence as a Moral Force

The idea of a "moral force" akin to a force of nature is, I suppose, upsetting to some, since it sounds too much like the old idea of natural law. And maybe it is. In any event, the idea of violence as a moral force is quite a challenging one, when one considers that historically it is by violence that most moral laws have gained recognition. The early history of punishments—or should I say most of the history of punishments—is very clearly a violent one, at least up until a hundred years ago.[6] Violence in the service of morality may be seen as the self-regenerative aspect of violence. The feuding model is perhaps the best example. In this situation, a person from one clan kills a person from another clan. This is repaid by a killing in kind, which is further repaid, and so on and on. The retributive elements of this violence are unmistakable. Violence must be repaid by violence. (Why it *must* be repaid is another question which I have dealt with elsewhere).[7] Our question here is, why is it specifically that *violence* is chosen as the "repayment" for a wrong? It is because of the sacred retributive doctrine of reflecting the crime in the punishment. Where this "law" originated we do not know. But it certainly is stated many times in the Bible and other ancient writings ("an eye for an eye"), and there are many historical examples of it. Thus, violence is repaid by violence.

There is more to it than this, since we know that many crimes that are not violent have historically been dealt with by violent punishment. This applies especially to such crimes as larceny which in England during the seventeenth and eighteenth centuries were punishable by death. The simple answer to this question is that violence when used during that historical period (and in others too) was used for the sake of inflicting terror, of establishing mass obedience. It thus was not an automatic repayment for wrongs done according to their deserts, as occurred in the feuding clans, but as an instrument of politics.

Since violent retribution in the sense of feuds does not exist in modern structured societies, and has occurred only in historical periods of social chaos, we may dismiss violence as a moral force in and of itself, although its importance as a moral force in feuding subcultures cannot be dismissed, and certainly many aspects of these subcultures, even though found at different historical periods and in many diverse parts of the world, appear to be strikingly similar: defense of honor, shame, scarcity, to name but a few. The conclusion is that whereas violence may be an important moral force in primitive social orders (i.e., unstructured), in complex, structured societies violence has been appropriated by the powerful political body (the State), which uses it partly as a moral force but much more as a political instrument.

It is to the instrumental use of violence that we must now turn.

Violence as a Rational Instrument

We have seen that violence may be used instrumentally in a variety of situations and for a wide variety of purposes. It may be used by terrorists in promoting political ends, it may be used by criminals in robbing or raping their victims, by antagonists as a means of evening up old scores, and in schools and families as a way of ensuring obedience.

The instrumental aspect of violence is, in my opinion, of much greater importance today in our understanding of violent behavior than ever before. My reason for this view is that the instrumental use of violence leans heavily on a cognitive rationalistic *plan* of behavior. It is a use of violence which makes claims to its rational use, and, inevitably, to its justification on the grounds of its rationality. Such an understanding of violence—and this applies equally to the students and the actors of violence—represents a great advance in our thinking, but it is also fraught with very serious dangers. These dangers lie in the uncertain realm of our thinking processes in relation to our emotional processes, or, in Freudian terminology, in the extent to which we are able to separate out what is "rational" from what is a "rationalization." In the realm of violence this problem is truly immense, for we know that one of the worst acts of violence in our very recent history was the cold-blooded, brutal, rational extermination of the Jews. The violent final solution was carried out on the basis of an *ideology,* presented as a rational theory concerning, among other things, racial purity and the preservation of Western civilization. It is easy for us today to reexamine that ideology and point out that it was not a *rational* theory and, incongruously, was in fact designed to appeal to the emotions. But at the time, it was not at all clear, or at least clear only to very few. In fact, many intellectuals developed rational theories to support the doctrine.

We face the same difficulty today in much worse proportions. Ideologies of various persuasions—espoused by persons ranging from political theorists and activists down to common criminals (who often have intellectuals speaking on their behalf)—are used in justifying violence. The robber (or his spokesman) argues that it is because he is poor, unemployed, discriminated against by society, that he must go out and beat people. The terrorist—whether from above or below—develops a sophisticated theory justifying violence, often indiscriminate, as a means to a lofty, laudatory goal. I am not suggesting that because these ideologies are used as rationalizations for violence that there is no truth in them. Violence may indeed be justifiable in many of these situations. But the important point we must recognize is that in this century violence is more and more being justified on rational grounds. The Red Brigades do not execute political enemies because they hate them. They do so because, according to their ideology, their victims deserve it, and it serves their political strategy. The robber does not kill his victim because he hates him, but because it serves his purposes. The two great powers build up a nuclear arsenal not because they are angry, or hate each other and would like to destroy each other, but because, they say, it would be irrational not to defend oneself, not to "keep the balance." And at this level we perhaps face the most difficult paradox involved in violence today: that it takes merely the press of a button to wreak wide-scale destruction, the extent of which is beyond our imagination. The series of behaviors involved in implementing nuclear aggression is, I would suggest, virtually opposite to those that we have in the past associated with aggressive behavior, such as anger, hate, rage, heated physical activity, and the like. Instead, there is a carefully worked out, rational plan which is carried out mechanically and carefully.

Herein lie both the advantage and the disadvantage of an instrumental understanding and use of violence. Because violence is seen as a rational, planned, "cool" act or sequence of behaviors, one should expect that it will only be used in carefully specified situations; that the possibility of accidents of violence is minimized. But on the other hand, because it is rational and planned and requires only the pressing of buttons and the taking of orders, to implement such violence takes much less physical effort. And the mental effort necessary to instigate this instrumental violence lies in the explication of various ideologies (of the left or right).

Thus, we continue on the brink. Competing ideologies battle for our support, both emotional and rational support, because the important attribute of ideologies is that they contain in them not only highly rational argument, but considerable emotional appeal. It is of the greatest importance today that we study and understand these ideologies and their implications and try to separate out their emotional appeal from their rational bases. We must react with much greater skepticism when confronted with theories that justify the use of violence. This applies especially to those "middlebrows" who tend to side with violence-from-below, as they did in Germany in support of the Baader-Meinhof gang, in Italy in support of the Brigate Rosso, in Uruguay in support of the Tupamaros, and in many other instances, all of which only served to extend and support the use of violence, with very doubtful, if any, gains.

The same skeptical view should also be developed in regard to criminal violence of the traditional kind such as homicide, aggravated assault, robbery, and rape. It is one thing to develop descriptive explanations of criminal violence, showing that it is related to such factors as age, sex, various subcultural attributes, and so on. But it is another thing to allow these explanations as excuses for violence. Once again, we need to look much more closely at the ideological bases of our explanation of criminal violence and, indeed, at the whole direction that research in criminal violence has taken.

Finally, if we take this notion of the cognitive bases of instrumental violence seriously, it follows that we should study violence as a *learned response*. Although I have suggested that a large part of this modern day learning of violence has to do with ideological justifications for its use, there are other ways of learning violence which do not necessarily, or even apparently, imply an ideological processing.

Violence as a Learned Response

The borderline between an ideologically learned use of violence and nonideologically learned violence is that of the subculture of violence. As we saw in Chapter 4, there is probably a wide variety of subcultures of violence, some of which emphasize the ideological use of violence, others which emphasize its nonideological use—so that, in other words, it is a learned "habit," or life style. I used as the prototypical example the Dukhobors, who emphasized both aspects of violence: they had developed a detailed ideological base to justify their violence, but they had also developed the practice of violence to such an extent that children were taught it as a value in itself and often performed acts of violence without really understanding their ideological significance.

The nonideological use of learned violence is also well illustrated by aspects of violence in the South, where it was clearly transmitted from one generation to the other that one had to avenge affronts to one's honor with violence. The question of why one should do it, simply did not arise.

The more intense example of violence as a learned response is that of family violence, especially the propositions that have recently been made concerning the generational aspects of family violence. The dynamics of this process, if it exists, are yet to be understood, and it is to be hoped that more research will be done in this area. I should add, however, that even in the case of family violence, it is not altogether clear to what extent ideology plays a part. Certainly there are theorists around who argue that the whole basis of the family structure is one of "violence,"[8] mainly because of its totalitarian structure or its enclosed nuclear structure. Most of these theories tend, however, to broaden the definition of the term "violence" to mean "violation", so in my view it is probably stretching it a bit to argue that violence in the home has an ideological base.

An exception may be the current literature on wife-beating, which is, perhaps, more evidence of the modern tendency to view violence instrumentally, and thus ideologically. Much of the work in this area has been done by women's liberationists who tend to explain the behavior of wife-beaters in terms of an ideology that sees society structured specifically to discriminate against women, so that men feel entirely justified in beating them. Had such studies been conducted in the fifties decade, explanations would no doubt have centered on sociopsychiatric types of theories. The fact that no studies were conducted on the issue until very recently supports the liberationist ideology. It also demonstrates that although violence occurs in diverse contexts, the contexts do not always (or even often) dictate the direction that research will take. Perhaps we should allow these diverse settings themselves to play a greater role in directing research on violence.

The Diversity of Violence

Three general conclusions follow from an understanding of violence as an incredibly diverse phenomenon:

1. Although it is clear that violence often occurs in relation to the oppression of small minorities, especially the ethnic poor, it does not at all follow that by elimination of poverty the problem of violence will be solved, because we know that violence occurs in these subcultures as a result of a complicated cultural process which involves generational transmission of values, perceptions, and life styles that are deeply dependent upon the major culture. This dependence is partly economic, but also psychological. A Marxist would argue that it is the poverty of economic dependence that produces the psychological dependence. We

know, of course, that this is an oversimplification. Jews have consistently borne the brunt of violence, especially at periods throughout history when they were thriving economically. It is true that Jews have not developed violent subcultures in the sense of perpetrating violence within their own group, as seems to have been the pattern with oppressed black minorities. The difference may well be explained by differences in economic well-being. It is clear that once again, we need a great many more intensive studies of subcultures—violent and nonviolent—if we are to understand the complex processes by which violence arises and is perpetuated. The development of a classification of subcultures, along with a further classification of subcultures of violence would be an important first step.

2. The fact that violence occurs in specific and diverse contexts—the football field, the classroom, the home, the prison, the policeman's beat, and so an—suggests that there is every reason to mount specific programs designed to deal with these situations and contexts. Once again, although certain continuous themes and lessons that we have learned from violence in other contexts may help when applied to these diverse contexts (for example, the maxim "violence breeds violence"), there is every reason to argue for the implementation and usefulness of small, narrowly focused programs to deal with violence in these situations and contexts. The chances are that the causes are situational, or, if not situational, can be alleviated by situational changes. Programs that try to apply what we know about aggression—its emotive base, its relation to frustration, its instrumental use, its subcultural attributes, and the many other explanations provided in this book—could be of great service in such settings. Indeed some have been developed and successfully implemented in regard to programs designed to train police in crisis management, dealing with family violence, and so on. Yet the police context appears to be the only area in which programs have been developed to deal with violence. I know of no others—not even in prisons.

3. Violence may, under certain conditions, be an illness in the medical sense. We do not know how much or even what kinds of violence may be accounted for by this body of research, but it would surely be foolish to discount or even minimize the evidence of various medical and physiological conditions related to aggression. Indeed, some of the studies, though they lack the usual features of control groups and sampling that sociologists prefer, have demonstrated startlingly *direct relationships* (something which a social scientist *never* finds) between certain physiological factors and aggressive behavior. Clearly, further

research is absolutely essential in this area, especially from the point of view of how much and what kinds of violence the medical-physical research can explain.

Can There Be Peace?

The answer is clearly no, and in the light of the material that I have presented in this book, it can be seen to be a silly question, because it implies that violence is a unitary phenomenon with a unitary solution. It is abundantly clear that violence occurs in so many different forms, under such a variety of social, psychological, economic, cultural and historical conditions, that to suggest that any single change—even the greatest of changes, such as a violent revolution—could eliminate violence is a gross over-simplification of the problem. We may charge the idealist theorists who envisage a society without violence with being romantics and impractical, for they have failed to understand the clearly diverse *and separate* conditions that lead to the many different varieties of violence.

The situation is even more complicated than this. It is not at all clear that if, say, it were possible to effect a change which reduced a particular form of violence (e.g., homicide) then other aspects of violence would remain the same. Would the incidence of suicide perhaps increase? The great theoretical and empirical difficulty that we face as researchers is to work out the extent to which different forms of violence are separate from each other and the extent to which others are interdependent. It is a sorry fact that with the exception of a few studies of the relationship between suicide and homicide, and of war and homicide, we are blissfully ignorant of the extent to which different types of violence either are or are not related to each other. In this book I have tried to show that there is some evidence to support the relationship between some kinds of violence and others, such as the history of various types of Southern violence. But the evidence is scant, and on the whole must be inferred, and probably applies only to a very small portion of violence in American society. Most of these propositions are reasoned guesses. It is a very important area for future research.

There is a final reason why we cannot expect violence in general to decrease or become controllable in the near future, and that is the clear biological bases of our culture, age and sex. We saw in Chapter 5 how deeply this biological division in all cultures cuts into the social fabric of society. We have also seen, that as far as empirical data are concerned, the age-sex factors are clearly *the* factors that account for variation in many types of violence. Nor can we assume that even if these cultural differences were wiped out (i.e., "equality" of the sexes or ages) that violence would decrease. I tried to show in Chapter 5 that violence may be partly an inevitable product of the peculiar relationship between biology and culture, a relationship that has remained largely unchanged for more than two thousand years (and maybe a million or so before that). But I also showed that there were culturally specific factors that contributed to the links between age, sex, and violence, and it is these that might have to be contended with if one looked towards reducing male youth violence. These factors are, however, not directly related to notions of "equality" among sexes and ages, but rather our understanding of the different processes of psychological development that boys and girls go through which may in large part be specific to each culture (e.g., "identity crises," "generation gap," sex-typing and many others). We need a greater understanding of these processes in relation to violence. There is very little research dealing directly with this question—most of the material I reviewed in that chapter drew upon works designed for other purposes, so that attention given to violence was either incidental or had to be inferred.

The conclusion is that, though we may work to understand the culturally specific factors that may contribute to the vast differences in sex and age in levels and types of violence, we should expect success only in specific and limited situations. The biological basis of the age-sex difference is so central to our culture—indeed to all cultures—that it is unlikely that violence related to this basic division will ever be entirely or even mostly eliminated. The difficulty is that we have not the slightest idea how much violence is attributable to culturally specific factors and how much to the biological base, or the extent to which the biological base can be minimized by cultural readjustments. At present, it seems that most cultures, to a fair degree, reflect the biological base. What would happen if they did not, I do not know. Certainly there is enormous variation in the extent to which the biological divisions of age and sex are carried out in each culture. And it is true that some primitive cultures have been found which have virtually reversed or equalized the male-female roles. But they are the exception. Certainly there are none to my knowledge that have reversed the age basis of the social order, or even equalized it.[9]

If we are serious about grappling with the broad and diverse problem of violence, it is a matter of identifying which aspects, types, patterns, processes, etc. of violence are so far least studied. Four basic issues emerge from the "big picture" that I have conveyed, and it is on these that future research should focus:

1. The study of the ideological bases of violence not only by the users of violence but also by the "explainers" of violence is crucial.

2. Factors contributing to the continuity and discontinuity of violence should be studied, both in historical context and through comparative studies of violent and nonviolent subcultures.

3. Much more work is needed on types of violence, the variety of conditions under which they occur, and their dependence on or interdependence with each other.

4. Large-scale "solutions" such as "the elimination of poverty" are probably fruitless, because they assume violence to be a unitary or near unitary phenomenon and also require deep structural changes in society. More useful would be detailed studies of the contexts of violence, on the twin assumptions that violence is in many cases context-specific, and that social contexts can more easily be changed than can social structures.

Violence is an old problem, only recently studied. The great difficulty with an old problem is that its explanation becomes so worn as to produce a cynicism that gnaws away at students who would try to comprehend it. In a space of less than 20 years, the same questions and answers to violence have been recited over and over, both theoretically and empirically. The work that I have reviewed in this book has been of immense value in adding to our knowledge of violence. But the time has come to ask new questions and to extend those pieces of research in directions that will force us to ask new questions. Only in this way can we avoid old answers.

Notes

INTRODUCTION
1. *Oxford Dictionary,* Compact Edition, pp. 3635–6.
2. *Ibid.,* p. 2405.
3. *Ibid.,* p. 82.
4. *Ibid.,* p. 1263.
5. E. van den Haag, *Political Violence and Civil Disobedience* (New York: Harper & Row, 1972), p. 55.
6. See also *ibid.,* pp. 64–65.

CHAPTER 1
POLITICAL VIOLENCE: REVOLUTION AND REPRESSION
1. E. van den Haag, *Political Violence and Civil Disobedience* (New York: Harper & Row, 1972), pp. 53–54.
2. The primitive society described by Malinowski comes closest to this model. See B. Malinowski, *Crime and Custom in Savage Society* (Paterson, New Jersey: Littlefield, Adams and Co., 1964).
3. See G. Newman, *The Punishment Response* (Philadelphia: Lippincott, 1978).
4. Errico Malatesta, *Il Programma Anarchico,* 1920. Also quoted in P. Berman, ed. *Quotations from the Anarchists* (New York: Praeger, 1972), p. 97. Malatesta, like many anarchists, spent countless years in prison and in exile. He was born in Italy in 1853, and died under house arrest in Mussolini's Italy.
5. See E. P. Thompson, *The Making of the English Working Class* (New York: Vintage, 1966).
6. R. Fogelson, *Violence as Protest: A Study of Riots and Ghettos* (New York: Doubleday, 1971), Chap. 2.
7. *Ibid.,* p. 51.
8. *Ibid.,* p. 51.
9. Marxists would argue, as does Hobsbawm, that rebellions and riots without a political ideology are "primitive" rebellions. See E. Hobsbawm, *Primitive Rebels* (New York: Norton, 1952).
10. E. V. Zenker, *Anarchism,* Methuen and Co. (London: 1898), p. 3.
11. E. Maletesta, *Umanita Nova,* August 12, 1920. Quoted in Berman, *Quotations from the Anarchists,* p. 108.
12. A. Berkman, Quoted in Berman, *Quotations from the Anarchists,* p. 116. Berkman, born in Russian Poland in 1870, emigrated to the United States where he served 14 years in prison for attempting the assassination of Henry Clay Frick, who was responsible for repressing the Homestead, Pennsylvania strike. He was eventually deported to Russia in 1919, fled after the Bolshevik suppression of Kronstadt, and committed suicide in 1936.
13. A. Berkman, Quoted in Berman, *Quotations from the Anarchists,* p. 116.

14. M. Bakunin, *Statism and Anarchy*, 1873. Quoted in Berman, *Quotations from the Anarchists*, p. 108.

15. Parsons was hanged as an accessory to the killing of a policeman during a clash between 200 police and a large public gathering which Parsons had addressed. A bomb was thrown by someone (still unknown) which killed or severely wounded seven policemen. The trial of Parsons and a number of his comrades was subsequently viewed as a national tragedy, especially as the sentences of some were commuted to life imprisonment, but Parsons refused to apply for clemency, and so was hanged. See M. M. Trumbull, *The Trial of the Judgment: Review of the Anarchist Case* (Chicago: Heath and House, 1888).

16. The Chicago *Alarm*, November 8, 1884. Letter from an Indianapolis member of the *International* to the Chicago *Alarm*, February 21, 1885.

17. Quoted in E.V. Zenker, *Anarchism*, p. 1.

18. A. Stumper, "Considerations à propos de L'Affaire Baader-Meinhof," *Revue de Droit Penal et de Criminologie* 1 (October 1973): 33–44.

19. F. J. Hacker, *Crusaders, Criminals, Crazies* (New York: Bantam, 1977), p. 71.

20. R. Dahrendorf, "Baader-Meinhof—How Come? What Next?" *New York Times*, October 20, 1977, p. 35.

21. Che Guevara, *Guerilla Warfare* (London: Pelican, 1969).

22. C. Marighela, *For the Liberation of Brazil* (London: Penguin, 1971), p. 95.

23. We should note that terrorism is not solely the domain of "left wing" organizations. There have been many terrorist groups that could be termed "right wing," such as the Brazilian death squad; the FLN in Algeria; the various Croatian terrorist groups, to name only a few. We are here dealing mostly with left wing terrorists mainly because they tend more often to write down their ideologies.

24. K. F. Johnson, "Guatemala—From Terrorism to Terror," *Conflict Studies* 23 (May 1972): 4–17.

25. B. M. Jenkins, *Soldiers Versus Gunmen—The Challenge of Urban Guerilla Warfare* (Santa Monica, Cal.: The Rand Corporation, 1974). A. Burton, *Urban Terrorism* (New York: The Free Press, 1975).

26. C. Wilson, *The Tupamaros: The Unmentionables* (Boston: Branden Press, 1974).

27. G. Jackson, *Surviving the Long Night: An Autobiographical Account of a Political Kidnapping* (New York: Vanguard Press, 1974).

28. O. Rammstedt, "Urban Guerilla and Social Movements," in J. Niezing, ed., *Urban Guerilla—Studies in the Theory, Strategy and Practice of Political Violence in Modern Societies* (Rotterdam, Netherlands: Rotterdam University Press, 1974), pp. 46–68.

29. For an excellent survey of terrorist theory and practice which clearly demonstrates this point see W. Laqueur, *Terrorism* (New York: Little, Brown, 1977).

30. U.S. Congress Senate Committee on the Judiciary, *Terrorist Activity*, Hearings before the Subcommittee to Investigate the Administration of Internal Security Act and Other Internal Security Laws, Part 1, 93rd Con., 2nd Sess., Washington, D.C.: U.S. Government Printing Office, 1974.
T. J. Deakin, "Legacy of Carlos Marighella," *F.B.I. Law Enforcement Bulletin*, 43, 10 (October 1974): 19–25.

R. Kroes, "Violence in America—Spontaneity and Strategy," in J. Niezing, ed., *Urban Guerilla,* pp. 81–93.

National Advisory Commission on Criminal Justice Standards and Goals, *Disorders and Terrorism,* Washington, D.C.: U.S. Government Printing Office, 1976.

31. R. E. Butler, "Terrorism in Latin America," in Y. Alexander, ed. *International Terrorism: National Regional and Global Perspectives* (New York: Praeger, 1976).

32. R. Ridenour, "Where are the Terrorists—and What Do They Want?" *Skeptic* 11 (January-February 1976): 18–23.

33. See J. F. Ianni, *A Family Business* (New York: Mentor, 1973). Also Hobsbaum, *Primitive Rebels.* The latter analyzes the structure of these "primitive" social movements.

34. Burton, *Urban Terrorism,* p. 248.

35. H. B. Hawthorn, *The Doukhobors of British Columbia* (London: Dent and Sons, 1955).

36. For example, G. Woodcock, and I. Irakumovic, *The Doukhobors* (Toronto: Oxford University Press, 1968).

37. F. Fanon, *The Wretched of the Earth* (New York: Grove Press, 1968).

38. F. Nietzsche, *Beyond Good and Evil,* trans. Walter Kaufman (New York: Vintage, 1966).

39. J. Genet, *The Balcony,* trans. B. Frechtman (New York: Grove Press, 1968).

40. See Chapter 8 for a more detailed treatment of this essentially psychological process.

41. J.-P. Sartre, *Preface* to Fanon, *The Wretched of the Earth.*

42. J. Rubin, *Do It!* (New York: Simon & Schuster, 1970), p. 150.

43. F. J. Hacker, *Crusaders, Criminals, Crazies,* passim.

44. See, for example, J. Black-Michaud, *Cohesive Force* (Oxford: Basil Blackwell, 1975).

45. Hacker, *Crusaders, Criminals, Crazies,* p. 80.

46. G. Sorel, *Reflections on Violence,* ed. T. E. Hulone (London: Allen and Unwin, 1915).

47. *Ibid.,* p. 205.

48. Mao Tse Tung, *Quotations from Chairman Mao Tse Tung* (Peking: Foreign Languages Press, 1967), p. 261.

49. Zenker's encyclopaedic and passionate review of anarchism ends by taking this view.

50. E. Kefauver, *Crime in America,* Sidney Shalett, ed. (Garden City: Doubleday, 1961).

51. J. F. Kirkham, S. Levy, and W. J. Crofty, *Assassination and Political Violence,* Staff Report to the National Commission on the Causes and Prevention of Violence, Washington, D.C.: U.S. Government Printing Office, 1970.

52. D. Abrahamsen, *Our Violent Society* (New York: Funk & Wagnalls, 1970), p. 160.

53. Erich Fromm, *The Anatomy of Human Destructiveness* (New York: Holt, Rinehart and Winston, 1973).

54. W. Reich, *The Mass Psychology of Fascism,* trans. V. Carfagno (New York: Farrar, Straus & Giroux, 1970).

55. B. Bettelheim, "Individual and Mass Behavior in Extreme Situations," *Journal of Abnormal and Social Psychology* 38 (1943): 417, 426.

56. S. Milgram, *Obedience to Authority: An Experimental View* (New York: Harper & Row, 1974).
    P. G. Zimbardo, "A Pirandellian Prison," *New York Times,* April 8, 1973.

CHAPTER 2
HISTORICAL VIOLENCE: CONTINUITIES AND DISCONTINUITIES

1. J. F. Kirkham, S. Levy, and W. J. Crofty, *Assassination and Political Violence,* Staff Report to the National Commission on the Causes and Prevention of Violence, Washington, D.C.: U.S. Government Printing Office, 1970.
2. C. Tilly, "Collective Violence in European Perspective," in H. D. Graham, and T. R. Gurr, eds. *Violence in America: Historical and Comparative Perspectives* (New York: Bantam, 1969), pp. 4–44.
3. *Ibid.,* p. 800.
4. A. C. Leiby, *The Revolutionary War in the Hackensack Valley* (New Brunswick, New Jersey: Rutgers University Press, 1962).
5. E. B. McCrady, *The History of South Carolina in the Revolution 1780–1783* (New York: Macmillan, 1902).
6. Graham and Gurr, *Violence in America,* p. 63.
7. R. M. Brown, "Historical Patterns of Violence in America," in Graham and Gurr, *Violence in America,* p. 62.
8. "The Difference of Race Between the Northern and Southern People," *Southern Literary Messenger,* XXX (June 1860): 406–407.
9. See W. Notestein, *The Scot in History* (New Haven: Yale University Press, 1946).
10. *Hatche Courier,* June 24, 1846.
11. *Southern Advocate,* May 9, 1828.
12. J. H. Franklin, *The Militant South* (Cambridge, Mass.: Harvard University Press, 1956), p. 70.
13. *Ibid.,* pp. 11–12.
14. *Ibid.,* pp. 70–71.
15. H. T. Catterall, ed. *Judicial Cases Concerning American Slavery and the Negro* (Washington, D.C.: Carnegie Institution of Washington, 1929), Part II, p. 57.
16. Quoted in Franklin, *The Militant South,* p. 76.
17. S. Acheson, and J. H. O'Connell, *George Washington Diamond's Account of the Great Hanging at Gainesville, 1862* (Austin, Texas: Texas State Historical Association, 1963), p. 90.
18. *Ibid.,* p. 62.
19. Brown, "Historical Patterns of Violence," in Graham and Gurr, *Violence in America,* p. 65.
20. R. Lane, "Criminal Violence in America: The First 100 Years," *Annals of the American Academy of Political and Social Science* 423 January 1976): 1–13.
21. Brown, in Graham and Gurr, *Violence in America,* p. 67.
22. M. Weber, *The Protestant Ethic and the Spirit of Capitalism* (New York: Scribner, 1958).
23. Graham and Gurr, *Violence in America,* passim.
24. R. Aron, *Progress and Disillusion* (New York: Mentor, 1969).
25. L. Morris, *Bald Knobbers* (Caldwell, Idaho: Caxton Printers, 1939).
26. R. M. Brown, "Pivot of American Vigilantism: The San Francisco Vigilance Committee of 1856," in John A. Carroll, ed. *Reflections of*

Western Historians (Tucson, Arizona: University of Arizona Press, 1969).

27. Kirkham, et al., *Assassination and Political Violence,* p. 216.
28. W. E. Washburn, *The Governor and the Rebel: A History of Bacon's Rebellions in Virginia* (Chapel Hill, North Carolina: University of North Carolina, 1957).
29. B. Hindle, "The March of the Paxton Boys," *William and Mary Quarterly,* 3 (1946): 461–486.
30. Graham and Gurr, *Violence in America,* passim.
31. Brown, "Historical Patterns of Violence," in Graham and Gurr, *Violence in America,* p. 73.
32. W. G. Broehl, *The Molly Maguires* (Cambridge, Mass.: Harvard University Press, 1964).
33. *Ibid.,* p. 361.
34. Argument of Franklin B. Gowen before a Joint Committee of the Pennsylvania State Legislature, Philadelphia, 1875, pp. 76ff. Quoted in J. W. Coleman, *The Molly Maguire Riots* (New York: Arno, 1969), p. 22.
35. See Allan Pinkerton, *The Mollie Maguires and the Detectives* (New York: Dover, reprint series, 1973).
36. L. Adamic, *Dynamite: The Story of Class Violence in America* (New York: Viking, 1934).
37. Brown, "Historical Patterns of Violence," in Graham and Gurr, *Violence in America,* p. 75.
38. *Ibid.*
39. R. Walsh, *Charleston's Sons of Liberty: A Study of the Artisans, 1763–1789* (Columbia, South Carolina: University of South Carolina Press, 1959), pp. 3–55.
40. Brown, "Historical Patterns of Violence," p. 54.
41. J. A. Inciardi, *Careers in Crime* (Chicago: Rand McNally, 1975).
42. *Ibid.,* p. 96.
43. H. C. Brearley, *Homicide in the United States* (Chapel Hill: University of North Carolina Press, 1932), pp. 54–56. Other examples are also reported in H. V. Redfield, *Homicide North and South* (Philadelphia: Lippincott, 1880).
44. L. Katcher, *The Big Bank Roll: The Life and Times of Arnold Rothstein* (New York: Harper, 1959).
45. E. Kefauver, *Crime in America,* Sidney Shalett, ed. (Garden City: Doubleday, 1961).
46. For two balanced accounts, see J. A. Inciardi, *Careers in Crime,* and F. Ianni, *A Family Business* (New York: Mentor, 1973). See also Chapter 8.

CHAPTER 3
CRIMINAL VIOLENCE

1. R. M. Brown, "Historical Patterns of Violence," in H. D. Graham, and T. R. Gurr, eds. *The History of Violence in America: Historical and Comparative Perspectives* (New York: Bantam, 1969), p. 45f.
2. See, for example F. H. McClintock, *Crimes of Violence* (London: Macmillan, 1965).
3. D. J. Mulvihill, M. M. Tumin, and L. A. Curtis, *Crimes of Violence,* Vol. 11, Staff Report to the National Commission on the Causes and

Prevention of Violence, Washington, D.C.: U.S. Government Printing Office, 1969, p. 4.

4. T. Sellin, and M. E. Wolfgang, *The Measurement of Delinquency* (New York: Wiley, 1964).

5. Adapted from Sellin and Wolfgang, *The Measurement of Delinquency.*

6. G. Newman, *Comparative Deviance* (New York: Elsevier, 1976).

7. Federal Bureau of Investigation, *Uniform Crime Reports* (Washington, D.C.: U.S. Government Printing Office). Issued annually.

8. M. E. Wolfgang, "Uniform Crime Reports: a critical appraisal," *University of Pennsylvania Law Review* 3 (April 1963): 708–738.
S. M. Robinson, "A critical view of the uniform crime reports," *Michigan Law Review* 64 (April 1966): 1031–1054.
P. Lejins, "Uniform crime reports," *Michigan Law Review* 64 (April 1966): 1011–1030.
Mulvihill and Tumin, *Crimes of Violence,* pp. 16–42.

9. M. E. Wolfgang, and F. Ferracuti, *The Subculture of Violence* (London: Methuen, 1967), p. 258.

10. H. Harlan, "Five hundred homicides," *Journal of Criminal Law and Criminology* 40 (1950): 736–752.

11. M. E. Wolfgang, *Patterns in Criminal Homicide* (Philadelphia: University of Pennsylvania Press, 1958).

12. *Sources:* (a) Mulvihill and Tumin, *Crimes of Violence,* p. 20; (b) U.S. Department of Justice, *Sourcebook of Criminal Justice Statistics,* 1975, p. 12; (c) F.B.I. *Crime in the United States: Uniform Crime Reports,* 1967 and 1974.
Direct comparisons between U.C.R. rates and victimization rates should be made with care, as the victimization rates are compared with a population base of 12 years old and over. F.B.I. rates use total population. For other difficulties in making direct comparisons, see M. Hindelang, *Victimization in Eight American Cities* (Cambridge, Mass.: Ballinger, 1976).

13. A. Blumstein, "Seriousness Weights in an Index of Crime," *American Sociological Review* 39, 6 (1974): 854–864.

14. *Sources:* Mulvihill and Tumin, *Crimes of Violence,* p. 57; F.B.I. *Uniform Crime Reports,* 1968–1973.

15. *Sources:* F.B.I. *Uniform Crime Reports,* 1960–1974.

16. *Source:* U.S. Bureau of Census, *Social Indicators,* Washington, D.C.: U.S. Government Printing Office, 1978, p. 290.

17. Here is a partial listing, mainly of homicide studies:
R. S. Banay, "A study of 22 men convicted of murder in the first degree," *Journal of Criminal Law and Criminology* 34 (July 1943): 106–111.
R. C. Bensing, and O. J. Schroeder, *Homicide in an Urban Community* (Springfield, Illinois: Thomas, 1969).
H. C. Brearly, *Homicide in the United States* (Chapel Hill: University of North Carolina Press, 1932).
J. H. Cassidy, "Personality study of 200 murderers," *Journal of Criminal Psychopathology* 2 (1941): 296–304.
J. V. De Porte, and E. Parkhurst, "Homicide in New York State. A statistical study of the victims and criminals in 37 counties in 1921–30," *Human Biology* 7 (1935): 47–73.
L. I. Dublin, and B. Bunzel, "Thou shalt not kill: a study of homicide in the United States," *Survey Graphic* 24 (March): 127–131.

C. Dunn, *The Patterns and Distribution of Assault Incident Character-istics Among Social Areas,* U.S. Department of Justice, Law Enforce-ment Assistance Administration, Washington, D.C.: U.S. Govern-ment Printing Office, 1976.

E. Gibson, and S. Klein, *Murder* (London: H. M. Stationery Office, 1961).

A. F. Henry, and J. F. Short, Jr., *Suicide and Homicide* (Glencoe, Illinois: Free Press, 1954).

F. L. Hoffman, *The Homicide Problem* (Newark, New Jersey: Pru-dential Press, 1925).

J. J. Kilpatrick, "Murder in the Deep South," *Survey Graphic* 32 (October 1943): 395–397.

F. H. McClintock, *Crimes of Violence* (London: Macmillan, 1963).

T. Morris, *The Criminal Area* (London: Routledge & Kegan Paul, 1958).

T. Morris, and L. Blom-Cooper, "Murder in microcosm," *The Ob-server* (London), March 26, 1961, and *A Calendar of Murder* (Lon-don: Michael Joseph, 1963).

S. Palmer, *A Study of Murder* (New York: Crowell, 1960).

D. J. Pittman, and W. Handy, "Patterns in criminal aggravated assault," *Journal of Criminal Law, Criminology and Police Science* 55 (1964): 462–470.

O. Pollak, *The Criminality of Women* (Philadelphia: University of Pennsylvania Press, 1950).

Royal Commission on Capital Punishment, 1949–1953 *Report* (Lon-don: H. M. Stationery Office, 1953).

S. Siciliano, "L'Omicidio," *Studio su un'Indagine Criminologica Com-piuta in Danimarca* (Padova: Cedam, 1965).

V. Swigert, and R. Farrell, *Murder, Inequality and the Law* (Boston: Lexington, 1976).

H. Von Hentig, *Crime: Causes and Conditions* (New York: McGraw-Hill, 1947).

M. E. Wolfgang, *Patterns in Criminal Homicide* (Philadelphia: Uni-versity of Pennsylvania Press, 1963).

Other studies establishing the age difference concerning the violent crimes of robbery and rape are cited in Chapter 9, where these crimes are dealt with in more detail.

18. There are many methodological difficulties with these computations. Wolfgang presents data from 1958 to 1964 recomputed for age-specific rates and shows that there was virtually no increase in crime for the 10–17 age group. Those data are, however, misleading as can be seen from Figure 3.4. The increases for 1958–64 were slight, but we can see that by grouping the 10–14 group with the 15–17 group the increase for the latter group would be considerably hidden. See M. E. Wolf-gang, *Youth and Violence,* U.S. Department of Health, Education and Welfare (Washington, D.C.: U.S. Government Printing Office, 1970), p. 29.

19. *Sources:* F.B.I. *Uniform Crime Reports,* 1958–1974: U.S. Bureau of Census, general population data. The Uniform Crime Report does not give age-specific rates. I have produced these calculations using the methods described in Mulvihill and Tumin, *Crimes of Violence,* Appendix 10.

20. *Source:* National Advisory Committee on Criminal Justice Standards

and Goals, *Disorders and Terrorism: Report of the Task Force on Terrorism,* Washington, D.C.: U.S. Government Printing Office, p. 509. Date were derived from F.B.I., National Bomb Data Program, and newspaper reports. They do not include threats or unsuccessful attempts.
21. *Ibid.,* p. 28.
22. Mulvihill and Tumin, *Crimes of Violence,* Appendix 10. See also Chapter 9.
23. C. Dunn, *Assault Incident Characteristics,* 1976.
24. Wolfgang, *Youth and Violence.*
25. As Wolfgang and Ferracuti observe in their *Subculture of Violence,* "there is no need to document this generalization about sex and homicide. Every study known to the authors reports this fact," p. 318.
26. F. Adler, *Sisters in Crime* (New York: McGraw-Hill, 1976).
27. R. Simon, "Women and Crime," in G. Newman, ed., *Crime and Justice in America 1776–1976, The Annals of the American Academy of Political and Social Science,* Vol. 423, January 1976, p. 37.
28. *Ibid.*
29. J. Davis, "Blacks and Crime," in G. Newman, ed., *Crime and Justice,* pp. 89–98.
30. See, for example H. Garfinkel, "Research note on inter- and intra-racial homicides," *Social Forces* 27 (1949): 369–381.
    G. Myrdal, *An American Dilemma* (New York: Harper & Row, 1944). Other studies are summarized in M. E. Wolfgang, *Crime and Race* 1964 ed. (New York: Institute of Human Relations Press, 1964).
31. *Sources:* F.B.I. Uniform Crime Reports, 1964–1974, U.S. Bureau of Census, general population data.
32. In a recent study, striking agreement was found in comparisons between victimization data for 1974 and U.C.R. data of that year in proportions of offenders classified as black. This study was also able to estimate the effects of differences in victims' reporting of crime. It found that ". . . once the victim's reporting (to the police) behavior is taken into account, differences between NCP crimes that are reported to the police and UCR data on arrestees remain only for assault." And in this instance, it was found that victims *underreported* assault. See M. Hindelang, "Race and Involvement in Common Law Personal Crimes: A Comparison of Three Techniques," *American Sociological Review,* in press.
33. *Sources:* Mulvihill and Tumin, *Crimes of Violence,* pp. 210–212, and U.S. Bureau of Census, general population data.
34. Mulvihill and Tumin, *Crimes of Violence,* p. 214. Various other studies have found differing interracial proportions of violent crime. See M. E. Wolfgang, *Patterns in Criminal Homicide* (Philadelphia: University of Pennsylvania Press, 1958), who found 6%; H. Harlan, "Five Hundred Homicides," *Journal of Criminal Law and Criminology* 40 (1950): 736–752 who found 3%; P. J. Pittman, and W. Handy, "Patterns in Criminal Aggravated Assault," *Journal of Criminal Law and Criminology* 55 (1964): 462–470 who found 4%; proportions reported in other studies for different crimes are reported in Chapters 7, 8, and 9.
35. Victim-offender relationships are dealt with in more detail in Chapters 7, 8 and 9.
36. *Sources:* F.B.I. *Uniform Crime Reports,* 1964–1974, U.S. Bureau of Census, general population data. Rates computed using the method outlined in Mulvihill and Tumin, *Crimes of Violence,* Appendix 10.

37. M. E. Wolfgang, R. Figlio, and T. Sellin, *Delinquency in a Birth Cohort* (Chicago: University of Chicago Press, 1972).
38. From G. Newman, and F. Ferracuti, "Assaultive Offenses," in D. Glaser, ed. *Handbook of Criminology* (New York: Rand McNally, 1974), p. 183.
39. This observation is based upon Mulvihill and Tumin, *Crimes of Violence,* Chap. 3, and U.C.R. data.
40. *Source:* F.B.I. *Uniform Crime Reports,* 1958–1974.
41. C. Shaw, and H. D. McKay, *Juvenile Delinquency in Urban Areas* (Chicago: University of Chicago Press, 1942).
42. *Source:* F.B.I. *Uniform Crime Reports,* 1974.
43. I have made these calculations using the method outlined by Mulvihill and Tumin, *ibid.* Also, this method is explained in T. N. Ferdinand, "Demographic Shifts and Criminology: an inquiry," *British Journal of Criminology* (April 1970): 164–175.
44. Mulvihill and Tumin, *Crimes of Violence,* Appendix 3.
45. The following is a partial listing:

In Italy
E. Ferri, *L'Omicidio* (Torino: Fratelli Bocca, 1895).
E. Morselli, *Il Suicidio* (Milano: Dumolard, 1879).

In the United States
M. Amir, "Patterns in forcible rape" (Ph.D. diss., University of Pennsylvania, 1965), and "Victim precipitated forcible rape," *Journal of Criminal Law, Criminology and Police Science* 58 (1967): 493–502.
Bensing and Schroeder, *Homicide in an Urban Community.*
Brearley, *Homicide in the United States.*
C. S. Dunn, *The Analysis of Environmental Attribute/Crime Incident Characteristic Interrelationships* (Ph.D. diss., S.U.N.Y. at Albany, 1974).
A. Normandeau, "Patterns and Trends in Robbery" (Ph.D. diss., University of Pennsylvania, 1968).
Swigert and Farrell, *Murder, Inequality and the Law.*
M. E. Wolfgang, *Studies in Homicide* (New York: Harper & Row, 1967).
M. E. Wolfgang, R. M. Figlio, and T. Sellin, *Delinquency in a Birth Cohort* (Chicago: University of Chicago Press, 1972).

In Denmark
K. Svalastoga, "Homicide and Social Contact in Denmark," *American Journal of Sociology* 62 (1956): 37–41.

In Finland
V. Verkko, *Homicides and Suicides in Finland and Their Dependence on National Character* (Copenhagen: Gads Forlag, 1951).

In England
McClintock, *Crimes of Violence.*
Morris and Blom-Cooper, *A Calendar of Murder.*
F. H. McClintock and E. Gibson, *Robbery in London* (London: Macmillan, 1961).

In India and Sri Lanka
C. H. S. Jayewardene, "Criminal homicide: a study of culture conflict" (Ph.D. diss., University of Pennsylvania, 1960); "Criminal cultures and subcultures," *Probation and Child Care Journal* 2 (June 1963): 1–5; "Criminal homicide in Ceylon," *Probation and Child Care Journal* 3 (January 1964): 15–30.
J. H. Strauss, and M. A. Strauss, "Suicide, homicide and social structure in Ceylon," *American Journal of Sociology* (1953) 58: 461–469.
A. L. Wood, "Crime and aggression in changing Ceylon," *Transactions of the American Philosophical Society,* new series 51, 8 (December 1961); "A socio-structural analysis of murder, suicide, and economic crime in Ceylon," *American Sociological Review* 26 (October 1961): 744–753.
E. D. Driver, "Interaction and criminal homicide in India," *Social Forces* 40 (1961): 153–158.
H. Bloch, "Research report on homicide, attempted homicide and crimes of violence," Colombo: Ceylon Police Report, 1960.

In Mexico
J. M. V. Alzaga, "Epidemiology of homicide in Mexico, D. F.", reported in M. E. Wolfgang and F. Ferracuti, *The Subculture of Violence* (London: Methuen, 1967).
M. E. Bustamante, and M. A. Bravo, B., "Epidemiologia del homicidio en Mexico," *Higiene* 9 (1957): 21–23.

In South Africa
A. M. Lamong, "Forensic psychiatric practice in South African mental hospital," *South Africa Medical Journal* 35, 40 (1961): 833–837.
46. These are K. Svalastoga, "Rape and social structure," *Pacific Sociological Review* 5 (1962): 48–53.
    Pittman and Handy, "Patterns in Assault."
    A. D. Pokorny, "A comparison of homicides in two cities," *Journal of Criminal Law, Criminology and Police Science* 56 (1965a): 478–487; "Human violence—a comparison of homicide, aggravated assault, suicide and attempted suicide," *Journal of Criminal Law, Criminology and Police Science* 56 (1965b): 488–497.
47. See M. E. Wolfgang, and F. Ferracuti, *The Subculture of Violence* (London: Methuen, 1967), p. 261, for a list of criticisms of such studies.
48. Further reasons for these data patterns are also considered in Chapter 6, in relation to the literature on crowding.
49. The method used was that described in Mulvihill and Tumin, *Crimes of Violence,* Appendix 3. A similar study was conducted for the period of 1958–1964, where it was found that 30–50% of the increase in absolute crime during that period could be attributed to age structure alone. See P. C. Sagi, and C. F. Wellford, "Age Composition and Patterns of Change in Criminal Statistics," *Journal of Criminal Law, Criminology and Police Science,* 59, 1 (1968): 29–36.
50. Mulvihill and Tumin, *Crimes of Violence,* p. 44.
51. *Ibid.,* p. 98.
52. *Ibid.*
53. *Source:* U.S. Bureau of Census, *Social Indicators,* p. 225. Based on data from National Health Statistics.

54. Mulvihill and Tumin, *Crimes of Violence,* p. 44.
55. F.B.I. *Uniform Crime Reports,* 1969, p. 10.

CHAPTER 4
CULTURES AND SUBCULTURES OF VIOLENCE
 1. See, for example, S. Hackney, "Southern Violence," in *Violence in America,* eds. H. D. Graham and T. R. Gurr (New York: Bantam, 1969), pp. 505–527.
    R. D. Gastil, "Homicide and a Regional Culture of Violence," *American Sociological Review* 36 (1971): 412–26.
    T. F. Pettigrew and R. B. Spier, "The Ecological Structure of Negro Homicide," *American Journal of Sociology* 67 (1971): 621–629.
 2. H. Blumenthal, R. Kahn, F. Andrews, and K. Mead, *Justifying Violence: Attitudes of American Men* (Ann Arbor, Michigan: University of Michigan Press, 1972).
 3. R. Clark, *Crime in America* (New York: Simon & Schuster, 1970).
 4. L. Berkowitz, and A. LePage, "Weapons as Aggression-Eliciting Stimuli," *Journal of Personality and Social Psychology* 7 (1967): 202–207.
 5. R. Clark, *Crime in America.*
    D. N. Daniels, M. F. Gilula, and F. M. Ochberg, eds. *Violence and the Struggle for Existence* (Boston: Little, Brown, 1970).
    L. P. Kenneth, *The Gun in America* (New York: Greenwood, 1975).
    H. S. Bloomgarden, *The Gun: A "Biography" of the Gun that Killed John F. Kennedy* (New York: Grossman, 1975).
 6. M. B. Clinard, *Cities with Little Crime* (New York: Cambridge University Press, 1978). The South has a higher rate of gun ownership than the North. One historian has argued that the attachment to guns is traceable to the frontier tradition: R. Lane, "Criminal Violence in America: The First 100 Years," in *Crime and Justice in America: 1776–1976,* ed. G. Newman, *Annals of the American Academy of Political and Social Science* (January 1976).
 7. Blumenthal, et al., *Justifying Violence* is the only study to provide empirical evidence that backs up the impressionistic evidence. However, this research has also been severely criticized. See H. Toch, Review in *Journal of Criminal Justice* 2 (1974): 179–181.
 8. H. D. Graham and T. R. Gurr, *Violence in America,* p. 800.
 9. The interpretation of comparative crime statistics is fraught with many difficulties. Specific comparisons should not be made, only general inferences. The reader is strongly urged to consult E. Vetere and G. Newman, "International Crime Statistics: An Overview from a Comparative Perspective," in *Abstracts in Criminology and Penology* (May 1977) for a review of these methodological difficulties.
10. These data are based on offenses reported to police, and were collected as part of a survey conducted by the United Nations Section on Criminal Justice and Crime Prevention, Department of Economic and Social Affairs. They are analyzed more extensively in G. Newman and E. Vetere, *World Crime* (New York: New York University Press) (in press).
11. There is no consistent classification of "developed" and "developing" countries. However, the classification used is based upon information presented in United Nations: *Report on the World Social Situation, 1974* (New York: Department of Economic and Social Affairs, 1975).

Developed Countries: Argentina, Australia, Austria, Canada, Chile, Cyprus, Denmark, Finland, France, German Federal Republic, Greece, Ireland, Italy, Japan, New Zealand, Norway, Poland, San Marino, Singapore, Spain, Sweden, Switzerland, United Kingdom, United States, Yugoslavia. *Developing Countries:* Algeria, Bahamas, Bahrain, Barbados, Costa Rica, Ecuador, Egypt, El Salvador, Guyana, Indonesia, Iran, Iraq, Jamaica, Kuwait, Malaysia, Maldives, Morocco, Oman, Pakistan, Peru, Qatar, Syrian Arab Republic, Trinidad and Tobago.

12. J. L. Freedman, *Crowding and Behavior* (San Francisco: Freeman, 1975).
13. J. Conklin, *The Impact of Crime* (New York: Macmillan, 1975).
14. C. R. Shaw, and H. D. McKay, *Juvenile Delinquency in Urban Areas* (Chicago: University of Chicago Press, 1942).
15. See, for example, M. Clinard, and D. Abbot, *Crime in Developing Countries* (New York: Wiley, 1975).
    D. Biles, ed. *Crime and Justice in Papua and New Guinea* (Canberra: Australian Institute of Criminology, 1977).
    Migration from country to city is not necessarily devastating and conducive to crime. It depends upon the patterning of kinship ties that is kept up. See G. Newman, *Comparative Deviance* (New York: Elsevier, 1976), Chap. 4.
16. M. E. Wolfgang, and F. Ferracuti, *The Subculture of Violence* (London: Tavistock, 1967).
17. See G. Woodcock, and I. Arakumovic, *The Doukhobors* (New York: Oxford, 1968).
18. S. Holt, *Terror in the Name of God* (New York: Crown, 1964), p. 46.
19. *Ibid.*
20. *Ibid.,* p. 67.
21. This and the following 6 points are from Wolfgang and Ferracuti, *The Subculture of Violence,* pp. 158–160.
22. The bureaucratic reasons as well as the "social control" reasons for this law are discussed in H. B. Hawthorn, ed. *The Doukhobors of British Columbia* (Vancouver: University of British Columbia Press, 1955).
23. Holt, *Terror in the Name of God,* p. 2.
24. *Ibid.*
25. *Ibid.,* pp. 230–232.
26. *Ibid.,* p. 231.
27. *Ibid.,* p. 232.
28. *Ibid.,* frontispiece.
29. Some of these are described very briefly by Wolfgang and Ferracuti, *The Subculture of Violence,* pp. 279–283.
30. E. A. Hooton, *Up From the Ape* (New York: Macmillan, 1946), p. 448.
31. F. B. Livngstone, "On the Non-Existence of Human Races," in A. Montagu, ed. *The Concept of Race* (London: Collier Macmillan, 1964).
32. P. L. Workman, "Genetic Analyses of a Hybrid Population," in M. H. Crawford, and P. L. Workman, eds. *Methods and Theories of Anthropological Genetics* (Albuquerque: University of New Mexico Press, 1973).
33. S. H. Katz, "Genetic Adaptation in Twentieth Century Man," in Crawford and Workman, pp. 405–410.
34. *Ibid.*

35. *Ibid.*
36. T. Hirschi and M. Hindelang, "Intelligence and Delinquency." *American Sociological Review* 42 (August 1977): 571–587.
37. Katz, "Genetic Adaptation," p. 417.
38. A. R. Jensen, *Genetics and Education* (New York: Harper & Row, 1973).
39. Katz, "Genetic Adaptation," p. 417.
40. F. Barth, *Ethnic Boundaries* (Boston: Little, Brown, 1969).
41. G. Newman, *The Punishment Response* (Philadelphia: Lippincott, 1978). There was a period of a few hundred years during the Middle Ages when feuding organized around bargaining was very common.
42. F. Ianni, *A Family Business* (New York: Mentor, 1975).
43. Marc Bloch, *Feudal Society,* trans. L. A. Manyon (Chicago: University of Chicago Press, 1961).
    J. Goebel, *Felony and Misdemeanor: A Study of the History of Criminal Law* (Philadelphia: University of Pennsylvania Press, 1976).
    G. Newman, *The Punishment Response.*
44. M. J. L. Hardy, *Blood Feuds and the Payment of Blood Money in the Middle East* (Leiden: E. J. Brill, 1963).
45. J. Black-Michaud, *Cohesive Force: Feud in the Mediterranean and Middle East* (Oxford: Basil Blackwell, 1975), p. 16.
46. *Ibid.*
47. S. Ball-Rokeach, "Values and Violence: A Test of the Subculture of Violence Theory," *American Sociological Review,* 30, 6 (1973): 736–744.
    H. S. Erlanger, "The Empirical Status of Subculture of Violence Thesis," *Social Problems,* 22, 2 (1974): 280–291.
48. G. Newman, *Comparative Deviance.*
49. J. Black-Michaud, *Cohesive Force* (Oxford: Basil Blackwell, 1975).
50. H. Hess, *Mafia and Mafiosi: The Structure of Power,* trans. Edward Osers (Lexington, Mass.: D. C. Heath, 1970).
    A. Pigliaru, *Il Banditismo in Sardegna: La Vendetta Barbaricina* (Milano: Giuffre, 1970).
    M. Hasluck, *The Unwritten Law of Albania,* ed. J. H. Hutton and J. E. Anderson (Cambridge: Cambridge University Press, 1954).
    C. L. Sonnichsen, *The Story of the Great Texas Feuds* (New York: Devin-Adan, 1962).
51. J. G. Peristiany, *Honour and Shame: The Valued Mediterranean Society* (London: Weidenfeld and Nicolson, 1965).
52. Hess, *Mafia and Mafiosi,* p. 94.
53. E. J. Hobsbawm, *Primitive Rebels: Studies in the Archaic Forms of Social Movement in the 19th and 20th Centuries* (New York: Norton, 1959), p. 92.
54. I. C. Horowitz, and G. Schwartz, "Honor, Normative Ambiguity and Gang Violence," *American Sociological Review,* 39 (1974): 238–51.
55. F. Fanon, *The Wretched of the Earth* (New York: Grove Press, 1963).
56. R. Coles, *Children of Crisis: A Study of Courage and Fear* (Boston: Little, Brown, 1967).
57. W. Miller, "Lower Class Culture as a Generating Milieu of Gang Deliquency," *Journal of Social Issues* 14 (1958): 5–19.
58. *Ibid.*
59. G. Newman, *The Punishment Response.*

60. See I. Taylor, J. Walton, and J. Young, *The New Criminology* (New York: Harper & Row, 1974).
61. W. Bonger, *Economic Conditions and Crime* (Bloomington, Indiana: Indiana University Press, 1969).
62. R. Quinney, *Critique of Legal Order* (Boston: Little, Brown, 1973).
63. R. Quinney, *Class, State and Crime* (New York: McKay, 1977).
64. R. K. Merton, *Social Theory and Social Structure,* 3rd ed. (New York: Free Press, 1968), p. 210.
65. R. A. Cloward, and L. E. Ohlin, *Delinquency and Opportunity* (New York: Free Press, 1960).
66. F. Ferracuti, and G. Newman, "Assaultive Offenses," in D. Glaser, ed. *Handbook of Criminology* (New York: Rand McNally, 1974), p. 188.
67. I. K. Feierabend, and R. L. Feierbend, "Aggressive Behaviors with Politics, 1948–1962; A Cross-National Study," *Journal of Conflict Resolution* 10 (1966): 249–272.
68. A. F. Henry, and J. F. Short, *Suicide and Homicide* (Glencoe, Illinois: Free Press, 1954). This finding is in contrast to that of J. L. McCary, "Ethnic and Cultural Reactions to Frustration," *Journal of Personality* 18, 3 (1949): 321–26.
69. A. Cohen, *Delinquent Boys* (Glencoe: Free Press, 1955).
70. This consensus across classes is now well established. See G. Newman, *Comparative Deviance* for a study and review of other research supporting this finding.
71. I. Illich, *Deschooling Society,* (New York: Harper & Row, 1972).
72. A. Turk, *Criminality and Legal Order* (Chicago: Rand McNally, 1969).
73. J. Newman, and G. Newman, "Crime and Punishment in the Schooling Process: An Historical Analysis," In E. Wenk, ed., *Theoretical Perspectives on School Crime* (Hackensack, N.J.: National Council on Crime and Delinquency, 1978).
74. F. Adler, *Sisters in Crime* (New York: McGraw-Hill, 1975).

CHAPTER 5
VIOLENCE AND THE ROOTS OF CULTURE: AGE AND SEX

1. For more detailed data on this fact, see G. R. Newman, and E. Vetere, *World Crime: A Comparative Analysis* (New York: New York University Press, 1978) (in press). See also Chapter 3.
2. See R. N. Johnson, *Aggression in Man and Animals* (Philadelphia: Saunders, 1972), pp. 52–56, for a review of all these studies.
3. I. Eibl-Eibesfeldt, *Love and Hate* (New York: Holt, Rinehart and Winston, 1972), 86–88.
4. There are many exceptions. In baboons, adolescent males fight against females, and probably never manage to dominate their mothers; weaker animals may form "alliances" and thus maintain dominance. See: Johnson, *Aggression in Man and Animals, passim.*
5. See R. A. Hinde, "The Study of Aggression: Determinants, Consequences, Goals and Functions," in J. Dewit, and W. W. Hartup, eds. *Determinants and Origins of Aggressive Behavior* (The Hague: Mouton, 1974), pp. 14–17.
6. There are many examples of this. See, for example, D. Lerner, *The Passing of Traditional Society* (Glencoe, Illinois: Free Press, 1958). A. Inkles, and D. H. Smith, *Becoming Modern: Individual Change in Six Developing Countries* (Cambridge, Mass.: Harvard University Press, 1974).

7. This is simply another way of restating Weber's dictum: that all authority presupposes a certain amount of voluntary submission on the part of subordinates. M. Weber, *From Max Weber: Essays in Sociology,* trans. and edited by H. Gerth, and C. W. Mills, (New York: Oxford University Press, 1946).

8. Newman and Vetere, *World Crime.*

9. Generally, anthropologists have observed that physical maturity is reached early in tropical cultures as against non-tropical cultures. However, it has also recently been suggested that nutrition may be a major factor, so that children in the U.S. and developed countries mature earlier on the average than those in starvation level cultures. Concerning the transition from child to adult, see A. van Gennep, *The Rites of Passage,* trans. M. B. Vizedom and G. L. Caffee (Chicago: University of Chicago Press, 1960). However, it should be recognized that this is a very general observation. Nutrition may play a small part in a more complex set of factors related to poverty, as we shall see below.

10. G. S. Hall, *Adolescence,* 2 Volumes (New York: Appleton, 1965).

11. J. Piaget, *The Moral Judgment of the Child* (New York: Free Press, 1965).

12. See Gary Y. Larsen, "Methodology in Developmental Psychology: An Examination of Research on Piagetian Theory." *Child Development,* 48 (1977): 1160–1166.

13. See T. Hirschi, and M. Hindelang, "Intelligence and Delinquency," *American Sociological Review* 42 (August 1977): 571–587 for a critical appraisal of all research concerning the relationship between intelligence and delinquency. It would appear that there is undoubtedly a relationship between low intelligence and delinquency, but the dynamics of this relationship remain unknown, except to point out that unhappy school experience is by far the most common factor related empirically to delinquency. See also F. Ferracuti and G. Newman, "Psychological Theories of Delinquency," in L. Sebba and F. Landau, eds. *Criminology in Perspective: Essays in Honor of Israel Drapkin* (Boston: Heath, 1977).

14. F. M. Fodor, "Delinquency and susceptibility to social influence among adolescents as a function of level of moral development," *Journal of Social Psychology* 86 (1972): 257–260. There is no research clearly linking defective moral development to aggressive behavior. However, one study addresses the other side of this question—that moral development is positively related to conformity: R. M. Diamond, and M. Belenky, "Moral Judgment Level and Conformity Behavior," *Developmental Psychology* 7 (1972): 327–336. Other studies found a relationship between "psychopathic delinquency" and moral development: G. Jurkovic, and N. Prentice, "Relation of Moral and Cognitive Development to Dimensions of Juvenile Delinquency," *Journal of Abnormal Psychology* 86, 4 (August 1977): 414–420; A. F. Campagna, and S. Harter, "Moral Judgment in Sociopathic and Normal Children," *Journal of Personality and Social Psychology* 31 (1975): 199–205.

15. See J. L. Tapp, "A Child's Garden of Law and Order," *Psychology Today* 12 (December 1970): 29–62, for empirical evidence on universality.

16. Newman and Vetere, *World Crime.* See also Chapter 4.

17. One study has shown that early childhood experience may be related to moral development. But again, this study addresses the dynamics of moral development, not its relationship to aggression: M. L. Hoffman,

"Father Absence and Conscience Development," *Developmental Psychology* 4 (1971): 400–406. One study did examine the possible relationship between moral judgment and attitudes to the use of war, and found no variation across six cultures. See H. Cook, and D. Jackons, "Moral Development and the Development of the Concept of War," in DeWit and Hartup, *Determinants of Aggressive Behavior,* pp. 473–480.

18. W. W. Lambert, "Promise and Problems of Cross-Cultural Exploration of Children's Aggressive Strategies," in DeWit and Hartup, *Determinants of Aggressive Behavior,* pp. 437–459.
19. See G. Newman, *The Punishment Response* (Philadelphia: Lippincott, 1978), for a review of this controversy.
20. P. Aries, *Centuries of Childhood* (New York: Alfred A. Knopf, 1962).
21. See S. Halleck, *Psychiatry and the Dilemmas of Crime* (New York: Harper & Row, 1967) for an excellent coverage of this aspect of the "generation gap."
22. T. Hirschi, *The Causes of Delinquency* (Berkeley, Calif.: University of California Press, 1969).
23. D. Matza, *Delinquency and Drift* (New York: Wiley, 1964).
24. There are many, many studies. The classic studies are L. Berkowitz, and E. Rawlings, "Effects of Film Violence on Subsequent Aggressive Tendencies," *Journal of Abnormal and Social Psychology* 66 (1963): 405–12; and L. Berkowitz, R. Corwin and M. Hieronimus, "Film Violence and Subsequent Aggressive Tendencies," *Public Opinion Quarterly* 27 (1963): 217–229.
25. See D. Howitt, and G. Cumberbatch, *Mass Media Violence and Society* (New York: Wiley, 1975) for a review of all these studies; and S. Brady, *Screen Violence and Film Censorship—A Review of Research* (London: Home Office Research Unit, His Majesty's Stationery Office, 1977).
26. *Ibid.,* p. 43.
27. I. Illich, *Deschooling Society* (New York: Harper & Row, 1972).
28. Lambert, "Promise and Problems of Children's Aggressive Strategies," in DeWit and Hartup, p. 451.
29. S. Feshbach, "The development and regulation of aggression: some research gaps and a proposed cognitive approach," in DeWit and Hartup, pp. 167–191.
30. F. M. Thrasher, *The Gang* (Chicago: University of Chicago Press, 1927). H. Asbury, *The Gangs of New York* (New York: Knopf, 1928).
31. National School Public Relations Association, *Violence and Vandalism* Arlington, Va.: 1975.
32. J. Newman, and G. Newman, "Crime and Punishment in the Schooling Process: An Historical Analysis," in E. Wenk (ed.) *Theoretical Perspectives on School Crime,* (Hackensack, N.J.: National Council on Crime and Delinquency, 1978).
33. C. F. Rosenthal, *Social Conflict and Collective Violence in American Institutions of Higher Learning,* Vol. 1, Washington, D.C.: U.S. Department of Commerce, 1971.
    I. Wallerstein, *University in Turmoil: The Politics of Change* (New York: Atheneum, 1969).
34. E. Erikson, *Childhood and Society* (New York: Norton, 1950).
35. S. Halleck, *Psychiatry and the Dilemmas of Crime.*
36. K. Moyer, *The Psychobiology of Aggression* (New York: Harper & Row, 1976).
37. F. Adler, *Sisters in Crime* (New York: McGraw-Hill, 1975).

38. See Newman and Vetere, *World Crime*. Of the fifty countries surveyed, the ratio of male to female crime was never less than 6:1. See also Wolfgang and Ferracuti, *The Subculture of Violence,* p. 258.
39. Newman and Vetere, *World Crime*.
40. Johnson, *Aggression in Man and Animals,* pp. 97–98.
41. J. P. Scott, *Aggresssion* (Chicago: University of Chicago Press, 1975), p. 128.
42. Johnson, *Aggression in Man and Animals,* p. 98.
43. *Ibid.*
44. *Ibid.*
45. D. R. Robertson, "Social Control of Sex Reversal in a Coral Reef Fish," *Science* 117 (1971): 1007–1009.
46. See D. D. Thiessen, *The Evolution and Chemistry of Aggression* (Springfield, Ill.: Charles C. Thomas, 1976), p. 55f, for an excellent review of the sex reversal literature, especially pp. 58–59, for a survey of all species in which reversal has been artificially induced.
47. Moyer, *Psychobiology of Aggression,* p. 60.
48. H. Persky, K. D. Smith, and G. K. Basu, "Relation of Psychological Measures of Aggression and Hostility to Testosterone Production in Man," *Psychosomatic Medicine* 33 (1971): 265–277.
49. L. E. Kreuz, and R. M. Rose, "Assessment of Aggressive Behavior and Plasma Testosterone in a Young Criminal Population," *Psychosomatic Medicine* 34 (1972): 321–332.
50. Moyer, *Psychobiology of Aggression,* pp. 62, 64, 65.
51. *Ibid.,* p. 63–64. The most well known study, and review of the literature is G. K. Sturup, "Correctional Treatment and the Criminal Sex Offender," *Canadian Journal of Corrections* 3 (1961): 250–265.
52. Personal Communication, Dr. Bent Svendson, formerly Deputy Director, Herstedvester Prison, Denmark.
53. Thiessen, *Evolution of Aggression,* pp. 62–65, for a review of all those studies.
54. Johnson, *Aggression,* pp. 101–102.
55. *Ibid.,* pp. 102–103.
56. Thiessen, *Evolution of Aggression,* p. 75.
57. *Ibid.,* p. 50.
58. *Ibid.*
59. Johnson, *Aggression in Man,* p. 93.
60. Thiessen, see Chapter 10 for a more detailed discussion.
61. K. Lorenz, *On Aggression,* (N.Y.: Harcourt Brace Jovanovich, 1966).
62. See Eibl-Eibelsfeldt, *Love and Hate,* (New York: Holt, Rinehart and Winston, 1972); A. Montagu, *The Nature of Human Aggression* (New York: Oxford University Press, 1976).
63. Freud's basic writings on sex-role development may be found in S. Freud, "Some Psychological Consequences of the Anatomical Distinction Between the Sexes," in *Collected Papers,* Vol. V., trans. J. Riviere (London: Hogarth Press, 1948), 186–197; and "Female Sexuality," *Ibid.,* pp. 252–272.
64. See W. B. Miller, "Lower Class Culture as a Generating Milieu of Gang Delinquency," *Journal of Social Issues* 14 (1959): 5–19.
65. B. G. Rosenberg, and B. Sutton-Smith, *Sex and Identity* (New York: Holt, Rinehart and Winston, 1972), p. 46.
66. K. Millett, *Sexual Politics* (New York: Doubleday, 1970), p. 178.

67. E. Maccoby, ed., *The Development of Sex Differences* (Stanford, Calif.: Stanford University Press, 1966). Appendix.
68. W. Mischel, "The Social Learning View of Sex Differences in Behavior," in E. Maccoby, ed. *The Development of Sex Differences.*
69. L. Zebrowitz, and J. Eisen, "Achievements of Male and Female Storybook Characters as Determinants of Achievement Behavior by Boys and Girls," *Journal of Personality and Social Psychology* 33, 4 (April 1976): 467–473.
70. Mischel, "The Social Learning View of Sex Differences," p. 63.
71. L. Kohlberg, "A Cognitive-Developmental Analysis of Children's Sex-Role Concepts and Attitudes," in Maccoby, *The Development of Sex Differences,* pp. 82–172.
72. Maccoby, *The Development of Sex Differences,* Appendix. L. Terman, and C. C. Milee, *Sex and Personality* (New York: Russell and Russell, 1936).
73. W. Mishel, in Maccoby, ed., p. 73–4.
74. *Ibid.,* pp. 74–6.
75. P. Mayo, "Sex Differences and Psychopathology," in B. Lloyd, and J. Archer, eds. *Exploring Sex Differences* (London: Academic Press, 1976), p. 213.
76. *Ibid.*
77. *Ibid.*
78. This hypothesis has been expounded in L. Phillips, "A Social View of Psychopathology," in *Foundations of Abnormal Psychology,* ed. P. London, and P. Rosenham (New York: Holt, Rinehart and Winston, 1968).
79. S. Dornbusch, "Afterword," in Maccoby, *The Development of Sex Differences* p. 216.
80. See C. Ounsted, and D. C. Taylor, eds. *Gender Differences: Their Ontogeny and Significance* (London: Churchill Livingstone, 1972), especially Chapter 10.

CHAPTER 6
RECYCLING VIOLENCE: THE FAMILY

1. F. Ferracuti, and G. Newman, "Assaultive Offenses," in D. Glaser, ed. *Handbook of Criminology* (New York: Rand McNally, 1974), p. 185. Many studies report these findings.
2. J. M. Reinhardt, *Sex Perversions and Sex Crimes* (Springfield, Ill.: Thomas, 1957).
   W. Stekel, *Sadism and Masochism: The Psychology of Hatred and Cruelty,* Vols. I and II (New York: Liveright, 1929).
   R. Krafft-Ebing, *Psychopathia Sexualis* (Philadelphia: Davis, 1892).
   G. Rothman, *The Riddle of Cruelty* (New York: Philosophical Library, 1971).
   D. Lunde, *Murder and Madness* Stanford, 1976.
3. K. Moyer, *Psychobiology of Aggression,* (New York: Harper & Row, 1976), pp. 205–6.
4. C. R. Carpenter, "Sexual Behavior of Free-Ranging Rhesus Monkeys," *Journal of Comparative Psychology,* 33 (1942): 113–142.
5. Moyer, *Psychobiology of Aggression, passim.*
6. R. N. Johnson, *Aggression in Man and Animals* (Philadelphia: Saunders, 1972), pp. 104–106.
7. Commission on Obscenity and Pornography, *Report of the Commission*

on Obscenity and Pornography (Washington, D.C.: U.S. Government Printing Office, 1970).

8. S. Freud, *Civilization and Its Discontents,* trans. James Strachey (New York: W. W. Norton, 1962).

9. For the best and basic discussion of social learning and how it relates to reinforcement theory, or "behaviorism," see A. Bandura, and R. H. Walters, *Social Learning and Personality Development* (New York: Holt, Rinehart and Winston, 1963).
R. H. Walters, "Some Conditions Facilitating the Occurrence of Imitative Behavior," in E. C. Simmel, R. A. Hopper, and G. A. Milton, eds. *Social Facilitation and Imitative Behavior* (Boston: Allyn & Bacon, 1968), Chapter 1.
J. B. Gilmore, "Toward an Understanding of Imitation," in Simmel, *et al., ibid.*

10. G. Tarde, *The Laws of Imitation* (New York: Holt, Rinehart and Winston, 1903).

11. A. Bandura, "Social Learning Through Imitation," in M. R. Jones, ed. *Nebraska Symposium on Motivation* (Lincoln, Neb.: University of Nebraska Press, 1962), pp. 211–269. The most powerful data supporting the notion that imitation may occur without rewards are those of Mowrer's study of mynah birds. Although Mowrer at the time interpreted this learning as "secondary reinforcement," recent interpretations of his work concluded that "one is left with the unsatisfactory alternative of saying that mynah birds have a tendency to imitate." See O. H. Mowrer, "On the Psychology of 'Talking Birds'—a contribution to the language of personality theory," in *Learning Theory and Personality Dynamics: Selected Papers* (New York: Ronald Press, 1950).
B. M. Foss, "Mimicry in Mynahs (Gragula Religiosa): A Test of Mowrer's Theory," *British Journal of Psychology,* 55 (1964): 85–88.
A. Bandura, "Vicarious Processes: A Case of No-Trial Learning," in L. Berkowitz, ed. *Advances in Experimental Social Psychology,* Vol. 2 (New York: Academic Press, 1965), pp. 1–55.

12. *Ibid.* This is a very difficult issue, made more difficult by Rieff's observation that it is strictly impossible to imitate an act unless the response to be imitated is already part of the observer's response repertoire. P. Rieff, *Introduction* in C. H. Cooley, *Human Nature and Social Order* (New York: Schocken, 1964).

13. Bandura and Walters, *Social Learning and Personality Development,* passim.

14. *Ibid.* Also W. Mischel, *Introduction to Personality* (New York: Holt, Rinehart and Winston, 1971).

15. Bandura and Walters, *Social Learning and Personality Development,* passim.

16. One study was unable to find support for the general theory of differential association, probably because of this theory's failure to take into account the distinction between learning and performance. A. J. Reiss, Jr., "An Empirical Test of Differential Association Theory," *Journal of Research in Crime and Delinquency* 1, 1 (1962): 5.

17. A. Bandura, "The Role of Modeling Processes in Personality Development," in W. Hartup and N. L. Smothergill, eds. *The Young Child: Reviews of Research* (Washington, D.C.: National Association for the Education of Young Children, 1967), p. 43.

18. H. Kaufman, *Aggression and Altruism* (New York: Holt, Rinehart and Winston, 1970), pp. 54–75.
19. See A. Bandura, *Aggression: A Social Learning Analysis* (Englewood Cliffs, N.J.: Prentice Hall, 1973).
20. A. Bandura, D. Ross, and S. A. Ross, "Vicarious Reinforcement and Imitation," *Journal of Abnormal and Social Psychology* 67 (1963): 601–607. This is one of but many such studies supporting generalization.
21. H. Toch, *Social Psychology of Social Movements* (London: Methuen, 1966).
22. S. Brownmiller, *Against Our Will: Men, Women and Rape.* (New York: Simon and Schuster, 1975).
23. Wilhelm Reich was clearly the first to see the functions of oppression in the family. See *The Mass Psychology of Fascism,* trans. V. Carfagno (New York: Farrar, Straus & Giroux).
24. D. Martin, *Battered Wives* (San Francisco: Glide Publications, 1976), pp. 1–3.
25. D. J. Mulvihill and M. M. Tumin and L. A. Curtis, *Crimes of Violence,* Vol. II, Staff Report to the National Commission on Causes and Prevention of Violence, Washington, D.C.: U.S. Government Printing Office, 1969, p. 360.
26. Definitive figures are hard to come by. Del Martin, *Battered Wives,* reviews much of the literature. See also S. Eisenberg, and P. Micklow, "The Assaulted Wife: 'Catch 22' Revisited," *Women's Rights Law Reporter,* 1976.
27. J. C. Barden, "Wife Beaters: Few of Them Ever Appear Before a Court of Law," *The New York Times,* October 21, 1974.
28. R. J. Gelles, *The Violent Home: A Study of Physical Aggression Between Husbands and Wives* (Beverly Hills Calif.: Sage Publications, 1972).
29. R. Stark, and J. McEvoy IV, "Middle Class Violence," *Psychology Today* (November 1970): 30–31.
30. Martin, *Battered Wives,* pp. 18–20.
31. Stark and McEvoy IV, "Middle Class Violence."
    M. Bard, "The Study and Modification of Intra-Familial Violence," in *The Control of Aggression and Violence* (New York: Academic Press, 1971), p. 154.
    S. Johnson, "What About Battered Women?" *Majority Report* (February 8, 1975): 4.
32. Gelles, *The Violent Home,* pp. 95–96.
33. M. E. Wolfgang, *Patterns in Criminal Homicide* (New York: Wiley, 1958), p. 125.
34. The history of man's inhumanity to woman is catalogued in E. Davis, *The First Sex* (New York: Putnam, 1971), pp. 254–255. An historical review of the legal and religious status of women and their punishments may be found in G. Newman, *The Punishment Response* (Philadelphia: Lippincott, 1978).
35. The question, of course, as to whether civilization has progressed in a humanitarian direction is often argued. See Newman, *ibid.*
36. J. E. Snell, and R. J. Rosenwald, "The Wife Beater's Wife," *Archives of General Psychiatry* 11 (August 1964): 107–112.
    E. Pizzey, "The Cultured Graduate Who Became a Thing," *Manchester Daily Express,* October 29, 1974, p. 11.

37. L. G. Schultz, "The Wife Assaulter," *The Journal of Social Therapy,* 6, 2 (1960).
B. M. Cormier, "Psychodynamics of Homicide Committed in a Marital Relationship," *Corrective Psychiatry and Journal of Social Therapy* 8 (1962): 187–194.
W. C. Pertue, "A Preliminary Investigation Into Uxoricide," *Diseases of the Nervous System* 27 (1966): 808–811.
38. Gelles, *The Violent Home.*
39. T. Johnston, "When He Stopped Beating His Wife," *City of San Francisco,* July 6, 1975, p. 24.
40. S. K. Steinmetz, and M. Straus, eds., *Violence in the Family* (New York: Dodd Mead, 1974), p. 9.
41. R. N. Whitehurst, "Violence in Husband-Wife Interaction," in Steinmetz and Straus, pp. 78–79.
42. J. S. Gayford, "Wife-Battering: A Preliminary Survey of 100 Cases," *British Medical Journal* 1 (January 25, 1975): 194–197.
43. W. J. Goode, "Violence Among Intimates," in Mulvihill and Tumin, eds., *Crimes of Violence,* Vol. 13, Appendix 19, p. 960.
44. Gelles, *The Violent Home.*
Eisenberg and Micklow, "The Assaulted Wife"
Martin, *Battered Wives,* pp. 52–53.
45. Goode, "Violence Among Intimates."
46. Gayford, "Wife Battering."
47. *Ibid.*
48. Martin, *Battered Wives,* pp. 74–75.
49. *Ibid.,* pp. 77–80.
50. There is much disagreement about all these propositions. It would appear that middle class parents use verbal rebuke more often, but that there is no difference in rise of physical punishment between the classes. See, for a review of all this literature H. Erlanger, "Social Class and Corporal Punishment in Child Rearing: A Reassessment," *American Sociological Review* 39 (1974): 68–85.
51. G. Newman, *The Punishment Response.*
52. L. DeMause, "The Evolution of Childhood," *Journal of Psychohistory* 1, 4 (Spring 1974): 503–705.
53. N. A. Polansky, and N. F. Polansky, "The Current Status of Child Abuse and Neglect in This Country," Paper prepared for the Joint Commission on Mental Health of Children (Washington, D.C.: U.S. Department of Health, Education and Welfare, U.S. Government Printing Office, 1967).
54. H. R. Jeter, "Children, Problems and Services in Child Welfare Programs," Children's Bureau Publication, N. 403, Washington, D.C.: U.S. Department of Health, Education and Welfare.
55. S. R. Zalba, "The Abused Child: I. A Survey of the Problem," *Social Work,* 11 (1966): 3–16.
56. D. Gil, and H. Noble, "Public Knowledge, Attitudes and Opinions About Physical Abuse in the U.S.," Papers in Social Welfare No. 14: Florence Heller Graduate School for Advanced Studies in Social Welfare, Brande University, Waltham, Massachusetts, 1967.
57. R. Gelles, S. Steinmetz and M. Strauss, cited in: J. Prescott, "Child Abuse in America: Slaughter of the Innocents," *Hustler Magazine,* October 1977, pp. 97–105.
58. Mulvihill and Tumin, *Crimes of Violence,* p. 109.

59. J. Prescott, "Child Abuse in America," p. 99.

60. Cited in Mulvihill, et al., p. 108.

61. D. Fergusson, J. Fleming, and D. O'Neill, Child Abuse in New Zealand, A. R. Shearer Government Printer, Wellington, 1972.
    D. Gil, Nationwide Survey of Legally Reported Physical Abuse of Children, Brandeis University, Waltham, Massachusetts, 1968.

62. E. Elmer, "Child Abuse: A Symptom of Family Crisis," in E. Pavenstedt, ed. *Crisis of Family Disorganization* (New York: Behavioral Publications, 1971).
    E. Elmer, "Child Abuse: The Family's Cry for Help," *Journal of Psychiatric Nursing* 5, 4 (1967): 332–341.
    E. Elmer, "Studies of Child Abuse and Infant Accidents," in *The Mental Health of the Child* (1971): 343–370. U.S. National Institute of Mental Health: U.S. Government Printing Office, Washington, D.C.

63. V. De Francis, "Child Abuse. Preview of a Nation-wide Survey," Paper presented at an associate group meeting jointly sponsored by the Children's Division of the American Humane Society, The American Public Welfare Association, and the Child Welfare League of America at the National Conference on Social Welfare, Cleveland, May 1963.

64. A number of studies are summarized in Ferracuti and Newman, "Assaultive Offenses," p. 186–187. See also T. Harder, "The Psychopathology of Infanticide," *Acta Psychiatrica Scandinavica* 43, 2 (1967): 196–245.
    N. Lokianowicz, "Attempted Infanticide," *Psychiatrica Clinica* 5, 1 (1972): 1–16.
    L. Uskiewiczowa, "Child Murder by Parents in the Light of Medicoforensic Material," *Psychiatria Polska* (Gdansk), 5, 2 (1972): 125–132.

65. R. Galdtson, "Observations on Children Who Have Been Physically Abused by Their Parents," *American Journal of Psychiatry* 122, 4 (1965): 440–443.
    R. Helfer, and C. Kempe, eds. *The Battered Child* (Chicago: University of Chicago Press, 1968).

66. Gil, *Nationwide Survey,* 1968.
    E. Elmer, *Children in Jeopardy* (Pittsburgh: University of Pittsburgh Press, 1967).
    M. Cohen, E. Philbrick, and R. Mulford, "Neglecting Parents: A Study of Psychosocial Characteristics," American Humane Association, Children's Division, Denver, 1967.
    K. Zuckerman, J. Ambuel, and R. Bandman, "Child Neglect and Abuse: A Study of Cases Evaluated at Columbus Childrens' Hospital in 1968–1969," *Ohio State Medical Journal* 68: (1972) 629–32.

67. L. Young, *Wednesday's Children* (New York: McGraw-Hill, 1964).
    J. G. Howells, "The Pathogenesis of Hard-Core Families," *American Journal of Psychiatry* 22 (1966): 1159–1164.
    V. Fontana, "Social Manifestations," in *The Maltreated Child* (Springfield, Ill.: Thomas, 1971).
    V. Fontana, "Which Parents Abuse Children?" *Medical Insight* 3, 10 (1971): 16–21.

68. De Francis, "Child Abuse," 1963.
    Elmer, *Children in Jeopardy,* 1967.

69. W. Becker, "The Problem of Maltreatment of the Child," *Therapie der*

Gegenwart (Berlin) 107, 2 (1967): 135–136, 138–140, 142–144, 147–149.

J. Holter, and S. Friedman, "Etiology and Management of Severely Burned Children: Psychosocial Considerations," *American Journal of the Disturbed Child* 118 (1969): 680–686.

B. Johnson, and H. Morse, "Injured Children and Their Parents," *Children* 15, 4 (1968): 147–152.

L. Terr, "A Family Study of Child Abuse," *American Journal of Psychiatry* 127, 5 (1970): 665–671.

70. J. C. M. Matheson, "Infanticide," *Medical Legal Review* 9 (1941): 135–52.

G. McDermaid, and E. Winkler, "Psychopathology of Infanticide," *Journal of Clinical and Experimental Psychopathology and Quarterly Review of Psychiatrical Neurology* 16 (1955): 22–41.

A. H. Chapman, "Obsession of Infanticide," AMA, *Archives of General Psychiatry* 1 (1959): 12–16.

71. S. Chaneles, "Child Victims of Sexual Offenses," *Federal Probation* 31, 2 (June 1967): 52–56.

72. *Ibid.*

73. G. Laury, "The Battered Child Syndrome: Parental Motivation, Clinical Aspects," *Bulletin, New York Academy of Medicine* 46, 9 (1970): 676–685.

B. Steele, and C. Pollock, "A Psychiatric Study of Parents Who Abuse Infants and Small Children," in R. Helfer, and C. H. Kempe, eds. *The Battered Child* (Chicago: University of Chicago Press, 1968).

74. R. Jenkins, et al., 1970, "Interrupting the Family Cycle of Violence," *Journal of the Iowa Medical Society* 60, 2 (1970): 85–89.

R. E. Helfer, and C. H. Kempe, *Child Abuse and Neglect: The Family and the Community* (Cambridge, Mass.: Ballinger, 1976).

C. Kempe, et al., "The Battered Child Syndrome," *Journal of the American Medical Association* 181, 1 (1962): 17–29.

A. Lascari, "The Abused Child," *Journal of the Iowa Medical Society* 62 (1972): 229–232.

B. Meinick, and J. Hurley, "Distinctive Personality Attributes of Child Abusing Mothers," *Journal of Consulting and Clinical Psychology* 33, 6 (1969): 746–749.

J. E. Oliver, et al., "Five Generations of Ill-Treated Children in One Family Pedigree," *British Journal of Psychiatry* 119 (1971): 473–480.

J. Spinetta, and D. Rigler, "The Child-Abusing Parent: A Psychological Review," *Psychological Bulletin* 77, 4 (1972): 296–304.

H. Steinhausen, "Sociomedical Aspects of Physical Maltreatment of Children," *Monatsschrift Fur Kinderheildunde* (Berlin) 120, 8 (1972): 314–318.

S. K. Steinmetz, *The Cycle of Violence* (New York: Praeger, 1977).

75. J. Weston, "The Pathology of Child Abuse," in Helfer and Kempe, *The Battered Child*, 1968.

76. W. Freidrich, and J. Boriskin, "The Role of the Child in Abuse," *American Journal of Orthopsychiatry* 46, (1976): 580–590.

77. L. Adelson, "The Battering Child," *Journal of the American Medical Association* 222, 3 (1972): 159–161.

78. H. De Young, "Homicide (Children's Division)," *Human Behavior* (February 1976): 16–17.

79. D. Sargent, "The Lethal Situation: Transmission of Urge to Kill From

Parent to Child," in J. Fawcett, ed. *Dynamics of Violence* (Chicago: American Medical Association, 1971).

80. A. P. Iskrant, and P. V. Joliet, *Accidents and Homicide* (Cambridge: Harvard University Press, 1968).

   E. B. McKnight, J. W. Mohr, R. E. Quinsey, and J. Erochko, "Matricide and Mental Illness," *Canadian Psychiatric Association Journal* 11 (1966): 99–106.

81. R. Campbell, "Violence in Adolescence," *Journal of Analytic Psychology,* 12, 2 (1967): 161–173.

   M. Katz, "Family Crisis Training: Upgrading the Police While Building a Bridge to the Minority Community," *Journal of Police Science and Administration* 1, 1 (1973): 30–35.

   J. Mecir, "Homicidal Behavior of Minors Directed Against Their Parents," *Ceskslovenska Psychiatrie* (Praha), 64, 5 (1968): 319–325.

82. P. Hellsten, and O. Katila, "Murder and Other Homicide by Children Under 15 in Finland," *Psychiatric Quarterly Supplement* 39, 1 (1965): 54–74.

83. J. Duncan, and G. Duncan, "Murder in the Family: A Study of Some Homicidal Adolescents," *American Journal of Psychiatry* 127, 11 (1971:) 74–78.

84. R. Sandoff, "Clinical Observations on Parricide," *Psychiatric Quarterly* 45, 1 (1971): 65–69.

85. Professor Megargee has studied the problem of the "overcontrolled" aggressive person, in an attempt to align it with social learning theory. E. I. Megargee, "Matricide, Patricide and the Dynamics of Aggression," Paper presented to the American Psychological Association Meetings, Washington, D.C., 1967.

86. F. Wertham, *Dark Legends: A Study in Murder* (New York: Duell, Sloan & Pearce, 1941).

87. E. B. McNeil, "Violence and Human Development," *Annals of the American Academy of Political and Social Science* 364, (1966): 149–157.

88. L. Bender, "Psychiatric Mechanisms in Child Murderers," *Journal of Nervous and Mental Disease* 80 (1934): 32–47.

   E. Podelsky, "Children Who Kill," *General Practitioner* 31, (1965): 98–102. Certainly the frustration-aggression theories would make this interpretation. See especially L. Berkowitz, *Aggression: A Social Psychological Analysis* (New York: McGraw-Hill, 1962), Chap. 11.

CHAPTER 7
VIOLENCE: AN OCCUPATIONAL HAZARD

1. U.S. Department of Health, Education and Welfare, National Center for Health Statistics, *Vital Statistics of the U.S.,* 1968, Vol. 2, Mortality, Part A, 1972.

2. G. D. Robin, "Justifiable Homicide by Police Officers," *Journal of Criminal Law, Criminology and Police Science* 54, (1963): 225–231.

3. H. Toch, *Police, Prisons and the Problem of Violence* (Washington, D.C.: U.S. Department of Health, Education and Welfare, 1977), p. 15.

4. F.B.I., *Uniform Crime Reports* (Washington, D.C.: U.S. Government Printing Office, 1974), p. 228.

5. A. L. Kobler, "Police Homicide in a Democracy," *Journal of Social Issues* 31, (1975): 163–184.

6. W. A. Westley, *Violence and the Police: A Sociological Study of Law, Customs and Morality* (Boston: MIT Press, 1970).

H. Toch, *Violent Men: An Inquiry Into the Psychology of Violence* (Chicago: Aldine, 1969).

Much of the exposition on police and prison violence closely follows the excellent monograph on the subject of Professor Toch. See H. Toch, *Police, Prisons and the Problem of Violence,* National Institute of Mental Health, U.S. Department of Health, Education and Welfare, 1977.

7. R. R. E. Kania, and W. L. Mackey, "Police Violence as a Function of Community Characteristics," *Criminology* 15, 1 (May 1977): 27–47.

8. Westley, *Violence and the Police,* p. 49.

9. *Ibid.*

10. J. H. McNamara, "Uncertainties of Police Work: The Relevance of Police Recruits Background and Training," in D. J. Bordua, (Ed.) *The Police: Six Sociological Essays* (New York: Wiley, 1967).

11. A. Niederhoffer, *Behind the Shield: The Police in Urban Society* (New York: Doubleday (Anchor Books), 1969).

12. *Ibid.*

13. Westley, *Violence and the Police.*

P. Chevigny, *Police Power: Police Abuses in New York City* (New York: Pantheon, 1969).

14. Toch, *Violent Men,* Chapter 5.

15. *Ibid.,* pp. 140–141.

16. *Ibid.,* pp. 162–163.

17. C. Wertham, and I. Piliavin, "Gang Members and the Police," in D. J. Bordua, ed. *The Police,* p. 87.

18. For a history of "professional heavy crime," see J. A. Inciardi, *Careers in Crime* (Chicago: Rand McNally, 1975), p. 96.

19. D. R. Cressey, *Theft of the Nation* (New York: Harper & Row, 1969).

20. J. F. Ianni, *A Family Business* (New York: Mentor, 1975).

21. Inciardi, *Careers in Crime.*

22. See, for example: D. Cressey, *Criminal Organization: Its Elementary Forms* (New York: Harper & Row, 1972).

23. Toch, *Police, Prisons,* p. 63.

24. *Ibid.,* p. 53.

25. *Ibid.,* p. 52.

26. Out of an estimated prison population (State and Federal Prisons) of 218,205 on December 31, 1974 (*Sourcebook of Criminal Justice Statistics, 1976,* p. 686). It works out to a rate of roughly 70 per 100,000 population—roughly 7 times the murder rate for the non-prison population.

27. *Ibid.,* p. 53.

28. *Ibid.*

29. *Ibid.*

30. In 1964, 10% of prison aggressors had been previously convicted of assault.

In 1974, 24% of aggressors were convicted for homicide, *ibid.,* p. 55.

31. Toch, *Violent Men,* p. 160.

32. Toch, *Police, Prisons,* p. 56.

33. *Ibid.,* p. 56.

34. *Ibid.*

35. *Ibid.*

36. J. H. Gagnon, "The Social Measuring of Prison Homosexuality," *Federal Probation* 32 (1968): 1ff.
    J. L. Ward, "Homosexual Behavior of the Institutionalized Delinquent," *Psychiatric Quarterly Supplement* 32 (1950): 301–314.
    R. M. Lindner, "Sexual Behavior in Penal Institutions," in A. Deutsch, ed. *Sex Habits of American Men* (New York: Prentice-Hall, 1948).
37. J. Irwin, *The Felon* (Englewood Cliffs, N.J.: Prentice-Hall, 1970).
    A. V. Huffman, "Problems Precipitated by Sexual Approaches for Youthful First Offenders," *Journal of Social Therapy* 7 (1961): 216–222.
38. A. J. Davis, "Sexual Assaults in the Philadelphia Prison System and Sheriff's Jails," *Trans-Action* 6 (1968): 14–15.
39. Toch, *Police, Prisons,* p. 58.
40. *Ibid.,* p. 59.
41. *Ibid.,* p. 67.
42. H. Toch, *Men in Crisis: Human Breakdown in Prison* (Chicago: Aldine, 1975).
43. E. Megargee, "Population Density and Disruptive Behavior in a Prison Setting," in A. K. Cohen, G. F. Cole, and R. G. Bailey, eds. *Prison Violence* (Lexington, Mass.: Lexington Books, 1976), pp. 135–144.
44. National School Public Relations Association, *Discipline Crisis in the Schools: The Problems, Causes, and Search for Solutions,* (Washington, D.C.: Education U.S.A. Special Report, 1973).
45. United States Senate, Committee on the Judiciary, *Our Nation's Schools —A Report Card: "A" in School Violence and Vandalism,* 94th Congress, 1st Session, April, 1975, p. 4.
46. *Ibid.,* p. 6.
47. *Ibid.,* p. 8.
48. *Ibid.,* p. 24.
49. J. Newman, and G. R. Newman, "Crime and Punishment in the Schooling Process: An Historical Analysis," in E. Wenk, ed. *Theoretical Perspectives on School Crime,* U.S. Department of Health, Education and Welfare, Washington, D.C.: U.S. Government Printing Office, 1978.
50. *Ibid.*
51. Quoted, *ibid.* from the writing of Francis Grund in 1837.
52. *Ingraham v. Wright,* 1977, *U.S. Law Week* 45: 4364.
53. Senator Birch Bayh, "Our Nation's Schools—A Report Card: 'A' in School Violence and Vandalism," Report to 94th Congress, 1st Session, by Committee on the Judiciary, April, 1975, p. 9.
54. *Ibid.,* p. 12.
55. *Ibid.*
56. Newman and Newman, "Crime and Punishment in the Schooling Process," 1978.
57. National School Public Relations Association, *Violence and Vandalism,* (Washington, D.C.: National Education Association Special Report, 1975), p. 8.
58. F. Redl, and D. Wineman, *The Aggressive Child* (Glencoe: Free Press, 1957).
59. *Ibid.*
60. S. K. Weinberg, and H. Arond, "The Occupational Culture of the Boxer," *American Journal of Sociology* (March 1952): 460.
61. N. Hare, "A Study of the Black Fighter," *The Black Scholar* 3 (November 1971): 2–8.
62. *Ibid.*

63. M. D. Smith, "Significant Others' Influence on the Assaultive Behavior of Young Hockey Players," *International Journal of Sport Sociology* 3–4, 9 (1974): 45–58.
64. K. G. Sheard, and F. G. Dunning, "The Rugby Football Club as a Type of 'Male Preserve': Some Sociological Notes," *International Journal of Sport Sociology* 3–4, 8 (1973): 5–25.
65. L. Tiger, *Men in Groups* (New York: Random House, 1970).
66. Smith, "Significant Others' Influence." Also R. R. Faulkner, "Violence, Camaraderie and Occupational Character in Hockey," Paper presented at the Conference on Sport and Social Deviances, New York: State University at Brockport, December 1971.
67. R. Stivers, *A Hair of the Dog: Irish Drinking and American Stereotype* (University Park: Pennsylvania State University Press, 1975).
68. I. Taylor, "Soccer Seriousness and Soccer Hooliganism," in S. Cohen, *Images of Deviance* (London: Penguin, 1971).
69. Personal Communication from R. W. Burnham, United Nations Criminal Justice and Crime Prevention Section, who has recounted to me his first-hand experiences.
70. H. Davies, *The Glory Game* (London: Weidenfeld and Nicholson, 1972), p. 108.
71. For a review of these theories see M. Schwartz, "Causes and Effects of Spectator Sports," *International Journal of Sport Sociology* 3–4, 8 (1973): 31–43. See also D. Ball, and J. Loy, *Sport and Social Order* (Reading, Mass.: Addison-Wesley, 1975).
72. J. P. Scott, "Sport and Aggression," in G. S. Kenyon, ed. *Contemporary Psychology of Sport* (Chicago: Athletic Institute, 1968).
73. T. Veblen, *Theory of the Leisure Class* (New York: Funk & Wagnalls, 1967).
74. Schwartz, "Causes and Effects of Spectator Sports."
75. R. Kraus, *Recreation and Leisure in Modern Society* (New York: Appleton-Century Crofts, 1971).
76. J. A. Harrington, *Soccer Hooliganism: A Preliminary Report to Mr. Denis Howell, Minister of Sport* (Bristol: John Wright and Sons, 1968).

CHAPTER 8
MOBS, RIOTS AND GANGS

1. G. Le Bon, *The Crowd* (London: Penguin, 1977).
2. N. Smelser, *Theory of Collective Behavior* (Englewood Cliffs, N.J.: Prentice-Hall, 1963).
3. *Report of the National Advisory Commission on Civil Disorders* (New York: Bantam; Dutton, 1968), pp. 10–11.
4. Gary T. Marx, "Issueless Riots," in J. Short, and M. Wolfgang, ed. *Collective Violence* (Chicago: Aldine Atherton, 1972).
5. See for a review S. P. Aiyar, ed. *The Politics of Mass Violence in India* (Bombay: Manaktalas, 1967).
6. M. K. Gandhi, *The Way to Communal Harmony* (Ahmedabad: Navajivan Publishing House, 1963), Chaps. V–VIII.
7. *Ibid.*, p. 183.
8. See, for a review of this process L. Berkowitz, *Aggression: A Social Psychological Analysis* (New York: McGraw-Hill, 1962), especially Chaps. 6 and 7.
K. R. Scherer, R. P. Abeles, and C. S. Fischer, *Human Aggression and Conflict* (Englewood Cliffs, N.J.: Prentice-Hall, 1975), Chaps. 4–6.

9. Gandhi, *The Way to Communal Harmony*, p. 186.
10. Prejudice as a conditioner of violence has also been extensively studied by Berkowitz, *Aggression;* see also G. W. Allport, *The Nature of Prejudice* (Reading, Mass.: Addison-Wesley, 1954).
11. Scherer, et al., *Human Aggression, ibid.*
    H. Toch, *Violent Men: An Inquiry into the Psychology of Violence* (Chicago: Aldine, 1969), Chap. 6.
12. Gandhi, *The Way to Communal Harmony*, p. 191.
13. Aiyar, *The Politics of Mass Violence*, p. 27.
14. Toch, *Violent Men,* Chap. 6.
15. T. R. Fyvel, *The Insecure Offenders* (London: Penguin, 1961).
    J. Patrick, *Glasgow Gang Observed* (London: Methuen, 1973).
16. See H. Asbury, *The Gangs of New York* (New York: Knopf, 1928).
17. W. Miller, *Violence by Youth Gangs and Youth Groups as a Crime Problem in Major American Cities,* National Institute for Juvenile Justice and Delinquency Prevention, Law Enforcement Assistance Administration, U.S. Department of Justice, Washington, D.C.: U.S. Government Printing Office, 1975.
18. L. Yablonsky, *The Violent Gang* (New York: Macmillan, 1962).
19. Miller, *Violence by Youth Gangs.* There are, of course, great difficulties in defining just what a "gang" is. The reader is urged to consult the original works for Miller's explanation of this problem.
20. *Ibid.*
21. *Ibid.,* p. 44.
22. W. B. Miller, "The Rumble This Time," *Psychology Today* (May 1977): 52–56.

CHAPTER 9
THE VIOLENCE OF STRANGERS: RAPE AND ROBBERY

1. For a review of the shortcomings and comparative validity of rape statistics, see M. Hindelang, and B. Davis, "Forcible Rape: A Statistical Profile," in D. Chappell, R. Geis, and G. Geis, eds. *Forcible Rape: The Crime, The Victim, The Offender* (New York: Columbia University Press, 1977).
2. *Ibid.,* p. 98.
3. M. Amir, *Patterns in Forcible Rape* (Chicago: University of Chicago Press, 1971).
4. a. Amir, *Forcible Rape,* p. 44.
   b. President's Commission on Crime in the District of Columbia, *Report,* Washington, D.C.: U.S. Government Printing Office, 1966, p. 54.
   c. D. J. Mulvihill, M. M. Tumin, and L. A. Curtis, *Crimes of Violence,* Vol. 11, Staff Report to the National Commission on Causes and Prevention of Violence, Washington, D.C.: U.S. Government Printing Office, 1969, p. 212.
   d. A. J. Reiss, Jr., *Studies in Crime and Law Enforcement in Major Metropolitan Areas,* Vol. 1, Sec. 1. Measurement of the Nature of the Amount of Crime, Field Survey III, President's Commission on Law Enforcement and Administration of Justice, Washington, D.C.: U.S. Government Printing Office, 1967, p. 34.
   e. M. W. Agopian, D. Chappell, and G. Geis, "Black Offender and White Victim: A Study of Forcible Rape," in Chappell, Geis and Geis, eds. *Forcible Rape,* Chap. 6.
   f. C. Hayman, C. Lanza, R. Fuentes, and K. Algor, "Rape in the Dis-

trict of Columbia," Paper presented to the American Public Health Association, October 12, 1971.

    g. National Crime Panel Survey. This was a national victimization survey conducted by the Bureau of Census. The source is M. Hindelang, M. Gottfredson, C. Dunn and N. Paresi, *Sourcebook of Criminal Justice Statistics,* (Washington, D.C.: U.S. Department of Justice 1974), p. 394.

5. B. Mintz, "Patterns in Forcible Rape: Review Essay," *Criminal Law Bulletin* 9 (October 1973): 703–710.

6. Sources for a, b, c, e and h are as for note 4. Other sourses are:

    i. C. R. Hayman, et al., "Sexual Assault on Women and Children in the District of Columbia," *Public Health Report* 83, 12 (December 1968): 1021–1028.

    j. J. M. Macdonald, *Rape Offenders and Their Victims* (Springfield, Ill.: Thomas, 1971).

    k. D. Chappell, and S. Singer, "Rape in New York City: A Study of Rape Materials in Police Files and Its Meaning," Mimeographed, Albany, New York: School of Criminal Justice, S.U.N.Y. at Albany, 1973.

7. C. R. Hayman, et al., "Sexual Assault on Women and Children in the District of Columbia," *Public Health Reports* 83, 12 (December 1968): 1021–1028, is of particular interest, because it found that in the case of children (under 17 years) the victim was much more likely to have known the offender. But beyond this age, the proportion attacked by strangers was much, much greater.

8. B. Mehrhof, and P. Kearon, "Rape: An Act of Terror," in *Notes from the Third Year* (New York: Women's Liberation Press, 1972), pp. 79–81.

9. Amir, *Forcible Rape,* p. 336.

10. *Ibid.*

11. J. Selkin, "Rape," *Psychology Today* 8, 8 (January 1975): 71–75. Many writers have identified feelings of powerlessness in women as a central factor in their submission to rape, although no formal studies have been conducted exactly on this topic. See S. Brownmiller, *Against Our Will: Men, Women and Rape* (New York: Simon & Schuster, 1975).
    S. Griffin, "Rape: The All-American Crime," *Ramparts* 10 (September 1971): 26–35.
    E. Hilberman, "Rape: The Ultimate Violation of Self," *American Journal of Psychiatry* 133, 4 (April 1976): 436–437.

12. G. Greer, "Seduction is a Four-Letter Word," in L. Schulz, ed. *Rape Victimology* (Springfield, Ill.: Thomas, 1975), 374–395.
    A. Hooper, "Fraud in Assault and Rape," *University of British Columbia Law Review* 3, 2 (May 1968): 117–130.

13. Greer, "Seduction," pp. 374–395.

14. S. Nelson, and M. Amir, "The Hitchhike Victim of Rape: A Research Report," in D. Chappell, R. Geis, and G. Geis, *Forcible Rape,* Chap. 13.

15. Amir, *Forcible Rape,* p. 200.

16. G. Geis, "Group Sexual Assaults," *Medical Aspects of Human Sexuality* 5, 5 (May 1971): 101–112.
    S. Thompson, "Gang Rape: Why It's Increasing," *Sexology* 41, 8 (March 1975): 16–19.

17. *Sourcebook of Criminal Justice Statistics,* 1974, pp, 391–392.

18. Geis, "Group Sexual Assaults," *ibid.*

19. Amir, *Forcible Rape,* ibid.
20. R. T. Rada, "Alcoholism and Forcible Rape," *American Journal of Psychiatry* 132, 4 (April 1975): 444–446.
21. Amir, *Forcible Rape,* ibid.
22. Mulvihill and Tumin, *Crimes of Violence,* p. 342. The study of Hayman, et al., however, found about half, but the cases were hospital reported alleged rapes, not police reported rapes.
23. M. Amir, "Victim Precipitated Forcible Rape," *Journal of Criminal Law, Criminology and Police Science* 58, 4 (1967): 493–502.
24. B. C. Glueck, Jr., *New York Final Report on Deviated Sex Offenders,* Albany, New York: Department of Mental Hygiene, 1956.
25. M. Amir, "Forcible Rape," *Federal Probation* 31, 1 (March 1967): 54.
26. D. Chappell, et al., "Forcible Rape: A Comparative Study of Offenses Known to the Police in Boston and Los Angeles," in J. Hanslin, ed. *Studies in the Sociology of Sex* (New York: Meredith, 1971), pp. 169–190.
27. Apart from the extensive findings of the *President's Commission on Obscenity and Pornography* Washington, D.C.: U.S. Government Printing Office, 1968, there are:
    M. J. Goldstein, "Exposure of Erotic Stimuli and Sexual Deviance," *Journal of Social Issues* 29, 3 (1973): 197–219.
    G. A. Kercher, and E. Walker, "Reactions of Convicted Rapists to Sexually Explicit Stimuli," *Journal of Abnormal Psychology* 81, 1 (February 1973): 46–50.
28. W. H. Manville, "Mind of the Rapist," *Cosmopolitan* 176, 1 (January 1974): 74–77.
29. Report of Cambridge Department of Criminal Science, *Sexual Offences* (London: Macmillan, 1957), pp. 156–179.
30. This was the more typical rape found in Boston by Chappell, et al. See note 26.
31. P. H. Gebhard, J. H. Gagnon, W. B. Pomeroy, and C. V. Christenson, *Sex Offenders: An Analysis of Types* (New York: Harper & Row, 1965), pp. 177–205.
32. Other clinical studies have also pointed to the inability of some rapists to separate aggressive from sexual urges. See M. L. Cohen, R. Garofali, R. B. Boucher, and T. Seghorn, "The Psychology of Rapists," in Chappell, et al., *Forcible Rape,* Chap. 14.
33. G. Fisher, and E. Rivlin, "Psychological Needs of Rapists," *British Journal of Criminology* 11 (1971): 182–185.
34. T. B. Garrett, and R. Wright, "Wives of Rapists and Incest Offenders," *Journal of Sex Research* 11, 2 (May 1975): 149–157.
35. Mulvihill and Tumin, *Crimes of Violence,* p. 217.
36. Hindelang, et al., *Sourcebook of Criminal Justice Statistics,* 1976, pp. 382–383.
37. From C. S. Dunn, *Patterns of Robbery Characteristics and Their Occurrence Among Social Areas,* U.S. Department of Justice, Analytic Report 15, 1976. *Sources:* a. F. H. McClintock, and E. Gibson, *Robbery in London* (London: Macmillan, 1961), p. 16, Table 6. These percentages are derived from the totals of robberies in 2 years (1956, 1957).
    b. A. Normandeau, *Trends and Patterns in Crimes of Robbery* (Ph. D. diss., University of Pennsylvania, 1968), p. 20, Table 41. These percentages are derived from data for a 7 year period, 1960–1966.
38. a. Normandeau, *Trends and Patterns in Crimes of Robbery,* p. 168.

b. Mulvihill and Tumin, *Crimes of Violence,* p. 214.

c. Reiss, *Studies in Crime and Law Enforcement,* p, 34.

d. Dunn, *Patterns of Robbery,* ibid.

e. Hindelang, et al., *Sourcebook of Criminal Justice Statistics,* 1974, p. 394.

39. G. Allport, *The Nature of Prejudice.*

40. There are, of course, other explanations. Dunn points out that the level of interracial robberies may depend considerably on the amount of racial mix in particular social areas. See C. Dunn, *Patterns of Robbery Among Social Areas,* 1976.

41. a. McClintock and Gibson, *Robbery in London,* 1961, p. 130. Averages of percentages for 2 years (1956, 1957).

b. Normandeau, *Trends in Robbery,* 1968, pp, 224–225, p. 244. Averages of percentages over 7 year period (1960–66). Note that the difference in percentages reported for London in Normandeau's Table 84 (p. 244) is due to the application of the averaging procedure to the McClintock/Gibson data in order to make it consistent with the data reported by Normandeau in his Table 79 (pp. 224–225) and Table 94 (p. 244). In order to calculate the overall percent distribution of location of robbery, Normandeau simply averaged the percent distributions across the 7 years. This averaging procedure has been reapplied to the McClintock/Gibson data for 2 years (1950, 1957) and to the Conklin data for 2 years (1964, 1968).

c. J. Conklin, *Robbery and the Criminal Justice System* (Philadelphia: Lippincott, 1972), p. 41. Averages of percentages for 2 years (1964, 1968).

d. C. Dunn, *The Analysis of Environmental Attribute/Crime Incident Characteristic Interrelationship* (Ph.D. diss., S.U.N.Y. Albany, 1974, p. 334.

e. Mulvihill and Tumin, *Crimes of Violence,* p. 221.

f. Hindelang, et al., *Sourcebook of Criminal Justice Statistics,* 1974, p. 376.

42. McClintock and Gibson, *Robbery in London.*

43. a. *Ibid.,* p. 24.

b. Normandeau, *Trends in Robbery,* ibid.

c. F.B.I. *Uniform Crime Reports,* 1975.

d. Dunn, *Patterns of Robbery Among Social Areas,* p. 13.

e. Hindelang, et al., *Sourcebook of Criminal Justice Statistics,* 1974, p. 384.

44. Conklin, *Robbery.*

45. a. McClintock and Gibson, *Robbery in London,* p. 24.

b. Dunn, *Patterns of Robbery,* p. 20.

c. Hindelang, et al., *Sourcebook,* p. 384.

CHAPTER 10
BORN TO KILL?

1. There is some argument as to whether Freud was actually talking about instincts, since the translation of the German word "Trieb" might more accurately have been "drive" rather than instinct. In any event, influential psychoanalysts and ethologists have freely used the same term: instinct. See A. Storr, *Human Aggression* (New York: Bantam Books, 1968), and K. Lorenz, *On Aggression* (New York: Harcourt, Brace Jovanovich, 1966).

2. See P. L. Van den Berghe, "Bringing the Beasts Back In: toward a bio-social theory of aggression," *American Sociological Review* 39, 6 (1974): 777–788.
3. Lorenz, *On Aggression,* Chapters 7, 11.
4. I. Eibl-Eibesfeldt, *Love and Hate: The Natural History of Behavior Patterns,* trans. Geoffrey Strachan (New York: Holt, Rinehart and Winston, 1972).
5. Lorenz, *On Aggression;* D. D. Thiessen, *The Evolution and Chemistry of Aggression* (Springfield, Ill.: Thomas, 1976).
6. This thesis is generally advanced by the ardent critic of the ethologists, Ashley Montagu in his many writings, the most recent being, *The Nature of Human Aggression* (New York: Oxford University Press, 1976).
7. For an excellent review, see Thiessen, *The Evolution and Chemistry of Aggression,* pp. 30–46.
8. A. Storr, *Human Aggression* (New York: Bantam Books, 1968). Experimental evidence for this thesis (a sub-category of frustration-aggression theory) may be found in L. Berkowitz, *Aggression: A Social Psychological Analysis* (New York: McGraw-Hill, 1962), pp. 132–164 and A. H. Buss, *The Psychology of Aggression,* (New York: Wiley, 1971), pp. 245–265.
9. K. E. Moyer, *The Psychobiology of Aggression* (New York: Harper & Row, 1976).
10. *Ibid.*
11. J. Delgado, *Physical Control of the Mind: Toward A Psychocivilized Society* (New York: Harper & Row, Colophon Books, 1969).
12. Moyer, *The Psychobiology of Aggression,* pp. 53–55.
13. R. N. Johnson, *Aggression in Man and Animals* (Philadelphia: Saunders, 1972), p. 78.
14. J. M. R. Delgado, V. Mark, W. Sweet, F. Ervin, G. Weiss, G. Bach-y-Rita and R. Hagiwara, "Intracerebral radio stimulation and recording of completely free patients," *Journal of Nervous Mental Disorders* 147, (1968): 329–340.
15. Moyer, *The Psychobiology of Aggression,* passim.
16. Thiessen, *The Evolution and Chemistry of Aggression,* pp. 133–171.
17. M. E. Wolfgang, *Patterns in Criminal Homicide* (Philadelphia: University of Pennsylvania Press), 1958.
18. R. H. Blum, "Drugs and Violence," in D. J. Mulvihill and M. M. Tumin and L. A. Curtis, eds. *Crimes of Violence:* A Staff Report to the National Commission on the Causes and Prevention of Violence, Vol. 13, Washington, D.C.: U.S. Government Printing Office, 1969, pp. 1462–1523.
19. Moyer, *The Psychobiology of Aggression,* p. 81.
20. *Ibid.*
21. *Ibid.,* p. 86.
22. *Ibid.,* p. 80.
23. *Ibid.,* p. 69.
24. E. M. Abrahamsen, and A. W. Pezet, *Body, Mind and Sugar* (New York: Holt, Rinehart and Winston, 1951).
25. Moyer, *The Psychobiology of Aggression,* pp. 74–78.
26. H. W. Dunham, *Community and Schizophrenia: An Epidemiological Analysis* (Detroit: Wayne State University Press, 1965).
See also H. W. Dunham *Social Realities and Community Psychiatry* New York: Behavioral Press, 1975).
27. Moyer, *The Psychobiology of Aggression,* p. 57.

CHAPTER 11
THE DYNAMICS OF VIOLENCE

1. A. Gesell, and H. Thompson, "Learning and Growth in Identical Twins," *Genetics and Psychology Monographs* 6 (1929): 1–123.
2. Z. Y. Kuo, *The Dynamics of Behavior Development: An Epigenetic View* (New York, Random House, 1967).
   H. F. Harlow, R. O. Dodsworth, and M. K. Harlow, "Total Isolation of Monkeys," *Proceedings of the National Academy of the Sciences* 54 (1965): 90–97.
   G. Mitchell, "Abnormal Behavior in Primates," in L. A. Rosenblum, ed. *Primate Behavior,* Vol. 1 (New York: Academic Press, 1970).
   Johnson, *Aggression in Man and Animals,* pp. 110–116.
3. K. Davis, "Extreme Social Isolation of a Child," *American Journal Sociology* 45 (1940): 554–565.
   K. Davis, "Final Note on a Case of Extreme Social Isolation," *American Journal of Sociology* 52 (1947): 432–437.
4. See H. Lane, *The Wild Boy of Aveyron* (Cambridge, Mass.: Harvard University Press, 1976).
5. See, for example, the extensive experimental research of Denenberg and his associates, J. H. Denenberg, and M. X. Zarrow, "Rat. Pax.," *Psychology Today* 3 (1970): 45–47 and 66–67
   See for a review, E. Maccoby, and J. C. Masters, "Attachment and Dependency," in P. H. Mussen, ed. *Carmichael's Manual of Child Psychology,* (New York: Wiley, 1970).
6. D. Abrahamsen, *The Murdering Mind* (New York: Harper & Row, Colophon, 1973), p. 29.
7. H. Kaufman, *Aggression and Altruism* (New York: Holt, Rinehart and Winston, 1970).
8. J. C. Dollard, L. Doob, N. Miller, O. Mowrer, and R. Sears, *Frustration and Aggression* (New Haven: Yale University Press, 1939).
9. *Ibid.,* p. 7.
10. J. S. Brown, and I. E. Farber, "Emotions conceptualized as intervening variables—with suggestions toward a theory of frustration," *Psychological Bulletin* 48 (1951): 465–495.
11. L. Berkowitz, *Aggression: A Social Psychological Analysis* (New York: McGraw-Hill, 1962), p. 28.
12. Some would think it appropriate to quote the study by Henry and Short at this point, which examined the relationship between homicide and suicide within the framework of frustration-aggression theory. However, it is not very relevant here. Henry and Short defined frustration narrowly (and irrelevantly to blacks) as variations in the business cycle, tending to support the Durkheimian view that with increased prosperity suicide rose both for whites and blacks. Nowhere did they test the hypothesis of whites being the source of frustration to blacks, although strangely, they did consider the possibility of blacks being frustrating to poor whites, which they used as the explanation of lynching. See A. F. Henry, and J. F. Short, *Suicide and Homicide* (Glencoe: Free Press, 1954).
13. Berkowitz, *Aggression,* p. 26.
14. *Ibid.,* pp. 27–28.
15. O. H. Mowrer, "An Experimental Analogue of 'Regression' with Incidental Observations of 'Reaction Formation,'" *Journal of Abnormal and Social Psychology* 35 (1940): 56–87.
    R. G. Barker, T. Dembo, and K. Lewin, "Frustration and Regression:

an experiment with young children," *University of Iowa Studies in Child Welfare* 18 (1941): 1–314.

16. Berkowitz, *Aggression,* pp. 29–32.

17. *Ibid.*

18. K. Menninger, *Love Against Hate* (New York: Harcourt Brace Jovanovich, 1942), p. 295.

19. Berkowitz, *Aggression,* p. 29.

20. A. Bandura, and A. C. Huston, "Identification as a Process of Learning," *Journal of Abnormal Social Psychology* 63 (1961): 311–318. J. P. Scott, *Aggression* (Chicago: University of Chicago Press, 1975). R. G. Geen, and R. Pigg, "Acquisition of an aggressive response and its generalization to verbal behavior," *Journal of Personality and Social Psychology* 15 (1970): 165–170.

21. Berkowitz, *Aggression,* p. 31.

22. S. Halleck, *Psychiatry and the Dilemmas of Crime* (New York: Harper & Row, 1967), see especially pp. 51–83.

23. K. Menninger, *The Vital Balance* (New York: Viking, 1963).

24. There are a lot of complications and difficulties with this theory when used in relation to stress. Menninger also posits *heterostasis* as well as homeostasis as an important element in adaptation which recognizes that man lives in an ongoing, constantly changing state. Thus, adaptation does not necessarily serve to bring the person back to a "rest" position. Increases in tension as well as decreases may be involved in this adapting process. After all, one could argue that the ultimate state of homeostasis, of complete rest and constancy is death.

25. Halleck, *Dilemmas of Crime,* p. 52.

26. *Ibid.,* pp. 52–58.

27. Berkowitz, *Aggression,* Chaps. 5, 6 and 7.

28. Halleck, *Dilemmas of Crime,* p. 68f.

29. See K. R. Scherer, R. P. Abeles, and C. S. Fischer, *Human Aggression and Conflict* (Englewood Cliffs, N.J.: Prentice-Hall, 1975).

30. E. I. Megargee, "Undercontrolled and Overcontrolled Personality Types in Extreme Anti-social Aggression," in E. I. Megargee and J. E. Hokanson, eds. *The Dynamics of Aggression* (New York: Harper & Row, 1970).

31. F. Redl and D. Wineman, *The Aggressive Child* (New York: Free Press), 1957.

32. Johnson, *Aggression in Man and Animals,* pp. 139–142.

33. J. R. Lion and M. Penna, "The Study of Human Aggression" in R. E. Whalen, ed. *The Neuropsychology of Aggression* (New York and London: Plenun, 1974), pp. 165–204.

34. Van den Berghe, "Bringing the Beasts Back in: Toward a Biosocial Theory of Aggression," *American Sociological Review* (1974) 39: 777–788, and replies to his paper in *American Sociological Review* 40 (1975): 674–682.

35. Halleck, *Dilemmas of Crime,* p. 101.

36. E. Sutherland, "The Diffusion of Sexual Psychopath Laws," *American Journal of Sociology* 56 (September 1950): 142–148.

37. Halleck, *Dilemmas of Crime,* p. 100.

38. W. McCord, and J. McCord, *Psychopathy and Delinquency* (New York: Grune & Stratton, 1956).

39. *Ibid.,* p. 103.

40. H. J. Eysenck, *Crime and Personality* (Boston: Houghton Mifflin, 1964), p. 37.

41. *Ibid.,* p. 40.
42. M. E. Wolfgang, and F. Ferracuti, *The Subculture of Violence* (London: Tavistock, 1967), p. 217.
43. E. Cumming, and J. Cumming, *Closed Ranks: An Experiment in Mental Health Education* (Cambridge: Harvard University Press, 1957).
44. S. Shah, and G. Weber, *The Problem of Individual Violence,* p. 80.
45. G. D. Gulevich, and P. G. Bourne, "Mental Illness and Violence," in D. N. Daniels, M. F. Gilula and F. M. Ochberg, eds. *Violence and the Struggle for Existence* (Boston: Little, Brown, 1970).
46. S. B. Guze, *Criminality and Psychiatric Disorders* (New York: Oxford University Press, 1976).
47. S. Palmer, *The Psychology of Murder* (New York: Crowell, 1962).
48. *Ibid.* See also Wolfgang and Ferracuti, *The Subculture of Violence,* pp. 217–219.
49. M. W. Kahn, "A Comparison of Personality, Intelligence, and Social History of Two Criminal Groups," *Journal of Social Psychology* 49 (1959): 3–40.
50. S. A. Pasternack, ed. *Violence and Victims* (New York: Spectrum, 1975).
51. Wolfgang and Ferracuti, *The Subculture of Violence,* p. 220.
52. M. E. Wolfgang, R. F. Figlio, and T. Sellin, *Delinquency in a Birth Cohort* (Chicago: University of Chicago Press, 1975), p. 89.
53. D. J. Mulvihill, M. M. Tumin, and L. A. Curtis, *Crimes of Violence,* Vol. 12, Staff Report to the National Commission on Causes and Prevention of Violence, Washington, D.C.: U.S. Government Printing Office, 1969, pp. 549–553.
54. D. Williams, "Neural Factors Related to Habitual Aggression," *Brain* 92 (1969): 503–520.
55. G. Bach-Y-Rita, and A. Veno, "Habitual Violence: A Profile of 62 Men," *American Journal of Psychiatry* 131, 9 (1974): 1015–1917.
56. J. J. Cocozza, and H. J. Steadman, "Some Refinements in the Measurement and Prediction of Dangerous Behavior," *American Journal of Psychiatry* 131, 0 (1974): 1912–1914.
57. Attempts to predict the dangerousness of those committed as dangerously mentally ill have been dismal failures. However, the diagnosis of "dangerously mentally ill" does not depend upon the four criteria listed here concerning previous criminal record. They very often have depended upon other clinical diagnoses such as "propensity to act out." See, for example, H. J. Steadman, "The Determination of Dangerousness in New York." Paper presented at 1974 Annual Meeting of the American Psychiatric Association, Detroit, Michigan.
58. This applies even when it is observed that prediction of future violence according to past records of violence produces many mistakes, a finding reported by Wenk and his associates. E. A. Wenk, J. O. Robinson, and G. W. Smith, "Can Violence Be Predicted?" *Crime and Delinquency* 18 (1972): 393–402. A moderately significant statistical correlation means just that: there may be many exceptions to the rule. A correlation is merely a method of summarizing a general relationship between two or more factors.
59. In Truman Capote's, *In Cold Blood,* the character "Perry" was portrayed as a psychopathic killer.
60. W. McCord, and J. McCord, *The Psychopath: An Essay on the Criminal Mind* (Princeton, N.J.: Van Nostrand, 1964), p. 172.
61. *Ibid.,* p. 173.

62. D. T. Lunde, *Murder and Madness* (San Francisco: Portable Stanford, 1976), p. 92.
63. L. E. Hinsie, and R. J. Campbell, *Psychiatric Dictionary* (New York: Oxford University Press, 1960).
64. Lunde, *Murder and Madness*, p. 49.
65. *Ibid.*, pp. 76–77.
66. Hans von Hentig, *The Criminal and His Victim* (New Haven, Conn.: Yale University Press, 1948). These general observations are always difficult to defend. It has also been found, for example, that there are significant increases in murder in periods directly following major wars. Thus, it is not clear whether murder decreases during wars, or increases after wars. See D. Archer, and R. Gartner, "Violent Acts and Violent Times: A Comparative Approach to Post-War Homicide Rates," *American Sociological Review* 41, 6 (1976): 937–962.
67. *Ibid.*
68. Henry and Short, *Suicide and Homicide,* 1954.
69. Wolfgang and Ferracuti, *The Subculture of Violence,* p. 145.
70. D. Abrahamsen, *The Murdering Mind,* passim.
71. S. Hurwitz, *Criminologia* (Firenze: Macri, 1954).
72. Lunde, *Murder and Madness,* p. 48.
73. *Ibid.,* p. 56.
74. Halleck, *Dilemmas of Crime,* pp. 167–168.

CONCLUSIONS

1. See: G. Zilboorg, "Introduction" to *Beyond the Pleasure Principle* by Sigmund Freed, trans. James Strackey (New York: Bantam Books, 1959), p. 13.
2. See Chapter 2.
3. See N. Brown, *Life Against Death* (Middletown, Conn.: Wesleyan University Press, 1959). Freud caustically noted that the purpose of life is death. He might just as easily have said that the purpose of death is life!
4. *Ibid.* See also E. Becker, *The Denial of Death* (New York: The Free Press, 1975).
5. In defense of murder, the Marquis de Sade argued that since death was a natural force of nature, killing a few people more or less was simply assisting nature in her work. The point of death as a natural force should lead to a quite opposite position, since it makes life finite and thus of much greater importance to lead it as long and as full as possible. Wanting a long life is not the same as wanting an eternal life. Interfering with nature on the grounds of Sade is clearly against the natural law.
6. See G. Newman, *The Punishment Response* (Philadelphia: Lippincott, 1978).
7. *Ibid.*
8. R. D. Laing is the extreme proponent of this view. See R. D. Laing, *The Politics of Experience* (New York: Ballantine, 1967). The point is also beautifully illustrated in the play *Friends* by Kobo Abe. Trans. Donald Keene (New York: Grove Press, 1969).
9. There are societies that allow children to become adults at a much earlier age than we do in Western society. Keeping children longer, one historian has suggested, is an especially modern phenomenon. See: P. Aries, *Centuries of Childhood* (New York: Knopf, 1962).

Index

79 80 81 7 6 5 4 3 2 1